A Raid Too Far

NUMBER 143

Williams-Ford Texas A&M University Military History Series

A Raid Too Far

Operation Lam Son 719 and Vietnamization in Laos

JAMES H. WILLBANKS

Texas A&M University Press
COLLEGE STATION

Manufactured in the United States of America

First edition
This paper meets the requirements of
ANSI/NISO, Z39.48–1992
(Permanence of Paper).
Binding materials have been
chosen for durability.

Library of Congress Cataloging-in-Publication Data

Willbanks, James H., 1947–
A raid too far : Operation Lam Son 719 and
Vietnamization in Laos / James H. Willbanks. — 1st ed.
p. cm. — (Williams-Ford Texas A&M University military history series ; no. 143)
Includes bibliographical references and index.
ISBN 978-1-62349-017-1 (cloth : alk. paper) —
ISBN 978-1-62349-117-8 (e-book) 1. Operation Lam Son 719, 1971.
2. Vietnam (Republic). Quân lu'c—History—Vietnam War,
1961–1975. I. Title. II. Series: Williams-Ford Texas A&M
University military history series ; no. 143.
DS557.8.L3W55 2014
959.704'342—dc23
2013022041

THIS BOOK IS DEDICATED

TO OUR BELOVED DAUGHTER JENNIFER

AND TO ALL THOSE BRAVE SOULS

WHO FLEW AND FOUGHT IN LAOS IN 1971.

Contents

List of Illustrations / ix
Acknowledgments / xi
Introduction / 1
1. Prelude: Vietnamization / 4
2. Deciding to Launch the Operation / 24
3. The Plan / 36
4. The Mission Receives a Green Light / 52
5. The Other Side / 60
6. The Battle Is Joined / 70
7. The Attack Grinds to a Halt / 87
8. On to Tchepone / 117
9. The Withdrawal / 132
10. Assessing Lam Son 719 / 158
11. Aftermath / 178

Epilogue: Endgame / 202

APPENDIX 1 / 207
Task Organization, ARVN and US
APPENDIX 2 / 212
Order of Battle, People's Army of Vietnam
APPENDIX 3 / 214
Casualties
APPENDIX 4 / 215
US Army Aviation Summary
APPENDIX 5 / 216
US Air Force Summary
APPENDIX 6 / 217
US/ARVN Artillery Summary

Notes / 219
Glossary / 245
Bibliography / 249
Index / 261

Illustrations

A gallery of photographs follows page 86.

PHOTOGRAPHS
CH-47 Chinooks depart Fire Support Base Vandegrift.
Aviation staging area at Khe Sanh.
Assault helicopter company flying west along Route 9 in Laos.
ARVN paratroopers en route to combat assault in Laos.
ARVN convoy en route to pickup zone at Lang Vei.
South Vietnamese column moves west along Route 9 in Laos.
Lt. Gen. Hoang Xuan Lam talks with reporters.
Staging area at Lang Vei.
Downed UH-1H Huey helicopter from B/101st Avn Bn (AH).
AH-1G Cobra attack helicopter from 4/77th ARA.
South Vietnamese soldiers walk along a trail in Laos.
UH-1C Huey gunship from 174th AHC "Sharks."
South Vietnamese troops move along Ho Chi Minh Trail.
Medevac helicopter lands in Laos.
USMC CH-53 at Khe Sanh.
One of the airborne brigade LZs north of Route 9.
ARVN soldiers with weapons captured in Laos.
Russian-built PT-76 light tank captured during a battle with the NVA.
Bags of rice captured during Operation Lam Son 719 in southern Laos.
Disabled vehicles and equipment along Route 9.
M41 tank from ARVN 17th Armored Squadron destroyed in March 1971.
South Vietnamese soldiers captured by the NVA along Route 9.
ARVN M41 tank relic in Xepon, 2010.

MAPS
Map 1. Southeast Asia / 22
Map 2. Area of Operations / 25
Map 3. Operation Lam Son 719, Phase I (Dewey Canyon II) / 41

Map 4. Operation Lam Son 719, Phase II / 44
Map 5. NVA Military Fronts and Regions / 62
Map 6. Plan for the Assault on Tchepone / 122
Map 7. Enemy Situation, Mid-March 1971 / 142

Acknowledgments

I would like to thank Rich Boylan and Tim Nenninger at the National Archives and Records Administration, College Park, Maryland, and archivists Meghan Lee and Jason Schultz at the Richard Nixon Presidential Library and Museum, Yorba Linda, California, for their invaluable assistance. I would also like to express my appreciation to the historians and archivists at the US Army Center of Military History at Fort McNair, Washington, DC; the Military History Institute at Carlisle, Pennsylvania; the US Army Combined Arms Research Library at Fort Leavenworth, Kansas; the Gerald R. Ford Presidential Library in Ann Arbor, Michigan; and the Vietnam Center and Virtual Archive at Texas Tech University in Lubbock, Texas, for their assistance. Special thanks go to the US Army Command and General Staff College for providing a sabbatical to work on this book and to the Command and General Staff College Foundation for providing funding for research in Vietnam and Laos.

I am particularly indebted to Lt. Col. (Ret.) Mike Sloniker, who provided invaluable information on the valiant army aviators who flew in support of the ARVN in Laos in 1971. Special thanks for providing photos and other information also go to Joe Kline, who flew as a door gunner with Company B, 101st Aviation Battalion, in 1971, and Donna Thompson, whose husband, the late Fred Thompson, flew with the 174th Assault Helicopter Company in Lam Son 719.

Last, but certainly not least, I would like to express my appreciation and that of many of my colleagues to Merle Pribbenow, who is an expert on all things Vietnamese and has given freely of his time and expertise to translate Vietnamese documents and educate a generation of Vietnamese War scholars; we are all forever in his debt. This book would not have been possible without his invaluable assistance and wise counsel.

A Raid Too Far

Introduction

1

On a Saturday in March 1971, Maj. Jack Barker flew his US Army UH-1H Huey helicopter into Laos as part of a rescue mission to pick up South Vietnamese soldiers in heavy contact with North Vietnamese regulars. When the flight of helicopters from Bravo Company, 101st Aviation Battalion, approached Landing Zone Brown, the first aircraft that attempted to land was driven off by intense ground fire. As Major Barker descended toward the LZ, the enemy unleashed a flurry of automatic weapons fire at his aircraft, forcing him to abort the attempt. On his second approach, his aircraft was again raked by enemy fire, sustaining severe battle damage and causing Barker again to abort the landing. He nursed the crippled aircraft back to his base at Khe Sanh, where he boarded another helicopter and departed for the besieged LZ. As Barker made his third descent into the LZ, his aircraft was struck by a rocket-propelled grenade and exploded in midair; there were no survivors.[1]

North Vietnamese soldiers swarmed the area where the wreckage fell, so the bodies of Barker and his crew could not be recovered. Thirty years later, a recovery mission by Joint Task Force—Full Accounting would be mounted to recover the remains of Barker and his three crewmen: Capt. John Dugan, Sgt. William Dillender, and Pfc. John Chubb. However, this mission was not successful, and their remains would not be recovered until a subsequent mission in October 2005 succeeded in locating the crash site.[2]

Major Barker's aircraft was one of more than one hundred US helicopters lost while flying in support of an operation called Lam Son 719. In early 1971, for the first time in their history, the Republic of Vietnam Armed Forces (RVNAF) launched a corps-level campaign alone on a foreign battlefield. On 8 February, the lead elements of what would eventually total more than seventeen thousand South Vietnamese soldiers crossed the border into Laos to strike at North Vietnamese Army (NVA) resupply areas and infiltration routes. It was a massive operation that would involve thirty-four South Vietnamese battalions, with nearly seven hundred helicopters and two thousand fixed-wing aircraft committed in their support.[3]

The North Vietnamese responded strongly to the South Vietnamese operation, committing more than sixty thousand troops to the battle. What followed was forty-five days of some of the heaviest fighting of the war. The last South Vietnamese forces withdrew from Laos during the last week in March 1971. The enduring image of Lam Son 719 was that of terrified ARVN soldiers hanging onto the skids of US helicopters as they were being driven from Laos in defeat. The prevalent story line at the time was that the poor performance of South Vietnamese soldiers in Laos clearly demonstrated that President Richard Nixon's Vietnamization policy was a failure and that the South Vietnamese would not be able to handle the North Vietnamese Army and Viet Cong once all US combat troops were withdrawn.

While the endgame is not disputable, the truth of the matter with regard to Operation Lam Son 719 and South Vietnamese performance on the battlefield in Laos is much more complicated than the enduring images of panic-stricken ARVN soldiers escaping Laos might suggest. During the course of the fierce battles that followed, some South Vietnamese units fought valiantly against overwhelming odds, but others did not. The US helicopters supporting the South Vietnamese troops received more combat damage, and more helicopters were shot down, than during any other comparable time in the Vietnam War. The bitter fight in Laos was different from most of the battles that both the South Vietnamese and their US supporters had ever fought; it was a mid- to high-intensity "attritional slugfest" and about as far removed from counterinsurgency operations as one could get.[4] As US Air Force historian Bernard C. Nalty observed, the operation "tested not only the skills and tenacity of a particular South Vietnamese task force and its leaders, but the entire concept of Vietnamization."[5]

In one sense, the operation proved to be, as Gen. Phillip B. Davidson, MACV chief of intelligence, observed after the war, "a raid too far."[6] Nevertheless, the South Vietnamese, although failing to achieve the operation's original goals, still inflicted heavy casualties on the North Vietnamese. The purpose of this book is to provide a comprehensive assessment of the planning, execution, and aftermath of the operation. In doing so, it will address not only what was happening in Laos and concurrently with the forces supporting the operation from the northern I Corps area in South Vietnam, but also what was transpiring at the same time in Saigon and Washington. Additionally, it will attempt to understand the response of the North Vietnamese that had such a seminal impact on the final outcome of the operation. Fortunately, that part of the effort has been assisted by a flurry of accounts released in Vietnam in 2011, the fortieth anniversary of the campaign. Ultimately, the intent is to weave all of these perspectives together into a comprehensive real-time narrative that seeks to put the incursion into Laos in the proper historical context of Nixon's approach to the war, Vietnamization, US withdrawal, and the subsequent fall of South Vietnam.

CHAPTER ONE

Prelude: Vietnamization

To understand how and why South Vietnamese troops found themselves crossing the border into Laos in February 1971, one must go back to 1968. By the fall of that year, US involvement in Southeast Asia had reached a pivotal point. The communist forces had suffered horrendous losses on the battlefield during that year's Tet Offensive, but in the process they had reaped a tremendous psychological victory. Although US troop levels were at an all-time high, and much had been said about the "light at the end of the tunnel," the sheer scope and ferocity of the communist attacks in 1968 had been stunning, and the cries to get out of Vietnam reached a new intensity. A shaken Lyndon Johnson announced that he would not run for reelection. During a tumultuous Democratic Party convention in Chicago, Hubert Humphrey won his party's nomination for the presidency. He and Richard Nixon, the Republican nominee, squared off in a battle for the soon-to-be-vacated White House.

During his campaign, Nixon made the war in Vietnam a major element of his platform, promising "new leadership that will end the war and win the peace in the Pacific." He proclaimed: "The nation's objective should be to help the South Vietnamese fight the war and not fight it for them. . . . If they do not assume the majority of the burden in their own defense, they cannot be saved."[1] Despite his later protestations to the contrary, such pronouncements gave many voters the impression that Nixon had a secret plan for ending the war.

The election was extremely close. In the end, Nixon won the popular vote by only 512,000 votes, only a plurality of 43 percent. On 20 January 1969, Nixon was inaugurated as the thirty-seventh president of the United States. He, in fact, did not yet have a plan for Vietnam; what resulted was, as historian Larry Berman suggests, "a series of improvisations."[2] Once in office, Nixon faced the same problems that had confronted his predecessor. Escalation and commitment of increased numbers of American troops had not worked; the Tet Offensive had demonstrated that fact only too clearly. The resultant bloody stalemate was unacceptable not only for those clamoring for a US pullout, but also for an ever-increasing number of the American people who had previously supported the war but would no longer tolerate a long-term commitment to what appeared to be an unwinnable war. In addition, the new president had to contend with a Democrat-controlled Congress that now, with a Republican in the White House, felt free to attack the war with a renewed fury. The president knew his only feasible option was an American withdrawal, but the problem for Nixon was how to devise an exit strategy that would allow the United States to withdraw gracefully without completely abandoning South Vietnam to the communists while at the same time demonstrating to America's other allies that the United States could be relied upon to maintain its international commitments.

No one understood this better than Henry Kissinger, who became Nixon's national security adviser. He believed that disengaging the United States from the war in an honorable fashion was the first order of business if the country was to maintain its rightful position on the world stage. He and Nixon saw eye to eye on this; Nixon told him, "You and I will end the war."[3] Kissinger would play a seminal role in the drama that would unfold over the next four years.

On his first day in office, the new president immediately set about to find a solution to the pressing problem at hand, issuing National Security Study Memorandum 1 (NSSM 1), titled "Situation in Vietnam," which was sent to selected agencies within the new administration, including, among others, the Department of Defense, the Department of State, the Central Intelligence Agency, the Joint Chiefs of Staff, the US Embassy in Saigon, and Headquarters, Military Assistance Command, Vietnam (MACV). The memorandum, designed "to develop an agreed evaluation of the situation in Vietnam as a basis for making policy decisions," requested responses to twenty-nine major questions and fifty subsidiary queries covering six broad categories: negotiations, the enemy situation, the state of the armed forces of South Vietnam, the status of the pacification effort, the political situation in South Vietnam, and American objectives. Kissinger would later write in his memoir of the time that the purpose of the memorandum was a fact-finding exercise designed "to sharpen any disagreements so that we could pinpoint the controversial questions and the different points of view."[4]

Chief among the new president's concerns were the viability of the Nguyen Van Thieu government in Saigon and the capability of South Vietnamese forces to continue the fight after any US withdrawal.[5] If Nixon wanted divergent views and opinions on the war, he certainly found them in the wide range of responses to the twenty-nine questions. Kissinger and his staff summarized the responses to NSSM 1 in a forty-four-page report, which revealed that the only general agreement among most respondents was that the Republic of Vietnam (RVN) could not in the foreseeable future defend itself against both the Viet Cong and the North Vietnamese Army (NVA).[6] In the same vein, most respondents agreed that the government of Vietnam (GVN) probably could not stand up to serious political competition from the National Liberation Front (NLF) and that the enemy, although seriously weakened by losses incurred during the Tet Offensive, was still an effective force capable of being refurbished and reinforced from North Vietnam.

Despite agreement on these points, the respondents disagreed about the progress achieved to that point and the long-range prognosis for the situation in Southeast Asia. There were two opposing schools of thought in this matter. The more optimistic group, best represented by the response from Gen. Creighton W. Abrams Jr., commander of MACV, and echoed by Ambassador Ellsworth Bunker in Saigon, the Joint Chiefs of Staff, and Adm. John S. McCain Jr., commander in chief, US Pacific Forces, held that the North Vietnamese had agreed to peace talks in Paris because of their military weakness, that pacification gains were real and "should hold up," and that the "tides are favorable."

Although the MACV opinion emphasized that significant progress was being made in modernizing the Army of the Republic of Vietnam (ARVN), it warned that the South Vietnamese could not yet stand alone against a combined assault, stating that "the RVNAF simply are not capable of attaining the level of self-sufficiency and overwhelming force superiority that would be required to counter combined Viet Cong insurgency and North Vietnamese Army main force offensives."[7] Accordingly, General Abrams stressed in his response that any proposed American troop withdrawal had to be accompanied by a concurrent North Vietnamese withdrawal.

Differing strongly with the MACV report and definitely representing a decidedly more pessimistic view were the responses from the State Department, Central Intelligence Agency, and civilians in the Defense Department, all of whom were highly critical of Saigon's military capabilities and US progress to date. The civilians in the Defense Department went so far as to say that the South Vietnamese could not be expected to contain even the Viet Cong, let alone a combined enemy threat, without continued and full American support. These respondents agreed that pacification gains that had been reported in the months after the Tet Offensive were "inflated and fragile" and that the communists had agreed to participate in the negotiations that began in Paris in May 1968 only for political and strategic reasons—to cut costs and to pursue their aims through negotiation—rather than because they perceived they were facing defeat on the battlefield.

Thus, there existed two divergent opinions about the long-term prognosis for the future of South Vietnam and its military forces. What had been designed as a means to clear the air on the Vietnam situation and assist in developing a viable strategy had only served to obfuscate things further for the new president. Henry Kissinger wrote, "The answers [to NSSM 1] made clear that there was no consensus as to facts, much less as to policy."[8]

Nixon faced a serious dilemma. He had promised to end the war and bring the troops home, but he could not, as Kissinger later observed in his memoirs, "simply walk away from an entire enterprise involving two administrations, five allied countries, and thirty-one thousand dead as if we were switching a television channel."[9] The new president had to devise an exit strategy to get the United States out of Vietnam without "simply walk[ing] away." While the survival of South Vietnam remained an objective, it manifestly was not the primary goal, which was to get the United States out of Vietnam. Nixon and his advisers needed to find a way that the United States could disengage itself from the conflict without completely abandoning the South Vietnamese.

Despite the difficulty involved in trying to strengthen the South Vietnamese armed forces so that US forces could be withdrawn, the president and his closest advisers, particularly Secretary of Defense Melvin R. Laird, agreed that this was the only feasible course of action if the United States were ever to escape from Vietnam. It was only the assumption of greater combat responsibility by the RVNAF that would facilitate a disengagement of American forces, which by that time totaled over 543,000.

To get a better sense for the situation on the ground in Southeast Asia, Nixon directed Laird to go to South Vietnam to conduct a firsthand assessment. On 5 March 1969, the secretary of defense, accompanied by Gen. Earle Wheeler, chairman of the Joint Chiefs, arrived in Saigon. There they were briefed by senior MACV officers, who emphasized the view that significant improvements were being made in the South Vietnamese armed forces. Laird instructed General Abrams to speed up the process so that the bulk of the war effort could be turned over to the Saigon forces as soon as possible. Abrams repeated his earlier warning that the South Vietnamese were not prepared to stand alone against a combined threat. Nevertheless, Laird, citing political pressures at home, directed Abrams to improve the RVNAF and turn over the war to them "before the time given the new administration runs out."[10] This was not really a new mission for Abrams, who had been working on this effort since his days as Westmoreland's deputy in Saigon.[11] However, the urgency was a new factor.

Despite Abrams's warnings about the current capabilities of the South Vietnamese armed forces, Laird returned to Washington convinced that the South Vietnamese could eventually take over prosecution of the entire war, thus permitting a complete US withdrawal. A former Republican congressman with seventeen years in the House, Laird was anxious to end the war because he realized the traditional grace period afforded a new president by the public, the press, and Congress following Nixon's election victory would be short-lived. Antiwar sentiment on Capitol Hill was growing, and Laird knew that Nixon would feel the brunt of congressional ire if he did not end the war quickly. Moreover, if the war in Vietnam continued much longer, Laird reasoned that it would weaken American strength and credibility around the world in places far more important to US security than Southeast Asia. Laird believed that any effort to prolong the conflict would lead to such strife and controversy that it would seriously damage Nixon's ability to achieve an honorable settlement. Therefore, according to Deputy Assistant Secretary of Defense Jerry Friedheim,

Laird was "more interested in ending the war in Vietnam rather than winning it."[12]

Laird told Nixon that he believed the president had no choice but to turn the entire war over to the South Vietnamese as quickly as possible in order to extricate US forces and placate both the resurgent antiwar movement and the ever-growing segment of the American population who just wanted the war to go away. He proposed a plan designed to make the South Vietnamese armed forces capable of dealing not only with the ongoing insurgency, but also with a continuing North Vietnamese presence in the south. Laird argued that the large US presence in the country stifled South Vietnamese initiative and prevented them from getting on with taking over the war effort. He told Nixon that he believed the orientation of American senior commanders in Vietnam "seemed to be more on operations than on assisting the South Vietnamese to acquire the means to defend themselves." Laird wanted the senior US military leaders in South Vietnam to get to work on shifting their focus from fighting the war to preparing the South Vietnamese to stand on their own. Accordingly, he declared that "it is essential that we decide now to initiate the removal from Southeast Asia of some US military personnel" and recommended withdrawing fifty thousand to seventy thousand American troops in 1969 and developing long-range plans to methodically replace American forces with the RVNAF.[13]

In a National Security Council meeting on 28 March 1969, the president and his advisers discussed Laird's recommendations. In attendance was Gen. Andrew Goodpaster, then serving as General Abrams's deputy in Saigon. He reported to the president that substantial improvement in the South Vietnamese forces had already been made and that MACV was in fact close to "de-Americanizing" the war. According to Henry Kissinger, Laird took exception to Goodpaster's choice of words, saying, "What we need is a term 'Vietnamizing' to put the emphasis on the right issue." In very short time, *Vietnamization* was adopted as the embodiment of Nixon's efforts to turn the war over to the South Vietnamese.[14]

Laird later described the objective of the new Vietnamization effort in an address before the House Armed Services Committee as "the effective assumption by the RVNAF of a larger share of combat operations from American forces" so that "US forces can be in fact withdrawn in substantial numbers." He concluded,

"Vietnamization provides the means for the orderly disinvolvement of American troops from combat without having to sacrifice our . . . objective—the right of self-determination for the people of Vietnam."[15]

Such statements were clearly aimed at selling the new policy to Congress and the American public. Brig. Gen. Alexander M. Haig, then a member of Nixon's national security staff, later described Laird's plan as a "stroke of public relations genius," but pointed out that it was "a program designed to mollify American critics of the war, not a policy for the effective defense of South Vietnam." Nevertheless, Laird, according to Henry Kissinger, had convinced himself that Vietnamization would work, and he became its most vocal proponent, making it his top priority.[16]

Nixon was quickly won over by Laird's arguments, later writing, "It was on the basis of Laird's enthusiastic advocacy that we undertook the policy of Vietnamization." It may not have taken very much to convince the president to endorse this approach; Haig maintains that Nixon had begun talking about troop withdrawals shortly after his inauguration, and Laird's Vietnamization plan provided the rationale he was looking for. It would enable the president to initiate a phase-down of combat operations by US troops with the ultimate goal of complete withdrawal. However, Nixon realized that American forces could not be pulled out precipitously. Although the situation was improving in South Vietnam, there was still a significant level of fighting. Time was needed to make the RVNAF sufficiently strong to continue the war alone. Thus, American forces would have to continue combat operations to gain the necessary time to build up the South Vietnamese forces. The outcome of the decisions made about Vietnamization and US withdrawals was addressed in National Security Decision Memorandum 9, which was signed on 1 April 1969.[17]

Concurrent with the effort to increase the combat capabilities of the South Vietnamese armed forces and the subsequent phased withdrawal of American troops, the administration would pursue the second part of what developed into a two-track strategy. With General Abrams focused on improving the RVNAF while holding off the North Vietnamese on the battlefield, Kissinger would initiate secret negotiations with the North Vietnamese in Paris in an attempt to forge a cease-fire and subsequent peace agreement. The objective was a negotiated settlement that would permit the United States to disengage from the war on favorable terms and guarantee at least a reasonable chance of survival for South Vietnam after US forces departed. In this way, Nixon hoped to extricate the United States from Southeast Asia and achieve "peace with honor."

On 10 April 1969, Nixon issued planning guidance for the way ahead in National Security Study Memorandum 36 (NSSM 36), which directed "the preparation of a specific timetable for Vietnamizing the war" that would address "all aspects of US military, paramilitary, and civilian involvement in Vietnam, including combat and combat support forces, advisory personnel, and all forms of equipment." The stated objective of the requested plan was "the progressive transfer . . . of the fighting effort" from American to South Vietnamese forces.[18]

The directive listed alternative completion dates of 31 December 1970, 30 June 1971, 31 December 1971, and 31 December 1972. The directive also listed the assumptions on which the timetable was to be based. First, the starting date for the plan would be 1 July 1969. Second, it was assumed that, lacking progress in the Paris peace talks, any US withdrawal would be unilateral and that there would not be any comparable NVA reductions. This was a significant change from previous assumptions that called for a mutual withdrawal of both US and North Vietnamese forces from South Vietnam; this meant that the South Vietnamese would have to take on both the NVA and the VC. Third, the US withdrawals would be on a "cut and try" basis, and General Abrams would make periodic assessments of their effects before launching the next phase of troop reductions.[19] Last, it was assumed that the South Vietnamese forces would willingly assume more military responsibility for the war. Based on these assumptions, the American troop presence in South Vietnam was to be drawn down eventually to the point that only a small residual support and advisory mission remained.

Thus, the Nixon administration, despite assessments from a wide range of government agencies that agreed that the RVNAF could never combat a combined VC-NVA threat, came up with a program to prepare the South Vietnamese to do just that, instructing the American command in Saigon to develop plans for turning over the entire war effort to Saigon so that US forces could be withdrawn.

In mid-May, the MACV commander was recalled to Washington for consultations on implementing the new strategy. Nixon and Kissinger told Abrams to proceed with Vietnamization and redeployment of US troops in a "systematic and orderly fashion" without accepting "undue risks." They warned him not to bend to "the pressures which were to develop for premature US disengagement" and that he was to make recommendations on the deployment schedule based on his personal assessment of the situation on the ground in South Vietnam.[20] With his marching orders in hand, Abrams returned to Saigon to plan the way forward. All that was left to institute the new strategy was a public announcement.

On 8 June 1969, President Nixon met with President Thieu at Midway and publicly proclaimed for the first time the new American policy of Vietnamization. Nixon stated that there would be a steady buildup and improvement of South Vietnamese forces and institutions, accompanied by increased military pressure on the enemy, while American troops were gradually withdrawn. He emphasized that the ultimate objective was to strengthen RVNAF capabilities and bolster the Thieu government so that the South Vietnamese could stand on their own against the communists. Before closing, Nixon announced that he was pulling out twenty-five thousand troops and that at "regular intervals" thereafter he would pull out more. According to the president, this withdrawal of US forces was contingent on three factors: (1) the progress in training and equipping the South Vietnamese forces, (2) progress in the Paris negotiations, and (3) the level of enemy activity.[21] The assessment of RVNAF progress and level of enemy activity would be left to Abrams's on-site evaluation. Unfortunately, as it turned out, once the withdrawals started, domestic political pressures would trump Abrams's judgment in determining the pace of withdrawals.

Privately, President Thieu was not pleased with the American president's announcement. According to Nixon, Thieu, realizing what the end state of US withdrawals meant, was "deeply troubled," but Nixon later claimed he "privately assured him [Thieu] through Ambassador [Ellsworth] Bunker that our support for him was steadfast." Thieu and many of his generals were upset with another aspect of Vietnamization, and that was the word itself. The South Vietnamese leaders took exception to the whole concept and the associated implication that the ARVN were finally stepping up to assume responsibility for the war. To the South Vietnamese, who had been fighting the communists since the 1950s, the idea that the war would now be Vietnamized was insulting. Nguyen Duy Hinh, a former ARVN general, wrote in an official US Army–commissioned monograph after the war, "It was after all our own war, and we were determined to fight it, with or without American troops. In my opinion, Vietnamization was not a proper term to be used in Vietnam, especially when propaganda was an important enemy weapon."[22]

Despite the sensitivities of the South Vietnamese, Henry Kissinger recorded that "Nixon was jubilant. He considered the announcement a political triumph. He thought that it would buy him the time necessary for developing our strategy."[23] A later memorandum revealed that Nixon hoped that his new policy of Vietnamizing the war would demonstrate to the American people that he "had ruled out a purely US solution to the problem in South Vietnam and indeed had a plan to end the war."[24]

To solidify the new strategy, Nixon met with Laird and General Wheeler upon his return from Midway. The purpose was to discuss a mission change for General Abrams. The current mission statement, which had been issued by President Johnson, charged MACV to defeat the enemy and force his withdrawal to North Vietnam. As a result of the discussions following the Midway announcement, a new order to Abrams that would go into effect on 15 August directed him to "assist the Republic of Vietnam Armed Forces to take over an increasing share of combat operations" and focus on (1) providing "maximum assistance" to the South Vietnamese to strengthen their forces, (2) supporting the pacification effort, and (3) reducing the flow of supplies to the enemy.[25]

Abrams was given an unenviable job. He had been directed to increase the capability of the South Vietnamese armed forces and hand over the war to them while at the same time hold off the enemy to provide time for the improvement of the RVNAF. However, he was also directed to reduce the number of US troops in country, which were the forces that he needed in order to hold off the enemy. Obviously, this was going to be a tall order.

The Vietnamization effort would be implemented in three phases. In the first phase, responsibility for the bulk of ground combat against Viet Cong and North Vietnamese forces would be turned over gradually to the RVNAF. During this phase, the United States would continue to provide air, naval, and logistic support. The second phase, which would proceed concurrently with the first phase, consisted of developing capabilities in the

RVNAF to help them achieve self-reliance through an increase in artillery, air, and naval assets and other support activities. The third phase involved the reduction of the American presence to strictly a military advisory role, with a small security element remaining for protection. It was assumed that the advisory and assistance presence would be gradually reduced as South Vietnam grew in strength, but the new strategy, at least as it was described initially, always included leaving a small residual force in South Vietnam "for some time to come," as Laird told a House subcommittee in February 1970.[26]

While the United States continued to conduct combat operations against the NVA and Viet Cong with American forces, the new Vietnamization policy focused initially on modernizing and developing the South Vietnamese armed forces. This effort was not a new initiative, but during the earlier years of US involvement in Vietnam, particularly during the period of American buildup (1965–67), it had been of secondary importance as US military leaders focused on the conduct of operations by American units in the field. With the election of Richard Nixon and his subsequent emphasis on Vietnamization, the effort to strengthen and modernize the South Vietnamese forces became a top priority for MACV.[27]

This effort focused on developing the RVNAF into a balanced force with command, administration, and self-support capabilities to continue the fighting successfully after the withdrawal of US and NVA troops. Laird would be the driving force in this endeavor, and he directed MACV to speed up its efforts to prepare the South Vietnamese to assume responsibility for the fighting.

In Saigon, the senior US commander was concerned about the way ahead. On 2 September 1969, Abrams responded to Laird's guidance, pointing out again in very clear terms that, in his opinion, proposed modernization and improvement programs would not enable the South Vietnamese to handle the current combined threat, the central premise of the Vietnamization effort. Citing poor leadership, high desertion rates, and corruption in the upper ranks of the RVNAF, Abrams reported that he thought that the South Vietnamese forces could not be improved either quantitatively or qualitatively to the extent necessary to deal with both the VC and NVA; he clearly stated that he thought what the secretary of defense wanted done simply could not be accomplished in the time frame expected and with the resources allocated.[28]

Abrams was not alone in this assessment. In July, General Wheeler, chairman of the Joint Chiefs, in a memorandum prepared for Laird after the chairman returned from his trip to Vietnam, had declared that "the resulting structure [called for in NSSM 36] is not designed to provide the South Vietnamese Armed Forces the capability to deal with both the full enemy guerrilla force in country and cope with the North Vietnamese armed forces." He stated further that unless the North Vietnamese could be induced to withdraw from both South Vietnam and their sanctuaries in Cambodia and Laos, a residual US force would be required "for some years to come." He closed by warning that the "RVNAF cannot in the near future maintain the integrity of South Vietnam."[29]

Laird could not accept Abrams's September assessment, nor the earlier observations of Wheeler, because if he did, it meant that he would have to admit that the United States could never gracefully exit South Vietnam, particularly in light of the increasingly obvious fact that the North Vietnamese were not going to agree to a mutual withdrawal of US and PAVN troops from South Vietnam. On 10 November, undeterred by the advice from his senior generals, Laird directed the Joint Chiefs of Staff to come up with a new plan that would, one way or the other, create a South Vietnamese military force that could "maintain at least current levels of security."[30] He told the military planners to assume unilateral US withdrawals that would reduce American military strength first to a "support force" of 190,000–260,000 troops by July 1971 and then to a much smaller advisory force by July 1973.

In Saigon, Abrams and his staff, despite their misgivings, realized that the die was cast with regard to eventual US withdrawal, and they attempted to formulate the best plan possible given Laird's increasingly adamant guidance. To comply with the secretary's orders, the military planners assumed a reduced Viet Cong threat and a declining PAVN presence in South Vietnam while virtually ignoring Hanoi's forces based just outside the borders of South Vietnam. Based on these questionable assumptions, MACV submitted its new recommendations at the end of December.

The new MACV proposal was not good enough or fast enough for Laird. In mid-February 1970 he flew to Saigon to meet with Abrams and Thieu to impress upon them the urgency of the situation. He voiced disappointment about what he perceived as the lack of any new or fresh approaches from MACV regarding the implementation of the Vietnamization program. When Laird got back to Washington, he ordered the Joint Chiefs of Staff to come up with a more comprehensive plan. Two months later, the Joint Chiefs submitted the revised plan, which became known as the Consolidated RVNAF Improvement and Modernization Plan, or CRIMP. This plan, which covered the 1970–72 fiscal years, raised the total supported South Vietnamese military force structure to an even 1.1 million.[31]

The CRIMP plan called for a number of equipment improvements for the ARVN, which eventually received 155-mm and 175-mm long-range artillery pieces, M42 and M55 antiaircraft weapons, M48 tanks, and a host of other sophisticated weapon systems and equipment. The new equipment and weapons received in the two years following the approval of CRIMP enabled the ARVN to activate an additional division (3rd Infantry Division) as well as a number of smaller units, to include twenty-five border ranger battalions, numerous artillery battalions, four armored cavalry squadrons, three tank battalions, two armored brigade headquarters, and three antiaircraft battalions. After two years under this program, the South Vietnamese army strength would increase to 450,000 and consist of 171 infantry battalions, twenty-two armored cavalry and tank squadrons, and sixty-four artillery battalions.[32]

The territorial Regional and Popular Forces (RF/PF) also benefited greatly from CRIMP. As Vietnamization gained momentum, MACV and Washington planned to fill the gaps left by departing US divisions with an expansion of the RF/PF, which would, it was hoped, be able to take over the major share of territorial security and support of the pacification program. This expansion effort involved a significant increase in numbers and improved equipment. Under CRIMP, the RF and PF received newer, more modern weapons, including M16 rifles, M60 machine guns, and M79 grenade launchers; all were vast improvements over the hodgepodge of older cast-off weapons with which they previously had been armed. The influx of new 105-mm howitzers enabled the South Vietnamese Joint General Staff (JGS) to activate eventually a total of 174 territorial artillery sections to provide support for the RF, PF, and border ranger forces, thus vastly improving the fire support available to the territorial forces while reducing the burden on the regular artillery forces, who could then focus on supporting the regular maneuver battalions in their combat operations.[33] In addition to the new equipment, the manpower strength of the Regional and Popular Forces was increased to get more government troops into the countryside to support the pacification effort.

In terms of the sheer volume of materiel and modern equipment, Vietnamization worked. By 1970, South Vietnam had made a quantum leap in terms of modernization and was one of the largest and best equipped military forces in the world. Unfortunately, however, equipment and sheer numbers were not the only answers to the problems facing South Vietnam as it prepared to assume ultimate responsibility for the war. The fighting ability of the South Vietnamese armed forces had to be improved. To do this, MACV placed more emphasis on training and the advisory effort, which had been ongoing since the earliest days of US involvement in Southeast Asia but which had increasingly become a sideshow with the influx of US ground combat troops that began in 1965. Under Laird's incessant urging, the advisory mission became one of the highest priorities in terms of manning and resourcing.

While Abrams focused on improving the advisory effort and increasing the capabilities of the South Vietnamese armed forces, President Nixon and Secretary Laird continued to push for more and faster troop reductions. Nixon had announced the first US troop withdrawal at Midway, but he and Laird were given new motivation to expand their withdrawal plans by former secretary of defense Clark Clifford. In June 1969, Clifford published an article in *Foreign Affairs* that urged the unilateral withdrawal of one hundred thousand troops by the end of the year and of all other personnel by the end of 1970, leaving only logistics and Air Force personnel.[34] Nixon, never one to shrink from a challenge, stated at a press conference that he could improve upon Clifford's schedule. This statement received a lot of attention in the press and effectively committed the United States to a unilateral withdrawal from South Vietnam, thus removing the promise of troop reductions (or the pace thereof) as a bargaining chip for Kissinger in his dealings with the North Vietnamese in Paris. This would have serious consequences for peace negotiations and the efficacy of the eventual cease-fire agreement.

The first redeployment of twenty-five thousand US troops promised by President Nixon was accomplished by 27 August 1969 when the last troops from the 1st and 2nd Brigades of the 9th Infantry Division departed the Mekong Delta. In the months following the Midway announcement, there were continuing discussions about the size and pace of the US withdrawal. Laird had come up with several options for the rest of 1969 that ranged from withdrawing a total of fifty thousand troops at the low end, to one hundred thousand at the high end; in between were a number of different combinations of numbers and forces. Although Laird was the one pushing for the troop withdrawals, even he realized that the troop reductions had to be done judiciously, and he cautioned the president to be careful about withdrawing too many troops too quickly, as this would have serious consequences for the pacification program.[35] Laird's warning proved timely.

On 6 August, as soldiers from the 9th Infantry Division prepared to depart South Vietnam, the communists attacked Cam Ranh Bay. Five days later, they attacked more than one hundred cities, towns, and bases throughout South Vietnam. An official North Vietnamese history of the war revealed that the politburo in Hanoi had concluded after the Midway announcement that the United States had "lost its will to fight in Vietnam" and thus the communists, believing they were in a position to dictate the degree and intensity of combat, launched the new round of attacks.[36]

When Nixon had made his announcement in June about the initial US troop withdrawal, he emphasized that one of the criteria for further reductions would be the level of enemy activity. These new communist attacks clearly went against Nixon's conditions, and accordingly, he announced that he was delaying a decision about additional troop withdrawals. This caused an uproar in Congress and the media. On 12 September the National Security Council met to discuss the situation. Kissinger reported that "a very natural response from us would have been to stop bringing soldiers home, but by now withdrawal had gained its own momentum." Kissinger had sent the president a memorandum two days before the meeting, expressing concern about the administration's "present course" in South Vietnam. He warned that "withdrawals of US troops will become like salted peanuts to the American public; the more US troops come home, the more will be demanded. This could eventually result, in effect, in demands for a unilateral withdrawal. . . . The more troops are withdrawn, the more Hanoi will be encouraged." Kissinger would be proven right, but during the NSC meeting he was the only dissenter to the decision to go ahead with the scheduled troop reductions. On 16 September, Nixon ordered a second increment of thirty-five thousand American troops to be redeployed by December. According to Kissinger, the withdrawals became "inexorable . . . [and] the President never again permitted the end of a withdrawal period to pass without announcing a new increment for the next."[37]

On the battlefield, the war continued. The scale and intensity of the fighting had lessened somewhat, but Americans were still dying in the field.[38] At the same time, Nixon's diplomatic approaches to Hanoi had failed to achieve any traction. The president's critics in Congress continued their criticism of his handling of the war. In the late fall of 1969, antiwar activists organized several mass rallies calling for an end to the war. On 15 October, Moratorium Day, between 500,000 and 1 million people participated in demonstrations in a number of large cities across the country.

Nixon responded on 3 November by appealing to "the great silent majority" in a nationally televised address in which he spelled out his Vietnam policy. He insisted that the only honorable way to end the war was do so in a way that enabled the South Vietnamese to defend themselves as US forces were withdrawn. Accordingly, he asked the American people for patience and continued support of Vietnamization, closing in speech by saying, "North Vietnam cannot humiliate the United States. Only Americans can do that."[39]

Nixon's speech seemed to achieve its objectives. A poll taken soon after the broadcast showed that 77 percent of the American people polled supported Vietnamization.[40] Even some antiwar senators and Congressman responded favorably to Nixon's speech. Attempting to build on this momentum, on 15 December, Nixon ordered a third increment of fifty thousand to be redeployed before April 1970.

In Vietnam, the increased pace of withdrawals meant that once the initial departure of US forces began, the RVNAF were forced to assume more responsibility for the war, regardless of the progress of Vietnamization and pacification. This was the situation that confronted General Abrams. Faced with a war that continued to rage, he had to increase the efforts to prepare the RVNAF to fill the void on the battlefield left by the redeploying US forces. He was essentially fighting for time.

By the end of 1969, Vietnamization had made progress in several areas. The modernization effort had resulted in the equipping of all ARVN units with modern equipment. The advisory effort had received new emphasis, and the RVNAF training system was improving. The redeployment of US troops had forced the South Vietnamese forces to assume more responsibility for the war, as the number of battalion-size operations conducted by ARVN almost doubled between 1968 and 1969. Still, combat performance of the South Vietnamese troops was uneven, at best. Some units, such as the 51st ARVN Infantry Battalion, did very well against their communist opponents, while others, such as the 22nd ARVN Infantry Division, were largely ineffective in the field (the 22nd had conducted eighteen hundred ambushes during the summer months of 1969 and netted only six enemy killed).[41]

The MACV Office of Information publicized the increased participation of the RVNAF, emphasizing that, in time, the South Vietnamese forces would be able to stand on their own.[42] Despite these claims, many US advisers felt that the South Vietnamese were still too dependent on US forces for support and worried about their ability to carry on the war by themselves after the United States withdrew. The MACV public relations statements were correct in one sense: it was clear that time would be necessary before the South Vietnamese could stand on their own against the North Vietnamese. By the spring of 1970, US ground combat strength in South Vietnam had dropped by 25 percent in the nine months since the first increment had been withdrawn. The key question was whether there was enough time left to increase the combat capabilities of the South Vietnamese forces before all US combat units were withdrawn.

Vietnamization received its initial test in the spring of 1970, when Nixon ordered an attack into the North Vietnamese sanctuaries in Cambodia. In March, Cambodian Prince Norodom Sihanouk was deposed in a bloodless coup by his prime minister, General Lon Nol. Prior to this, the North Vietnamese had occupied large sections of the relatively unpopulated eastern part of the country, using them as base areas to store supplies and sanctuaries from which to launch attacks into South Vietnam. US B-52s attacked these areas during the covert Menu bombing campaign that began in March 1969, but the raids were less than effective in shutting down the base areas and sanctuaries. When Lon Nol took control of Cambodia, Nixon, wanting to provide support to the new pro-western government and buy time for Vietnamization and the continued withdrawal of US troops, seized the opportunity. He realized that the only sure way to secure the necessary time was to destroy the border sanctuaries and the vast amounts of war materiel stored in them. In Saigon, General Abrams, who had long advocated attacking the enemy sanctuaries in Cambodia, agreed with the president, characterizing a thrust into Cambodia as "the military move to make at this time in support of our mission in South Vietnam both in terms of security of our own forces and for advancement of the Vietnamization program."[43]

Accordingly, on 28 April 1970 the president authorized a US–South Vietnamese assault on the Parrot's Beak and Fishhook areas of Cambodia that jutted into South Vietnam west and northwest of Saigon (see Map 1).[44] This operation was a combined attack that involved thirty-two thousand American soldiers and forty-eight thousand South Vietnamese troops. The main attack into the Fishhook region was made by a fifteen-thousand-man force that included elements of the 1st Cavalry Division and the 11th Armored Cavalry Regiment. At the same time, an eighty-seven-hundred-man task force made up of South Vietnamese forces and elements of the US 25th Infantry Division conducted an attack into the Parrot's Beak. Both attacks were very successful, and the allied forces overran all but one of the enemy's base areas in Cambodia, destroying numerous large communist base camps, capturing an impressive array of supplies and material, to include sixteen million rounds of various caliber ammunition; 143,000 rockets; 22,892 individual weapons; 5,487 land mines; sixty-two thousand grenades; fourteen million pounds of rice; and 435 vehicles.[45] This was enough materiel to support enemy actions in the area for a full six months. Additionally, the various operations that made up the Cambodian incursion accounted for more than eleven thousand NVA dead.[46]

The South Vietnamese forces, most of which were under the command of Lt. Gen. Do Cao Tri, accompanied by US advisers and supported by US artillery, tactical air, and helicopter gunships, performed well, accomplishing all assigned missions. At a White House meeting on 31 May, General Abrams provided his assessment, saying, "The ARVN has done better than I would ever have expected." In a subsequent press conference, Nixon announced that the South Vietnamese performance in Cambodia was "visible proof of the success of Vietnamization."[47]

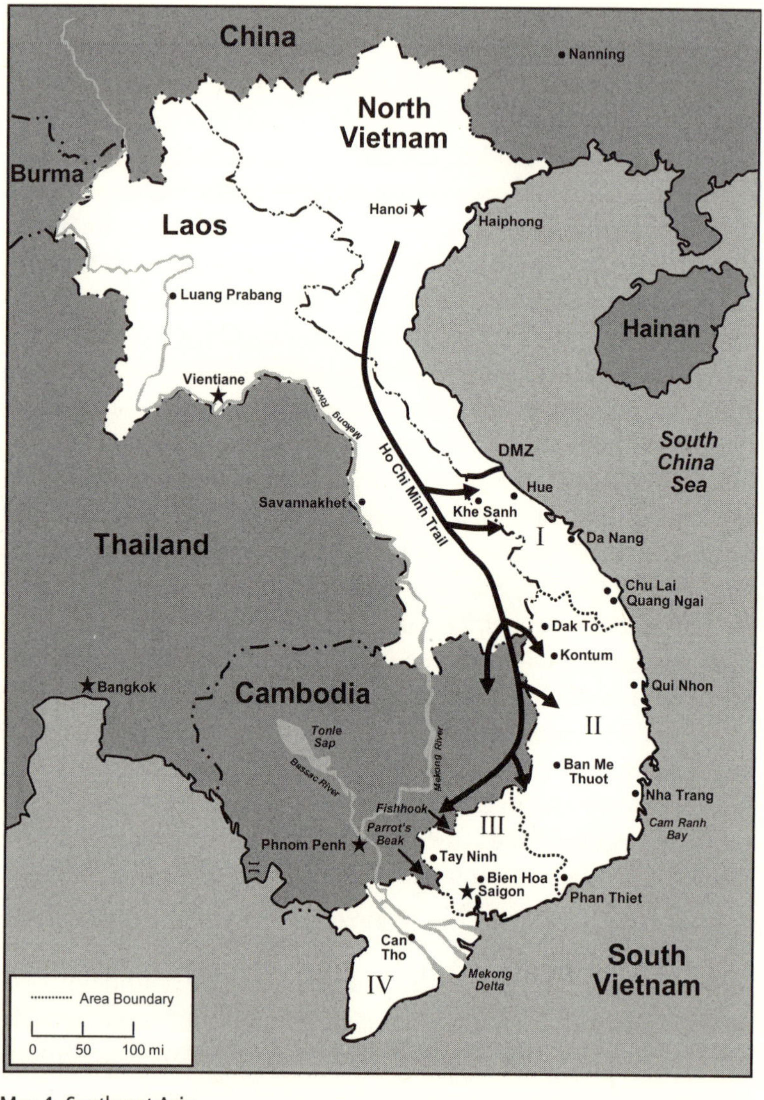

Map 1. Southeast Asia

The truth of the situation was somewhat less than Nixon wanted to believe. Many of the South Vietnamese units that had participated in the incursion were mostly from the better ARVN units rather than from the mainstream of South Vietnamese troops. In addition, there had been no intense fighting in the ARVN sector, because most of the communist soldiers there fled when the allied forces launched the invasion. South Vietnamese forces continued to demonstrate an inability to conduct combined arms operations and difficulty in coordinating fire support for their own troops, so the ARVN commanders continued to rely heavily on US fire support.[48] Even acknowledging these continuing problems, it is, nevertheless, true that South Vietnamese combat performance in Cambodia indicated that modest progress had been achieved in the Vietnamization effort.

Sustaining that progress was imperative, because the US troop withdrawals had continued unabated. On 20 April 1970, President Nixon announced that even though 110,000 US troops had been scheduled to be redeployed during the first three increments, a total of 115,000 had actually departed Vietnam. The second phase of the withdrawal, from April 1970 to April 1971, would reduce the total US strength by a further 150,000. By the end of 1970, only about 344,000 US troops remained in South Vietnam; the 9th Infantry Division, the 3rd Brigade of the 82nd Airborne Division, the 1st Infantry Division, the 3rd Marine Division, two brigades of the 25th Infantry Division, and the entire 4th Infantry Division were gone. As these US forces prepared to depart, they suspended combat operations, and the RVNAF took over responsibility for their respective operational areas.

It was against this backdrop of regular US troop withdrawals and continuing efforts to increase the combat capabilities of the South Vietnamese forces that the decision was made that would further test the efficacy of Vietnamization and result in the crossing of the border into Laos in 1971.

CHAPTER TWO

Deciding to Launch the Operation

Nixon believed that the Cambodian incursion of 1970 had "gravely undermined Hanoi's capacity to conduct offensive operations," thus buying much-needed time for the allies.[1] The North Vietnamese had long depended on the overland route from the port of Sihanoukville in Cambodia to supply their forces in South Vietnam. The coup that deposed Prince Sihanouk and put Lon Nol in power, together with the subsequent allied invasion of Cambodia in April 1970, had effectively closed that route. Additionally, a second route that involved shipment from North Vietnamese ports down the South China Sea to many points on the South Vietnamese coast had been severely curtailed by the fall of 1970 by an increasingly effective coastal interdiction campaign under Operation Market-Time. Deprived of its sanctuaries and bases in Cambodia, and with the coastal infiltration route from Sihanoukville effectively interdicted, Hanoi had to turn almost entirely to cross-country routes through the panhandle of Laos from North Vietnam for the resupply of its forces in the south.[2]

By 1971 the Ho Chi Minh Trail in Laos was a system of roads, command centers, transshipment points, base areas, and way stations, which were called *binh trams*. The *binh trams* were located about a day's march from each other, and each operated as a complete logistical center with an assigned area of responsibility and its own medical, engineering, storage, transportation, and maintenance support as well as infantry and antiaircraft troops to provide security.

The trail stretched from North Vietnam through the Mu Gia, Ban Karai, and Ban Raving Passes in the Annamite (or Truong Son) Mountains southward to Base Area 604, a key base in Laos near Tchepone, located on Route 9 about forty kilometers from the border with South Vietnam, adjacent to Khe Sanh in Quang Tri Province. From Base Area 604, men and supplies moved to

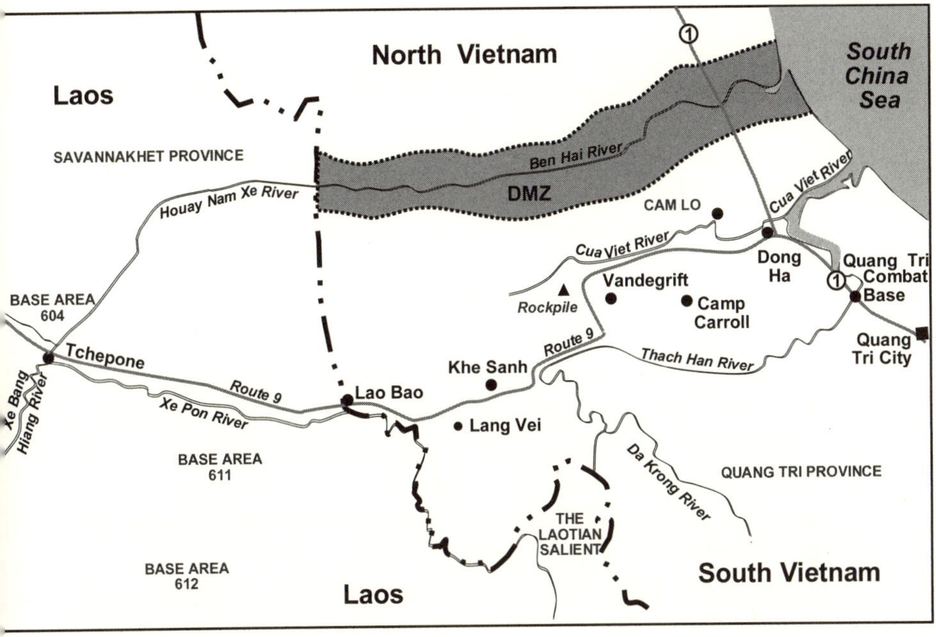

Map 2. Area of Operations

two other key NVA base areas, 611 to the southeast and 612 to the south near Saravane (see Map 2). From these intermediate base areas, replacements, reinforcements, and supplies could be readily moved into South Vietnam via Route 9 or through the A Shau Valley.

The North Vietnamese boasted after the war that they had built over thirteen thousand kilometers of trails and roads as part of the system. Beginning in 1959, the trail network had been built, maintained, and defended by Transportation Group 559 using an estimated one hundred thousand NVA and Laotian volunteers and forced laborers.[3] US intelligence estimated that between 1966 and 1971, 630,000 NVA troops, one hundred thousand tons of foodstuffs, four hundred thousand weapons, and fifty thousand tons of ammunition moved from North Vietnam down the Ho Chi Minh Trail.[4]

In the fall of 1970, joint MACV and South Vietnamese JGS intelligence estimates indicated that the North Vietnamese had two primary goals for the approaching 1971 dry season. First, they would conduct an intensified resupply and reinforcement operation in southern Laos. Then, using this buildup, they would strike from Laos with large-scale operations in the spring and summer of 1971 against the lowlands of Quang Tri and Thua Thien Provinces in South Vietnam's Military Region I.[5]

After the allied invasion of Cambodia, the NVA initiated a vast program to increase the capabilities of the Ho Chi Minh Trail and sanctuaries in Laos. In the fall of 1970, work crews and bulldozers were seen in the Ban Karai pass and at Tchepone. Not only were the North Vietnamese attempting to improve the trafficability of the trail network, they were also trying to further fortify the route so that it could be used without interference from US or South Vietnamese forces. While North Vietnamese engineering troops worked to improve the trail, twenty antiaircraft battalions were moved into Laos to provide air cover for the North Vietnamese forces against allied aircraft. These new units came equipped with a wide range of sophisticated weaponry, including 12.7-mm (.51 caliber) and 14.5-mm machine guns, 23-mm cannons, and more than two hundred heavier antiaircraft guns (37 mm, 57 mm, 85 mm, and 100 mm). These weapons provided a significant improvement of the NVA air defense umbrella over the Ho Chi Minh Trail.

Besides the insertion of air defense units, other NVA combat units were also moved to Laos to protect the vital supply line, bringing the total communist troop strength in Laos to an estimated twenty-two thousand (seven thousand NVA combat troops, ten thousand men in logistics and support units, and five thousand communist Pathet Lao). Under the protection of these forces, intelligence reports estimated that by the end of 1970 the NVA were infiltrating six thousand combat troops down the Ho Chi Minh Trail every month into South Vietnam.[6] In addition to reports of increased infiltration, US intelligence also had picked up indications that an unusually heavy stockpiling of weapons, ammunition, and equipment was taking place in Base Area 604. Other intelligence reports indicated that the North Vietnamese were also intent on rebuilding their sanctuaries in Cambodia.

Unless something was done, the North Vietnamese would soon be in position to directly threaten Quang Tri, the northernmost province in South Vietnam, and, by a short march from Base Area 611 through the A Shau Valley, could easily attack the ancient capital of Hue and other cities in the region. Intelligence analysts believed that the influx of troops and new weapons into Laos and Cambodia might be in preparation for a communist offensive against the two northern provinces of South Vietnam either early in 1971 or more likely in the US election year of 1972, when less than fifty thousand US troops would remain in South Vietnam and Nixon would be busy running for reelection.[7]

President Nixon and his advisers were alarmed at the buildup in Laos and the renewed enemy activity in Cambodia. In a meeting with the president and Henry Kissinger, his national security advisor, in Washington on 19 October 1970, Ambassador Ellsworth Bunker, home from Saigon for consultation, expressed concern with the step-up in infiltration on the Ho Chi Minh Trail and urged that more be done to interdict the routes.[8]

Bunker's concern was well-placed; the enemy buildup was very troubling. The president faced the same problem that had confronted him when the communists had threatened Phnom Penh in 1970. He had to do something about the North Vietnamese forces in Laos, or the enemy buildup there could have a devastating effect on Vietnamization and plans for US withdrawal from Southeast Asia. Nixon could not afford to wait, because US strength and combat power in-country were dwindling daily (by that time, US division strength was down to six from a high of ten, with the total troop number down by two hundred thousand), and he did not think the South Vietnamese could handle such an attack into Laos entirely on their own. Because US ground troops were barred from operating outside South Vietnam by the Cooper-Church Amendment, which had been passed in the furor following the Cambodian incursion, the ground fighting would have to be done by the South Vietnamese, and it was questionable whether they could stand alone against the North Vietnamese Army.[9] If the president waited, however, the NVA would continue their buildup until they launched a new general offensive at a time of their choosing.

Soon after Bunker's visit, the president, reviewing a series of new intelligence studies commissioned in early November, came to the conclusion that his only option was to conduct a preemptive strike against the communists. In that case, early 1971 would be the last feasible time to do so, because after that, given the continuing US troop withdrawals, there would not be enough US forces left to provide the necessary support to a large-scale South Vietnamese operation, nor fill in behind the South Vietnamese troops when they launched their attack.[10]

Once the decision was made to launch a preemptive strike,

the next question was where to focus the attack. An amphibious thrust into North Vietnam, aimed at Vinh, was initially considered, but Kissinger countered with a recommendation to repeat the Cambodian incursion to take advantage of the gains made by the earlier operation. He believed that an operation that took on the communists in Cambodia "was almost certain to succeed," since the North Vietnamese forces in Cambodia were occupied containing Lon Nol's forces, and there were not a lot of NVA reserves available to respond to another South Vietnamese incursion there.[11]

However, there were other ideas about where the allies should launch the attack. One of these can be traced back to an August 1970 cable from Admiral McCain, CINCPAC, to the Joint Chiefs of Staff that discussed concepts for potential operations in Laos and Cambodia that might be conducted by South Vietnamese, Cambodian, Lao, or Thai forces.[12]

Adm. Thomas H. Moorer, who had replaced Gen. Earle Wheeler as chairman of the JCS, believing that North Vietnamese defenses along the Ho Chi Minh Trail in Laos made any attack there problematic, agreed with Kissinger, favoring a thrust into Cambodia instead. From his perspective in Saigon, General Abrams expressed his belief that there were insufficient forces to support a major move into Laos.[13]

Admiral McCain, however, was insistent that Laos should be the focal point for operations in the coming dry season; he cabled Abrams in October that "the enemy's dependence on the logistics corridor through the Laos panhandle presents us with an unprecedented challenge. There is little doubt as to the damage which could be dealt to North Vietnam's aspirations by effectively blocking or even significantly hindering the southward movement of men and materiel."[14] Thus, to McCain, an operation to bottle up the Ho Chi Minh Trail in Laos was very attractive.

On 5 November, Admiral Moorer sent a message to McCain asking him to submit plans for the next six months. McCain responded that he anticipated a massive logistics buildup by the North Vietnamese in the coming dry season. Accordingly, he proposed two courses of action. The first consisted of coordinated operations by Thai, Lao, and South Vietnamese forces, each operating within their own national boundaries. The second course of action reiterated his earlier idea in which Thai, Laotian, and South Vietnamese troops would conduct combined operations to cut the Ho Chi Minh Trail in the Laotian panhandle in southeastern Laos. Aside from the obvious benefits that would ensue from attacking the communist supply route there, such an attack, in McCain's opinion, would compel Prince Souvanna Phouma, the ruler of Laos, to abandon the supposed neutrality imposed by the 1962 Geneva Accords and actively enter the war against the communists.[15] However, any operation into Laos would have to be conducted before the northeast monsoon season ended in May 1971. After that, the prevailing winds would shift around to blow from the southwest, bringing heavy rains to southern Laos that would inhibit both air support and movement on the ground.

By early December, the White House was considering three plans that could be executed simultaneously: (1) a major drive by one, two, or three South Vietnamese divisions into the Laotian panhandle, using extensive air cover, to cut the Ho Chi Minh Trail; (2) a strong spoiling attack by South Vietnamese forces into Cambodia, again with strong US air support; and (3) covert operations by South Vietnamese units into North Vietnam.[16]

The idea of attack into Laos was not a new one. Gen. William C. Westmoreland, commander of MACV from 1964 to 1968, had, almost from the beginning of his command, sought authority to conduct cross-border operations to cut the Ho Chi Minh Trail in Laos. In November 1968 he directed the preparation of Operations Plan El Paso, which included a corps-sized attack into the Laotian panhandle to seal off and block the trail.[17] However, for a number of reasons, not the least of which were political constraints imposed by the Johnson administration, the attack into Laos never materialized.

With Johnson out of the White House and the Nixon administration in office, the attack into Laos became an attractive idea for a number of reasons. As former ARVN major general Nguyen Duy Hinh recalled after the war, such an operation would "retain the initiative for the RVNAF [Republic of Vietnam Armed Forces], disrupt the flow of enemy personnel and supplies to South Vietnam, and greatly reduce the enemy's capability to launch an offensive in 1971."[18] As previously stated, with US troops being steadily drawn down, early 1971 would be the last opportunity for the South Vietnamese to go on such an offensive while substantial US combat forces would still be in South Vietnam to provide support.

Despite these obvious advantages, determining who was the

most vocal proponent for the Laos option is subject to conjecture. Complicating the issue is that after the operation turned out the way it did, there was significant effort on many of the principals involved in putting together the plan to distance themselves from the original decision to launch the operation. In his memoir, Kissinger puts the blame on General Abrams for having misled him about the operation's prospects for success.[19] This appears to be a case of Kissinger wanting to absolve himself from responsibility after the fact.

The South Vietnamese also disavowed any responsibility for the decision to launch the operation when it became controversial later; one former ARVN officer, Col. Hoang Ngoc Lung, in a postwar study wrote: "The Cambodian foray in 1970 and the Laos operation to Tchepone in 1971 came into being only because MACV originated them, promoted them, and supported them."[20] This was not entirely the case, since Gen. Cao Van Vien, chairman of the South Vietnamese JGS, had been proposing a similar operation to cut the North Vietnamese supply lines since 1965.[21] Moreover, Vien and President Thieu both agreed to the raid into Laos when General Abrams presented it to them; they realized that if the offensive did not take place in early 1971, it would not take place at all.[22] Former South Vietnamese ambassador Bui Diem later recalled that Thieu and his generals were optimistic, saying "that their enthusiasm came as no surprise," citing the high morale in the ARVN after the successes in the Cambodian operation the previous year.[23]

Historian Lewis Sorley maintains that when the option was first discussed, Abrams warned against "the ever present danger of RVNAF indigestion from too much too soon" and that the plan was pushed by Alexander Haig and Admiral McCain. It is clear from the message traffic that Abrams received his marching orders from Washington via CINCPAC and that he responded to the guidance that he was given to come up with a plan. Haig himself later claimed that, "prodded remorselessly by Nixon and Kissinger, the Pentagon finally devised a plan" for the thrust into Laos. Gen. Bruce Palmer later wrote, "The more immediate origins of the March 1971 incursion into Laos, namely the White House, illustrate how closely President Nixon and his NSC staff dominated the overall control and conduct of both the war and the closely interrelated negotiations to end the war."[24]

On 6 December 1970, Admiral McCain sent a message to General Abrams advising him that the president wanted to see concepts for multidivision South Vietnamese attacks into Cambodia and Laos. He directed Abrams to contact General Vien and the JGS to discuss the contemplated operations and secure President Thieu's support for them.[25]

On 8 December, Admiral Moorer further directed Abrams to prepare contingency plans for the South Vietnamese cross-border operation into the Laotian panhandle via Route 9, supported by full US air support and a concurrent, but smaller, South Vietnamese attack into Cambodia to destroy a major enemy base area being developed in the Chup Rubber Plantation, about sixty miles northeast of Phnom Penh. At this juncture, Nixon and Kissinger still placed primary interest on the attack into Cambodia, where they hoped to prevent the NVA from rebuilding their bases that were destroyed during the 1970 Cambodian incursion. Nevertheless, the focus was rapidly shifting to the proposed operation in Laos.[26]

Abrams already had a plan in place for the thrust into Cambodia. It involved a drive by the ARVN III Corps into the Chup area with up to twenty-eight South Vietnamese battalions to open Route 7 from the South Vietnamese border to the Mekong River, clear enemy base areas, and disrupt any North Vietnamese offensive planned for Military Region III.[27] The White House subsequently approved this plan.

There was no existing plan for the attack into Laos. Two days after receiving the guidance from Admiral McCain to prepare a plan for Laos, Abrams held a meeting with Gen. Fred Weyand, his deputy; Lt. Gen. James W. "Jock" Sutherland, commanding general of US XXIV Corps; Lt. Gen. Michael S. Davison, commander of II Field Force; Maj. Gen. Donald Cowles, MACV J3 Operations; and Brig. Gen. William C. Potts, MACV J2 Intelligence. The J2 briefed the enemy situation, citing intelligence reports that indicated that the NVA was initiating a full-scale logistical effort to move additional men and equipment south along the Ho Chi Minh Trail. He then predicted a four-part NVA offensive as soon as the logistical buildup was completed: (1) a multidivision invasion of Quang Tri and Thua Thien Provinces, focused on the cities of Quang Tri and Hue; (2) a renewed attack in Cambodia, aimed at capturing Phnom Penh and overthrowing the Lon Nol government; (3) a rebuilding operation along the Cambodian–South Vietnamese border to reclaim lost sanctuaries; and (4) a continuation of the buildup in southern Laos throughout the dry season to support follow-on operations.[28]

Based on the earlier guidance from Admiral McCain and the current enemy situation as briefed by the J2, Abrams directed Sutherland and Davison each to develop concept plans for attacks into Laos from Military Regions I and III, respectively, to counter the NVA buildup there.

In a follow-on meeting, Abrams reviewed their recommended courses of action and selected Sutherland's proposal for a main ARVN attack by I Corps supported by US XXIV Corps to cut the Ho Chi Minh Trail in the vicinity of Tchepone along Route 9. This would be conducted concurrently with the second ARVN offensive in Cambodia to counter the NVA buildup against Phnom Penh. Abrams then presented this concept to Ambassador Bunker, President Thieu, and General Vien. After this meeting, the South Vietnamese began their own planning.[29]

As this planning evolved, Admiral Moorer cabled Abrams on 10 December, forwarding a message from the president. In that message, the president again charged Abrams to "undertake, in coordination with the armed forces of South Vietnam and Cambodia, an intensive planning effort . . . to carry the battle to the enemy to the greatest extent possible."[30] Additionally, he informed Abrams that the president was dispatching Brigadier General Haig to Saigon to secure approval for the proposed operations from President Thieu and to receive the initial concept briefing from General Abrams.

On 12 December, Abrams forwarded to Admiral McCain a more fully developed concept for the proposed operation in Laos, which called for a two-division force, spearheaded by a South Vietnamese armored brigade, from northern I Corps attacking along Route 9 "to sever the enemy [line of communication] at Tchepone . . . and to deny to the enemy the logistic corridor vital for continued prosecution of the war." He emphasized that "speed of execution is essential to the success of this operation," saying further, "An operation dependent solely on air mobility would be subject to the vagaries of the weather and the considerable enemy AAA [antiaircraft artillery] threat in the objective area." The message also addressed the attack into Cambodia to strike at the enemy bases in the Chup Rubber Plantation area. Three days later, McCain forwarded the concept to Moorer, saying that the operation provided "an excellent opportunity to strike the enemy where he least expects it, to destroy his resupply effort at the heart of the system." He closed saying, "I wholeheartedly concur with the concept of this plan." When Moorer received the concept plan on 15 December, he cabled Abrams and McCain back generally concurring with the plan for the attacks into both Laos and Cambodia, saying that he was "already sold on the plan and just need[ed] additional ammunition to sell it to higher authority."[31]

In the interim, General Haig arrived in Saigon on 13 December. He met with Abrams and Ambassador Bunker. Then they met together with President Thieu and General Vien in the Presidential Palace to discuss the proposed thrusts into Laos and Cambodia. After the meeting, Haig cabled the White House that Abrams, Bunker, and Thieu favored the bolder course of action: the attack into Laos to strike a decisive blow against the Ho Chi Minh Trail, with a supporting attack into Cambodia.[32]

After meeting with Thieu, General Abrams met again with Haig and presented the details of the concept for the proposed operation, describing the attack along Route 9 into Laos by ARVN I Corps. US forces, specifically prohibited from a ground role in Laos, would furnish air support, airlift, and the majority of the supporting firepower. Additionally, to support the ARVN attack to seize Tchepone, US forces would set up blocking positions along the DMZ in South Vietnam and establish a forward support base adjacent to the Laotian border at Khe Sanh, the site of the former US Marine combat base that had been closed in 1968.[33]

The South Vietnamese thrust into Laos was envisioned as a two-pronged attack to the west from Khe Sanh using ground and airmobile operations on and parallel to Route 9. The initial assault would be followed by search and clear operations to destroy communist base areas and interdict traffic along the Ho Chi Minh Trail inside Laos. Concurrently, a smaller South Vietnamese supporting attack by elements of ARVN III Corps into Cambodia would seek to open Highway 7 from the South Vietnamese border to the Mekong River and destroy a new enemy base area being constructed in the vicinity of the Chup Rubber Plantation, some twenty-five miles inside Cambodia.

According to the concept presented by Abrams, the Laotian operation would be conducted in four phases. In Phase I, a US mechanized brigade would open and secure Highway 9 to the Laotian border and establish a forward operating base, airfield, and several firebases within South Vietnam to support subsequent South Vietnamese operations in Laos. In Phase II, ARVN armored forces supported on the flanks by helicopter-inserted infantry, would advance rapidly along Highway 9 into Laos to seize Tchepone, the site of an old French airbase, which, according to Abrams, was "the vital NVA/VC logistic nerve center providing logistic support not only to Cambodia and southern Vietnam, but to Laos and I and II Corps as well."[34]

In Phase III, ARVN forces would improve the airfield at Tchepone to support follow-on logistics operations, while other forces would destroy NVA forces and supply caches in the area. In Phase IV, ARVN forces would withdraw either back down Highway 9 or through Base Area 611, which they could destroy as they moved through it. As the main ARVN forces withdrew, "stay behind" guerrillas would be inserted. It was envisioned that operations would last about three months and would start in late January or early February. This would provide sufficient time to complete the operation before the Laotian rainy season began in late April.

Summarizing the concept plan, Abrams stated that the operation would "strike at the heart of the logistic/infiltration network in the Laos panhandle" and would "substantially disrupt the enemy timetable for 1971 and significantly impact on his effort in 1972." Further, he argued that if the communist supply routes could be interdicted in Laos and Cambodia for just one dry season, their ability to launch large-scale offensives in South Vietnam in Military Regions I and III would be "significantly curtailed, if not eliminated, for an indefinite future."[35]

Haig returned to Washington and related Abrams's plan to Kissinger and the president, noting that Bunker, Thieu, and Vien were all in favor of the plan but pointing out that Thieu insisted on US air and logistical support as conditions.[36] According to Kissinger, Nixon liked the plan immediately, but, concerned with public, international, and congressional reaction, he "was determined not to stand naked in front of his critics as he had the year before on Cambodia."[37] Therefore, he set about to build a working consensus in favor of the offensive among his advisers. To do this, he set up a series of briefings for his cabinet members and other key advisers in which he could take them on one at a time. He targeted Secretary of Defense Melvin R. Laird first.

On the morning of 23 December, Nixon met with Laird, Moorer, and Kissinger. Haig briefed the plan, saying that General Abrams had described the operation as "potentially the most decisive operation of the war." Nixon told Laird that he was in favor of the proposed operation and asked the secretary of defense what he thought. Laird replied, "Let's take a crack at it."[38] According to Kissinger, Laird fully backed the concept of a cross-border operation to cut the Ho Chi Minh Trail, arguing that it would buy at least a year and that a successful major offensive operation by the South Vietnamese without US ground support would confirm the modernization and self-reliance of ARVN ground troops and serve as clear evidence of the success of Vietnamization. Nixon then gave his general approval of both plans "in principle," subject to review after Laird returned from his scheduled trip to Saigon early in January.[39]

The restrictions of the Cooper-Church Amendment, forbidding American ground troops from crossing the border, also meant that no US advisers could accompany ARVN units into Laos. US support was limited to tactical air, helicopter, and long-range artillery support (operating from South Vietnamese firebases along the border). Nevertheless, the president believed that the ARVN was capable of conducting these attacks supported by the American combat forces that remained at the beginning of 1971. Admiral Moorer assured him that the South Vietnamese could do the job if protected by American airpower.[40]

CHAPTER THREE

The Plan

As the initial concept for the operation was being developed and briefed, Lieutenant General Sutherland was at first told, because of operational security concerns, not to discuss the plan with his South Vietnamese counterpart, Lt. Gen. Hoang Xuan Lam, commander of ARVN I Corps. However, Sutherland soon learned that Lam already knew about the upcoming operation. On 22 December 1970, the US advisor to the 1st ARVN Division, Col. Ben Harrison, discovered that Lam and Brig. Gen. Pham Van Phu, commander of the 1st ARVN Division, had already discussed a possible operation in Laos. Phu then asked Harrison and his staff to provide assistance in drafting a division plan for the cross-border operation. When Harrison contacted Sutherland for guidance, Sutherland, following Abrams's orders, denied permission for Harrison to assist the ARVN in the planning for the operation.[1] Therefore, both corps commanders were independently preparing plans for the operation that one would conduct and the other would support. This surreal situation continued until the first week in January.

On 7 January, Admiral Moorer sent Abrams a message authorizing him to finalize planning for the Laotian operation. That same day, General Abrams sent Lieutenant General Sutherland a message instructing him to prepare a detailed plan for the attack into Laos. The deadline for submission of the final plan was no later than 16 January, giving Sutherland and his planners just nine days to complete the planning cycle.

Subsequently, Sutherland, finally given approval to coordinate with his counterpart, met with Lam to discuss how to proceed. A combined planning cell was established, and as General Sutherland later observed, "the tempo of planning increased and with it more personnel were added to the combined planning staff." Sutherland offered the XXIV Corps headquarters as a secure area for the planning, and the two corps commanders agreed to assign two members of their respective staffs to form the combined planning cell. The planners were instructed to be prepared to brief the completed plan on 16 January 1971.[2]

On 21 January, Sutherland and Lam flew to Saigon, where they met with Generals Vien and Abrams at MACV headquarters. There they presented a detailed briefing of the plan. Later that day, Lam briefed the plan to President Thieu.

Operation Lam Son 719, named for the birthplace of Le Loi, a Vietnamese national hero who had defeated an invading Chinese army in the early fifteenth century, was to be a combined RVNAF-US operation conducted under several constraints.[3] No joint command headquarters was established for the control of the operation. As previously stated, the overall ground commander of the operation in Laos was to be Lieutenant General Lam, who would respond directly to orders and guidance from President Thieu; ultimately, this relationship would govern the complete course of the operation, reducing US control and influence once the South Vietnamese forces crossed into Laos.

General Sutherland would command all involved US Army forces and coordinate American support in Military Region I for the operation; as part of that effort, he also would coordinate and direct all airmobile operations in support of General Lam's ground plans in both South Vietnam and Laos. Gen. Lucius D. Clay Jr., commander of the Seventh Air Force, would command and coordinate all US Air Force resources that would support the operation.

Lam and Sutherland would control their respective phases of the operation from forward command posts at Dong Ha and Quang Tri, respectively; I Corps would establish a forward command post at FSB Kilo, just south of Khe Sanh. Because of the congressional restrictions against US ground personnel crossing the border, the ground action in Laos would be the sole responsibility of South Vietnamese forces; as previously stated, there would be no US ground combat troops in Laos, and American advisers with the ARVN units would remain in South Vietnam. This would have a major impact on normal operating procedures, particularly with regard to fire support coordination. The South Vietnamese had grown dependent on their advisers to help coordinate fires, tactical air support, and logistics; in Laos they would have to accomplish these critical functions themselves.

The operation was envisioned to be a spoiling attack, one that was designed not so much to take and hold terrain objectives, but rather to strike at the enemy's lines of communication in Laos, disrupt his plans, and forestall a new offensive. The primary objective of the coordinated air and ground attack along Route 9 into Laos would be to seize Base Area 604 west and south of Tchepone, a small town located at a strategic junction of supply routes along the Ho Chi Minh Trail forty-two kilometers from the border with South Vietnam. Additional South Vietnamese forces would block enemy routes to the north and south of the town. After securing Tchepone, the South Vietnamese would, for the remainder of the dry season, interdict the trail and destroy logistical facilities in the area before sweeping southwest from Tchepone down Route 914 through a major enemy storage and staging area called Base Area 611 en route back into South Vietnam through the A Shau Valley.

This operation would be conducted on the enemy's home court. The area had been occupied, developed, and defended in order to secure the segment of the Ho Chi Minh Trail that transited Laos en route to bases and staging areas in Cambodia. As such, it was the hub of a vast network of trails and communication with its own organic and assigned defense units. This meant that when enemy combat units arrived in the region, they would have access to supply stockpiles that were cached throughout the area. Additionally, the NVA units could tap into already existing radio and wired communications networks.

The terrain in the objective area was generally mountainous and heavily covered with thick vegetation that favored the defender. Through the center of the area of operations, the Xe Pon River flowed from east to west, with Route 9 generally paralleling the north bank of the river from the Vietnamese-Laotian border to Tchepone, where it met the Xe Bang Hiang River. The first major terrain feature in the area was the Co Roc, a rectangular plateau about four kilometers long, located on the Laotian side of the border southeast of Route 9. The second prominent terrain feature was a thirty-five-kilometer-long, fifteen-hundred-foot-high escarpment that rose abruptly from the river valley about two kilometers south of the river, stretching east-west twenty-five kilometers from twenty kilometers west of the border to a point south of Tchepone, where it abruptly turns southward.

The floor of the valley varied in width from two to five kilometers and provided a natural flight route into the area, particularly under marginal weather conditions. The terrain on the northern side of the Xe Pon River was broken, uneven, very hilly, and heavily vegetated.

Route 9 itself was a single-lane road, originally built by the French, that ran three hundred kilometers from Dong Ha in South Vietnam's I Corps Tactical Zone east to Savannakhet on the Mekong River on the western border of Laos and Thailand. The road from the South Vietnamese border to Tchepone was characterized by high shoulders on both sides of the road in most places, leaving very little maneuver room in those areas. The road was overlooked by high ground from Co Roc to the escarpment and almost its entire length from the border to Tchepone. The north-south feeder roads to Route 9 generally ran along ridges or streams.

Due to the topography and vegetation, there were few natural landing zones in the operational area. Most of those available were only large enough for one or two helicopters, requiring hovering approaches and departures; this situation usually precluded the landing of large helicopter formations at one time and increased the vulnerability of subsequent landings by helicopters that followed the first aircraft to put down in the LZs.[4] The limited number of areas that could be used for LZs would reduce flexibility for airmobile operations and have severe consequences for troop insertions and resupply by helicopter during the coming operation.

The weather in the area of operation during the period selected for the attack, a transition time between two monsoon seasons, was characterized by intermittent periods of rain, drizzle, haze and fog. In February and March, cloud cover would usually prevail except for a window of perhaps four to six hours in the middle of the day. This would limit ceilings and visibility, restricting both US Army helicopters and Air Force fixed-wing aircraft once the operation was launched.[5] The operation would have to be completed before the end of May, when the prevailing winds would be blowing from the southwest and heavy rains would drench southern Laos, severely inhibiting both air support and movement on the ground.

At the time planning began for the operation, North Vietnamese strength in the objective area was estimated to be between twenty-two thousand and twenty-five thousand troops. It was acknowledged that the enemy would have the capability to reinforce with up to seven regiments by D-Day plus 21 (D+21). These forces would be equipped with tanks, rockets, mortars, artillery, and antiaircraft weapons.[6]

After a preparatory phase that included movement to attack positions along the Laotian border, the actual invasion of Laos would commence on 8 February and last ninety days until monsoon rains would force the curtailment of operations. The attack was to be made by some of the ARVN's best troops, including the ARVN 1st Division and 1st Armored Brigade, three Ranger battalions from I Corps, and most of the elite Airborne and Marine Divisions from the JGS's strategic reserve. Initially, sixteen thousand South Vietnamese troops would be employed when the operation was launched; later, reinforcements would increase this number to over twenty thousand. A total of forty-two ARVN maneuver battalions, plus supporting elements, would be committed to the operation; of these, thirty-four would actually operate in Laos at some time during the operation. The ground action in Laos would be supported by US artillery, tactical air support, B-52 bombers, fixed-wing gunships, and helicopters. Approximately ten thousand US combat, engineering, and other troops, including eleven maneuver battalions, would support the operation from Quang Tri Province.[7]

The complex plan was divided into four phases. Phase I would involve the clearance of Route 9 from Dong Ha to the Laotian border and the establishment of forward logistical bases. This phase would be primarily a US operation, named Dewey Canyon II, that would commence with the 1st Brigade of the US 5th Infantry Division (Mechanized), commanded by Brig. Gen. John G. Hill, a highly decorated Korean War veteran, clearing and securing Route 9 from Dong Ha to the western border with Laos (see Map 3).[8] Additionally, during this phase fire support bases would be established at Ca Lu, near Fire Support Base (FSB) Vandegrift, an abandoned US Marine firebase located west of Quang Tri, and Khe Sanh, where a headquarters would be established to coordinate all helicopter assaults, close air support, long-range artillery fires, and logistical support.

Khe Sanh had become famous during the Tet Offensive of 1968, but it had been abandoned for three years. In fact, there had been no major allied operations west of Vandegrift since 1968, and the mountainous area between there and the South Vietnamese–Laotian frontier effectively belonged to the NVA.

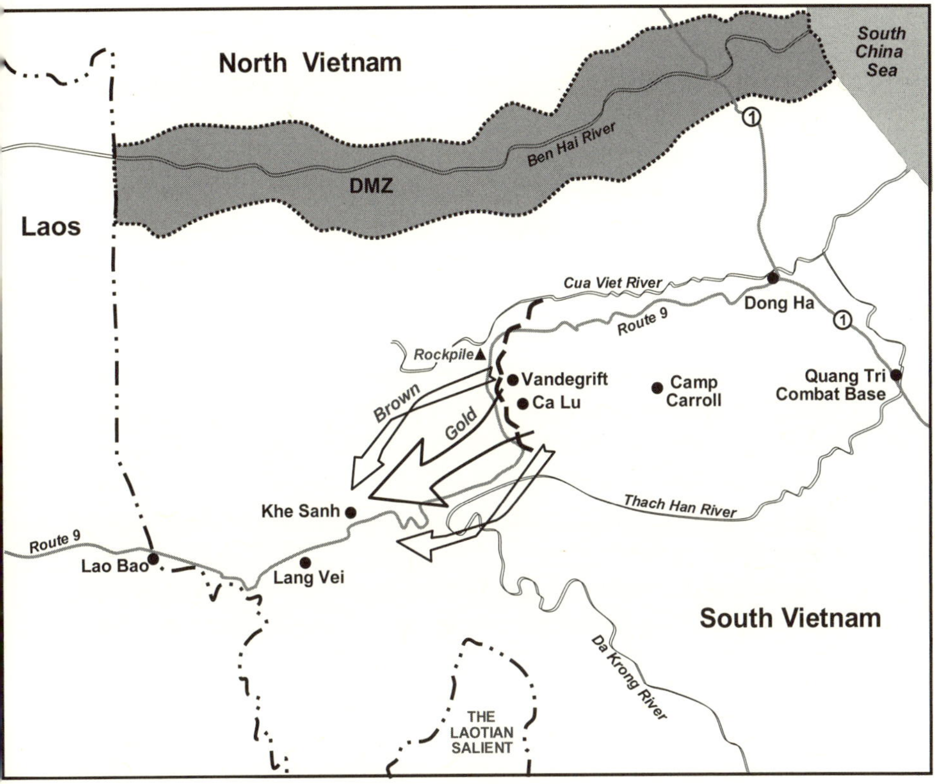

Map 3. Operation Lam Son 719, Phase I (Dewey Canyon II)

In addition to securing Khe Sanh, the 1st Brigade, 5th Infantry Division, would also cover and protect the deployment of US heavy artillery battalions to western Quang Tri Province and establish a screen southward to the Laotian border to protect ARVN troop assembly areas. The US 45th Engineer Group would repair the airfield at Khe Sanh and prepare it for C-130 traffic. The engineers would also repair Route 9, which was paved from Dong Ha to Vandegrift but not much more than an unimproved dirt path from Vandegrift to the Laotian border.

Simultaneous with the operation of the 1st Brigade, 5th Infantry Division, the US 101st Airborne Division (Airmobile), under the command of Maj. Gen. Thomas M. Tarpley, would take over responsibility for the ARVN 1st Infantry Division area of operation in Quang Tri and Thua Thien provinces when the ARVN moved to attack positions along the border and while they were committed in Laos. The 101st would also conduct artillery attacks into the A Shau Valley, west of Thua Thien Province as a diversionary action. Other US forces would secure the area south of the DMZ and adjacent to the Vietnamese-Laotian border.

Tactical air support for the operation would be provided through the US Seventh Air Force. The South Vietnamese Air Force would play a role within South Vietnam and would assist with air support against the more lightly defended areas in the Cambodian operation; however, it lacked the numbers and appropriate types of aircraft to handle the intense air defense threat that would no doubt exist over the Ho Chi Minh Trail in Laos.

Seventh Air Force would control air operations in Laos through forward Direct Air Support Center (DASC) Victor, which would be collocated with XXIV Corps (US) forward command post (CP) at Quang Tri. English-speaking Vietnamese military personnel would be assigned to the 23rd Tactical Air Support Squadron (TASS), which would be deployed to Quang Tri Army Air Field to provide airborne forward air controller (FAC) support; these Vietnamese speakers would assist the FACs in communicating with the South Vietnamese forces on the ground once they crossed into Laos. In addition to US Air Force fighter-bombers, additional close air support sorties would be provided by the 1st Marine Air Wing flying from bases at Da Nang, Phu Bai, and Chu Lai, along with US Navy and Marine strike aircraft flying from aircraft carriers *Hancock, Kitty Hawk,* and *Ranger* on Yankee Station in the Gulf of Tonkin.

Arc Light (B-52) aircraft would be provided by commander, Strategic Air Command under operational control of deputy commander, MACV. "Arc Light" was the code name for the use of B-52 Stratofortresses as a platform to provide close air support for ground tactical operations. The aircraft, based in Guam and Thailand, usually flew in three-ship cells, and each carried a massive amount of ordnance. During the operation, the B-52s would provide high-altitude area saturation air strikes against selected targets deemed appropriate for heavy aerial bombardment in support of the South Vietnamese ground forces in Laos.

With the command and control arrangements established and the combat support in place, an ARVN task force from the 1st Armored Brigade was to follow the 1st Brigade of the 5th Infantry Division, secure objective Ham Nghi, a few miles southwest of the Khe Sanh airfield, and conduct operations to the northwest to screen the northern flank.[9] Concurrent with this effort was the pre-positioning of sixty-five hundred troops from the ARVN

Airborne Division and three thousand troops from the Vietnamese Marine Corps. These forces were to be airlifted from Saigon and Bien Hoa airfields by US Air Force cargo aircraft to airfields at Quang Tri and Dong Ha in Military Region I during the period D+1 through D+4. Additionally, it was expected that about two hundred airlift sorties would be needed to support US forces in Phase I.[10] All of Phase I was expected to require five to eight days for completion.

Once Route 9 was secured, Phase II would begin with a three-pronged ARVN attack west along the highway to Tchepone, supported by Seventh Air Force tactical air support, US helicopters, and long-range artillery (see Map 4). The main thrust along the highway would be made by the ARVN Airborne Division reinforced by the 1st Armored Brigade, consisting of the 11th and 17th Armored Cavalry Squadrons; this attack would be accompanied by a combination of ground movement and successive heliborne assaults by the airborne brigade ultimately aimed at seizing Objective A Luoi, the intersection of Routes 9 and 92 at Ban Dong. Two other airborne battalions were to establish fire support bases nine kilometers northwest and eight kilometers northeast of Ban Dong.

As the main thrust was being made along Route 9 by the airborne-armored task force, the north and southern flanks would be secured by additional ARVN forces. The flanks of the main attack along Route 9 were to be protected in the south by a parallel attack conducted by Brig. Gen. Pham Van Phu's 1st ARVN Division, one of the most well regarded South Vietnamese divisions. Phu's 1st and 3rd Regiments would be inserted by helicopter to establish firebases initially on the high ground in the Co Roc area south of Route 9. In the north, the South Vietnamese flank would be protected by the 21st, 37th, and 39th Battalions of the ARVN 1st Ranger Group, which would conduct helicopter assaults from Khe Sanh to establish blocking positions sixteen kilometers northeast of A Luoi and to provide early warning and prevent the enemy from moving south to impede the main attack along the road.

Once Objective A Luoi was secured, the 2nd Airborne Brigade would assault by air into Tchepone, while the 1st Armored Brigade would continue the attack westward from A Luoi along Route 9 to link up with the airborne troops in Tchepone.

Once the border was crossed, the attack helicopters of the

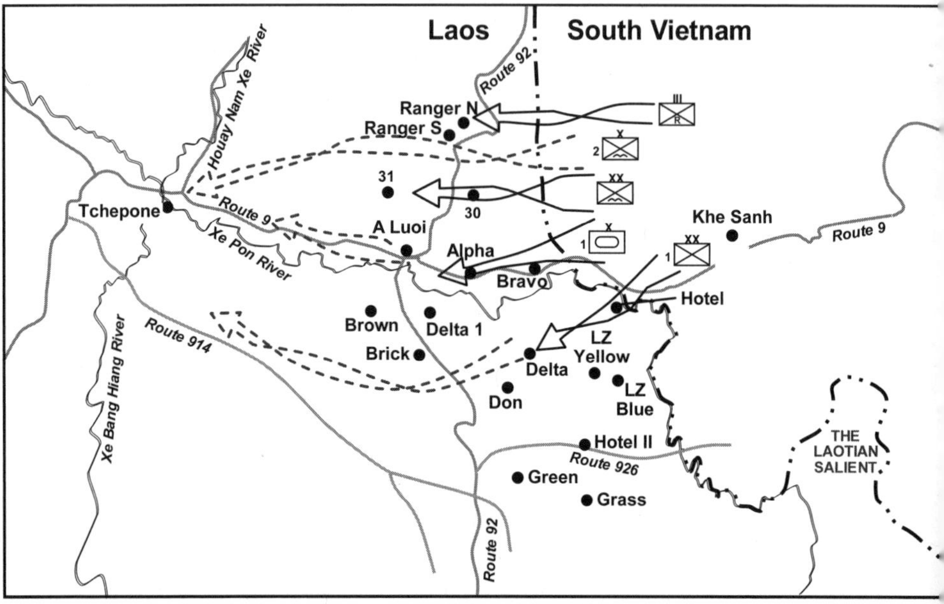

Map 4. Operation Lam Son 719, Phase II

US 2nd Squadron, 17th Cavalry (Air), were to locate and destroy antiaircraft weapons, find enemy concentrations, and carry out reconnaissance and security missions, which included the rescue of aircrews downed in Laos.[11] The 147th and 258th South Vietnamese Marine brigades would be held in I Corps reserve at Ham Nghi, just south of Khe Sanh. During this phase, US 1st Brigade, 5th Mechanized, would continue security operations west of Quang Tri Province and provide combat support as required from inside South Vietnam. The US 101st Airborne Division would continue to provide security operations in its assigned area as in Phase I.

Two days before the start of Phase II, US tactical air support would begin a concentrated campaign to suppress enemy air defenses (lasting from three to seven days). It was envisaged that Phase II would last until on or about 6 March 1971.

Phase III, which would commence after the capture of Tchepone, called for the South Vietnamese forces to conduct search-and-destroy missions in Base Area 604 and throughout the area south of Tchepone. The ARVN Airborne Division was to establish blocking positions northwest of Tchepone along Route 91 and southeast of Tchepone along Route 9 in order to isolate the area. At the same time, the 1st Infantry Division was to conduct search and destroy operations in its assigned area just to the south of the Xe Pon River, while the 1st Ranger Group would continue its blocking and screening mission on the northern flank. The ARVN forces would be limited to a corridor no wider than fifteen miles on either side of Route 9 and to a penetration no deeper than Tchepone. During this phase, the mission of the US forces remained unchanged. It was envisioned that this phase would last until the beginning of the southwest monsoon season in early May.

Phase IV, the final phase, addressed the withdrawal of the South Vietnamese forces from Laos. This was to be done in one of two ways. Under the first option, the Airborne Division, along with the 1st Armored Brigade, would withdraw directly to the east along Route 9 to Objective A Luoi to cover an attack to the southeast into the western portion of Base Area 611 by the 1st ARVN Division on the way back into South Vietnam. In this course of action, two Marine Brigades, 147th and 258th, were to conduct operations in the Ngok Tavak area also known as the Laotian Salient, a part of Laos south of Route 9 that jutted into South Vietnam, while the 1st ARVN Division focused on Base Area 611.

The second option was an attack by both the Airborne and 1st Infantry Divisions into Base Area 611; however, after both divisions attacked through the western portion of Base Area 611, they would turn north in an attack through the Laotian Salient rather than continue to the southeast.[12] Both options included provisions for the insertion of guerrilla units and other RVNAF elements left behind to harass the enemy in Base Areas 604 and 611 after the main body of South Vietnamese troops had withdrawn back into South Vietnam. The final decision on which option would be selected would depend on the situation at the time.

The US 101st Airborne Division was assigned the mission to provide rotary-wing support for the South Vietnamese forces. The assistant division commander for operations of the 101st, Brig. Gen. Sidney B. Berry Jr., was designated as the aviation support coordinator for the entire operation. Because the 101st still had responsibility for its assigned operational area, which had been greatly expanded with the redeployment of ARVN forces in I Corps in preparation for the upcoming operation, the division had to be augmented with additional helicopter units from other US divisions.[13] The commander of 101st Aviation Group would exercise command and control over all aviation assault, assault support, and aerial weapons units, to include both the US aviation units that were attached for this operation and the few South Vietnamese helicopters that participated. By the time this augmentation was completed, the 101st controlled an additional four assault helicopter companies, two assault support helicopter companies, two air cavalry troops, two assault helicopter battalion headquarters, and an aerial rocket artillery battalion.[14] This was a force of more than six hundred helicopters that would provide transportation, aerial fire support, resupply, and medical evacuation for ARVN troops attacking into Laos. Just putting this force together was a complicated task, and the aviators had to scurry to establish command and control relationships and accomplish the myriad of other coordination tasks that had to be completed before the operation was initiated. Maj. John A. G. Klose, operations officer from the 223rd Combat Aviation Battalion, later observed that this hectic time was "like twelve football games going on at the same time."[15]

Initially, each US assault helicopter battalion would provide dedicated direct support to a specific ARVN major unit. The 158th Assault Helicopter Battalion (from the 101st) would support the Airborne Division, the armored brigade, and the 1st ARVN Ranger Group. The 223rd Combat Aviation Battalion would support the 1st ARVN Division, and the 14th Combat Aviation Battalion would support the Vietnamese Marine brigades.

The 159th Assault Support Helicopter Battalion had responsibility for coordinating and conducting all medium and heavy lift support to both US units in Vietnam and South Vietnamese units in Laos. The Army CH-54A Flying Cranes from 478th Aviation Company would provide heavy lift north of Route 9, while CH-53D Sea Stallions from US Marine Corps Heavy Helicopter Squadron 463 (HMH-463), 1st Marine Air Wing, would cover the area south of Route 9.[16]

The 2nd Squadron, 17th Cavalry, from the 101st, would have the responsibility for coordinating and conducting all air cavalry and reconnaissance missions, to include the employment of the supplemental air cavalry units attached for the operation. As such, the squadron commander would receive missions directly from ARVN I Corps. Once the operation began, C Troop, 2nd Squadron, 17th Cavalry, and C Troop, 7th Squadron, 17th Cavalry, would support the armored, airborne, and Ranger units astride and north of Route 9, while A Troop, 2nd Squadron, 17th

Cavalry, and B Troop, 7th Squadron, 1st Cavalry, would support the 1st ARVN Division and the Vietnamese Marine Corps units south of Route 9.[17]

Because US ground troops were prohibited from crossing the border into Laos, the air cavalry troops would not be accompanied by their normal aero-rifle platoons, which were responsible for securing downed aircraft and recovering crews. Instead, the Hac Bao "Black Panther" Company from the 1st ARVN Division would perform those missions in Laos.[18] The Black Panthers were the division reaction force and enjoyed a very good reputation, having performed brilliantly during the 1968 Tet Offensive in Hue.

In addition to the critical support provided by US and Marine rotary-wing aircraft, the success of the plan also depended heavily on massive American air support in the form of B-52s, close air support, and tactical airlift. As previously stated, Seventh US Air Force would coordinate this effort with C-130 airborne command and control aircraft operating around the clock to coordinate air strikes and ensure timely air support for the operation. US FACs with Vietnamese interpreters aboard would control the two hundred sorties planned for each day of the operation. To assist in times of bad weather, a US Marine air support radar team from Quang Tri would be located at Khe Sanh to provide radar coverage of the entire area of operation in southern Laos.

The operation would also depend significantly on US artillery firing into Laos from South Vietnam. This support would be provided by the 108th Artillery Group, which included the 8th Battalion, 4th Artillery (with four 8-inch howitzers and eight 175-mm guns); 2nd Battalion, 94th Artillery (with the same number of artillery pieces); and B Battery, 1st Battalion, 396th Artillery (with four 175-mm guns). Additionally, the 108th Group would be augmented as required by 5th Battalion, 4th Artillery (with eighteen 155-mm self-propelled howitzers), which was the direct support unit of the US 1st Brigade, 5th Infantry Division (Mechanized). The plan called for 108th Artillery Group to augment ARVN I Corps artillery with long-range 155-mm, 175-mm, and 8-inch fires and to establish direct liaison with each RVNAF division and separate brigade.[19] The 4th Battalion, 77th Aerial Rocket Artillery (Airmobile) and their AH-1G Cobra attack helicopters would provide general support aerial field artillery fires to South Vietnamese forces in Laos and provide reinforcing fires to the 108th Artillery units providing long-range fires from inside South Vietnam.

Coordinating the support that would be critical for this operation would normally be the responsibility of the US advisers assigned to the South Vietnamese units, but because the advisers would not be crossing the border into Laos with their counterparts, the South Vietnamese company and battalion commanders would have to handle that critical support coordination themselves, most for the first time. The language barrier and lack of familiarity with procedures along with other issues would make this problem infinitely more difficult once the battle in Laos was joined.

To assist with facilitating US support, General Lam decided to establish divisional tactical operations centers near Khe Sanh, where Americans would be on hand to give advice and help with coordination while remaining on South Vietnamese soil. As Air Force historian Bernard C. Nalty pointed out, this "reflected the dependence of South Vietnamese commanders on American advice" but proved to be a poor substitute for an American presence on the ground in Laos and, in fact, "complicated the coordination of tactical air support and helicopter operations" because of the distance of the tactical operations centers from the fighting once the battle was joined.[20]

Logistics would also be a prime consideration in the conduct of the operation, particularly since there was only one ground line of communication, Route 9, once the South Vietnamese forces crossed into Laos. Because of security considerations, the ARVN 1st Logistics Command was excluded from operational planning until just before the operation was launched. Consequently, the brunt of the initial logistics requirements fell on the US Army Support Command, Da Nang, and the 101st Airborne Division Support Command.

According to the combined plan, I Corps units would receive the same logistical support from US log channels as US units from D-Day to D+8. During the period D+9 to D+17, the ARVN 1st Logistics Command was to gradually take over support for the ARVN operational forces.

US 26th General Support Group would establish a base support area (BSA) at Quang Tri in order to be operational on D-Day. US log units would deploy early to the ARVN assembly areas and provide support as the South Vietnamese forces assembled for the attack. Additionally, two forward logistic areas were to be established by US forces: Forward Support Area (FSA) 26-1 would be established in the Ca Lu–Vandegrift area to begin operations on D-Day, and FSA 26-2 would be established at Khe Sanh to handle support from D+4 to D+6.

To supply the ARVN units once they were in Laos, ARVN ground transportation would be used when possible, but as the South Vietnamese advanced further westward, their supply lines would grow longer and become more vulnerable to enemy interdiction, so there would be a heavy reliance on helicopters for resupply, particularly for those units in blocking positions on the high ground on the northern and southern flanks. Additional logistical support would be provided by tactical airlift from the Seventh Air Force's 834th Air Division.

To support the planned thrust into Laos, there was an associated plan for a diversion that involved a two-carrier US Naval task force with an embarked fifteen-hundred-man Marine Amphibious Unit steaming in the Tonkin Gulf some seventy kilometers off the North Vietnamese port of Vinh, which was located about two hundred kilometers north of the DMZ. The mission of this task force was to feign preparations for an amphibious assault on Vinh to draw North Vietnamese attention away from Laos and prevent the communists from rushing reinforcements from the area north of the DMZ to Laos when the South Vietnamese forces crossed the border.[21]

Additionally, the Vietnamese Marine Corps would execute a smaller deception operation in hopes of adding to the confusion of the North Vietnamese and drawing their attention away from the thrust into Laos, at least for a few days. The 147th Marine Brigade was ordered to conduct a practice river crossing, supported by M2 motorboats, across the Dong Ha River south of the DMZ. At a specified point after the river crossing, one Marine battalion would move to Cua Viet and simulate preparations to board ships to sail north of the 17th Parallel to conduct a landing in North Vietnam.[22]

As detailed plans were being finalized in South Vietnam, Nixon and his advisers continued to discuss the proposed operations. Laird, accompanied by Admiral Moorer, made his third trip to Vietnam on 9–12 January 1971 to take the pulse of the progress of Vietnamization and speak with President Thieu and General Abrams about the upcoming operations in Laos and Cambodia. According to Laird's record of this trip, Abrams, while acknowledging that "enemy troop movements introduced an element of uncertainty into the military situation," was insistent that the Laotian panhandle and the northern provinces of South Vietnam comprised the key to the military situation in early to mid-1971 and that "the proposed actions had the possibility of affecting the war at least as much as the Cambodian operation" the previous year. President Thieu concurred with Abrams on the necessity of the operations, agreeing "that military movement into the Laos panhandle would shorten the war," but Thieu was concerned about "political repercussions" over any perceptions of a widening of the war.[23]

A message sent on 12 January 1971 reveals that perhaps Abrams had more reason to be concerned than he indicated. In this message Abrams forwarded an intelligence update from MACV J2 Brigadier General Potts that estimated the combined Pathet Lao and NVA strength in Laos at more than forty-two thousand. More troubling was the prediction that the NVA could reinforce with two additional divisions from North Vietnam and up to twenty additional battalions from I Corps area within South Vietnam.[24] As it turned out, this prediction proved to be fairly close to what happened once the operation was launched.

Following the return of Laird and Moorer from Saigon, the president held a meeting in the Oval Office on 18 January 1971 attended by Kissinger, Laird, Moorer, Haig, Secretary of State William P. Rogers, and Richard Helms, director of the Central Intelligence Agency. Laird reported on his trip and recounted his conversations with Abrams, Bunker, and Thieu. In an almost three-hour briefing, Laird reviewed the military and political situation in South Vietnam and then discussed the proposed operations in Laos and Cambodia. In the discussion that followed, the consensus was that the campaign, if successful, would interrupt the North Vietnamese buildup, delay any planned communist general offensive, gain at least six more months for the Vietnamization program to proceed, buy more time and safety for the continued withdrawal of US troops, and dissuade the communists from further "adventures." Additionally, Nixon felt that a successful operation might convince the communists to negotiate in good faith and further stressed that the operations might "prove decisive in the overall conduct of the war."[25] Another key factor that came into play in the discussions was, as Admiral Moorer had observed in an earlier memorandum to Laird, that the operation represented the last opportunity for the South Vietnamese to mount a major operation against the enemy's sanctuaries while American forces were strong enough to provide substantial support and backing.[26]

Secretary Laird acknowledged that the North Vietnamese, no doubt, anticipated that the allies might launch an operation into Laos, "since they obviously held the bulk of their forces there for some reason." Director Helms of the CIA agreed, observing that "it was probable that the ARVN would run into a very tough fight in Laos." Admiral Moorer agreed that this might be so, but added that "it would probably be the enemy's last gasp."[27] It appears that despite the new intelligence estimates and the concerns on the part of Helms and others, it was determined that the potential gain from the operation outweighed the acknowledged risk.

This would be the first real test of Vietnamization in which the South Vietnamese forces would be expected to conduct the first major operation of its kind—a cross-border operation that would involve large South Vietnamese ground forces operating on their own without US Army and Marine ground advisers. It would serve as a critical test of South Vietnamese combat capability and have a great impact on the plans for American withdrawal from the war in Vietnam.

CHAPTER FOUR

The Mission Receives a Green Light

On 21 January, Lieutenant General Sutherland briefed the detailed XXIV Corps/I Corps plan to General Abrams and the Joint General Staff. Abrams subsequently approved the plan. In a follow-on meeting later that day, General Lam briefed the plan to President Thieu. Shortly thereafter, MACV dispatched a briefing team to CINCPAC and JCS to secure final approval.

It was believed that communist espionage cells were active within the RVNAF high command; therefore, General Abrams directed that the number of personnel involved in joint planning for the operation be held to a bare minimum.[1] Even General Lam's chief of operations, Col. Cao Khee Nhat, was not permitted to attend the plans briefing at XXIV Corps headquarters despite the fact that he had helped write the plan being discussed.[2]

D-Day was set for 30 January. South Vietnamese forces would cross the border into Laos on 8 February. Due to continuing concerns with security, I Corps did not disseminate its orders to subordinate commanders until 2 February; this delayed coordination among participating units while doing little to conceal friendly intentions from the enemy.[3]

The Airborne Division was to be the main effort, but the division commander, Lt. Gen. Du Quoc Dong, was not informed of the role his division would play until 18 January. He and his division did not begin detailed planning until they received the corps order on 2 February, giving them less than a week before they were to cross the line of departure.

General Dong assigned the 3rd Airborne Brigade (consisting of the 2nd, 3rd, and 6th Battalions) to occupy Objectives 30, 31, and A Luoi. Meanwhile, the armor-infantry task force consisting of the 1st Airborne Brigade (1st, 8th, and 9th Battalions), 1st Armored Brigade (11th and 17th Squadrons), 44th Artillery Battalion (155-mm towed), and the 101st Engineer Battalion would advance westward along Route 9, repairing the road as it advanced to link up with the airborne forces in A Luoi. The 2nd Airborne Brigade (5th, 7th, and 11th Battalions) would then seize Tchepone to link up with the armor-infantry column that would continue along Route 9 to Tchepone. Lieutenant General Lam approved the Airborne Division plan on 3 February.

In an attempt to preclude premature press coverage of the operation, the decision was made at MACV to impose an embargo on reporting troop movements until the operation was actually launched. This would prove to be an unwise move, because the imposition of the embargo was itself an indication of an upcoming operation and served to alienate the press, who would quickly become aware of the preparations being made for the coming offensive.

Despite the difficulties with maintaining secrecy about the operation, US and ARVN commanders were very optimistic about the potential outcome of the ambitious plan. Col. Arthur W. Pence, the senior adviser to the ARVN Airborne Division, reported after the operation: "It was apparent at this time that . . . Intelligence felt the operation would be lightly opposed and that a two-day preparation of the area prior to D-Day by tactical air would effectively neutralize the enemy antiaircraft capability, although the enemy was credited with having 170 to 200 antiaircraft weapons of mixed caliber in the operational area. The tank threat was considered minimal, and the reinforcement capability was listed as fourteen days for two divisions from north of the DMZ."[4]

Still, General Abrams was under no illusions that the operation would be easy, believing that the North Vietnamese had a significant fighting force in the area of operations and could "be expected to defend his base areas and logistics against any allied operation."[5] Radio intercepts beginning on 24 January reflected the enemy's concern over anticipated US and ARVN operations in northern Military Region I and the contiguous areas of Laos; they would not be caught unaware by the coming thrust into Laos.[6]

Nevertheless, both US and ARVN commanders and planners appear to have been emboldened by the modest success of the earlier Cambodian incursion in 1970. However, three significant differences between the attack into Laos and the Cambodian incursion exerted major influence on the ultimate outcome of Lam Son 719. Lam Son was to be a combined operation, but although US XXIV Corps would provide logistical support, long-range artillery, and helicopters, US personnel, unlike in the Cambodian operation, would be prohibited from operating on the ground in Laos. This meant that for the first time the ARVN would go into battle without their American advisers, whom they had become accustomed to relying upon to coordinate US close air, assault helicopter, medical evacuation, long-range artillery, and logistical support. In Operation Lam Son 719, once they crossed into Laos, the South Vietnamese forces would be on their own against the NVA.

The second difference between the Laotian operation and the Cambodian incursion was that the terrain and, to a great extent, the associated weather would favor the defenders and play major roles in the outcome of the battle. Whereas the terrain in Cambodia had been relatively easygoing, the target area for Lam Son 719 was rugged, covered with dense undergrowth and, along the Xe Pon River, which paralleled Route 9 to the south, double-canopy jungle. Route 9 itself was an unimproved road, characterized by deep ruts and washed out in a number of places. The single-lane route was dominated on both sides by high ground that provided excellent defensive terrain for the NVA defenders. Despite the problems presented by Route 9, it was the only logical overland avenue of advance for South Vietnamese ground forces attacking across the border. Additionally, to protect that route, the ARVN would have to occupy the high ground on both the north and south of the river in order for any column moving along the road to survive. Therefore, the NVA did not have to guess where to site their defenses.

In this and several other significant ways, the terrain in the area of operations overwhelmingly favored the North Vietnamese defenders. The nature of the terrain dictated the few areas where helicopters could be landed and the NVA could set up their air defenses in advance.[7] The objective area was close to North Vietnam, and the terrain and vegetation were good for concealing large numbers of troops and moving forces around. Additionally, since the area was part of the Ho Chi Minh Trail complex, the NVA troops were familiar with the area, and there was already a logistical network in place to provide necessary support.

The weather was also a significant factor. By the time of the operation, the northeast monsoon would be just ending, and flying weather would be marginal, often limiting flight operations by helicopters and fixed-wing aircraft. Additionally, the area would be subject to intermittent rainfall that at times could be heavy and inhibit trafficability for armored vehicles. Thus, terrain and weather would not favor the attacker in this operation.

The third key difference between Lam Son 719 and the Cambodian operation was that this time the enemy would stay and fight. After the loss of massive amounts of materiel and equipment in Cambodia the previous year, the North Vietnamese could not stand idly by and allow the South Vietnamese forces to cut the Ho Chi Minh Trail and interdict their logistical lifeline. They would have no choice but to put up a hard fight.

Besides these significant differences between Laos and Cambodia, there were a number of additional challenges involved in conducting an operation of this scope. First of all, the ground commander, Lieutenant General Lam, had never commanded such a large operation that involved more than one division. Nevertheless, his US counterpart, Lieutenant General Sutherland, before the operation considered Lam "a strong, positive leader who could be very decisive with his commanders in I Corps."[8] Unfortunately, despite Sutherland's earlier assessment, Lam would prove not up to the task at hand once his forces entered Laos.

Compounding the situation, the Airborne and Marine Divisions had never worked as divisions and were accustomed to brigade and battalion operations only. They had no experience in large-unit maneuver warfare. The commanders and staffs were not accustomed to working together, and the lack of sufficient planning time only made the situation worse. Additionally, the Airborne and Marine Divisions were national strategic reserve forces and answered normally to President Thieu and the JGS. Subordinating them under Lieutenant General Lam and I Corps did not sit well with either the airborne or the Marine generals. The Marine commander, Lt. Gen. Le Nguyen Khang, actually outranked Lam and was, moreover, critical of the plan from the beginning.[9]

The overall plan stressed speed and surprise, but the reliance on the occupation of fixed fire support bases, which was the normal practice in South Vietnam, would prove problematic in Laos. If the ARVN were not careful, the FSBs would tie down considerable forces and become tempting targets for NVA counterattacks.

According to Gen. Bruce Palmer, Abrams was more than aware of the potential dangers posed by the differences between the Cambodian incursion and Lam Son 719. It may have looked "very much like sending a boy to do a man's job" in an extremely hostile environment, but the US commander was counting heavily on US B-52 strikes, suppressive fires by US tactical air support, and the tactical mobility provided by US assault helicopters accompanied by their own armed escort helicopters to "even the odds" for the South Vietnamese. If the operation succeeded, it would place three South Vietnamese divisions astride the Ho Chi Minh Trail where they could prevent the flow of enemy logistics until the rains came in early May. If this could be accomplished, enemy plans for offensive action in Military Region I for the coming dry season would be severely crippled. The operation was not without risk, but if it worked, it would be a boost for the South Vietnamese and validate the Vietnamization process. However, if anything went wrong, it would be a disaster for both South Vietnam and the United States. As General Palmer later observed, the situation was "a big gamble"; failure would bring Vietnamization into serious question, further embolden the North Vietnamese, and "might result either in keeping US forces in Vietnam longer, or in generating such pressure at home as to cause the United States to abandon its hapless ally."[10]

The inherent risks in the Lam Son plan were only too clear to Henry Kissinger, who began to have doubts about the operation. On 21 January a CIA report prepared at Kissinger's request indicated that analysts did not think that the North Vietnamese forces "would be unduly surprised" by the impending South Vietnamese attack into Laos and that the move "would prompt strong military countermeasures by the Communists." Moreover, the report concluded that Hanoi would likely "do whatever it could to make the position of the South Vietnamese in Laos untenable and . . . [would] be prepared to accept the heavy manpower losses this might entail."[11]

On 25 January an anxious Kissinger met with Admiral Moorer to discuss the situation. The president's national security advisor reasoned that if the Tchepone area was so clearly critical to the North Vietnamese resupply effort, then they would no doubt fight hard to retain it. Concerned about the potential for high South Vietnamese casualties, he questioned the ability of the ARVN forces to operate by themselves without US advisers and air controllers on the ground with them.[12] As an alternative, Kissinger asked what could be done in northern Cambodia if the thrust into Laos were canceled. Moorer agreed to forward Kissinger's concerns and questions to McCain and Abrams but assured him that the South Vietnamese forces were capable of handling the attack in Laos and that US airpower could isolate the battlefield there to keep the force ratios at a manageable level.

Moorer sent Kissinger's questions in a message to McCain and Abrams on 26 January. General Abrams, responding in what struck Kissinger as a petulant tone, cabled back. He recommended canceling the Laos operation rather than substituting something somewhere else. He closed by again giving the operation along Route 9 in Laos his "unqualified support."[13] Moorer later wrote in his official diary, "It appears that after eighteen months of measured, unemotional, and statesmanlike responses to the endless questions from Washington, Abrams's one intemperate message has caused him to lose Kissinger's confidence."[14]

On 27 January the president met again with Laird, Rogers, Helms, Moorer, Kissinger, and Haig to discuss the situation further. Admiral Moorer reported that intelligence intercepts indicated that Hanoi was aware of the general plan for the upcoming operation in Laos but not the specific timing. Moorer acknowledged that "from the North Vietnamese reaction it was obvious that they considered Tchepone to be a vital area." He reported that he had discussed this situation with Abrams, who still "favored the operation provided full US support was assured," and reiterated that he, Moorer, was "confident that the South Vietnamese, with our support, could do the job."[15] Concluding his argument, the chairman reminded the president and the others in attendance at the meeting that Admiral McCain had weighed in earlier, calling the operation "an exceptional opportunity to inflict maximum damage against enemy personnel, materiel, and psychological pressure."[16]

When Laird was asked his opinion, he replied that he thought a successful operation in Laos would aid Vietnamization and "might lessen our long-term requirements for supporting ARVN forces for the next three or four years." However, in case the North Vietnamese reinforced in Laos, the allies should keep their options open on executing Phase II.[17]

Secretary of State Rogers was unconvinced of the wisdom of launching such an ambitious operation in Laos. He stated that, in his opinion, the whole issue depended on whether the operation would succeed. He reasoned that if the Ho Chi Minh Trail was as critical as Abrams maintained, the enemy would probably fight hard to protect it. If that were the case, the risks incurred in the operations would be too high, since during the operations the South Vietnamese ground forces would be expected to operate independently without US Army ground advisers. It would be a critical test of Vietnamization that would have a great impact on plans for American withdrawal. Rogers argued that when General Westmoreland as MACV commander had looked at a similar operation, he had estimated that it would take four US divisions to accomplish the mission. The current plan under consideration involved the use of far fewer South Vietnamese troops. Therefore, to Rogers, an ARVN defeat was almost assured, and he felt that such a setback "would serve as a defeat for both Vietnamization and for Thieu."[18] Additionally, he was concerned about international repercussions, particularly with regard to the response to the operation by Laotian prime minister Souvanna Phouma and possible Chinese reactions. Rogers also made the point that he believed Nixon's opponents in Congress would charge that the operation was contrary to the spirit, if not the letter, of the Cooper-Church Amendment. According to Kissinger, Nixon had heard the same kinds of objections before he ordered US and South Vietnamese forces into Cambodia. He had already considered most of Rogers's objections and "simply did not believe that his Secretary of State knew what he was talking about."[19]

Kissinger maintains that even though Nixon ultimately approved the mission, he continued to be concerned with follow-on phases of the initial assault that called for the ARVN airborne forces to be lifted by US helicopters to overwatch positions along Route 9. The president questioned whether the touching down of American helicopters on Laotian soil constituted "ground combat in Laos," proscribed by the Cooper-Church Amendment. There was a brief discussion about sending the South Vietnamese troops into Laos without US helicopter support or shifting the whole operation further south into Cambodia. Kissinger asserts that Nixon had already made up his mind to go through with the whole operation but that his questions added a level of uncertainty among his senior military advisers. He wrote after the war, "The uncertainty and hesitation suggested by his [Nixon's] request for further study of the airborne operation was bound to be magnified as it moved down in the military hierarchy."[20]

Despite any reservations the president may have had, the repeated assurances that he had received from General Abrams, Admiral McCain, and Admiral Moorer were persuasive. Nixon closed the meeting by giving final approval for Phase I of the southern Laos operation; he had previously approved the Chup Plantation operation in Cambodia, code-named Toan Thang 1-71, which would launch in early February.[21] Admiral Moorer confirmed that he would instruct General Abrams to move out with Phase I but to await further authorization for Phase II and subsequent phases, which Moorer assured the president could be canceled on forty-eight hours' notice if necessary.[22]

Alexander Haig wrote later that those who briefed the president on the plan for the attack into Laos were optimistic about its success, but all agreed that the "key factor was all-out US military support of ARVN." This is a rather revealing commentary on the prevalent thinking on the state of the Vietnamization process in early 1971, but as Haig pointed out in his memoirs, the success of Vietnamization "had little to do with its military effectiveness. Vietnamization was a success not in Vietnam but in the United States, where as the Secretary of Defense [Laird] and his faction had hoped and intended, it has lessened opposition to the war in Congress and the news media by offering a program that promised a definitive end to American casualties. These had fallen dramatically . . . , but reduced American casualties had little to do with the military effectiveness of the armed forces of South Vietnam."[23] That military effectiveness and the outcome of the decision to take the war to the enemy would soon play out along Route 9 in Laos.

CHAPTER FIVE

The Other Side

The success of Lam Son 719 depended greatly on secrecy, and whether the North Vietnamese had advanced warning of the impending operation has long been a controversial subject. There have been assertions that the North Vietnamese learned of the attack early in the planning process. Larry Berman, in his biography of *Time* magazine reporter and Vietnamese communist spy Pham Xuan An, writes that in January 1971 An picked up information from one of his ARVN sources about planning for an impending cross-border attack into Laos that was to begin before the rainy season set in. According to Berman, An passed this intelligence on through his normal clandestine reporting channels.[1]

Writing after the war, journalists Richard Pyle and Horst Faas of Associated Press claimed that northern spies were inside the Da Nang headquarters of I Corps during the planning for Lam Son 719. In a postwar assessment of the operation, former ARVN generals Cao Van Vien and Dong Van Khuyen wrote that "the enemy was not surprised by LAM SON 719 and was fully prepared to meet our forces head-on." There were fears at the time that this might be the case. In a January meeting in Saigon when Generals Sutherland and Lam went to present their plans to Abrams and Vien, Sutherland later recalled, "By then I knew, and so did General Abrams, that the [other side] had been alerted that something was going on." This suspicion went as high as the White House; in his diary for 26 January, Nixon aide H. R. Haldeman wrote, "Hanoi has our plan we've discovered."[2]

Whether the North Vietnamese actually knew about the planned operation is subject to conjecture; the evidence is contradictory. Even postwar Vietnamese narratives provide conflicting accounts about North Vietnam's prior knowledge of the impending operation. Several North Vietnamese accounts agree with the aforementioned assertion that Pham Xuan An provided intelligence on Operation Lam Son 719, but most assert that he did not pass on the battle plans for the operation and that the intelligence he provided was very general in nature, consisting of vague hints that the Airborne and Marine Divisions were being sent to conduct an operation at some unspecified distant location.

It appears that most of the reports that the North Vietnamese received prior to the crossing of South Vietnamese forces into Laos lacked details about the size, the actual timing, operational objectives, and specific location of the attack. A recent article on the 1971 southern Laos operation in the official Vietnamese Army newspaper acknowledges that prior knowledge of South Vietnamese intentions was "very general." Citing the "enemy's tightened security," the article continues: "Because of this, during the last two months of 1970 our efforts to obtain information about the enemy's plan to attack southern Laos did not achieve any significant results." Another account in that article admits that one of Hanoi's best covert agents, Dinh Van De, who served as deputy chairman of the Saigon government's National Assembly, was not aware of any plans to launch an operation into Laos.[3]

Additional evidence also points to further North Vietnamese uncertainty about the coming attack. For example, Gen. Dong Si Nguyen, commander of Group 559, responsible for maintaining the Ho Chi Minh Trail, took a trip down the trail to Central Office for South Vietnam (COSVN) headquarters, located in Cambodia, in late January.[4] It is highly unlikely that General Nguyen would have been absent from his headquarters in the Route 9–Southern Laos area at that time if he and the high command had known when and where the South Vietnamese planned to launch their offensive.

Still, Gen. Nguyen Huu An, former commander of the NVA 308th Division in 1970–71, in his postwar memoir asserts that "a number of things that the Americans had tried to conceal gradually were exposed to our view," maintaining that the Central Party Committee received a report on 3 February that Nixon had signed an agreement with Thieu to provide maximum support for a South Vietnamese operation into Laos.[5]

It is clear that the North Vietnamese suspected that the Americans and South Vietnamese were planning another large operation, but it is also clear that they were less certain about the specific details of that operation. However, Hanoi did not need advance notice to realize that the area they called the Route 9–Southern Laos area was a potential target for allied cross-border operations,

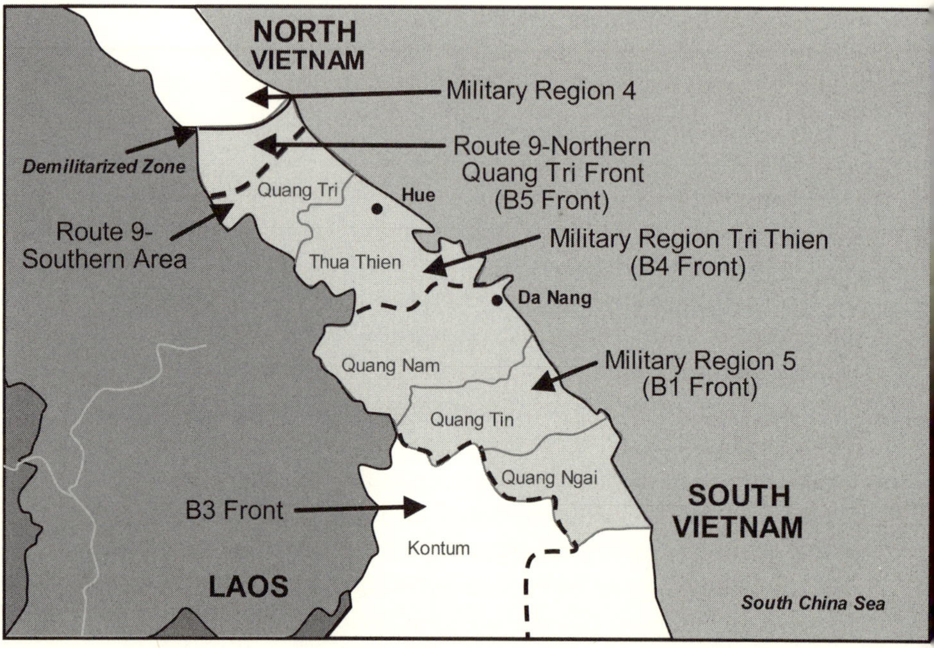

Map 5. NVA Military Fronts and Regions

and they predicted that the South Vietnamese "puppet forces" might launch a number of medium-sized and large offensives during the 1970–71 dry season (see Map 5).[6]

The leaders in Hanoi had concluded that the next logical step for the US and South Vietnamese forces after the Cambodian incursion would be to try to cut off the flow of supplies down the Ho Chi Minh Trail to communist forces in South Vietnam. They reasoned that there were three places that the United States might attempt such an operation: southern Military Region 4 in North Vietnam (where the Ho Chi Minh Trail began), the Route 9 area in Laos, and the triborder area where the borders of Laos, Cambodia, and South Vietnam meet.[7] They felt that the Route 9 area was the most logical place for the operation, and that is where they concentrated their preparations.

With the increased importance of Laos in light of the losses of materiel and equipment sustained during the Cambodian incursion in 1970, the North Vietnamese began drawing up plans and deploying forces to protect the area. An official history of one unit involved in the coming battle related, "Our Party's Politburo concluded that after the coup in Cambodia, it was clear that the

Ho Chi Minh Trail would be an immediate and priority target of enemy attack so that they could achieve their goals of splitting the Indochina military theater in half, cutting off our flow of logistics support down from North Vietnam, and weakening the resistance forces of the Vietnamese, Cambodian, and Laotian nations. Based on this assessment of the situation, the Politburo directed all battlefields to make preparations for battle all along our strategic transportation corridor, with special focus on the Route 9–Southern Laos area. The Politburo also ordered that a plan be drafted to defend against the possibility of a rash and reckless enemy invasion of North Vietnam itself."[8]

In October of 1970 the North Vietnamese established B70 Corps headquarters to exercise tactical command and control over the forces that would defend the Ho Chi Minh Trail where it ran through Laos. The new headquarters would initially assume command of the forces already in the area and, ultimately, reinforcements that would be rushed to the area when the fighting began in earnest. Sr. Col. Cao Van Khanh assumed command of the new corps, and Sr. Col. Hoang Phuong was named political commissar.

In preparation for the anticipated South Vietnamese thrust into Laos, North Vietnamese engineers began to improve the road network in the area to provide better mobility for their troops committed in the area. Additional North Vietnamese soldiers prepared defensive positions around the most likely landing zones and helicopter routes. Meanwhile, Group 559, responsible for the maintenance and support of the Ho Chi Minh Trail, accumulated supplies and equipment to support troops in battle for four or five months. The General Rear Services Department formed a forward command headquarters to work with the troop stations (*binh trams*) and other units of Group 559 to stockpile equipment and ammunition in order to build a supply network south of the Gianh River.[9]

By January 1971 the supplies stored by the *binh trams* amounted to more than six thousand tons, which, combined with the High Command's supply reserves, was sufficient to support fifty thousand to sixty thousand troops in combat for four to five months. In addition, more than thirty thousand tons of supplies were stored in warehouses along Group 559's strategic transportation corridor.[10]

While the North Vietnamese leaders had concluded that the

most logical place for an allied attack would be along Route 9, it appears that they did not have any actionable intelligence on the timing of the attack into Laos.[11] However, based on weather considerations they believed that any such attack would begin in late 1970. When this did not occur, they decided that the United States and South Vietnam must be planning something else, but they were not sure where. This uncertainty had a significant impact on subsequent North Vietnamese troop dispositions in Laos, southern North Vietnam, and northern South Vietnam.

Indicative of this uncertainty, Col. Gen. Nguyen Huu Ann, commander of the 308th Division during 1970–71, reports in his memoir that he had a meeting with Gen. Vo Nguyen Giap in the summer of 1970. Giap asked, "Where do you think the Americans will set up their bases to support the puppets? Will they attack Military Region 4, or will they attack Route 9 and southern Laos?" After discussing the courses of action open to the US and South Vietnamese forces, Giap directed, "You must make preparations in both areas, but focus the bulk of your effort on southern Laos. If the enemy makes a ground attack into Region 4, we will have to defeat him there, but your unit must always be ready to move out immediately if the enemy enters the Route 9 area of southern Laos."[12]

In a briefing to the 19th Plenum of the Party Central Committee on 12 December 1970, General Giap reviewed the military situation as he saw it, indicating that US and South Vietnamese intentions for the coming dry season were still unclear. He discussed the battlefields in South Vietnam, Cambodia, and Laos and talked about the potential courses of action that the US and South Vietnamese forces might take in the coming year. Acknowledging the possibility of enemy thrusts into Cambodia and southern Laos, Giap also talked about a potential enemy landing at some location along the coast in Military Region 4 north of the DMZ.[13]

When the attack along Route 9 did not materialize, the North Vietnamese leadership began focusing their attention on a possible US–South Vietnamese attack into the southern portion of the North Vietnamese panhandle in Military Region 4.[14] By late December 1970–early January 1971, however, the North Vietnamese were in the process of preparing an offensive of their own, sending elements from their 2nd and 320th Divisions down to mount attacks against the northern half of Kontum Province in the Central Highlands.[15] At the same time, the 324th Division was ordered to attack the northern portion of Route 12, northwest of Hue in Military Region Tri Thien.[16]

Nevertheless, the North Vietnamese hedged their bets somewhat and continued to prepare the battlefield in Laos by conducting reconnaissance and selecting potential assembly areas, fighting positions, and routes of travel, but as of the time that Lam Son 719 actually kicked off, they had only deployed one regiment of the B70 Corps (24th Regiment, 304th Division) inside Laos to block Route 9, while a regiment of the 320th Division, B70 Corps, was fighting Lao forces west and south of Route 9 and the 320th Division's 64th Regiment was beginning to move into Laos, on the way to the Central Highlands to join the 320th Division's 52nd Regiment, which was already there. The rest of the 304th Division, the entire 308th Division, and other combat support units were all being held back in the rear in the southern portion of North Vietnam's Military Region 4 to guard against the possibility of an amphibious landing along the coast inside North Vietnam.[17] This force included eighty-eight PT-76, T-34, and T-54 tanks from the two battalions of the 202nd Tank Regiment and one battalion from the 203rd Tank Regiment.[18]

The North Vietnamese do not seem to have been entirely sure what the United States and the South Vietnamese were up to until the end of January and early February 1971, when Operation Dewey Canyon II was launched.[19] It was clear then that US forces were intending to open up Route 9 and reoccupy Khe Sanh. The most logical reason for this was to use the old Marine base as a springboard for an attack into Laos. When it became apparent that the US–South Vietnamese forces were indeed planning a thrust along Route 9 into Laos, the North Vietnamese hurriedly responded, creating an ad hoc organization called Headquarters 702 to assume overall control of the coming fight. However, the NVA commander did not arrive to set up the new headquarters until 14 February, almost a week after South Vietnamese forces first crossed the border into Laos.[20]

In a very real sense, the North Vietnamese saw operations against the forces involved in and supporting Lam Son 719 on both sides of the Lao-Vietnamese border as a single campaign rather than dividing operations between those on the South Vietnamese side of the border and those inside Laos. Headquarters 702 was set up to oversee and coordinate the entire effort regardless of the border that ran through the area of operations.

This made sense, since each of the subordinate area headquarters elements involved (Military Region 4 headquarters, Group 559 headquarters, the B5 Front headquarters, and the Tri Thien Military Region headquarters) had other responsibilities beyond that of directing the battle against Lam Son 719, and B70 Corps headquarters had its hands full directing its own subordinate elements and probably was not capable of controlling and coordinating the efforts of all the other forces involved.

Additionally, the B70 Corps commander, Cao Van Khanh, was junior in rank to most of the other commanders involved (he was certainly junior to Military Region 4 commander Vuong Thua Vu, Group 559 commander Dong Si Nguyen, and Tri Thien Military Region commander Tran Van Quang), so a more senior officer was needed to be able to command all the headquarters elements involved.[21] Problems with sensitivities over seniority and rank were not confined to the South Vietnamese army; the NVA had to deal with such considerations as well. Accordingly, Maj. Gen. Le Trong Tan, deputy commander of the General Staff, who had commanded the Viet Minh 312th Division at the Battle of Dien Bien Phu in 1954, was placed in overall command of Headquarters 702.[22]

The new headquarters would have full command authority over all forces participating in the campaign, including B70 Corps, Group 559, the Route 9–Northern Quang Tri Front, the Tri Thien Military Region, Military Region 4, and Pathet Lao armed forces in southern Laos. Hanoi saw the coming confrontation in Laos as potentially the decisive battle of the war and gave the following instructions to the Central Military Committee: "It is vital for you to win this victory, no matter how many men or how much equipment and supplies you must use, and no matter how many men and how much equipment we have to sacrifice, because this is a battle of strategic significance."[23] Accordingly, the North Vietnamese forces would react in a strong and forceful way when the South Vietnamese crossed into Laos.

To support the forces that were being moved into the area in anticipation of the impending South Vietnamese attack, Headquarters 702 placed logistics under the direction of the deputy commander of Headquarters 702 for Rear Services (Logistics), who was a deputy director of the General Department of Rear Services. He was able to call on support from the preexisting logistics support elements of B70 Corps, forward elements of the

General Department of Rear Services in the southern panhandle of North Vietnam, and Group 559 (the Ho Chi Minh Trail Group) for logistics support organizations, stockpiles, and facilities.

Once the South Vietnamese intentions became clearer, the North Vietnamese did a lot of hurried scrambling, pulling out their previously prepared Route 9 plans. They rushed to send units down from North Vietnam and westward from the B4 Front area (Tri Thien) and mobilized some units that just happened to be on the Ho Chi Minh Trail headed south when Lam Son 719 kicked off.

The B70 Corps assumed control of the three divisions that were en route or already in the area: the 304th, 308th, and 320th Divisions. The 308th Division, which had fought at Dien Bien Phu in 1954, initially operated from Khe Sanh to the South Vietnamese border. The 304th Division, which had operated almost continuously in the Route 9 area since 1968, with the 24th, 66th, and 9th Regiments had responsibility for the area from the border west to A Luoi.[24] The 320th Division would operate west of A Luoi once the battle was joined.

Additionally, the 2nd Division from Military Region 5 was ordered to leave its heavy equipment behind and move from the Que Son area in Quang Nam Province to the Route 9 area. There, the division, including its 1st and 141st Regiments, was brought up to full strength in personnel and equipment. It would be assigned the mission to blunt the ARVN thrust westward down Route 9 inside South Vietnam from Dong Ha to the border. Later in February, the 324th Division would move into the area and join the 2nd Division to put pressure on the ARVN southern flank.

In addition to B70 Corps inside Laos, Headquarters 702 was also able to call on the forces of B5 Front, Military Region Tri Thien, and Military Region 5 in South Vietnam as part of the overall effort to destroy the South Vietnamese forces as they launched their offensive into Laos from South Vietnam. Inside South Vietnam, the B5 Front directed the 27th and 270th Infantry Regiments, 84th and 38th Artillery Regiments, and 15th Sapper Battalion in the conduct of attacks against US forces in the area between Dong Ha and Khe Sanh that would support any South Vietnamese thrust into Laos. In addition, they were charged with cutting the line of communication along Route 9 between the two allied bases.

To guard against the possibility that the South Vietnamese

forces might extend their operations into the southern portion of Military Region 4, the area north of the DMZ, the General Staff gave the B70 Corps the added responsibility for preparing plans in coordination with Region 4 forces to blunt any enemy incursion in that area. The General Staff sent ten additional antiaircraft battalions to Military Region 4 to strengthen the forces defending the strategic supply corridor and critical positions. At the same time, the General Staff sent ten companies of local forces to reinforce the coastal districts from Thanh Hoa to Nam Ha to defend against enemy amphibious landing forces.[25]

The North Vietnamese were intent on protecting their vital base areas in Laos, but they also wanted to inflict a decisive defeat on the attacking South Vietnamese forces. They were well aware of Nixon's efforts to Vietnamize the war, and they wanted desperately to show that the South Vietnamese were not ready for major conventional operations.

Demonstrating how important they considered the coming confrontation, Col. Gen. Van Tien Dung, deputy chairman of the Politburo's Central Military Committee and chief of the General Staff, was dispatched to the front as an "emissary" to Headquarters 702 to oversee and monitor operations.[26]

On 31 January, in an address to the troops on the Route 9–Southern Laos front, the Communist Party Central Committee made clear the operation's objectives: "The coming engagement will be a strategically decisive battle. We will fight not only to retain control of the strategic transportation corridor, but also to annihilate a number of units of the enemy's strategic reserve forces to . . . deal a significant defeat to a portion of their 'Vietnamization' plot, to advance our resistance effort to liberate South Vietnam and defend North Vietnam, to gloriously fulfill our international duty, and to hone our main force troops in the fires of combat. Our Army must certainly win this battle."[27]

The North Vietnamese leadership acknowledged that the coming battle would not be easy. A postwar history of the Route 9–Southern Laos Counteroffensive Campaign, as the operation would be known in the North, listed the concerns as they prepared for the coming fight. Chief among these was that a large portion of the forces necessary to combat the South Vietnamese thrust into Laos would have to move some distance to the area and deploy quickly for battle. Additionally, the force would require a large quantity of supplies and technical support, but available transportation was limited. Last, and not least, they admitted that "the level of skills of our cadres in organizing and commanding combined arms combat operations was still limited." Accordingly, in the run-up to the operation, the Central Committee exhorted the forces in Laos to "use this opportunity to hone our main force troops and ensure that they reach a new level of maturity in large-scale massed combat operations involving many different specialty branches fighting in a coordinated fashion."[28]

By the time the ARVN launched their operation, there were over twenty-three thousand NVA troops in the area surrounding Tchepone. Hanoi ordered that Base Area 604 was to be held, sending additional reinforcements that would bring the total enemy troop strength to over thirty-six thousand. By the end of the campaign, the North Vietnamese were to throw elements of five main-force divisions, two separate regiments, eight artillery regiments, three engineer regiments, three tank battalions, six antiaircraft regiments, and eight sapper battalions plus associated logistical and transportation units into the battle.[29]

Why there was not more concern with the enemy and his potential for rapid reinforcement is unknown. Gen. Phillip Davidson, former MACV J-2 (Intelligence), wrote after the war that there were ample US intelligence reports that estimated that the NVA could reinforce the Tchepone area with at least eight NVA infantry regiments with associated artillery support within two weeks.[30] Thus, he points out, it was apparent that the ARVN assault troops, numbering less than three divisions, might find themselves fighting at least four NVA divisions, with possibly more on the way. Discounting these estimates was clearly a failure in the planning process that would have dire consequences for the ultimate outcome of the operation.

CHAPTER SIX

The Battle Is Joined

As the North Vietnamese situation in Laos developed, the allied plan was initiated as scheduled. XXIV Corps (US) established a forward command post at Quang Tri on 29 January, and I Corps (ARVN) concurrently established a forward CP at Dong Ha. Additionally, I Corps would establish a small command element at Ham Nghi, just south of Khe Sanh.

Phase I of the operation, Dewey Canyon II, was launched by US forces at 0400 hours, local time, 29 January, when Task Force 1-77 from the 1st Brigade, 5th US Mechanized Infantry Division, departed from Camp Carroll and moved west along Route 9 to establish a fire support base at Ca Lu, near FSB Vandegrift. The task force was composed of 1st Battalion, 77th Armor, commanded by Lt. Col. Richard Meyer, with two of its tank companies, two attached cavalry troops from 3rd Squadron, 5th Cavalry, and two attached infantry companies from 1st Battalion, 61st Infantry (Mechanized). The mission of the task force was to establish a fire support base at Ca Lu and secure the main supply route from the vicinity of Camp Carroll to the point where Route 9 turned west toward Khe Sanh.

By nightfall Task Force 1-77 had occupied Ca Lu, and one medium 155-mm self-propelled battery and two heavy artillery batteries were in place and prepared to provide fire support. With the fire support base established, one cavalry troop from the task force reconnoitered southwest of the Rockpile, a large karst outcropping south of the Demilitarized Zone, and one tank company reinforced with an infantry platoon probed north and northeast of the Rockpile. The other tank company, reinforced with the battalion's scout platoon, conducted local security and established outposts on the high ground that overlooked the firebase from the west.

The next morning, one troop of the 3rd Squadron, 5th Cavalry, advanced westward along Route Gold to clear Route 9 to

Khe Sanh; they were accompanied by engineers from the 14th Engineer Battalion and three D7 bulldozers from Company A, 7th Engineers, which improved the route and installed eighteen tactical bridges and twenty culverts between Vandegrift and Khe Sanh as the column advanced. Additional engineer equipment and crews were airlifted in front of the armor column to speed up repair time on the road.

The rest of the cavalry squadron advanced along Route Brown, a parallel axis that ran southwesterly from the Rockpile area to north of Khe Sanh. Following them, a company from the 7th Engineers began building a road to link the Rockpile and Khe Sanh; it would become known as Red Devil Road. Once the second phase of the operation began, this road would assist greatly in keeping Khe Sanh resupplied, providing a route for empty trucks to return to pick up new loads without clogging Route 9.

At 0830 on 30 January, 1st Battalion, 11th Infantry, commanded by Lt. Col. Raymond E. Farrar, conducted a combat assault by helicopter into Khe Sanh. The occupation of Khe Sanh was completed by 1530 with no enemy contact. At the same time, the 45th Engineers began building an assault airstrip that would be used until the damaged main airstrip could be repaired so it could again handle C-130 aircraft. Additional engineer equipment and supplies were brought in by helicopter.

To support the move into Khe Sanh, 3rd Battalion, 187th Infantry, and 4th Battalion, 3rd Infantry, were inserted by helicopter into landing zones along Route 9 to protect the movement of the ground column west along the road. At the same time, the US 101st Airborne Division (Airmobile) conducted diversionary moves from FSB Bastogne to FSB Veghel (27 kilometers southwest of Hue), then eight kilometers southwest to FSB Zon. From Zon, heavy artillery fires were directed into the A Shau Valley, where attack helicopters and fighter-bombers struck targets to draw the enemy's attention away from Khe Sanh and Route 9.

Also that day, in Saigon, MACV public affairs personnel briefed the media on background. General Abrams had imposed the news embargo on 29 January, asking reporters not to file stories about operations in Military Region I, except those described in the daily MACV press releases, until authorized to do so. When the embargo was announced, the reporters were told, "This announcement constitutes a part of the embargo, and is not for publication."[1]

The media silence would not last long. Word leaked, and there were already speculative stories in both US and international newspapers about the news blackout, most concluding that there would soon be an allied attack into Laos. Communist and other news sources not bound by the embargo also published reports about the preparations for a new operation in the I Corps area; even before the embargo was lifted, word of the impending operation was on the front pages of newspapers in the United States. According to Henry Kissinger, TV newscasters and the Washington press corps, not bound by the embargo, "not only dropped the broadest possible hints of an imminent allied operation in Laos; they also treated the embargo as a major story itself, a sinister plot of deception and coverup."[2]

As the looming confrontation with the media unfolded, the preparations for the upcoming attack into Laos continued. By 1230 on 31 January, Route 9 was open from Dong Ha to Khe Sanh for tracked and lightweight wheeled vehicles. With the road open, elements of the US 108th Artillery Group began their move to Khe Sanh. On 1 February, 8th Battalion, 4th Artillery (175-mm and 8-inch self-propelled [SP]) moved from Vandegrift to a position on the Khe Sanh plain that was given the name FSB Flexible. The 5th Battalion, 4th Artillery (155-mm SP) and 2nd Battalion, 94th Artillery (175-mm and 8-inch SP) moved to positions near Lang Vei.

As the occupation of Khe Sanh continued, a task force from US 1st Squadron, 1st Cavalry, conducted a reconnaissance in force along Route 9 from Khe Sanh toward the Laotian border. To screen this move, 1st Brigade, 5th US Mechanized Infantry Division, sent armor and infantry task forces on sweeps to the north of Route 9 and south of Khe Sanh toward the Laotian Salient, where the border caused a small finger of Laos to jut into South Vietnam. Meanwhile, the engineers continued to work on Route 9 and the airstrip at Khe Sanh.

On 2 February, 1st Squadron, 1st Cavalry, established a screen approximately four kilometers west of Lang Vei along the border to cover the movement of the South Vietnamese forces into their attack positions. Simultaneously, 2nd Squadron, 17th Cavalry, conducted a raid eighteen kilometers south of Khe Sanh in an area where enemy presence was expected, but no contact was made. However, they did discover a hastily abandoned enemy hospital located in a tunnel complex.[3]

As these actions unfolded, the airlift of troops and equipment into Military Region I in preparation for Lam Son 719 had begun on 26 January and continued for twelve days. The movement of the ARVN Airborne Division and the 258th Vietnamese Marine Brigade from Tan Son Nhut in Saigon to airfields at Dong Ha and Quang Tri in Military Region I began on 30 January and was completed by 6 February, requiring 247 sorties to lift 9,254 passengers and seventeen hundred short tons of cargo. In all, almost 600 sorties by C-130s and a dozen by C-123s delivered 12,000 troops and forty-six hundred tons of cargo to airfields in the northern provinces.[4]

The first combined operational meeting of I ARVN Corps at Dong Ha was held at the forward CP on 2 February, during which detailed operations orders were issued to subordinate South Vietnamese and US commanders.

On 3 February, the 1st ARVN Ranger Group (21st, 37th, and 39th Battalions) was inserted by troop-carrying helicopters into the Phu Loc area northwest of Khe Sanh to establish a firebase there. Eventually, the rest of the South Vietnamese units selected for the assault into Laos began to make their way toward the Khe Sanh area.

On 4 February the first contact with enemy forces occurred when a US engineer unit was attacked twenty-four kilometers northwest of Khe Sanh. Elements of the 2nd Squadron, 17th Air Cavalry, responded, killing five enemy soldiers in the ensuing engagement.

That same day, the US Army engineers completed construction of a thirty-two-hundred-foot assault airstrip located on the plateau at Khe Sanh. However, when lightly loaded C-130 aircraft made several test landings, they sank six inches into the dirt of the runway, revealing that additional compacting was necessary before the strip would be fully operational.[5] The engineers estimated that they would need four days to make the assault strip ready, but they were off by over a week, and the first aircraft would not be able to land there until 15 February. While the engineers worked on the new strip, they also began repairing the old thirty-nine-hundred-foot airstrip that had been heavily damaged during the Tet 1968 fighting. The first thing they had to do was clear the bunkers and minefields left by the Marines when they had pulled out after the intense fighting at the former Marine combat base during the 1968 Tet Offensive. Four D7E bulldozers were destroyed or damaged in the mine clearing operations. The repair of the old airstrip would not be completed until 1 March.

Previously, on 2 February, Nixon had given the go-ahead for launching Phase II, Lam Son 719, and authorized Abrams to commit MACV's airpower to the battle. Secretary Laird had approved an execute message for the operations that would terminate operating authorities on 5 April, which would effectively limit the Laos operation to six to eight weeks; Admiral Moorer told General Haig that he had implored Laird not to impose a termination date, as had been done during the Cambodian incursion, and the White House subsequently agreed that 5 April would not be treated as a hard and fast deadline.[6] Kissinger said, "If we get a bloody nose, we will get out early—on the other hand, if things go well we will stay."[7]

There were others in the administration who were still concerned about the upcoming operation. One of Kissinger's advisers, Dick Smyser, warned in a memorandum dated 6 February that "we should be prepared for the ARVN to have a tougher time than our planners predicted. Hanoi cannot afford to lose this one, and its forces will fight hard."[8] Unfortunately for the South Vietnamese, Smyser's prediction would prove only too prescient.

On 4 February, at Admiral Moorer's direction, General Abrams lifted the news embargo.[9] The order to lift the embargo was actually from Nixon, who was concerned about the mounting media response to the press blackout. With the lifting of the embargo, a new round of stories immediately appeared in the US press about the continuing buildup of South Vietnamese and American troops in western I Corps, to include the reopening of Khe Sanh and the improvement of the roads to the Laotian border. As previously noted, the media blackout had proved to be ineffective, and there had already been a number of reports and speculations about the upcoming operation. US officials tried further to manage the press by withholding military transportation from the reporters clamoring to cover the operation as the ARVN moved into Laos. In a transparent ploy, MACV invoked an obscure Department of Defense rule against competing with civilian airlines in carrying passengers across international boundaries, despite the obvious fact that there was no civilian transport to the area. Consequently, the newsmen could only get there on the few South Vietnamese Air Force (VNAF) helicopters that flew in the operation. The media was already extremely hostile due to the ham-handed way both US and South Vietnamese officials had tried to manage both the news and access to the battlefield; the situation would only get worse as the operation continued to unfold.[10]

By 5 February the US forces had finished most of their tasks and had taken over security for the ARVN assembly areas near the border; by that point the better part of two ARVN divisions had massed in the Khe Sanh area in preparation for the cross-border attack.

That day, the 1st ARVN Armored Brigade and attached elements of the 1st ARVN Airborne Brigade moved along Route 9 to occupy their assigned attack positions adjacent to the border in preparation for D-Day and the crossing into Laos. During the course of the day, the first US helicopter was lost when an AH-1G Cobra attack helicopter from Delta Troop, 3rd Squadron, 5th Cavalry, flew into the side of a cliff during bad weather northwest of Khe Sanh; both pilots were killed on impact.

The next day around 1900 hours, foreshadowing the difficulties that would be incurred in coordinating US firepower in support of the mission, a Navy pilot from the USS *Ranger* mistook elements of the armor-airborne task force assembled at the border awaiting commencement of the operation as enemy forces and dropped several cluster bombs on the formation, killing six ARVN soldiers, wounding fifty-one, and destroying an armored personnel carrier.[11] These were the first South Vietnamese casualties of Operation Lam Son 719. This incident underscored the difficulties ARVN and US support faced in coordinating firepower without US advisers on the ground, and it would contribute to a growing reluctance on the part of the ARVN to trust US tactical air support in close quarters as the operation unfolded.

As the South Vietnamese combat units moved to assume their attack positions, US logistics units displaced forward following the engineers who were repairing Route 9. Forward Support Area (FSA) 26-1 was opened at Ca Lu, south of Vandergrift, on 30 January. Advance elements of FSA 26-2 arrived at Khe Sanh on 3 February, and the facility became operational two days later.

Ground movement along Route 9 was difficult, since the road between Vandegrift and Khe Sanh was trafficable in only one direction at a time. Nevertheless, US and ARVN convoys moved day and night. During the first days, as originally planned, ARVN units were logistically supported by US logistic units. As soon as the ARVN units arrived in their assembly areas, they were issued supplies in preparation for the operation. This went fairly well, but there were some difficulties.[12] While the ARVN received supplies for the operation, ARVN logistics units dispatched advance teams to Khe Sanh to set up their own support facilities, including ammunition and fuel supply points, which were scheduled to initiate operations on D+17 (16 February).

By that time there were some major problems with fuel. The delay in opening the airstrip at Khe Sanh meant that aviation fuel had to be brought in overland via Route 9, but there was a shortage of large fuel tankers to haul the critical commodity. A short-term fix was to haul in loaded five-hundred-gallon fuel blivets by US heavy helicopters directly to the staging area for the lift helicopters at Khe Sanh. The fuel situation would worsen in the early morning hours of 8 February, when a convoy of tankers moving along Route 9 was ambushed, and six of the large twelve-hundred-gallon tankers were destroyed or damaged.

Fuel was not the only problem. The weather had been favorable during the first few days of February, and air support was effective. However, the weather turned bad on 4 and 5 February, with low clouds and intermittent rain. This delayed some troop landing plans and interfered with the engineer units working on the Khe Sanh airstrip. The weather took a turn for the better on 6 February, but was still not good enough to conduct effective close air support, and the air strikes that were supposed to neutralize NVA antiaircraft guns along Route 9 had to be canceled.

Lieutenant General Sutherland transmitted this information to Lieutenant General Lam, but Lam decided to go ahead with the attack across the border as planned despite the lack of expected preplanned air strikes. Lam was reluctant to change the plan, because it had already been approved by President Thieu.[13] There was also the supposition that the enemy was now well aware of ARVN intentions to enter Laos along Route 9 and would no doubt begin to move reinforcements to the area. Therefore, to Lam, delaying the operation was out of the question.

To compensate for the loss of the air strikes, Lam requested that the US air cavalry fly ahead of the lead ARVN units. However, the air cavalry was prohibited from crossing the border ahead of the ARVN; Lam and Sutherland agreed that the ARVN Airborne Division would send troops across the border precisely at 0700 on D-Day, to be followed by the US air cavalry, thus satisfying both US political restrictions and I Corps's desire for additional support.

Phase II of Operation Lam Son 719 commenced as planned at 0700 hours on 8 February 1971 when ARVN engineer elements from the two attacking units crossed the border to begin repairing the road. With the engineers on the Laotian side of the border, helicopters from C Troop, 2nd Squadron, 17th US Air Cavalry, flew across the border and began to conduct reconnaissance along the axis of advance.

With the air cavalry screening forward of their advance, the lead tanks and armored personnel carriers (APCs) from the 17th Armored Cavalry Squadron crossed the line of departure at 1000 hours and began rolling toward the border. They were followed by the remainder of the 1st ARVN Armored Brigade, which included the 11th Armored Cavalry Squadron and two attached South Vietnamese airborne battalions (the 1st and 8th), followed by the 101st Combat Engineer Battalion and a platoon of bulldozers.

The armored brigade was commanded by Col. Nguyen Trong Luat. This was Luat's first major operation as brigade commander, but he had won national acclaim for his actions during the Battle of Plei Me in 1965. The mission of Luat and his brigade was to open and secure Route 9 to Ban Dong, twenty kilometers inside Laos, then to push the final twenty-two kilometers to Tchepone; the ARVN were expected to reach Tchepone in three days.

Prior to the initiation of the attack, eleven B-52 Arc Light sorties were flown against targets in lower Laos to prepare for the ARVN thrust along Route 9, and shortly after the attack began, supporting artillery from the US 108th Artillery Group began a two-hour bombardment of long-range targets in Laos in an attempt to isolate the immediate battlefield.

With the US air cavalry providing cover, the four-thousand-man ARVN column, led by M41 tanks and M113 APCs from the 2nd Troop of the 17th Armored Cavalry Squadron, advanced along Route 9 into Laos, taking only sporadic enemy fire but meeting no real resistance. A sign at the border read, "Warning, No US Personnel Beyond This Point." On the other side of the sign, some wag had added: "No North Vietnamese Troops Permitted Beyond This Point." As the ARVN soldiers crossed into Laos, they waved at members of the foreign and local press, who were gathered at the border.

Ahead of the column, US Army air cavalry gunships struck at enemy air defense positions on the mountain slopes north and south of the axis of advance. At 0820, gunships engaged four enemy tracked vehicles, one of which was towing a 37-mm antiaircraft gun, two kilometers south of Ban Na on the northern flank.

Back in Saigon, President Thieu broadcast a statement over Radio Saigon to inform the people that South Vietnamese forces had crossed the border into Laos. Speaking as the supreme commander of the Armed Forces of the Republic of Vietnam, the president said, "This operation will be limited in both time and space, and its only objective is to destroy the North Vietnamese communist logistics and infiltration network in Laos, which they had occupied and used for many years to attack the Republic of Vietnam. In addition, the Republic of Vietnam has no territorial designs on Laos because the Republic of Vietnam has always respected the territorial integrity of the Kingdom of Laos."[14]

As the armored column advanced along Route 9 toward Ban Dong, the air cavalry continued to screen forward and to the flanks. A Pink Team of two AH-1G Cobra gunships, two OH-6 observation helicopters, and a command and control (C&C) UH-1H Huey from Bravo Troop, 7th Squadron, 1st Cavalry, was screening west of the 1st ARVN Division insertions when they began to take fire. The C&C helicopter was hit and went down, crashing upside down in a field of elephant grass. The crew chief and the pilot survived the crash, but the other two crew members were killed; this was the first helicopter shot down during the operations. The cavalry troop's aero-rifle platoon (Blue Team) was on alert at Lang Vei with the Hac Bao Company. When the call went out for the Hac Baos, the American Blue Team boarded the helicopters and took part in rescuing the downed Americans in violation of the standing order against US ground troops crossing the border into Laos. Lt. Col. Robert Molinelli, commander of 2nd Squadron, 17th Air Cavalry from the 101st Airborne Division, who had control of all the air cavalry assets, reported the violation up the chain of command to General Berry, assistant division commander of the 101st; the report eventually made it to the White House. Sometime later, the president changed the policy so that US troops could be inserted to rescue downed airmen, but none were ever committed.[15]

While the air cavalry screened forward and to the flanks, seven ARVN battalions were inserted by helicopters from the 223rd and 158th Aviation Battalions into prearranged landing zones on both the northern and southern flanks to establish blocking positions to secure the route of advance.[16] The 2nd Airborne Battalion was inserted into LZ 30, ten kilometers north of Route 9, with no enemy contact; they immediately began to build a fire support base at that location.

About five kilometers northwest of LZ 30, ARVN Rangers from 21st Battalion were inserted by the 158th Aviation Battalion into an LZ on the high ground overlooking Route 92 and the Namxe Samou River, a position that would eventually become known as Ranger South. The helicopters carrying the Rangers began taking fire as soon as they crossed the border; the third aircraft in the formation, flown by WO Paul Stewart and WO Thomas Doody, sustained hits in the tail boom from a 12.7-mm machine gun, which severed the driveshaft of the tail rotor. The aircraft went inverted, crashed upside down in the jungle, and exploded on impact; there were no survivors. The other aircraft pressed on to the designated landing zone. As they landed, the antiaircraft fire increased, wounding eleven Rangers aboard the helicopters, but the assault continued under cover of attack helicopters from the US air cavalry. Once on the ground, the Rangers established defensive positions to screen the northern flank and sent out patrols to search for the enemy in their assigned area of responsibility.

At 1100 hours, air cavalry gunships attacked two armored vehicles eight kilometers north of Ban Dong (Objective A Luoi) with undetermined results. Since this position was very near LZ 31, which would be used later in the day, General Lam requested additional aerial reconnaissance of the area. Subsequently, air cavalry gunships engaged an enemy position just two kilometers east of the landing zone. The attack caused numerous secondary explosions and resulted in a fire with flames reaching fifteen hundred feet in the air; the fire would last until just before daylight of the following morning. Shortly after this engagement, 3rd Airborne Brigade headquarters and 3rd Airborne Battalion were inserted by helicopter and occupied LZ 31 without any further contact with the enemy. Additional helicopters brought in a battery of six 105-mm howitzers, and a fire support base was soon established. Shortly thereafter, gunships spotted additional armored vehicles northwest of the airborne position, but the enemy did not engage the airborne troops at FSB 31. By the end of the day, the ARVN had effectively established a string of four mutually supporting firebases to cover the northern flank of the armored task force thrust along Route 9.

Meanwhile, to the south of Route 9, troops from the ARVN 1st Infantry Division were helicoptered into landing zones on the southern flank, securing their initial objectives with little enemy contact. At the same time, 1100, US helicopters from the 223rd Combat Aviation Battalion transported 4th Battalion, 3rd Infantry Regiment, to LZ Hotel in the Co Roc escarpment, where the ARVN soldiers landed with no enemy contact. However, one aircraft from the 174th Assault Helicopter Company was hit after departing the LZ, and the aircraft commander, WO Robert B. Gentry, was killed.[17]

Later in the afternoon, elements of the 223rd picked up the 2nd Battalion from the 3rd Infantry Regiment and inserted them in the vicinity of LZ Blue, four kilometers southwest of LZ Hotel. The helicopters from the 48th Assault Helicopter Company began taking fire as they approached the landing zone; one helicopter was hit and had to crash-land on a sandbar in the river, but the crew was rescued by another helicopter in the flight.

Once on the ground, the ARVN were immediately taken under fire, sustaining five wounded and killing nine enemy soldiers in the battle that ensued. The intensity of the fire convinced the regimental commander to divert his 3rd Battalion from its proposed landing at LZ Yellow to another landing zone near LZ Blue to reinforce the 2nd Battalion. Additional ARVN forces were landed at LZs Delta, Delta I, and Don. The NVA had staked out all the likely landing zones, and each attempt to land troops in those LZs encountered heavy enemy antiaircraft fire from well-placed 12.7-mm machine-gun positions. During the course of this effort, another Huey was shot down near LZ Blue. The commander of the 223rd, Lt. Col. Gerald W. Kirklighter, an experienced aviator on his second Vietnam tour, landed his helicopter to pick up the downed crew and their ARVN passengers, but his aircraft took heavy fire while he did so and sustained severe damage to the engine's transmission. Somehow Kirklighter was able to get the helicopter safely back to Lang Vei. En route, he radioed ahead to the personnel from the 101st Division Support Command, who were manning the staging area and refuel/rearm pad there, to get another command and control (C&C) helicopter ready for his arrival. Once he landed, he changed aircraft and flew back across the border into Laos. The intensity of this action and the damage sustained by the helicopters in this opening phase of the operations were only a portent of what was to come.

While the helicopter crews braved intense enemy fire to insert ARVN troops into landing zones north and south of the river, the ARVN armored column on Route 9 had an easier time of it, pushing nine kilometers (about six miles) into Laos on the first day. However, the column was slowed by dense jungle and huge bomb craters, some twenty feet deep, adjacent to the route that limited their advance. Additionally, the heavy foliage that came up to the road on both sides and the high shoulders greatly hampered the progress of the two airborne battalions that were trying to screen the flanks of the armored advance; at the same time, the thick vegetation limited maneuver room for the tanks and armored personnel carriers. Japanese photographer Akihiko Okamura, who had defied the press ban and hid in one of the APCs that crossed into Laos, later said, "It was like battering down a bamboo tunnel."[18]

The road itself, a single track through heavily forested mountains cut in a number of places by streams, was in disrepair, and the ARVN 101st Combat Engineer Battalion had to construct several detours where the road was totally destroyed, further slowing the advance of the armored column. Despite the best efforts of the ARVN engineers to repair the road, it remained virtually impassable to all but tracked vehicles for the remainder of the operation. As no wheeled vehicles could negotiate the terrain, the ARVN forces in Laos would be completely dependent on overtaxed US helicopters for resupply of fuel, ammo, food, and spare parts.

On the first day of the operation, in addition to the eleven B-52 sorties flown in support of the attack, the US Air Force also flew fifty-two tactical air support missions. During the same period, the US Army flew 468 gunship missions in support of the advance along Route 9 and the concurrent occupation of the ARVN positions along the northern and southern flanks. This continuing support would prove crucial in the coming battles.

At the end of the first day, there were sixty-two hundred South Vietnamese troops inside Laos. Contact had been relatively light, and the ARVN had suffered only three killed in action, thirty-eight wounded, and three missing in action. While the fighting on the ground had not been heavy, the antiaircraft fire had been intense and continuous since the very beginning of the operation; during the course of the day, when the helicopters made up to fifteen trips each into Laos, a total of seven helicopters were shot down by enemy fire, and several others were damaged. Still, the ARVN commanders were optimistic that the linkup between the armored column and the paratroopers would be made the next day.

However, the next morning, 9 February, the weather deteriorated and transformed Route 9 into a quagmire. Heavy rains prevented the engineers from working and impeded helicopter insertions, virtually halting logistical buildup efforts. Under these conditions, the 1st Armored Task Force advanced only five kilometers for the day. The other units already in Laos took the opportunity to improve their fire support bases and increased their patrols in their respective areas of operation.

There were only two enemy contacts on the second day of the operation. The 21st Ranger Battalion near Ranger South sighted three enemy tanks and other vehicles towing artillery pieces moving on the road north of their position. The Rangers called for tactical air support, but low ceilings and poor visibility prevented the fighter-bombers from engaging the tanks. Attack helicopters engaged but were unsuccessful in destroying the tanks. The 8th Airborne Battalion north of LZ Alpha, which was approximately ten kilometers west of the border along Route 9, also engaged the enemy, but the engagement produced undetermined results.

In the first few days of the operation, the North Vietnamese were slow to respond; a postwar history of the campaign admitted there were "a number of weaknesses" in the effort of the North Vietnamese to understand the enemy situation and noted that they "did not correctly predict the timing of the enemy's attack."[19] Because of these shortcomings, they had to react quickly to the rapidly developing situation. As the ARVN operation extended into Laos, General Giap and the commander of B70 Corps were restraining their forces until they decided whether the ARVN attack along Route 9 was for real or merely a deception to cover the main attack elsewhere.[20]

By 9 February they had decided that the ARVN thrust along the highway was in fact the main attack, and the commander of B70 Corps ordered the 308th "Iron" Division, located in an assembly area near the DMZ, to begin moving toward the area north of Route 9 to reinforce the NVA units already there. The division had only five hours' notice to move out, and it would take eight to ten days for the preponderance of the division to arrive in the battle area. At the same time that orders were issued to the 308th Division, the North Vietnamese high command ordered the 2nd Division to move from positions further south to the Tchepone area and eastward to blunt the ARVN armored column moving west along Route 9. The division's 1st Regiment (the Ba Gia Regiment) reacted quickly to position itself to block the road west of Ban Dong. However, the 2nd Division commander and several other key leaders were in the Central Highlands conducting reconnaissance and other preparations for a new attack there when the South Vietnamese force crossed into Laos; they had to hurry back to join the rest of the division along Route 9.[21]

With South Vietnamese intentions now clear, the Party Central Committee in Hanoi issued a resolution directing a vigorous response against the ARVN attempt to cut the Ho Chi Minh Trail in Laos. The resolution directed, "Mass our forces in a determined effort to annihilate large numbers of enemy troops and destroy large quantities of US and puppet military equipment; protect the supply route to the front lines at all costs; and, coordinated with the other battlefields and with the fraternal peoples of the nations of Laos and Cambodia, crush this American imperialist and puppet military adventure."[22] The Central Committee set the target goals for the campaign: kill approximately twelve thousand enemy troops, capture approximately one thousand enemy troops, annihilate two or three enemy regiments, and shoot down three hundred enemy helicopters. To have a chance to accomplish these goals, the North Vietnamese would have to scramble to reposition their forces to stop the South Vietnamese thrust down Route 9 toward Tchepone. They would operate under the slogan, "Let them come to us, but do not let them return home."[23]

On 10 February the weather cleared, and the ARVN armored column began moving slowly west on Route 9, inhibited by the muddy road conditions. The plan was for paratroopers from the airborne brigade to combat assault into Ban Dong, approximately twenty kilometers from the border near the intersection of Route 9 and Route 92, which connected Ban Dong and the DMZ. There they were to link up with the armored column, but it took a while for the weather to clear sufficiently for heliborne operations, which would not be possible until the afternoon.

At 1630, 4th Battalion, 1st Infantry Regiment, completed an assault into LZ Delta, ten kilometers due west of LZ Hotel. The LZ had been defended by NVA antiaircraft positions, which managed to down one OH-6 light observation helicopter and one

AH-1G Cobra with 12.7-mm machine-gun and small-arms fire; both crews were successfully extracted, and the operation continued.

At 1700, 9th Airborne Battalion was inserted by US helicopters into LZ A Luoi, near Ban Dong. The air assault came under heavy enemy antiaircraft fire from truck-mounted 12.7-mm machine guns, but US air cavalry gunships and US Air Force fighter-bombers suppressed the enemy fire, and the operation was competed at 1720 hours.

Two hours later, the armored column linked up with the paratroopers from the 9th Airborne Battalion at A Luoi. The South Vietnamese main attack along the road had reached a point halfway to Tchepone, opposed only by light enemy sniper fire. Armored cavalry elements reconnoitering Route 9 west of A Luoi reported that the road ahead was in better condition, capable of sustaining speeds of up to thirty-five miles per hour.

So far, the South Vietnamese had made good progress against relatively light resistance. However, earlier that afternoon, at 1300, a flight of four VNAF helicopters bound for Ranger South was hit by NVA 37-mm antiaircraft fire. Two of the helicopters were shot down, and all aboard were presumed killed. The first helicopter carried the G3 operations and G4 logistics officers of I Corps; the second one reportedly carried several foreign correspondents. The helicopter carrying the G3 and G4 crash-landed, but the aircraft carrying the newsmen exploded in midair.[24] It was suspected that the G3 was carrying a detailed map of the operation with him along with signal codes; a thorough search of the area for the helicopters proved fruitless, and it was assumed that the plans had fallen into enemy hands. Surprisingly, no effort was made to change the battle plans or the signal operating instructions.

Despite the loss of the two key staff officers from I Corps and the possible compromise of the plan, the linkup between the armored and airborne troops at A Luoi nearly twenty kilometers deep into NVA territory was encouraging; the South Vietnamese forces in Laos at this point totaled 7,500 men. Lieutenant General Lam ordered that the armored column push westward, but only after additional reinforcements were inserted on the northern and southern flanks. The 3rd Regiment of the 1st ARVN Division was ordered to occupy LZ Yellow, but when last-minute intelligence reports indicated enemy concentrations nearby, the helicopters carrying them were diverted to LZ Don, about four kilometers southwest of LZ Delta. This lift was completed at 1730 hours without further incident.

To the north, the 39th Ranger Battalion was airlifted into LZ Ranger North, two kilometers west of Ben Na and three kilometers northeast of Ranger South, which had been occupied by the 21st Rangers since 8 February. Lightly armed infantry troops, without armor, the Rangers were expected to provide early warning and delay any NVA reinforcements coming south along the Ho Chi Minh Trail until heavier firepower could be brought to bear. The positions at Ranger North and South were critical; if the NVA overran the Rangers, the North Vietnamese would effectively be able to cut Route 9.

Having established their initial defensive positions, the ARVN forces north and south of Route 9 began to search their respective areas of operation. A patrol from Ranger North engaged an unknown NVA unit, killing forty-three North Vietnamese and capturing two 37-mm antiaircraft guns. In the vicinity of FSB 31, the 3rd Airborne Battalion captured six NVA trucks loaded with ammunition; additionally, they discovered several ammunition caches.

South of Route 9, 3rd Battalion, 1st Infantry Regiment, searching near FSB Delta, found a weapons and fuel cache that contained 60 Soviet-made SKS rifles, 202 AK-47 assault rifles, four antiaircraft machine guns, large quantities of ammunition, 16,400 liters of fuel, fifty boxes of uniforms, and a large quantity of food. They also found two locations where enemy soldiers had been killed by US air strikes, with thirty bodies in one area and fifty in the other.

In a search operation along Route 9, 2nd Troop, 17th Armored Cavalry Squadron, also found fifty enemy bodies believed to have been killed by artillery or air strikes. Elsewhere, elements of the Airborne Brigade and 1st Battalion, 1st Infantry, found more sizeable caches of ammunition and supplies.

The ARVN forces on the ground in Laos were supported by three forward air controllers (FACs) and at night by three C-123 flare ships and three fixed-wing gunships (either AC-119 Stingers or AC-130 Spectres). Additionally, B-52 Arc Light strikes were used during the early days of the operation against enemy artillery emplacements, known storage areas, and suspected enemy troop concentrations.

By this time the US 175-mm artillery batteries had moved

from Lang Vei to Lao Bao, near where Route 9 crossed the border into Laos. They were now farther west than any US maneuver battalion, and this allowed them to range targets deeper in Laos but at the same time put them in range of enemy 122-mm and 152-mm guns.

By the evening of 10 February, the South Vietnamese forces in Laos were in reasonably good shape. At that point the South Vietnamese now had a string of ten blocking positions on both the northern and southern flanks of Route 9. While the Rangers had been busy in the north, elements of 1st ARVN Division had established a line of fire support bases in the south at LZs Brown, Hotel, Delta, Don, and Delta 1 (just six kilometers southeast of Ban Dong) to support the move westward by screening the southern flank. The South Vietnamese forces in Laos now totaled more than ten thousand troops in thirteen infantry battalions, two ranger battalions, two artillery battalions, and one engineer battalion.

There had not been a lot of significant contact since the ARVN had crossed into Laos. It appears that Hanoi's attention was at least initially drawn away from Laos by the diversion being conducted by the US naval task force, which had been augmented by two aircraft carriers, operating in the Tonkin Gulf seventy kilometers off the North Vietnamese port of Vinh. The task force, with 3rd Battalion, 9th Marines, embarked, feigned preparations for an amphibious assault and conducted air operations in the area. Apparently the threat was real enough to cause Hanoi to reposition some troops from the DMZ north to guard against any over-the-shore attack. An official US Marine Corps history notes that the diversion attracted much enemy attention, resulting in reports that NVA ground formations were moving northward toward Vinh from the DMZ.[25] However, if the North Vietnamese were fooled, they would not be so for very long, because the South Vietnamese buildup in Laos soon became readily apparent to the North Vietnamese high command, which would react vigorously, and the battle would be rapidly joined in earnest.

(top) CH-47 Chinooks depart Fire Support Base Vandegrift in Military Region I. (Courtesy of Joe Kline)

(bottom) Aviation staging area at Khe Sanh. (Courtesy of Joe Kline)

(top) Assault helicopter company flying west along Route 9 in Laos. (Courtesy of Donna Thompson)

(bottom) ARVN paratroopers en route to combat assault in Laos. (Courtesy of Joe Kline)

(top) ARVN convoy en route to pickup zone at Lang Vei. (Courtesy of Joe Kline)

(bottom) South Vietnamese column moves west along Route 9 in Laos. (Douglas Pike Photograph Collection, Vietnam Archive, Texas Tech University)

(top) Lt. Gen. Hoang Xuan Lam, commander of ARVN I Corps, talks with reporters at his forward headquarters near the Laotian border. (Douglas Pike Photograph Collection, Vietnam Archive, Texas Tech University)

(bottom) Staging area at Lang Vei. (Courtesy of Joe Kline)

(top) UH-1H Huey helicopter from B/101st Aviation Battalion (AH), downed by engine failure in Laos, is transported back to Khe Sanh by CH-47. (Courtesy of Joe Kline)

(bottom) AH-1G Cobra attack helicopter from 4/77th Aerial Rocket Artillery returning to Lang Vei from Laos. (Courtesy of Joe Kline)

(top) South Vietnamese soldiers walk along a trail in Laos. (Douglas Pike Photograph Collection, Vietnam Archive, Texas Tech University)

(bottom) UH-1C Huey gunship from 174th Assault Helicopter Company "Sharks." (Courtesy of Joe Kline)

(top) South Vietnamese troops on M113 armored personnel carrier move along the Ho Chi Minh Trail in Laos. (Douglas Pike Photograph Collection, Vietnam Archive, Texas Tech University)

(bottom) Medevac helicopter lands in Laos to pick up the crew of a downed helicopter from the 174th AHC. (Courtesy of Donna Thompson)

(top) USMC CH-53 at Khe Sanh. (Courtesy of Joe Kline)

(bottom) One of the airborne brigade landing zones north of Route 9 in Laos. (Courtesy of Joe Kline)

(top) ARVN soldiers with weapons captured in Laos during Operation Lam Son 719. (Douglas Pike Photograph Collection, Vietnam Archive, Texas Tech University)

(bottom) Russian-built PT-76 light tank captured during a battle with the NVA in Laos. (Douglas Pike Photograph Collection, Vietnam Archive, Texas Tech University)

(top) Bags of rice captured during Operation Lam Son 719 in southern Laos. (Douglas Pike Photograph Collection, Vietnam Archive, Texas Tech University)

(bottom) Disabled vehicles and equipment along Route 9 in Laos. (Douglas Pike Photograph Collection, Vietnam Archive, Texas Tech University)

(top) M41 tank from ARVN 17th Armored Squadron destroyed during Lam Son 719 in March 1971. (Douglas Pike Photograph Collection, Vietnam Archive, Texas Tech University)

(bottom) South Vietnamese soldiers captured by the NVA during the fighting along Route 9 in Laos. (Douglas Pike Photograph Collection, Vietnam Archive, Texas Tech University)

ARVN M41 tank relic in Xepon, 2010. (Author's private collection)

CHAPTER SEVEN

The Attack Grinds to a Halt

On 11 February, for reasons that were inexplicable at the time, the main attack along Route 9 came to a halt. The South Vietnamese forces stopped their advance about five kilometers beyond FSB A Luoi as they continued to search for enemy weapons caches in their respective areas of operation. General Abrams and his advisers had expected a much more rapid thrust, but the ARVN were less concerned about speed and more worried about securing their flanks. The armor column waited for orders from General Lam, but there was nothing but silence from I Corps. In the absence of orders from their higher headquarters, the ARVN commanders along Route 9 demonstrated little initiative or inclination to move aggressively toward Tchepone. At that point the westward thrust lost all momentum.

The pause in the attack along Route 9 gave the North Vietnamese an opportunity to move in additional reinforcements and provided the enemy "both time and opportunity to organize his reaction in a more effective way."[1] On 10 February the Department of Defense had released a report depicting the enemy threat in the immediate Lam Son 719 area of operations as approximately fifteen thousand combat troops and some ten thousand administrative and logistical personnel, for a total of twenty-five thousand troops. However, the report also included another forty thousand enemy combat and logistical personnel in other parts of the panhandle of Laos, raising the total number of enemy troops who could be brought to bear on the situation to over sixty-five thousand. This reflected an increase of thirty thousand troops over the last figures previously released on North Vietnamese strength in Laos.[2]

These intelligence reports were not far from wrong. By that time the North Vietnamese 70B Corps had the preponderance of three infantry divisions at its disposal in southern Laos, with two more on the way. This force included an artillery regiment that employed guns ranging from 105 mm to 240 mm; it also had a tank regiment that included T-54 tanks and numerous other armored and wheeled vehicles. Each of the assigned divisions was given a specific area of operation. The 308th Division, the Iron Division of Dien Bien Phu fame, operated from Khe Sanh to the South Vietnamese–Laotian border and by mid-February had one regiment engaged, with others en route. The 304th Division had responsibility for the area from the border west to A Luoi, with the 24B Regiment and advance elements of the 66th and 9th Regiments. The 320th Division, with only the 64th Regiment assigned in mid-February, operated west of A Luoi. The 102nd Regiment (Reinforced) was located north of Route 925 opposite the ARVN Ranger positions. By then the bulk of B70 Corps was located north of Route 9 and oriented on the northern flank of the South Vietnamese forces. However, elements of the 2nd Division and rear service units opposed the 1st ARVN Division on the southern flank. Later in February, the 324th Division would move into the Laotian Salient and join with the 2nd Division and rear service units to keep the pressure on the 1st ARVN Division and the Vietnamese Marine brigades that would be inserted into the area.[3]

As part of the thickening North Vietnamese defenses along Route 9, the enemy rushed additional air defense assets to the area. Eventually, they established an extensive air defense umbrella, characterized by overlapping fires from 12.7-mm, 14.5-mm, 23-mm, 37-mm, 57-mm, and some 100-mm guns. The Lam Son area of operations was fairly small, roughly thirty-five by sixty kilometers, and given the characteristics of the area, which included only a limited number of landing zones and fairly constrained low-level flight routes, the North Vietnamese did not have to be too imaginative to place their antiaircraft guns in the most advantageous positions. Therefore, they triangulated all clearings and much of the high ground with antiaircraft weapons. Additionally, they preregistered their mortars and artillery to zero in on the potential LZs. This would result in a highly hazardous situation for the helicopter pilots ferrying troops and supplies in support of the I Corps plan and would ultimately have a disastrous impact on the outcome of the operation.

Meanwhile, to keep up the pressure on the units in South Vietnam, the B5 Front, with the 31st and 27th Infantry Regiments, 84th and 38th Artillery Regiments, and the 15th Engineer Battalion, operated between Dong Ha and Khe Sanh with the mission of cutting the allied lines of communication and harassing US forces supporting the operation in Laos. During the period 10–16 February, the North Vietnamese increased artillery and rocket attacks against the allied fire support bases from Dong Ha to A Luoi, which greatly impeded the support for the operation in Laos.

As the additional North Vietnamese forces began to close on the area, the firebases in Laos and South Vietnam came under increasing enemy fire. At the same time, the South Vietnamese force along Route 9 remained stationary. It was clear that the ARVN attack needed to get moving to regain momentum before the enemy forces gained the initiative, but still General Lam was silent. Without orders, the South Vietnamese forces in Laos continued to sit where they were, assuming static positions that played right into the enemy's hands.

General Abrams, knowing that the best hope for the South Vietnamese forces was to maintain the initiative by pushing down the road as quickly as possible, was concerned that if the ARVN did not advance, the North Vietnamese Army would have time to react in a more forceful way to the invasion. He was also afraid that President Thieu might settle for less than the originally planned advance on Tchepone and the destruction of the North Vietnamese supplies there. Abrams was worried that the South Vietnamese president might yield to "a sense of caution," perhaps motivated by the number of American helicopters that had already been lost to hostile fire or, more probably, the desire to hold down casualties. He expressed these concerns to General Vien, pointing out the disadvantages of failing to advance, "giving the enemy both time and opportunity to organize his reaction in a more effective way."[4]

After the operation, it was determined that President Thieu had a hand in the halting of the ARVN attack. On 12 February, when several intense firefights broke out near A Luoi, he flew to Dong Ha to confer with Lam and his commanders. He ordered Lam to be careful as he moved west and to cancel the operation if he incurred three thousand casualties.[5] Thieu was apparently worried about how potentially high casualty figures in Laos would affect the upcoming national elections to be held in the fall. Also, he was concerned about damaging or losing the ARVN general reserve (which consisted of the Airborne Division and the

South Vietnamese Marines). Maybe more significantly, the Airborne Division was effectively Thieu's palace guard and provided protection against any potential coup; thus, he was reluctant to expose these critical units to possible destruction at the enemy's hand.

Regardless of Thieu's motivation, the attack effectively came to a halt as the ARVN commanders became more focused on destroying enemy supply caches and preventing casualties than on continuing the advance. Once the attack lost momentum and came to a standstill, it became almost impossible to get it started again.

As part of the consolidation of forces that Lam ordered in the wake of his discussion with Thieu, the 2nd Battalion, 3rd Regiment, of the 1st ARVN Division was inserted into an LZ twelve kilometers northwest of Moung Nong with the mission to conduct search operations in Base Area 611. With the introduction of the 6th Airborne Battalion into Objective 31 on 13 February, the total strength of South Vietnamese forces in Laos rose to 10,288. Still, the focus of these forces remained on platoon- and company-sized search operations in close proximity to their fire support bases.

It was at this point that General Lam and his commanders complained to General Sutherland that the Americans were not keeping their part of the bargain. Lam asserted that he had been promised the support of 130 helicopters, but after five days, only about half that number were available.[6] Sutherland tried to convince Lam that he had sufficient helicopters to support ARVN requirements, but this did not quiet Lam's concern, and it would grow as the battle in Laos unfolded.

Meanwhile, it became apparent to the South Vietnamese that the NVA high command was rushing even more forces to the area of operations. Two prisoners disclosed that the 320th Division had arrived in Laos on 4 February and had begun operating in the Ban Dong area.[7] This brought to four the number of NVA divisions that had been identified in the area of operations.

On 14 February, Abrams went to see General Vien at the JGS to see why the ARVN advance had stopped. He had hoped to convince the ARVN general to energize the attackers, but two more days passed without any western movement. In a subsequent message to Admiral Moorer, Abrams noted that "execution to date has been somewhat more deliberate than originally envisioned," citing three reasons: (1) General Lam considered it "prudent" to ensure flank security before advancing further, (2) the roads in Laos were far worse than expected, and (3) General Lam was determined to secure his lines of communication on the ground against contingencies of prolonged bad weather and enemy interdiction. Nevertheless, Abrams stressed that "the task that was initially laid out will be done."[8]

By 16 February, however, six days after the capture of Ban Dong, there still had been no further advance toward Tchepone. That day, Abrams and Sutherland met with Vien and Lam at Lam's forward command post in Dong Ha. In a meeting that lasted two hours, Abrams urged Lam to get the force moving; that was the only way they could keep the North Vietnamese off balance. It was subsequently decided to move the 1st ARVN Division further west along the southern escarpment to establish additional fire support bases from which to support the resumption of the airborne-armored thrust westward along Route 9 to Tchepone. It was estimated that it would take three to five days for the 1st Division elements to get into position. The order was given, but unfortunately for the attackers, by that time the NVA had positioned reinforcements to block the resumption of the South Vietnamese attack. The ARVN had lost the initiative and never regained it for the duration of the battle.

When the speed and momentum of the attack, which provided the ARVN their only chance for success, evaporated, the would-be attackers soon found themselves under attack by a much stronger enemy than they had anticipated and were coming under heavy rocket and long-range artillery fire. Additionally, the increased number of enemy antiaircraft weapons on the mountain slopes to the south, as well as north of Route 9, made airmobile operations and aerial resupply more and more dangerous as Lam Son continued. On 15 February a CH-47 Chinook helicopter from C Company, 159th Assault Support Helicopter Battalion (ASHB), ferrying a load of gasoline into Laos, was hit by enemy antiaircraft fire, exploded, and broke in half. There were no survivors.[9] Despite the increasingly lethality of the air defense environment, the large two-engined, twin-rotor aircraft were kept busy throughout the duration of the operations in Laos, not just hauling supplies, but also recovering downed Hueys and Cobras.

All of the helicopters, regardless of the type of mission they were flying, came under heavy fire every time they entered Laos. Later, Lieutenant Colonel Molinelli, commander of 2nd Squadron, 17th Cavalry, noted that for the first fifteen to eighteen days of the operation, every aircraft in his unit was hit every day, many of them taking "a tremendous number of hits."[10] His unit was no exception; every US Army aviation unit supporting the ARVN in Laos had experienced the same intensity. By the end of the first week of the operation, the number of damaged and destroyed helicopters from the fleet supporting Lam Son far exceeded the normal rates experienced by army aviation unit operations in South Vietnam and was rapidly approaching a point at which the assigned units would not be able to support the ARVN operations.[11] The situation only worsened as the North Vietnamese rushed additional antiaircraft guns to the area. The readiness rate of the helicopters eventually became a point of friction between Sutherland and Abrams; ultimately, it would take several weeks and extraordinary measures to repair or replace the increasing number of aircraft lost or damaged to the intense enemy antiaircraft fire in Laos.[12] As might be expected, the high-intensity antiaircraft environment was having an impact on the pilots as well as the aircraft; the repeated flights into and out of the swirling maelstrom took a toll on the nerves of many of the aircrews. Still, they carried on with the mission.

The increase in enemy pressure on the ground began on 14 February, when patrols from the 39th Ranger Battalion at Ranger North began engaging NVA troops, who were wearing new uniforms and carrying weapons, ammunition, and grenades but no packs. By late afternoon all companies of the Ranger battalion were in contact with the enemy. The Rangers called for artillery, which drove the North Vietnamese back. The following day, the fighting continued. Patrols discovered the bodies of forty-three NVA soldiers and captured two 37-mm antiaircraft guns. This indicated that there was a large unit in the immediate area. In fact, the 308th NVA Division and its three regiments, which had moved from North Vietnam, were closing on the Ranger positions.[13]

Unknown to the South Vietnamese and Americans, the North Vietnamese leadership in the Politburo in Hanoi had come to a momentous conclusion. They believed that they had an opportunity to hand the ARVN a decisive defeat. In a 15 February cable, they declared that the developing battle in Laos was a "strategically important and decisive battle because not only will it decide what strategic steps we will take next to inflict a major defeat on the enemy's 'Vietnamization' scheme, it will have a political impact in South Vietnam, in the United States, and throughout the world." The cable closed by charging the forces in Laos to "make the maximum possible effort" to defeat the South Vietnamese Route 9–Southern Laos operation.[14] As Gen. Dave Palmer wrote later, "Political and psychological gains reaped from such a victory would be so great as to justify sacrifices of whatever magnitude."[15] Therefore, the North Vietnamese pulled out all the stops. The result of the NVA's "maximum possible effort" would result in some of the heaviest sustained fighting since the 1968 Tet Offensive.

On 17 February, rain grounded the helicopters, but ground elements from the 17th Armored Cavalry Squadron and 8th Airborne Battalion operating north of Ban Dong began engaging NVA forces in the early morning. One contact resulted in four ARVN killed and thirty-six NVA killed. Another contact around noon resulted in the capture of a PT-76 tank and several Russian trucks. It was clear that the situation on the ground was changing, and the ARVN troops were becoming only too aware that it was. "The first week everybody was happy and confident, writing letters and trading souvenirs," reported Japanese photographer Akihiko Okamura with the lead tankers. "Now they are homesick and worried."[16] As it turned out, their worry was fully justified.

With the South Vietnamese attack stalled along the road and the ARVN on the flanks in largely static defensive positions, additional NVA reinforcements were committed to the battle area. The NVA moved on the more lightly defended Ranger and airborne bases on the northern flank, while other NVA forces kept up the pressure on the southern flank. In the early morning hours of 18 February, the 308th NVA Division was positively identified in action for the first time on the northern flank when the 1st Airborne Battalion engaged a small NVA force two kilometers north of LZ Bravo. During the course of the fight, they found an enemy command post in which there were documents with 308th Division markings. Later that morning, US air cavalry reconnaissance spotted and attacked an enemy truck convoy nine kilometers west-northwest of Ban Dong. Early that afternoon, another air cav reconnaissance team working west along Route 9 engaged another NVA unit, destroying several trucks and damaging a tank. In the course of that battle, a scout helicopter discovered three six-inch fuel pipelines running across the jungle floor.[17] The scout directed several Cobra attack helicopters in cutting one of the pipelines and setting the other two afire, but one of the Cobras was shot down during the engagement. The two pilots were wounded but were immediately rescued by another helicopter.

As the fighting on the northern flank intensified, there were eight B-52 strikes, 133 tactical air sorties, and many more helicopter gunship sorties flown against elements of the 308th Division. These strikes resulted in thirty-three secondary explosions and reports of thirty-seven vehicles, thirteen gun sites, and two cache sites destroyed.[18] In another engagement, attack helicopters from B Troop, 2nd Squadron, 1st Cavalry "Dutchmasters," destroyed ten fuel trucks, two large fuel blivets, and several telephone poles and communication lines.

The heavy fighting was not confined to Laos. At dusk on 18 February, the NVA launched an attack against the forward staging area at Lang Vei, which was maintained by elements of the 101st Division Support Command (DISCOM). The NVA encircled the base and opened up with mortars and rocket-propelled grenades (RPGs). Mortar fragments tore holes in a ten-thousand-gallon fuel blivet, spilling aviation fuel all over the ground. An RPG round destroyed one helicopter as pilots rushed to their aircraft to get airborne. Cobra attack helicopters and artillery from nearby US firebases eventually turned away the attack.

It was clear that the North Vietnamese were striking back with all they had, both in Laos and inside South Vietnam. They could not afford to let the South Vietnamese thrust along Route 9 succeed; despite the problems that the ARVN were having, they were hitting the NVA where it hurt. As a result, the intensity of the fighting would continue to spiral upward.

About midnight on 18 February, the 39th Rangers at Ranger North were attacked by a two-battalion enemy force. Following a heavy mortar barrage, and accompanied by recoilless rifle fire, NVA troops from the 102nd Regiment of the 308th Division, all in new uniforms and carrying new weapons, launched an intense attack on the eastern flank of the position where the Ranger defenses were weakest. The Rangers fought back with artillery support firing from Phu Loc and FSB 30. In massing for the attack, the NVA exposed themselves to the concentrated firepower of artillery, attack helicopters, and tactical air support. The enemy dead numbered more than six hundred, many of them killed by aircraft.

As the battle raged that morning, an emergency medevac call

went out from the Rangers. A Huey "Dustoff" from the 237th Medical Detachment, 61st Medical Battalion, on alert at Khe Sanh, responded. Attempting to land at Ranger North, the aircraft was shot down by a mortar round that hit the LZ. Of the two pilots, crew chief, and two medics on board, all were wounded except one, who helped the others find cover. Another American helicopter landed on the hot LZ and extracted all the downed crewmen except Sp5 Dennis Fujii, one of the medics, who was unable to board because of intense enemy fire directed at him. Rather than further endanger the lives of his comrades aboard the second helicopter, Fujii, who had shrapnel wounds in his back, waved the aircraft off and remained behind as the only American on the battlefield in Laos.

The Rangers held off the initial attack, but the bitter battle continued through the day and into the following night, during which USAF gunships and flare ships were employed in support of the South Vietnamese defenders. During the course of the battle, the enemy troops breached the Ranger lines and occupied the outer trenches.[19]

As the situation in Laos continued to unfold, President Thieu visited I Corps forward command post in Dong Ha late in the day on 19 February to meet with Lam and his division commanders. Lam briefed the president on the situation, stressing the sightings of new NVA units in the area and the increasing pressure on the northern flank. He told Thieu that enemy reinforcement in the area made the push toward Tchepone extremely risky. In response, Thieu told Lam "to take his time" and to expand search activities toward the southwest in an effort to cut Route 914, which ran between Tchepone and Route 92.[20] This was a meaningless order that essentially told Lam to keep doing what he was doing, which was effectively nothing. The ARVN continued to patrol in the vicinity of their respective positions, but they were not very aggressive. The ARVN fire support bases became friendly islands in hostile territory that increasingly depended on air support for survival.

The enemy situation in Laos with regard to strength and intention was becoming clearer to both the Americans and the South Vietnamese at their headquarters back in South Vietnam. On Route 9, elements of the 1st Regiment, 2nd NVA "Yellow Star" Division, were identified in front of the lead ARVN units; an enemy prisoner from the division disclosed that his unit had been moving east from the Tchepone area since early February to block the ARVN advance. South of Route 9, ARVN troops identified elements of the 24th Regiment of the 304th NVA Division and the 675th Artillery Regiment. Further south in the 1st ARVN Division area, captured documents confirmed the location of Binh Tram 41 two kilometers south of LZ Blue and indicated that it was supported by the 4th Air Defense Battalion, the 75th Engineer Battalion, and an unidentified infantry regiment. It was clear that the North Vietnamese had sent in additional reinforcements. More ominous, South Vietnamese forces began to sight enemy tanks, and a captured North Vietnamese soldier stated that there was an NVA tank regiment in the area. Additionally, indirect fire on the ARVN positions increased substantially, including the fires from 122-mm and 105-mm field guns and howitzers and possibly 85-mm and 130-mm guns as well.

The NVA, with elements of four divisions, increased the intensity of their attacks on the South Vietnamese positions. They intended to isolate the fire support bases and defeat them one at a time. As part of this effort, they would ring the ARVN positions with antiaircraft weapons to cut aerial resupply lines while demoralizing the defenders with around-the-clock mortar, rocket, and artillery fire. Having done that, they then would assault the ARVN positions using combined infantry-armor forces where possible.[21] In an attempt to negate the impact of B-52 strikes, the NVA forces would refrain from massing until just before they attacked. Once they attacked the ARVN positions, they would "hug the ARVN's belt," moving in as close as possible to the South Vietnamese defenders. The NVA often closed to within twenty to thirty meters of the ARVN so that the American fighter-bombers, B-52s, attack helicopters, and artillery could not get at the NVA without putting the South Vietnamese troops at risk. This also permitted the NVA to direct a heavy volume of short-range small arms, antiaircraft, and RPG rocket fire against helicopters attempting to fly in and out of the friendly positions.[22] There were even reports that helicopters were taking direct fire from tanks in some locations.[23]

While the situation developed north of Route 9, General Abrams, predicting that Lam Son could become "one of the most decisive operations of the Southeast Asia conflict," asked CINCPAC for immediate action to make available forty B-52 sorties per day through May, with the possibility of providing more if the situation dictated.[24] Admiral McCain concurred, and Admiral Moorer issued the appropriate orders on 21 February. To provide the additional B-52 sorties, the Strategic Air Command transferred a fourteen-plane alert force from Andersen Air Base in Guam to U-Tapao in Thailand, where it would remain through the month of May.[25] Because the distance from the B-52 base in Thailand to Tchepone was shorter, the B-52s there could carry out more missions per day than those flying from Guam. The resulting additional B-52 sorties would prove crucial as the battles in Laos unfolded and the NVA increased the pressure on the beleaguered ARVN.

By the morning of 20 February, back in Laos, NVA forces had completely isolated the 39th Ranger Battalion at Ranger North. US helicopters braved intense enemy antiaircraft fire to bring ammo in to the besieged Rangers. Specialist Fujii, who had been on the ground with the Rangers since the 18th, spent his time well, treating the mounting numbers of ARVN wounded. When the Ranger position came under heavy ground attack, Fujii grabbed an ARVN radio and directed armed helicopter and fixed-wing air strikes against the attackers, preventing the Rangers from being overrun. However, the situation was becoming dire; some of the ARVN officers began to panic. Removing their rank insignia and destroying their ID cards, they believed it was better to be captured as a "puppet soldier" rather than a "warmongering officer."[26]

Later that day, a rescue mission to pick up Fujii was mounted by C Company, 158th Aviation Battalion. Maj. Jim Lloyd, company commander, landed at Ranger North under heavy fire; Fujii jumped aboard, but Lloyd's aircraft took a number of hits as it took off. It caught fire and began to lose altitude. Lloyd managed to get the helicopter four kilometers to Ranger South, where he made an emergency landing. He, his crew, and Fujii made it out of the aircraft before it exploded. Lloyd and his crew were rescued by another helicopter, but Fujii decided to remain behind with the Rangers for two more days directing air strikes against the attacking North Vietnamese.[27] Fujii would be on the ground for a total of five days before finally being extracted.

The same afternoon that Major Lloyd attempted to rescue Fujii, aerial reconnaissance aircraft reported sighting four hundred to five hundred NVA troops encircling the 39th Ranger positions; in actuality, however, the situation was much worse, because the NVA had surrounded the base with more than two thousand troops. The fighting continued throughout the day. Capt. William Cathey, an F-4 pilot with the 40th Tactical Fighter Squadron, said Ranger North "looked like World War II must have. . . . We put a napalm strike within 100 meters of [ARVN] troops. That was tight. We could see them in their trenches."[28]

About to be overrun by encircling NVA forces, the battalion commander of the 39th Rangers ordered the survivors of his unit to break out and withdraw toward the 21st Ranger Battalion's position at Ranger Base South, six kilometers away. Carrying their wounded, the Rangers fought their way through the North Vietnamese lines toward the friendly position.

After the Rangers at LZ North began their breakout, radio contact was lost with the battalion at 1710, but two hours later the I Corps forward command post received word that the survivors of the battalion had fought their way out and had reached the 21st Ranger positions at LZ Ranger South with most of their wounded and all of their weapons. Of a total of 430 Rangers when the battle started, 178 were killed or missing and 148 were wounded. The 39th was finished as a unit, but they had exacted a heavy toll on the 102nd NVA Regiment; reconnaissance photo analysts counted 639 NVA bodies on the ground around Ranger Base North.[29]

It was during the battle for Ranger Base North that an incident occurred that set the tone for the lasting public perception of Lam Son 719. Although most of the Rangers there stood and fought valiantly against overwhelming odds, a few unwounded soldiers lost their nerve and tried to climb aboard helicopters attempting to evacuate seriously wounded soldiers. The aircrews tried to prevent these troops from escaping the battle, but some panicked soldiers deserted by clinging to the helicopters' skids and riding back to South Vietnam. Several of those individuals were photographed hanging on to the helicopters for dear life, and this became the enduring image of operation Lam Son 719.[30]

Many Americans involved in the fight in Laos protested this perception. Lieutenant Colonel Molinelli, who flew in support of the battle at Ranger Base North, said, "The ARVN Rangers were outnumbered six or eight to one. For three days we were unable to get supplies to them. When they were low on ammunition, they went out and took NVA rifles and fought on. When they decided to move off their hill, they beat their way right through that North Vietnamese regiment, killing them with their own guns and ammunition. . . . Seventeen of their men [Rangers] did panic and they did leave hanging on helicopter skids. There were a lot more who did not."[31]

The Rangers had shown remarkable courage and tenacity in the face of overwhelming odds, standing as long as they could against intense rocket, mortar, and artillery fire and repeated human wave attacks. Later, Specialist Fujii, who spent three days with the Rangers during the bitter fighting at Ranger North and two more at Ranger South, defended them, saying, "I think the Vietnamese Rangers are some of the most professional and qualified Vietnamese soldiers I ever worked with, and I would like to work with them again."[32]

Regardless of such positive assessments, the damage was done, and the fact that the Rangers had fought so tenaciously in the face of overwhelming odds was overlooked. It would be almost impossible to overcome the initial impression given by the media coverage of panic-stricken ARVN soldiers fleeing the communists. There would be several similar instances before the operation was over, and they would prove to be blows not only to ARVN pride, but also, by extension, to the policy of Vietnamization itself.

Despite the turn of events along the northern flank, General Abrams, while acknowledging the difficulties that were being incurred, continued to be optimistic in his situation reports. In a message to Moorer and McCain, Abrams pointed out that the Rangers at LZ Ranger North had tied down an entire NVA regiment, rendering two combat battalions ineffective before they were forced to withdraw; but even withdrawing, they made it out in good order with all their weapons and equipment. McCain agreed with Abrams, saying, "The orderly withdrawal of the 39th was omitted, and figures quoted were inflated in favor of the enemy." He concluded, "The impression derived from press articles was totally misleading."[33]

With the loss of LZ North, Washington became increasingly concerned and pressed Abrams for more timely and accurate reports. In a conversation with Admiral Moorer, the president, worried about the mounting negative stories in the press, said, "The main thing that I am concerned about is the SVN [South Vietnamese]. I don't want them to lose confidence in themselves—I don't want them to suffer defeat and hope that they can stay in there [Laos] for another month."[34]

In a follow-up phone conversation with the JCS chairman, an

exasperated Kissinger told Moorer, "I do not understand what Abrams is doing. . . . I think the units north of . . . [Highway] 9 are just dug in a static position in the sort of thing the North Vietnamese know how to fight. . . . And I don't see anything aggressive [to the] south . . . of 9 either." Clearly exasperated, he continued, "If we are getting our pants beaten off in here, we've had it in Vietnam for psychological reasons." Closing, he asked, "What we want to know is, 'is he cutting the road?'" Moorer answered, "When they get logistics and the combat situation in hand."[35]

Unconvinced, Kissinger decided to send General Haig to Vietnam for an on-the-spot assessment, but Laird and Moorer strongly advised him against doing so. They believed that sending a White House emissary at this point would be a clear demonstration of a lack of confidence in General Abrams, "which they could not countenance."[36] During a White House meeting on 25 February, the president, reiterating his "utmost confidence" in Abrams, stated that the issue of a visit by Haig to Saigon was not a "question of confidence" but rather a question of getting better information and that "he could see no harm in a trip."[37] Admiral Moorer recommended that the trip be rescheduled to coincide with better news from the battlefield. Haig's trip was subsequently postponed.

Nevertheless, Nixon remained disturbed about the turn of events in Laos. He believed that there was more at stake in Laos than just cutting the Ho Chi Minh Trail. This echoed an earlier discussion in December 1970, when he acknowledged that the operation, above all, would be seen as a test of Vietnamization. The South Vietnamese could not be allowed to suffer a decisive defeat in Laos that could jeopardize Thieu's reelection bid in the fall and damage the entire Vietnamization effort.

As Washington's concern escalated, the NVA had turned their efforts on LZ Ranger South, pouring in artillery and rockets on the embattled Rangers there; the number of wounded Rangers soared. At noon on 22 February, following a two-hour prep by tactical air strikes, helicopter gunships, and artillery, thirteen helicopters made it into LZ Ranger South to pick up 122 wounded ARVN troops and Specialist Fujii. By that time there were about four hundred ARVN, including about one hundred from the 39th Battalion, left at Ranger South. The battle continued to rage for the next four days and nights. The Rangers held tenaciously to their position, beating back attack after attack but suffering heavily from continuous pounding by NVA 122-mm and 130-mm shells.

Back in Saigon, President Thieu met with General Abrams and told him that he thought Phase III, the destruction of enemy forces, stockpiles, and facilities in the Tchepone area, could begin in about three days. He also said that he favored withdrawing his forces over Route 22 through Base Area 611 when the Tchepone area had been cleaned out.

When Abrams sent a message to Washington relaying Thieu's intent, Kissinger told Moorer that he interpreted the message to mean that the ARVN planned to go in, spend some time, and then pull right out. Concerned that Thieu might pull his forces from Laos prematurely, Kissinger said he hoped Abrams "did not entertain any thoughts of getting out of there because he has to stay in until April."[38]

After Kissinger briefed Nixon on Abrams's new assessment, the president telephoned Moorer to ask for his take on the situation. Moorer replied, "It is tough going but we are coming along all right." Nixon said that the ARVN "must continue to take whatever casualties they have to in order to hold their ground and stay in there because that is all we need."[39] That may have been the president's desire, but the situation on the battlefield was going to change the thrust of the operation.

Back in Laos, the fighting had intensified throughout the area of operations. At A Luoi, the situation was rapidly deteriorating. The armored column stalled along Route 9 continued to take artillery and rocket fire. Attempts to resupply the tankers by helicopter resulted in extremely intense antiaircraft fire. Tank patrols that ventured very far from ARVN lines immediately ran into withering enemy fire.

In the air, the supporting helicopters continued to sustain heavy damage as they flew in and out of Laos. The North Vietnamese had devised a very effective tactic for dealing with the armed escort helicopters. Where two or more antiaircraft weapons were situated in the same general area, one would open fire on approaching helicopters to attract the gunships and draw them into range of the other weapons, which could then open fire, catching the helicopters in a usually very effective crossfire.[40]

Cliff Whiting, a pilot from the 48th Assault Helicopter Company, later recalled, "Usually we put up ten slicks a day with support from our own gun platoon. Within weeks, we lost the entire gun platoon due to ships shot up, shot down, or pilots being killed." Despite the dire risks involved in crossing the border, the aviators courageously continued to fly missions in support of the embattled ARVN. They paid a terrible price. Whiting said, "Throughout the whole ordeal of Lam Son, there wasn't one aircraft command in the 48th that had not been shot down at least once inside Laos."[41]

This situation put a severe strain on MACV's aviation replacement and repair capabilities and threatened to seriously degrade the availability of helicopters to support the operation. This was particularly true with regard to armed helicopters. On 23 February, Lieutenant General Sutherland sent a message to Lt. Gen. William McCaffrey, deputy commander of US Army, Vietnam, reporting that "aviation support provided by XXIV Corps has been necessarily curtailed during the past several days as a result of an increase in non-availability of AH-1G and UH-1C gunships." Citing combat losses that had not been replaced, he further reported that "resupply, medevac, and combat assaults were curtailed because of the lack of gunship support."[42] At MACV headquarters, Abrams was not happy with Sutherland and sent Col. Sam Cockerham, acting commander of the 1st Aviation Brigade, to Sutherland's headquarters to straighten out the maintenance situation so that the readiness rate could sustain the operational tempo in Laos.[43]

While the Americans worked to increase helicopter availability, elements of the 1st ARVN Division engaged NVA units south of Route 9 along Route 92. Elsewhere, other 1st Division positions sustained heavy attacks by fire. On 23 February, 2nd Battalion, 3rd Regiment, of the 1st ARVN came into heavy contact with NVA forces near Objective A-Ro, about twelve kilometers southeast of Delta I along Route 92. Their sister battalion was brought in to reinforce, but the enemy continued to attack. On 24 February the division commander requested an Arc Light strike on the ARVN position. He notified the two ARVN battalions holding the position, and they withdrew an hour before the arrival of the B-52s, allowing the NVA to occupy their earlier lines. In the wake of the bombing, the ARVN quickly launched a counterattack to retake their original positions. They encountered only light, sporadic resistance and found 159 NVA dead and numerous weapons.[44]

Despite the outcome of this engagement, the South Vietnamese had by this time completely lost the initiative in the area of operations. Supported by heavy artillery and Soviet-made T-54 and PT-76 tanks, the NVA struck hard with repeated frontal assaults against most of the ARVN positions, focusing particularly on the airborne and Ranger units manning the northern flank. The T-54 was a Soviet-made main battle tank that mounted a 100-mm cannon and 12.7-mm machine guns; the ARVN had never faced these formidable weapons before.

Virtually every South Vietnamese unit was soon in heavy contact with the enemy. The NVA tactics were to surround the ARVN positions and cut their aerial resupply lines with heavy antiaircraft fire while pounding them continually with mortar, rocket, and artillery fire. Next they would storm the positions, using combined infantry-armor assaults where possible. The ARVN fought back, but they were usually severely outnumbered and compounded matters by repeatedly demonstrating the inability to coordinate maneuver and artillery fire support. Additionally, the NVA's 122-mm and 130-mm guns, which could fire a shell seventeen miles, far out-distanced the eleven-mile range of the ARVN 155-mm howitzers. Consequently, the ARVN gunners could not provide effective counterbattery fire to shut down the enemy guns. As a result, the South Vietnamese depended on US close air support and attack helicopters for survival. However, for a number of reasons, the allied air support was less effective than planners had anticipated. First, the weather was often bad, grounding both helicopters and fixed-wing aircraft or degrading their effectiveness when they could fly. Additionally, the North Vietnamese did their best to try to negate support by both fixed-wing aircraft and helicopters. To neutralize the close air support, they encircled the fire support bases so closely that B-52s could not attack them without endangering the defenders. The North Vietnamese waited until weather or darkness prevented accurate bombing by attack aircraft to launch their ground attacks against the South Vietnamese positions. Complicating the problem, the absence of US advisers meant that the air strikes that were flown were not closely coordinated. At the same time, the North Vietnamese set up automatic weapons and light antiaircraft guns to prevent helicopters from bringing in supplies and reinforcements. Nevertheless, the helicopters' pilots persevered against the ever-increasing volume of antiaircraft fire, providing support that was critical to the survival of the ARVN. However, the aircrews continued to pay a heavy price to provide that support.

As the battle unfolded in Laos with Ranger North in NVA hands and Ranger South about to go under, President Thieu became more and more upset with General Lam's indecision and poor conduct of the battle. On 23 February he summoned Lt. Gen. Do Cao Tri, hero of the Cambodian incursion, from his III Corps headquarters in Bien Hoa to Saigon and turned over command of Lam Son 719 to the more dynamic Tri. But as he was leaving Saigon to take over his new position, Tri's helicopter crashed, and he was killed.[45] General Lam retained command of the operation in Laos.

That same night another instance of fratricide occurred near FSB 31. During a resupply mission, movement was spotted outside the perimeter. Cobra gunships were directed against the supposed NVA force; they attacked, only to find out that it was a paratrooper patrol, not the enemy. Before the attack could be called off, twelve ARVN soldiers were killed and another thirty-one wounded.[46] This incident only exacerbated the growing mistrust of US close air support that began to mount after the aircraft from the *Ranger* hit the armored column the night before the South Vietnamese crossed into Laos on day one of the operation.

Further to the north, the fighting continued at Ranger Base South, where the 21st Ranger Battalion and the remnants of the 39th held out against repeated NVA attacks. After four days of heavy fighting, General Lam decided that the Rangers' position was no longer tenable. He reasoned that he had more pressing need for the air and artillery support required to protect the base, and since the position was not an objective itself, no useful purpose would be served by sacrificing another ranger battalion in a doomed attempt to hold it.[47] He ordered the Rangers to abandon Ranger South.

About 1000 in the morning on 25 February, four Cobra gunships circled above Ranger South, covering the extraction of the Ranger survivors by a US helicopter battalion, which picked them up and transported them to FSB 30. Later, they were picked up at FSB 30 and evacuated on to Phu Loc, less one company that remained with the 2nd Airborne Battalion at FSB 30.

The withdrawal of the Rangers left the northern flank of the Airborne Division exposed, and Fire Support Bases 31 and 30 now became the full focus of the NVA attack. Fire Support Base 31, located eight kilometers north of A Luoi and west of a NVA north-south supply line on Route 92, was occupied by the headquarters of the 3rd Airborne Brigade, commanded by Col. Nguyen Van Tho and defended by two severely depleted companies from the 3rd Airborne Battalion, a Ranger reconnaissance company, and a 105-mm howitzer battery. The airborne battalion's other two companies patrolled the mountainous area to the northeast. As enemy pressure mounted, an additional battalion, the 6th Airborne, which had been inserted into the area northwest of FSB 31 on 13 February, came under intense fire, sustaining twenty-eight killed and fifty wounded in action. It was evacuated on 19 February.

On the same day that the Rangers were evacuated from Ranger South, 25 February, a company from the 3rd Airborne Battalion patrolling southwest of FSB 31 captured an NVA soldier who turned out to be a platoon leader from 24th Regiment, 304th Division. He reported that the NVA had been preparing to counter any ARVN thrust into Laos since October 1970.[48]

Meanwhile, the other ARVN paratroopers in and around FSB 31 were taking a pounding as NVA gunners increased the volume of artillery and mortar fire on the defenders. Following this punishing barrage, the NVA launched a three-pronged attack by some twenty PT-76 and T-54 tanks in conjunction with an estimated two thousand infantry troops.

As the attack unfolded in the afternoon, an overhead FAC reported three enemy tanks within thirty meters to the east of the airborne positions; he subsequently directed air strikes by four A-7 fighter-bombers against the tanks, destroying all three and killing thirty enemy soldiers. Three more tanks were seen coming up the hill from Route 92, but tactical air support once again destroyed these attackers. However, the NVA continued to press the attack. A thunderstorm broke over the area, making it impossible to get fighters in to assist the defenders, and it was during this period that the NVA tanks and infantry penetrated the ARVN defenses and occupied the north and northwest sides of the position, forcing the defenders to the southern edge. The battle continued into the night, but the greatly outgunned and outnumbered paratroopers managed to hold on, with US Air Force gunships and flare ships providing much-needed support.

As the situation at FSB 31 continued to deteriorate, the Airborne Division commander, Lt. Gen. Du Quoc Dong, according to his senior adviser, Col. Arthur Pence, became increasingly unhappy with Lieutenant General Lam's plan and his use of his men in static positions, which he believed stifled the paratroopers' usual aggressiveness. Pence later said, "He [Dong] remarked on many occasions that General Lam considered the Rangers the first cousins, the Airborne the distant cousins, and the 1st ARVN Division the son."[49]

Dong also criticized US air support for its inability to resupply FSB 31, but enemy antiaircraft fire drove away any helicopter that attempted to land in the area. Pence suggested resupply by parachute, but Dong did not want to further demoralize his troops by letting them know how dire their situation was becoming.

The battle for FSB 31 continued to rage for four days as the number of paratrooper casualties mounted. With the situation desperate, several helicopters, led by Lt. Col. William N. Peachey, commander of the 158th Aviation Battalion, braved intense enemy fire and flew into FSB 31 to evacuate the wounded. However, as the aircraft landed, a new round of artillery fire began, and most of the ARVN soldiers stayed in their fighting positions. With no one to load them, the seriously wounded remained behind, and only a few walking wounded made it to the aircraft.

General Dong, wanting to save his forces at FSB 31, ordered Col. Nguyen Trong Luat, commander of the armored task force under Dong's control, to move some of the tanks from 17th Armored Cavalry Squadron north from A Luoi to reinforce the beleaguered defenders at FSB 31. At the same time, Dong ordered the two companies, 31st and 32nd, from the 3rd Airborne Battalion, which had been patrolling in the mountains northeast of the fire support base, to move south from their positions to link up with the tanks from the 17th Armored Cavalry and lead them into the fire support base.

During the night on 22 February, NVA sappers tried to penetrate FSB 31 from the west but were repelled, with fifteen sappers killed in the fighting. On 23 February, the fire support base again came under intense artillery fire, including shelling from 130-mm guns. Later that afternoon, 31st Company to the south of the firebase reported enemy armor moving near its location. These tanks were headed toward FSB 31. The ARVN responded with artillery and called for air support; the first aircraft on the scene destroyed a number of attacking tanks and turned back the enemy from the southern perimeter.

The defenders at FSB 31 waited in vain for the arrival of the ARVN tanks that had been dispatched to relieve them. They would never arrive; the reason why has remained controversial. Lieutenant Colonel Pence maintained that Colonel Luat simply ignored Dong's orders, as well as a follow-up order from General Lam. Although the armor was attached to the Airborne Division, and thus under Dong's command, "General Dong had absolutely no control over the task force commander," said Pence. "General Dong did everything he could do . . . except call the commander in and shoot him."[50]

The American adviser to the 1st Armored Brigade, Col. Raymond Battreall, later said that the armor commander had received conflicting orders from Generals Lam and Dong, and the column of five M41 tanks with accompanying paratroopers halted as ordered by the Airborne Division commander south of FSB 31. Perhaps, in the confusion, the inexperienced Airborne Division staff simply forgot about the armored element and neglected to issue any further orders.[51] Whatever the reason, the tankers failed to demonstrate any initiative and just "sat there," still several kilometers southeast of FSB 31 on 25 February, while their beleaguered brothers waited for relief that was not coming.

That day, elements of the 66th Regiment of the NVA 308th Division again hit FSB 31 from the northwest and east, supported by an estimated twenty camouflaged T-54 tanks from the 9th NVA Tank Company, which knocked over presawed trees and assaulted up the slope toward the defending paratroopers.[52] The appearance of the thirty-two-ton main battle tanks was a great shock to the ARVN defenders, most of whom had never before faced North Vietnamese tanks on the battlefield.

The defenders reeled in the face of this furious attack, but US Air Force A-7 and F-4 fighter-bombers took advantage of improved weather, dropping napalm and general-purpose bombs to turn back several assaults. However, an F-4 was hit by ground fire and burst into flames; the pilot ejected, and the FAC on station turned his efforts toward rescuing the pilot.[53] This left no one to guide the remaining aircraft, interrupting the flow of close air support crucial to the defenders. With no tactical air support to worry about, another column of NVA tanks and infantry attacked the fire support base from the north. A lone US helicopter attacked the tanks with M60 machine guns but was driven away by NVA ground fire when the enemy soldiers rolled on their backs and fired at the aircraft. Artillery from A Luoi and FSB 30 continued to fire in support of FSB 31, but the incoming fire did not stop the NVA tanks, which continued their assault up the hill toward the ARVN positions. Once the air support was diverted to assist in rescuing the downed pilot, the NVA breached the defenses and overran the firebase in forty minutes. Some of the paratroopers broke out and made their escape, but most were captured. Capt. Nguyen Van Duong, commander of a paratroop artillery battery, fought to the last minute, refusing to surrender; he was captured and subsequently executed by the NVA.[54]

Lieutenant Colonel Peachey returned to the area to see if and his unit could provide assistance, but it was apparent that the base was being overrun. He saw tanks inside the perimeter wire. He later observed, "There they were, big and ugly. They were on top of the bunkers, doing 360 degree turns, driving around and around."[55]

During the course of the fighting, Col. Nguyen Van Tho, the brigade commander, his entire staff, and the commander of the artillery battalion were trapped in a collapsed bunker. They called FSB A Luoi and, reporting that the NVA were tearing the roof off their bunker, requested artillery to be fired on their position. The subsequent artillery mission was fired, but apparently it was without effect, and shortly thereafter the NVA dug Tho and his officers out of the rubble and took them prisoner. Tho was sent back to the rear for interrogation. He was later forced by the communists to make a radio statement denouncing the South Vietnamese attack into "neutral" Laos.[56]

Lieutenant General Dong ordered a counterattack by 31st and 32nd Companies, but it ultimately failed, partly because the weather worsened, precluding further air support. In the course of the defense of FSB 31 and subsequent counterattack, the ARVN airborne forces suffered 155 killed and more than 100 captured, rendering the 3rd Airborne Battalion combat ineffective. Not surprisingly, the survivors were embittered toward the tankers who had failed to come to their rescue. This battle was arguably the first time that ARVN troops had faced a large-scale tank-infantry combined arms attack in the war, and they had come out on the wrong side of the engagement. Nevertheless, the paratroopers, left to their own devices by the failure of the armor relief column and the diversion of air support to search for the downed pilot, still made the NVA pay a butcher's bill, killing 250 soldiers from the NVA 64th Regiment and destroying fifteen PT-76 and T-54 tanks.

As these events unfolded, the airborne-armored task force that had failed to come to the aid of the defenders at FSB 31 had its own problems. On 25 and 27 February, and on the night of 1 March, the task force, consisting of elements of the 17th Armored Cavalry Squadron, reinforced with the 8th Airborne Battalion, still some distance southeast of FSB 31, fought three major battles with elements of the 36th Regiment, 308th NVA Division.[57] During the intense fighting, which included the first battle between North Vietnamese and South Vietnamese tanks, the ARVN sustained twenty-seven killed in action and had three M41 tanks and twenty-five APCs destroyed. However, with the help of US tac air, including aircraft from 1st Marine Air Wing and B-52 strikes, they claimed over a thousand NVA soldiers killed and seventeen PT-76 and six T-54 tanks destroyed.[58] Interrogation of NVA prisoners of war after the battled revealed that the 24th and 36th Regiments of the 308th NVA Division, reinforced by the 202nd Tank Regiment, had taken part in the battle. The airborne-armor task force had fought well, destroying the equivalent of an NVA regiment, but they had not arrived in time to save the paratroopers and prevent the fall of FSB 31.

With the fall of FSB 31, the airborne-armor task force, still under heavy enemy pressure, was left on its own. The commander of the Airborne Division failed either to support the task force or pull it back, despite recommendations by the US advisers to both the armored brigade and the Airborne Division. Eventually, the South Vietnamese chief of armor, after consulting with Lieutenant General Lam, intervened and directed the task force to move to more defensible terrain.

As these events unfolded in Laos, the situation was viewed with mounting concern in Washington. Henry Kissinger was stunned by the news of the fall of FSB 31, but even moreso by what he saw as Abrams's and Moorer's failure to keep him informed about the deteriorating situation in Laos. In a telephone conversation with Melvin Laird, Kissinger said, "I got a briefing this morning and they didn't even mention Hill 31, and I pick up the newspapers and if someone asks me I don't know what's going on."[59]

As Kissinger's ire increased, the situation on the northern flank in Laos worsened. While the ARVN were still fighting for their lives at FSB 31, the NVA had also hit FSB 30. There, the 2nd Airborne Battalion came under heavy indirect fire from weapons of all sizes, but the ARVN occupied a strong position on the high ground that was characterized by vertical drops on three sides. The NVA could not easily get up the steep slopes to attack the ARVN position directly, so they chose to pound the ARVN with mortar fire while their tanks, having a hard time because of the muddy conditions, supported with direct fire. After nearly a week of this continual bombardment, ARVN morale was low; they were running short of supplies, and nearly all the bunkers had been flattened by incoming rounds.

Throughout the area of operations, NVA forces had beefed up their antiaircraft capability to prevent helicopter resupply. Nevertheless, on 28 February an attempt was made to resupply the surrounded paratroopers at FSB 30, under the cover of smoke, artillery, helicopter gunships, and tac air, by a flight of ten CH-47 Chinook helicopters led by Lieutenant Colonel Peachey and Lt. Col. George Newton, commander of the 159th Assault Support Helicopter Battalion. Lieutenant Colonel Newton controlled the CH-47s, while Lieutenant Colonel Peachey directed and coordinated air strikes, called in artillery, and directed armed helicopter fires on all sides of the Chinooks as they approached the LZ at treetop level. However, the NVA shot down one of the Chinooks, which crash-landed in a cluster of trees near the LZ. The aircraft caught fire and exploded, but the crew escaped; Peachey and Newton landed to pick them up before returning to Khe Sanh.

Despite the resupply effort and continual support from B-52 strikes and close air support, including fires from fixed-wing gunships, the situation at FSB 30 was rapidly becoming untenable. The NVA launched a major tank-supported infantry attack late in the afternoon of 2 March. With the aid of AC-119 and AC-130 gunships supported by C-123 flare ships, the ARVN held on as darkness fell, and the battle continued to rage into the evening. During the course of the battle, an AC-119 Stinger gunship spotted a column of PT-76 tanks and took them under fire. The tanks attempted diversionary moves, but the Stinger's 20-mm cannon destroyed eight enemy tanks.[60] The bitter fighting continued until 2100 hours, when a lull occurred.

As that battle unfolded, Lieutenant General Sutherland described the developing situation in a message to General Abrams: "I am very concerned about the discipline and morale of the airborne division. General Dong [division commander] has developed a defeatist attitude and this same attitude is reflected in some of his subordinate commanders. For example, an operation was planned and executed today [2 March] to resupply FSB 30, evacuate dead and wounded and transport some 21st Rangers to the Ranger FSB. The wounded and four bodies were evacuated. Ninety-four healthy troops, but not including all the rangers, rushed to the choppers and boarded. The airborne infantry commander was among those who managed to get aboard the choppers. I have been told, but it has not been confirmed, that the brigade commander went to FSB 30 at approximately 1800 hours to take charge of the situation. I suspect that before this night is finished, the airborne troops may walk off and abandon FSB 30."[61]

The paratroopers made it through the night, but fighting at FSB 30 began in earnest again in the early morning hours of 3 March. It would last for the next ten hours. At one point when there was a lull in the fighting, a search of the perimeter found ninety-eight enemy bodies and numerous infantry weapons.[62] By late in the afternoon, however, the situation rapidly deteriorated. All the ARVN artillery—six 105-mm and six 155-mm howitzers—had been damaged by enemy fire, and the ARVN were locked in deadly close combat with the enemy. With the situation so far gone, the decision was made to extract the artillery pieces and evacuate the 2nd Airborne Battalion. Chinook helicopters were sent in to pick up the guns, but they were driven away by antiaircraft fire. Subsequently, the ARVN were ordered to destroy the guns and abandon the base; the evacuation was finally completed three days later.

That night, a battalion-size NVA force attacked the 17th Cavalry and 8th Airborne Battalion five kilometers north of A Luoi. The fighting continued throughout the night; during the course of the battle, more than two hundred enemy soldiers were killed and fourteen tanks were destroyed. The ARVN force suffered more than one hundred casualties, and ten vehicles were knocked out in the heavy fighting.[63]

A clear pattern had developed in the battles along the ARVN northern flank. It was becoming rapidly apparent that the NVA strategy was to isolate and overwhelm the ARVN fire support bases one by one. While attempting to drive away the tac air and helicopter support with antiaircraft positions entrenched on the hillsides in the area, the NVA then poured large volumes of indirect fire from mortars and long-range artillery into the firebases, eventually following with massed ground attacks. The enemy was taking heavy casualties but was showing no sign of letting up. Lieutenant General Sutherland sent a message to Abrams saying, "Use of tanks in daylight hours is an indication of enemy determination to stand and fight to keep RVNAF from advancing." He estimated that the North Vietnamese were losing the equivalent of one combat regiment a week but reported that enemy prisoners of war indicated morale of the North Vietnamese forces remained high.[64] It was clear that NVA B70 Corps was intent on halting the ARVN advance, inflicting heavy casualties, and forcing the South Vietnamese forces to withdraw from Laos, regardless of the cost to its own forces.

While the Rangers and paratroopers fought for their lives on the northern flank, the same pattern was developing south of Route 9. The NVA attacked the 2nd Battalion of the 3rd ARVN Regiment, 1st ARVN Division, at Hotel II, seven kilometers southeast of LZ Don. Additional NVA forces attacked the regiment's 3rd Battalion operating along Route 92. On 23 February, a US Marine CH-53 Sea Stallion, flown by Maj. Michael J. Wasko Jr. from HMH-463, was trying to sling-load a howitzer into FSB Hotel II when it was hit by antiaircraft fire and crashed; despite intense ground fire, the two Marine pilots were later rescued by a helicopter from 223rd Combat Aviation Battalion.[65]

Given the enemy situation at Hotel II, Gen. Pham Van Phu, commander of the 1st ARVN Division, decided to close the firebase and send the 3rd Regiment northwestward to interdict and disrupt Route 914. This proved easier said than done, because there was still a 105-mm artillery battery at Hotel II, and it was going to be difficult to extricate the guns, given the deteriorating situation. During the night, I Corps headquarters ordered that the artillery pieces on the base be destroyed and that the defenders break out and proceed on foot. The 2nd and 3rd Battalions were ordered to move their wounded north to find a suitable pickup zone (PZ). En route, the ARVN came upon an area that had been hit by an Arc Light strike, finding the bodies of 157 NVA killed in the bombing. During the march to the PZ, several medical evacuation attempts were made, but each time the helicopters were driven away by intense antiaircraft fire. One UH-1H helicopter was hit by enemy antiaircraft fire, burst into flames, and crashed.

That afternoon, a small detachment of twenty-three ARVN soldiers were unable to break out and were trapped within the perimeter of Hotel II. They radioed that they were about to be overrun. Three UH-1Hs from the 48th Assault Helicopter Company, who were operating in the area, responded to the pleas for help. Supported by two Cobras and two UH-1C Huey gunships who joined the effort, the three Huey slicks attempted to land to pick up the ARVN. However, they had to abort the first attempt due to intense ground fire and falling mortar rounds. With the gunships firing everything they had, the slicks made another attempt, and despite the continuing intense fire, two were able to land and pick up the ARVN troops. As the helicopters pulled away, the NVA overran the fire support base. Air strikes were called in on them and the artillery pieces that had been left behind.

By this time the ARVN were in heavy contact throughout the area of operations. What had been envisioned as a lighting raid on a key node of the Ho Chi Minh Trail had devolved into a pitched conventional battle of pure attrition. The antiaircraft fire had increased, the artillery was constant, and the convoys along Route 9 were attacked seemingly at will. General Sutherland noted that the performance of the armored brigade had been "disappointing." The northern flank was clearly crumbling, but the 1st ARVN Division on the southern flank, despite abandoning FSB Hotel II, was fighting very well, living up to its reputation as the best unit in the ARVN. US advisers later reported that the division had demonstrated "outstanding fighting ability, inspirational leadership, and sound tactics" during the fighting in Laos.[66]

The US aviation units had been very busy during these actions and had paid a heavy price for their efforts. Helicopter crews were flying multiple back-to-back missions throughout each day against ever-increasing antiaircraft artillery and small-arms fire. They were landing to provide resupply and evacuate the wounded, often in the midst of intense fire; virtually every aircraft that flew into Laos sustained hits every time it crossed into Laotian airspace. Some pilots were shot down more than once in a twenty-four-hour period. One CH-47 pilot from 159th ASHB later recalled, "I can honestly say that I don't remember a time when a Chinook returned from Khe Sanh for the evening without a Huey or a Cobra slung under it [headed] for the repair yards. Sometimes I'd make two trips late in the afternoon. Those ships were really shot to pieces!"[67] Yet the pilots and crews pressed on, providing support to the beleaguered South Vietnamese soldiers as best they could despite increasingly heavy losses.

The fire support provided by the US Army helicopters was essential to the survival of the ARVN in Laos. Because of the heavy enemy antiaircraft fire, by far the most intense of the war to date, it became difficult for OH-6s and OH-58s to perform their usual scout missions. That role was largely shifted to the AH-1G Cobra attack helicopters working in conjunction with UH-1H command and control ships. Making use of their speed and maneuverability, these teams were very effective in providing close fire support to the embattled ARVN. However, there was a problem when the Cobras engaged the enemy tanks, because initially high-explosive antitank (HEAT) rockets were not available; the Cobras were forced to use whatever ordnance they had on board when the tanks were sighted. They used their 2.75-inch flechette rockets to eliminate enemy troops riding outside the tanks and to force the crews to button up. Then they would use high-explosive (HE) and white phosphorus (WP) rockets and 20-mm cannon fire against the tank itself. Eventually, HEAT rockets became available, but direct hits were necessary to defeat the heavily armored T-54 tanks. This meant that engagements had to be initiated at ranges between one thousand and twelve hundred meters, which exposed the Cobras to the tank's heavy machine guns and to the weapons of the supporting infantrymen. Nevertheless, between 8 February and 24 March, Cobra air cavalry teams would sight sixty-six tanks, destroy six, and immobilize eight.[68] Most of the tanks were turned over to fighters or fixed-wing gunships, which could attack them with heavier ordnance from greater ranges. Still, the presence of NVA tanks had a tremendously negative effect on South Vietnamese morale.

Despite the massive amount of air support being provided by helicopters and fixed-wing attack aircraft, the South Vietnamese forces, having lost the initiative, were fighting for their lives just to hold on to their bases in Laos. In the final days of February and continuing into March, the North Vietnamese, according to an American adviser at the tactical operations center of the South Vietnamese Marines, simply "plucked those bases like ripe grapes, one by one."[69] As part of this effort, the North Vietnamese increased the intensity of indirect fire on all of the ARVN positions in Laos using 85-mm, 122-mm and 130-mm field guns. Additionally, NVA gunners fired counterbattery fire against the supporting US artillery units across the border in South Vietnam.

As these bitter battles in Laos continued to unfold, the American media began to suspect that the operation had gone awry and that the ARVN were bogged down. In response, Secretary of Defense Melvin Laird held a press briefing on 24 February. During the course of a ninety-minute question-and-answer session, Laird said that Lam Son 719 was not focused on any terrain objectives, but rather was designed to "slow up, to disrupt, the logistics supplies, to cut off and to downgrade the capability of the North Vietnamese to wage any type of warfare in South Vietnam."[70]

Despite Laird's efforts, the media continued to be critical of the Nixon administration over the conduct of the operation. They were still upset with the news embargo and were really livid that the South Vietnamese were prohibiting them from going into Laos. Laird was worried about the impact of the media and particularly about negative reporting. In a White House meeting he said, "We must bear in mind that we don't want to make these operations into either a victory or defeat at the present time. We don't want the psychology in the country to end up like it did after the enemy's Tet Offensive of 1968. Here an allied victory was turned into a defeat. The TV and newspaper assessments that Tet was a defeat could never be turned around."[71]

In truth, the reporting of the fighting in Laos was having a significant impact on the perceptions about the operation. A lot of critical stories in the press left little doubt that the operation was going badly. The Associated Press repeated claims by MACV spokesmen that the invasion had disrupted the enemy's dry season offensive plans, but the same piece quoted an unidentified source who maintained that the ARVN had not improved as much as some American generals were claiming and that some of the South Vietnamese units had abandoned their wounded and "bugged out."[72] Such reports were not helpful to the administration, which needed to sell the idea that the operation was going well and, by extension, that Vietnamization was working.

In Washington, Kissinger called Westmoreland to a meeting at the White House to get his assessment of the operation in Laos. Westmoreland, US Army chief of staff, was acting chairman of the JCS while Moorer was absent from Washington. By this time, MACV intelligence had reported the presence of the newly identified B70 Corps, which was thought to be controlling the 320th, 304th, and 308th NVA Divisions, with an additional three regiments that could be committed to the battle in Laos.[73] With this new intelligence, Westmoreland's assessment was bleak, asserting that the South Vietnamese forces in Laos were inadequate for the task at hand. He pointed out that during his tenure as COMUSMACV he had contemplated a cross-border drive into Laos (Operation El Paso), and his planners determined that four American divisions would be needed to take and hold the Tchepone area. The South Vietnamese were trying to do it with two. In Westmoreland's opinion, the commander of the ARVN Airborne Division, which was staggering under the NVA assault along the northern flank in Laos, was "not a fighter" and, "The airborne troops will die easily. . . . If they are defeated it will be a tremendous setback for Thieu."[74] When Kissinger brought up Westmoreland's assessment with Moorer, upon his return to Washington, the JCS chairman was less than happy with Westmoreland's comments. Moorer pointed out that Westmoreland had not made any objections when the Lam Son plan had been briefed to the JCS on 18 December.[75] It appeared that Westmoreland was trying to distance himself from the operation; he would not be the only one to do so in the aftermath of Lam Son 719.

On 26 February, Kissinger provided the president an update on the situation in Laos. He wrote, "The North Vietnamese not only have moved substantial forces into the area, but they also seem to have s[h]elved the cautious, economical style of fighting that has been the hallmark of Communist forces for the most of the past two years."[76] Kissinger's assessment would be borne out in the coming days and weeks.

CHAPTER EIGHT

On to Tchepone

The situation in Laos by the end of February was that the South Vietnamese northern flank was collapsing, the southern flank was under intense enemy pressure, and the column along Route 9 was effectively stalled and also under heavy attack. General Sutherland reported on the developing situation to Abrams, saying, "The enemy is all over that god-damn area, and seems to be getting stronger, if anything."[1]

At this point, President Thieu inserted himself into the action once again. Given the strong reaction of the enemy to the South Vietnamese thrust along Route 9, he had decided that the mission of Lam Son 719 should shift from destroying the NVA base areas to taking Tchepone, which by itself had no real military value. Although the surrounding jungles and mountains contained enemy supply caches, the town had been abandoned by the civilian population years before and was now nothing more than a collection of broken-down hovels. Focusing on Tchepone was purely a public relations ploy that, if the town were captured, would permit Thieu to declare victory and withdraw his forces from harm's way, thereby saving face and gaining political capital for the upcoming fall elections. Another factor that may have influenced Thieu was that the BBC announced that South Vietnamese troops had already occupied Tchepone.[2] Failure to do so at this juncture would have resulted in a public relations nightmare. Accordingly, Thieu gave the order to take Tchepone.

Effectively, the objective of occupying and destroying the enemy base areas in Laos had been given up in favor of what was largely a meaningless effort to get South Vietnamese forces into Tchepone for political rather than sound military reasons. Although Tchepone stood near the center of NVA logistics activity in the Laotian panhandle, the enemy supplies and war materiel were stored in the jungle, not in the town. Therefore, there was no intrinsic military value to occupying Tchepone. However, its capture had become the measuring stick by which the operation would be judged. Thus, the town became a psychological symbol, and just reaching it would become the priority rather than the destruction of the NVA logistical system, which had been the original objective of the operation.

Thieu's position was somewhat understandable. After two months of bloody fighting, many battalions, particularly those in the north, had been badly battered, and some were close to being ineffective for combat. The enemy was reinforcing his troops in the area, and sustained bad weather might deprive the South Vietnamese forces of the air support needed to ensure continued survival. Thieu, facing an election in the fall, could ill afford to sustain more casualties. In the end, Abrams, believing that the South Vietnamese had a chance to strike a forceful and meaningful blow against the NVA, was unable to convince Thieu to do anything other than launch a token attack against Tchepone before withdrawing.

On 27 February, Thieu directed that the Airborne Division be replaced by the remainder of the Marine Division, which had been moved to Khe Sanh. Apparently, according to former ARVN major general Nguyen Duy Hinh, Thieu gave this order because he "was really worried over the additional losses that the Airborne Division would sustain in protracted combat."[3] However, the order was ill-advised for several reasons. First, the Marine Division had never fought as a division and, as such, was an unknown quantity; it was not clear that they could pull off what Thieu wanted them to do. To make matters worse, the relief of one division with another in the face of intense enemy opposition is one of the most difficult tasks in modern warfare. Nevertheless, Thieu was apparently not prepared to risk the destruction of the Airborne Division, since it normally functioned as the palace guard and could be relied on to act as deterrent to any coup attempt.

The difficulties in replacing the Airborne Division with the Marine Division were not lost on General Lam, who flew to Saigon on 28 February to propose an alternate plan. He recommended to Thieu that his own 1st Infantry Division, reinforced with its 2nd Regiment, which had been moved from its previous position near the DMZ, conduct an assault by helicopter into Tchepone; the division, still maintaining eight firebases along the escarpment on the southern flank, was in pretty good shape, and it was, after all, one of I Corps's organic divisions. The Marine Division, less 369th Brigade, which would remain at Ham Nghi base (Khe Sanh) as the corps reserve, would follow the 1st Division, while the Airborne Division would be given an order to assume the mission of securing Route 9 while continuing to protect the northern flank. Thieu agreed with Lam's alternate plan and the next day, 1 March, informed Abrams and Ambassador Bunker of the change in the original plan. He told them that Lam planned to relieve the Airborne Division and wanted to insert two regiments from the 1st ARVN Division into Tchepone by helicopter. He also informed Abrams and Bunker that the Marine Division was being sent to Laos.

In Washington, concern escalated with the news of the change in plans. Clearly still worried about the reporting from Saigon and now confronted with the most recent turn of events, Henry Kissinger cabled Ambassador Bunker in Saigon: "Since receiving information on these various conceptual approaches, events on the ground have not confirmed our ability to accomplish them. . . . We will do our best to hold the fort [here]. But we must know what we are up against. There is no chance to keep panic from setting in if we are constantly outstripped by events." Further, addressing Abrams's performance, Kissinger told Bunker, "Everyone here has full confidence in him [Abrams]," but that he, Kissinger, was "profoundly concerned by the way the situation is evolving." He closed by requesting a frank and candid assessment "so that the President will be best able to handle any difficulties which may arise here and prepare himself for hard choices."[4] With this new turn of events and the negative reporting coming out of Laos, Kissinger knew that the administration would have a difficult time putting a good face on the operation.

As the Tchepone operation was being planned, the helicopter situation was becoming critical. The helicopters and their crews were almost at the breaking point. Coordinating the massive helicopter support necessary to sustain the ARVN in Laos was extremely demanding, and the sheer number of aircraft in the airspace was difficult to control. General Abrams did what he could to remedy the situation, directing on 3 March that a joint coordinating group of general officers be established to provide coordination and liaison between General Lam's headquarters and XXIV Corps. The group became operational at I Corps tactical command post on 1 March. Brig. Gen. Jack Hemingway assumed the role as adviser for aviation to oversee rotary-wing support for the forces in Laos. Additionally, a US Air Force brigadier general was assigned to the coordinating group as an adviser for air support and an ARVN brigadier general was assigned to help coordinate ARVN artillery. Once established, the group met with Lieutenant General Lam daily to ensure that quick and responsive aviation and fire support was provided to the South Vietnamese forces in Laos.[5]

In preparation for the push to Tchepone, I Corps requested US XXIV Corps to send troops to replace the 2nd ARVN Regiment operating along the DMZ. XXIV Corps concurred and ordered the 101st Airborne Division to send its 3rd Brigade to the DMZ to replace the ARVN regiment. Four battalions from the US brigade began to redeploy on 28 February. The next day, 11th Brigade from the US 23rd Infantry Division was pulled out of its area of operation south of the Hai Van Pass and sent to reinforce the northern sector. Concurrently, all US forces operating in northern Quang Tri Province were placed under the operational control of 101st Airborne Division.

Between 2 and 4 March, 147th Brigade of the Marine Division, with its 2nd, 4th, and 7th Battalions, along with 2nd Artillery Battalion, was inserted into Fire Support Base Delta; elements of the brigade moved to occupy a blocking position, called Objective Alpha, south of the firebase. During the same period, the 258th Marine Brigade, consisting of the 1st, 3rd, and 8th Battalions along with the 3rd Artillery Battalion, was airlifted into Fire Support Base Hotel; one battalion was left to secure the firebase, but the other two battalions moved south toward Objective Bravo, which was meant to serve as a blocking position to keep the NVA away from the critical LZs or at least out of range of direct-fire weapons. Thus, the Marines assumed responsibility for the security of the southern flank, releasing 1st ARVN Division troops to move westward in accordance with the new plan to take Tchepone. This left only one Marine brigade in reserve, not only for the Lam Son operation, but also for the entire country; the rest of the strategic reserve, to include the Airborne Division, was now fully committed. During this period, four CH-53D Sea Stallions from US Marine Corps squadron HMH-463 provided heavy helicopter lift support to emplace 155-mm guns in the FSBs south of Route 9. The Sea Stallions were escorted by four new Bell AH-1J Sea Cobra gunships that were attached to Marine squadron HML-367.[6]

By this time the NVA had gained control of the high ground overlooking Route 9 from the north, but they had paid a high price. Repeated B-52 strikes took a terrible toll on the North Vietnamese, inflicting casualties that MACV estimated to be one combat effective NVA regiment a week.[7] This probably prevented the North Vietnamese from concentrating enough forces to completely annihilate ARVN units along the highway.

Nevertheless, at this juncture the North Vietnamese had massed over forty-five thousand regular troops and outnumbered the South Vietnamese forces by almost two to one. Heavy mortar and large-caliber artillery fire increased on all South Vietnamese positions. To make matters worse for the South Vietnamese, intermittent rain and dense fog repeatedly grounded all aircraft. The few helicopters that were able to fly had to be kept at low altitude, and this made them very vulnerable to enemy ground fire. Resupplying the ARVN attack became particularly difficult and dangerous under these conditions.

Despite the difficulties involved in conducting helicopter operations in Laos, there was really no other way to get the troops positioned to continue the attack toward Tchepone. The plan was for the 223rd Combat Aviation Battalion to lift ARVN soldiers into three landing zones located along the escarpment south of Route 9 and the Xe Pon River, which were to be sequentially assaulted in accordance with Lam's new plan. Once these LZs were secured, another force would be inserted by helicopter into another LZ just a few kilometers from Tchepone to make the final assault on the town itself. These LZs were named for four actresses—Lolo for Gina Lollobrigida, Liz for Elizabeth Taylor, Sophia for Sophia Loren, and Hope for Hope Lange (see Map 6). Communist propagandists later charged that the Americans chose the names, thus proving the South Vietnamese to be their puppets. In fact, Col. Vu Van Giai, the deputy commander of the 1st ARVN Division, chose the names; he had long worked with US units in northern I Corps Tactical Zone, and he wanted names familiar to the Americans who would support the assault on Tchepone.[8]

From 3 to 6 March, US forces at Khe Sanh mounted one of the largest protracted airmobile operations of the war; the combat assault on Tchepone involved more helicopters in a single lift than any other previous combat air assault in US Army aviation history. It was carried out in what proved to be the most hostile air defense environment encountered to that point in the war; the

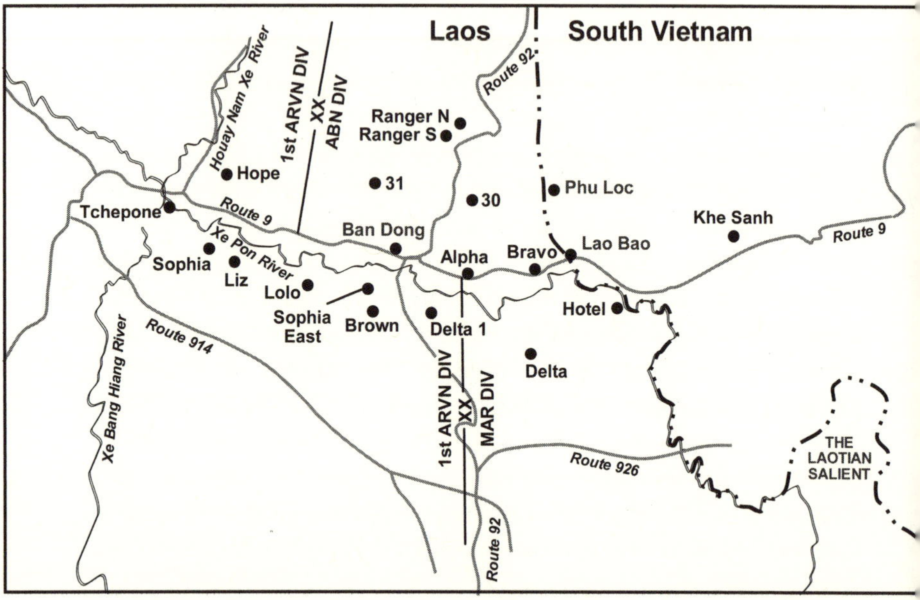

Map 6. Plan for the Assault on Tchepone

helicopter crews would have their work cut out for them. Brig. Gen. Sidney Berry later said of this operation, "Probably no one unit in the history of airmobile operations was presented a more demanding and challenging task than that assigned to the 223rd Combat Aviation Battalion to conduct the assaults 3 to 6 March."[9]

LZ Lolo was atop the highest peak on the southern escarpment, thirteen kilometers southeast of Tchepone. The plan for the assault on Lolo called for the insertion of three infantry battalions and one reinforced artillery battery. On the morning of 3 March, the same day that the South Vietnamese troops abandoned FSB 30, the last ARVN outpost north of Route 9, 223rd Combat Aviation Battalion, with additional helicopters from the 14th and 158th Aviation Battalions, airlifted ARVN troops of the 3rd Battalion, 1st Infantry Regiment, from LZ Delta into LZ Lolo. The insertion was preceded the night before by eight B-52s that bombed enemy positions south of the LZ and six fighter strikes on and around the LZ. As it turned out, this firepower had little effect.

The first helicopters landed, and ARVN soldiers got off and began to deploy. Initially, there was only light enemy response to the landing. However, when the next flight tried to land to offload their troops, the enemy opened up with everything they had. Seven of the next ten Hueys into the landing zone took hits as the enemy fire increased. Of the first twenty troop-carrying helicopters participating in the insertion at Lolo, North Vietnamese gunners shot down one en route and destroyed four others at the landing zone; another eight were damaged when they touched down to unload. Two Huey gunships were also shot down just east of the LZ. Maj. Bob Clewell, commander of A Company, 101st Aviation Battalion, led his unit into Lolo that day. He later commented on the intensity of enemy fire at the LZ, recalling, "They [the North Vietnamese soldiers] were like ants coming out of the ground."[10] Another pilot in the lift to Lolo observed, "They put in five hours of airstrikes and Cobras on the hillside. Then we went in and it sounded like a million people opened up on us."[11]

Lt. Col. Gerald Kirklighter, commander of the 223rd, suspended the assault and called for additional close air support and artillery fires. The 223rd attempted a second assault, but the enemy fire was still too intense, so that insertion was also called off. More close air support was called in, and this suppressed the enemy fire so that the assault could be continued.

During the course of the battle, the crew of one of the helicopters that was shot down in the landing zone found itself on the ground and in the middle of the fight in a ravine west of the crest of the peak on which Lolo was located. After using one of the ARVN radios to call in air strikes and armed helicopters against the NVA, they called Kirklighter and recommended that the LZ be shifted below the crest so the helicopters could insert their troops masked from the direct fire of the NVA covering the original LZ. Discharging the troops on a steep slope required skillful flying, but somehow the aviators pulled it off. By the end of the day, the ARVN had occupied Lolo, but in the process a total of eleven helicopters were shot down by the withering fire in the vicinity of the LZ, and forty-four others were damaged during the course of the operation.[12] This was one of the darkest days in US Army aviation history. At one point, Lieutenant Colonel Kirklighter, with the battlefield almost obscured by smoke and dust from the Cobra gunship strikes, the falling artillery, and the close air strikes, directed his incoming helicopters to "land to the burning aircraft!"[13]

Despite their losses, the US Army aviators pressed on with the mission as the antiaircraft fire intensified. Once the infantry troops were on the ground and the area was secured, 105-mm howitzers were airlifted in by helicopter to establish a fire support base so that supporting fires would be available for the next day's operation.

The next morning after they were inserted into LZ Lolo, troops from the 3rd Battalion, conducting search operations, made contact with an enemy force, killing eighty-three of them and capturing more than forty weapons. Shortly thereafter, helicopters from the 101st and 158th Aviation Battalions lifted the regimental command post and 2nd Battalion of the 1st Infantry Regiment into Lolo. That was followed by lifts of artillery, ammunition, supplies, and finally the 4th Battalion to complete the buildup of the fire support base.

At the same time, sixty-five helicopters lifted the 1st Battalion, 1st Infantry Regiment, into LZ Liz, five kilometers further to the west along the southern escarpment, completing the operation late in the afternoon. Once on the ground, the ARVN soldiers began constructing a fire support base on the high ground adjacent to the landing zone.

On that day back in Washington, Admiral Moorer received a message from General Abrams, who told the chairman, "I think we are going to get done what we set out to get done." He lauded General Lam as "tough, determined, careful and his spirits are good today." He rated the 1st ARVN Division as "solid from top to bottom." President Nixon, at a press conference that evening, quoted Abrams's evaluation of the ARVN in Laos, saying, "The South Vietnamese by themselves can hack it and they can give a better account of themselves even than the North Vietnamese units."[14]

While Washington tried to put the best face on the unfolding situation in Laos, the preparations for the assault on Tchepone continued. On 5 March the 4th and 5th Battalions from the 2nd Regiment were inserted by helicopter into LZ Sophia, four kilometers west of Liz and just four and one-half kilometers southeast of Tchepone. Once again the insertion was heavily contested by the NVA antiaircraft gunners, who shot down three helicopters in the first lift.[15] Nevertheless, the US Army aviators again pressed on against heavy enemy antiaircraft fire; in the process of inserting the ARVN troops at Sophia, two Cobras, two UH-1C Huey gunships, and two more Hueys were shot down. Most of the other aircraft in the flight sustained heavy damage from enemy fire.

Once on the ground, the 4th Battalion immediately began to

set up defensive positions to protect eight 105-mm howitzers, which were also brought in by helicopters. These guns could easily range Tchepone from that location. As preparations continued on the fire support base, the 5th Battalion pushed out from the landing zone to search the surrounding area. During their search they discovered an enemy camp that apparently had been destroyed by air strikes. There they found 124 enemy dead, thirty-three damaged or destroyed huts, seventy-one weapons, and eight tons of rice.[16]

By the end of the day on 5 March, the South Vietnamese forces had established a string of landing zones and fire support bases along the escarpment south of Route 9 and the Xe Pon River. They included FSBs Sophia, Lolo, Liz, Brown, and Delta 1. With the string of positions established along the southern escarpment, the next phase of the final assault on Tchepone began on the afternoon of 6 March, preceded by a heavy pounding of the NVA positions around Tchepone by fighter-bombers, B-52s, and long-range 175-mm guns firing from inside South Vietnam. Meanwhile, the 2nd and 3rd Battalions from the 2nd Regiment of the 1st ARVN Division waited seventy-seven kilometers away at Khe Sanh aboard 120 US UH-1H Huey helicopters. The operation had to lift off ninety minutes early due to incoming artillery and mortar fire, but the aircraft, lifting off all at once, were able to get airborne without incident. The airlift from Khe Sanh to LZ Hope, four kilometers northeast of Tchepone, was controlled by 223rd Combat Aviation Battalion and supported by Cobra gunships, aerial rocket artillery, and fighter-bombers in what was one of the largest and longest helicopter assaults of the war. Apparently, the NVA had not anticipated the landing at Hope.[17] Only one helicopter was hit by antiaircraft fire en route; it crash-landed in the LZ, and the crew was picked up later by an aircraft assigned to a follow-on wave; the rest of the flight and those that followed landed their troops amid only sporadic enemy ground fire.[18] By the end of the day, 276 helicopter sorties (some aircraft making three trips) landed about five thousand ARVN soldiers at LZ Hope.

Once on the ground, the "Black Wolves" of the 2nd Battalion, led by Maj. Tran Ngoc Hue, set up a perimeter and awaited the arrival of their sister battalion. Upon 3rd Battalion's landing, the two battalions moved rapidly off the landing zone and began to search the surrounding area to the north and east. The 2nd Battalion discovered a large cache of 122-mm rockets and an area where several burnt-out North Vietnamese tanks had been struck from the air. During the 3rd Battalion's search, they discovered over a hundred enemy soldiers killed by a B-52 strike, along with five trucks, six 12.7-mm machine guns, assorted small arms, and a large quantity of fuel.

While the airlifts into LZs Liz and Hope came under fire, they incurred fewer casualties and loss of helicopters than those at Lolo. After the heavy losses in the Lolo insertion, American planners back in South Vietnam demanded more intensive artillery preparation and tactical air support to suppress the North Vietnamese before the subsequent landings were attempted. Thus, Lolo resulted in a drastic increase in the Air Force sortie rate for the rest of the campaign, doubling from 104 sorties per day prior to 3 March to 211 sorties in the latter part of the operation. This included B-52 strikes the night before the landings at Liz, Sophia, and Hope, bombing by fighter-bombers the morning of the landing, and, at least in one case, the use of a fifteen-thousand-pound BLU-82 "Commando Vault" bomb dropped from a C-130 to blast the objective before the helicopters came in.[19]

The assault on Tchepone itself began on 7 March, when three battalions from the 2nd Regiment that had landed at LZ Hope entered the town. The ARVN troops occupied the town and patrolled in the surrounding area for the next two and one-half days; while the 2nd Battalion searched in and north of the town, the 3rd Battalion searched southeast of the town on the north bank of the Xe Pon River, and the 4th Battalion moved northwest from FSB Sophia to search on the south bank of the river.

During the course of their searches, the South Vietnamese troops seized enough rice to feed 159 battalions for thirty days; enough rifles, small arms, machine guns, mortars, and artillery pieces to equip seventeen infantry battalions; and 714 tons of ammunition. Almost four thousand captured enemy weapons were airlifted out and taken back to South Vietnam. Thousands of tons of supplies were destroyed. What the soldiers themselves could not destroy, they destroyed with artillery, gunships, and tactical air support; over two thousand secondary explosions were recorded from these strikes. In addition to the supplies found and destroyed, the ARVN discovered a number of sites where earlier air strikes had inflicted serious carnage on the NVA; for example, the 2nd Battalion, about a kilometer northeast of Tchepone, discovered fifty-two dead bodies and a cache of stored weapons.[20]

The ARVN had reached their objective; they had taken Tchepone and struck a blow against the enemy and his supply buildup. This was the high-water mark for the South Vietnamese forces in Laos. At this point in the campaign, South Vietnamese strength in Laos was 16,844 troops, which included eighteen battalions of infantry (including airborne), four artillery battalions, three armored cavalry squadrons, two engineer battalions, and six Marine battalions. By this time the Rangers, who had originally gone into Laos in the initial wave, had been withdrawn and were back with the 1st Ranger Group headquarters at FSB Phu Loc.

With the ARVN on the ground in Tchepone, some of the reports in the American press became more positive, but many were still somewhat cautious. Alvin Shuster of the *New York Times* wrote that the capture of Tchepone had provided an important psychological boost to the Saigon government. Michael Parks of the *Baltimore Sun* wrote that the ARVN had fought well in Laos, but he questioned their dependence on US air support and firepower.[21]

The helicopter crews who made possible the leapfrog movement of ARVN forces westward along the southern escarpment toward Tchepone paid a high price. Many of them flew multiple missions each day; some made eight to twelve trips daily into Laos. They were under fire constantly from the moment they crossed into Laos until they completed their missions and flew back over the border into South Vietnam; crews figured they stood a fifty-fifty chance of being shot down every time they entered the airspace in Laos along Route 9.[22] Both crews and aircraft were taking a beating, but replacement aircraft were brought in, and the helicopter crews kept flying, even though they knew full well what waited for them when they took off for Laos.

Contact with the enemy forces had been light during the operation in and around Tchepone; the North Vietnamese had failed to anticipate the South Vietnamese airmobile operation to seize the town. However, they recovered quickly. While they rushed reinforcements to the area, campaign headquarters broadcast a tape recorded statement from Van Di, the chairman of the Tchepone district, in which he said, "Not one single enemy soldier has set foot in the town of Tchepone, and the people are still going about their normal daily activities and are ready for battle." At the same time, campaign headquarters ordered all units to attack the enemy on all fronts; they were not going to let the South Vietnamese occupation of Tchepone go without a strong response.[23]

This became only too apparent to the South Vietnamese when intelligence reports indicated that enemy traffic was increasing on all routes into the contested area during the week of 3–10 March; these reports included a number of tracked vehicle sightings. The B70 Corps and attached units had suffered approximately twelve thousand casualties since the Lam Son operation began, but during the first two weeks in March the North Vietnamese would introduce five more regiments into the area of operation. This meant that the NVA forces had increased to twelve infantry regiments, two tank battalions, an artillery regiment, and at least nineteen antiaircraft battalions.[24] With these new forces added to the battle and the initial units that began the battle replenished with supplies and fresh troops, the North Vietnamese commanders were ready to renew their efforts to destroy the South Vietnamese forces in Laos.

As the NVA made preparations for the coming battles, US helicopter pilots flew resupply missions to all the firebases on 7 and 8 March. Contact with enemy continued to be light with the exception of FSBs Lolo and Delta, which both sustained mortar and rocket attacks followed by multicompany ground assaults.

The ARVN troops in and around Tchepone continued their search operations on 9 March; a total of fifty-nine enemy bodies and numerous destroyed supply caches were discovered in areas previously hit by tactical air strikes. South of Route 9, the headquarters of the 1st ARVN Regiment observed enemy tanks near its command post, but a subsequent artillery strike by 155-mm howitzers and 175-mm guns destroyed three of the tanks and left five burning.

Ground searches confirmed additional enemy soldiers killed by earlier Arc Light strikes. Six kilometers southeast of Sophia, 391 bodies were found; another 144 enemy bodies were discovered in the 1st Infantry Regiment area of operations. These reports were encouraging, but there was no attempt by the ARVN to cross the Xe Bang Hiang River west of Tchepone, where intelligence sources indicated that the NVA had moved most of its supplies.

As the operation at Tchepone continued to unfold, General

Abrams cabled Admiral Moorer on 8 March to provide a situation report on the operation. He reported that the "morale and confidence of the ARVN commanders has risen appreciably during the last three or four days." However, he warned that there was a "general feeling" among the senior ARVN officers "that their mission has been accomplished and it is now time to withdraw. They do not concede that there is still much to be done."[25]

Despite Abrams's warning, back in Washington the president was overjoyed by the reports from Tchepone. However, he was still very unhappy with the press coverage of the operation in Laos. In a message to Ambassador Bunker, Kissinger acknowledged that the president was pleased with the events at Tchepone, but noted, "The president made the additional comment that our worst enemy seems to be the press."[26]

On 9 March, General Lam flew once again to meet with Thieu and General Vien. This time he went to make a case for doing just what Henry Kissinger back in Washington was so worried about: rather than have his forces remain in Laos until the beginning of the rainy season, in line with the original concept, Lam was there to recommend a plan for the withdrawal of his forces from Laos. Having stressed the exposed position of South Vietnamese forces, Lam proposed to disengage and extract them by helicopter, with the 1st Division, the westernmost unit, leaving first, followed by the Airborne Division and last, the Marines. General Vien agreed with Lam. Abrams and Ambassador Bunker, also in attendance, strongly disagreed with the withdrawal. They hoped that the ARVN would stay in Laos until the rainy season started in May in order to destroy the NVA logistical network in the area and then withdraw through Base Area 611 and the A Shau Valley, fighting as they went. Abrams believed that if Thieu would insert one more division at Tchepone, the ARVN could cripple the NVA and perhaps win a decisive battle. He urged Thieu to reinforce his forces in Laos with the ARVN 2nd Infantry Division, then in Quang Ngai Province, and fight it out to the finish with the communists. General Vien said that he would do so, but only if Abrams inserted the 1st Brigade, 5th Mechanized, and two brigades of the 101st Airborne Division into Laos. Because of the restrictions imposed by the Cooper-Church Amendment, Abrams could only reply that "under no circumstances would US ground forces be inserted in Laos."[27]

Several days after the meeting, Abrams enumerated his concerns with the political and public relations problems involved in the withdrawal in a message to the chairman of the Joint Chiefs. He was worried about "whether it might not appear the RVNAF forces had been forced to withdraw despite the heavy casualties inflicted on the enemy; how such a move would be interpreted by the South Vietnam, American, and international press; [and] the effect this would have on the political situation in South Vietnam [where national elections would be held in the following fall]."[28] His worries would turn out to be well-founded.

Abrams's concerns notwithstanding, from Thieu's perspective the objective of Lam Son 719 had been accomplished; the NVA troops had suffered heavy losses in the bitter fighting, and ARVN troops had found and destroyed a large volume of enemy supplies. With his battered forces now outnumbered about two to one and strung out all along Route 9 from the border to Tchepone, Thieu was unwilling to risk more casualties as well as the potential destruction of his best division (the Airborne Division) and the bulk of his general reserve. Even though Tchepone had not been heavily defended, the ARVN positions at Lolo, Liz, and Sophia were still being shelled daily, and patrols routinely made contact with the enemy. Intelligence reports indicated that the North Vietnamese were rushing reinforcements to the area, and their air defenses showed no signs of weakening; it was clear that the NVA were not going to abandon the area without a fight. Accordingly, Thieu decided that it was time to get out before the situation got worse, so he gave the order to terminate the operation and begin the withdrawal. According to Gen. Bruce Palmer, Abrams privately observed that Thieu had lost his nerve and never forgave him.[29]

Abrams and Bunker were not the only ones who were concerned with this new turn of events. When Kissinger got word of Thieu's intent to change the mission, he sent a back-channel message to Ambassador Bunker urging him to impress upon President Thieu "the need not to allow the potentially significant benefits of this operation to be sacrificed for short lived publicity based on more limited gains achieved thus far. . . . From our perspective, every week ARVN stays in Laos represents a serious blow to the enemy's offensive capability, not only for this dry season but, more importantly, for the next." He concluded, "We have not gone through all this agony just for the favorable headlines achieved as a result of recent successes and would hope that

President Thieu would view the situation from the same perspective."[30] It soon became apparent that Kissinger and Thieu did not share the same perspective.

On 11 March, Kissinger told Admiral Moorer that the president wanted the ARVN to still be in Laos when he announced the next round of US troop withdrawals on 7 April. Such was not to be the case, because by that time the withdrawal was already under way. According to General Hinh, "It was apparent that President Thieu had decided, at the outset, that once Tchepone had been entered . . . the withdrawal would begin without delay." In fact, the 2nd Regiment had already begun to depart Tchepone, climbing the ridge south of town toward FSB Sophia.[31]

CHAPTER NINE

The Withdrawal

The I Corps plan for the withdrawal from Laos called for a "phased delay operation," in which ARVN forces would fall back toward South Vietnam, destroying base areas and supplies in their path as they went. The operation would begin with 2nd Regiment from the 1st ARVN Division closing FSB Sophia and subsequently occupying a new base, FSB Brick, near Route 92 about nine kilometers south of Ban Dong. Then the 1st Regiment would join them, and they would conduct operations in the area between Routes 92 and 914 for seven to ten days, hoping to find and destroy Binh Tram 33, which was thought to be in that area.

After this was accomplished, the order of withdrawal would be the 1st ARVN Division followed by the Airborne Division. FSBs Lolo and Brick would be closed; subsequently, 3rd Regiment from the 1st ARVN Division operating in the area of LZ Brown and FSB Delta 1 would pull out after clearing FSB A Luoi.

After withdrawal of the Airborne and 1st ARVN Divisions, the 147th and 258th Marine Brigades would pull back from FSBs Delta and Hotel. According to Lam's plan, the entire operation was to be completed by 31 March. Then, after resting and reorganizing for about two weeks, the 1st ARVN Division, two Marine brigades, and one airborne brigade would conduct operations into the eastern sector of enemy Base Area 611, the A Shau Valley, and the Laotian Salient.

Withdrawal of a force in contact was an extremely difficult maneuver, but particularly so when that force was greatly outnumbered by the enemy. The situation was further compounded by the terrain and weather, which favored the enemy, who were prepared to do everything they could to block the ARVN penetration deep into what had been their sanctuary. Additionally, there were other complicating factors. At this point the ARVN troops, which included three understrength divisions and the 1st Armored Brigade, had little or no artillery of their own; many of their guns had been destroyed in the fighting or left in place when the ARVN withdrew from their earlier positions. Many of the units in Laos were running low on ammunition, and the troops were worn out from weeks of pitched battle. This maneuver, quickly planned, would have been challenging and risky under the best circumstances; given the existing situation and Lam's deteriorating relationship with the airborne and Marine commanders, which would greatly complicate matters, the withdrawal would prove to be an agonizing and bloody affair.

By this time the NVA had moved more than sixty thousand troops into the area to inflict as much damage on the ARVN as possible.[1] When they saw that the ARVN were withdrawing, the NVA stepped up their efforts to annihilate as many of the South Vietnamese forces as possible. This was a great opportunity to demonstrate to the world that they had thrown the South Vietnamese out of Laos and prove that Nixon's Vietnamization policy was failing. Placing heavy antiaircraft fire on the evacuation helicopters, ambushing ARVN elements moving by road, and keeping pressure on the South Vietnamese firebases, the NVA turned the withdrawal into a nightmare.

While the ARVN disengagement was being planned, the enemy buildup continued. ARVN 1st Regiment reported sighting tanks near Ta Luong on Route 9, about ten kilometers southeast of Tchepone. In the area between Ta Luong and Route 914, they found the bodies of seventy-two NVA soldiers and a number of destroyed vehicles and artillery pieces, apparently the result of a very effective B-52 strike.

On the morning of 10 March, the 2nd ARVN Regiment at FSB Sophia received a mix of over a hundred 82-mm and 122-mm mortar rounds, which wounded thirteen soldiers and knocked out six of the eight 105-mm howitzers on the base. These were effectively the opening shots of the renewed effort by B70 Corps to destroy the ARVN forces in Laos before they could escape.

On 11 March, in accordance with the I Corps plan, the 1st and 2nd Regiments of the 1st ARVN Division began to withdraw. The 2nd Regiment headquarters, the 2nd and 5th Battalions, and a 105-mm howitzer battery were picked up by US helicopters at LZ Liz and taken to LZ Brown, leapfrogging over the 1st Regiment at Lolo. The 4th Battalion continued to secure FSB Sophia and the 3rd Battalion secured LZ Liz.

On 12 March, the 2nd Regiment headquarters and its two accompanying battalions established a new fire support base at Sophia East, also known as Sophia II, one kilometer west of LZ Brown. Later that afternoon, the 3rd Battalion was then moved by helicopters from LZ Liz to LZ Moon, adjacent to FSB Sophia East. The 4th Battalion was extracted from Sophia and arrived at LZ Moon about 1830 hours. With these moves complete, the 2nd Regiment consolidated its position and prepared to attack south to interdict Route 914 at Cua Viet and Cua Tang. After the 2nd Regiment departed Sophia, leaving their artillery in place, US fighter-bombers bombed the base, hoping to destroy the abandoned howitzers to keep them from falling into enemy hands. The withdrawal of the 2nd Regiment left the 1st Regiment at FSB Lolo, the westernmost ARVN position in Laos.

Back in Washington, Kissinger was briefed in detail on the withdrawal plan. He could not believe his ears, concluding, "Then they are really bugging out in the next ten days, those sons of bitches. It's their country and we can't save it for them if they don't want to. We would never have approved the plan if we thought they were only going to stay for a short time, six to eight weeks."[2] Admiral Moorer met with Kissinger and the president; Nixon was very concerned that the withdrawal might be seen as a defeat, thereby damaging Thieu's position, not only in Vietnam, but also around the world.[3]

In Saigon on 12 March, Ambassador Bunker and General Abrams met with President Thieu. They expressed Washington's concerns about the withdrawal plan, particularly with regard to potential public relations problems if it appeared that the South Vietnamese forces were being forced to withdraw from Laos prematurely. Thieu replied that the plan was to rotate in fresh troops and continue to exploit the Route 914 area before moving south to clear Base Area 611. Bunker, in a back-channel message to Kissinger, said that he and Abrams felt this was a "satisfactory plan."[4]

In Laos, the ARVN 4th Armored Battalion (Composite), heretofore uncommitted, moved westward along Route 9 toward FSB Alpha to assist in route security for the withdrawal. The 260-man unit had thirty M41 tanks, nine M113 armored personnel carriers, and two light tracked recovery vehicles. The insertion of this unit into the operation brought the total number of South Vietnamese troops committed to its peak of 17,104.

While the 2nd Regiment had been in the process of withdrawing from LZ Liz to the east, the enemy remained active in the airborne and Marine sectors, where ground assaults and attacks by fire continued. The situation was improved somewhat by more effective tac air, which resulted when Vietnamese interpreters were put in the cockpits with the US forward air controllers so they could talk to their countrymen on the ground to coordinate close air strikes. At the same time, US Army helicopters were still braving intense antiaircraft fire to keep the ARVN outposts resupplied.

With the withdrawal of the 2nd Regiment, the NVA turned their attention on the 3rd Regiment, attempting to surround the ARVN forces operating in the Ta Luong area southwest of FSB Sophia with the 1st and 141st Regiments of the 2nd NVA Division. At the same time, they increased the attacks by fire on the 1st ARVN Regiment at FSB Lolo, pounding the base around the clock with 122-mm rockets and 130-mm artillery fire. The incoming fire reached a new high on 14 March, when the defenders received an estimated two hundred rockets and over a hundred artillery rounds. Due to solidly built bunkers, the ARVN sustained only light casualties, but two 105-mm artillery pieces were severely damaged by the incoming fire. It soon became only too clear to the ARVN troops at Lolo that they were encircled by a much larger NVA force. The continuous enemy barrage had made resupply and evacuation of the wounded virtually impossible. The ARVN were able to hold the NVA at bay with artillery support from US firebases inside South Vietnam and close support from the Cobra attack helicopters of 4th Battalion, 77th Aerial Rocket Artillery. The Cobra support was provided in response to calls from a very fluent English-speaking South Vietnamese soldier on the ground whom the pilots came to know during the battle by his radio call sign, Quebec Whiskey.[5]

By this time, not only Lolo was under intense incoming fire, but Delta and A Luoi were as well. Indirect fire on the ARVN positions had greatly increased, and the enemy was doing everything it could to prevent aerial resupply and medical evacuation efforts, which mirrored the pattern of the attacks that had eventually resulted in the fall of FSBs 30 and 31. By that point the ARVN at Lolo were running out of ammunition, and the wounded could not be evacuated. Sometime during the period, contact was lost with Quebec Whiskey; apparently he had been killed or wounded in the ongoing battle.

With Lolo about to go under, the commander of the 1st ARVN Regiment made an emergency request for small-arms ammunition. Five aircrews from the 223rd Combat Aviation Battalion volunteered to attempt a resupply mission. Subsequently, the flight of five UH-1H helicopters, led by Maj. John A. G. Klose, S-3 operations officer of the 223rd, picked up five one-thousand-pound sling loads of small-arms ammunition and headed for Lolo. The LZ was now completely surrounded by NVA antiaircraft guns. As the resupply helicopters approached Lolo, one of the escorting Cobra gunships took fire from the ground; it crash-landed and burst into flames, but the two pilots were able to crawl away before the helicopter exploded, and they were later rescued. Despite what pilots described as the most intense display of enemy antiaircraft fire they had ever seen, the resupply helicopters continued their descent, taking hits all the way but delivering the much-needed ammunition to the ARVN defenders; all five helicopters sustained multiple hits during the mission.

At about 2200 hours on the night of 15 March, the decision was made to abandon Lolo. The plan was for the 1st Regiment command post to break out from the firebase, join the battalions operating from positions outside the base, break contact, and move to the high ground two kilometers to the east of the LZ. Meanwhile, the 4th Battalion would serve as rear guard to protect the regiment as it withdrew. Additionally, the ARVN would destroy four 155-mm howitzers that could not be taken with them; one 155-mm and four 105-mm howitzers had already been damaged by incoming enemy fire. As the regimental headquarters and the 1st, 2nd, and 3rd Battalions began to withdraw, they came under intense NVA attack. The regimental commander called two B-52 strikes within five hundred yards of his lead position, which wrought havoc on the North Vietnamese attackers, breaking the back of their attack. The ARVN troops fought their way north and east off the escarpment, eventually reaching a position two thousand meters southwest of FSB A Luoi, where they were picked up on 18 March by helicopters and flown to Khe Sanh.

The news from MACV that FSB Lolo was being abandoned met with more than a little consternation in Washington. At Secretary Laird's staff meeting on 17 March, General Westmoreland severely criticized the performance of the South Vietnamese in Laos. Admiral Moorer later recalled that Westmoreland "badmouthed the whole Lam Son 719 operation." The next day, the

JCS chairman reassured President Nixon that "things were going pretty well," that the ARVN had "severely disrupted" enemy movements throughout the Lam Son area of operations, and that the ARVN who had been reported as fleeing their positions were merely repositioning to higher ground.[6]

Privately, Moorer was less positive. He had received a message from Abrams saying that General Lam had apparently abandoned the idea of continuing the interdiction of Route 914 and any move eastward through Base Area 611. Moorer worried that perhaps the South Vietnamese had suffered many more casualties than they had reported and that this was the reason for the change in plans. Late on 17 March, he sent a message to Abrams warning that "the redeployment of ARVN forces . . . could [add] fuel to the current pessimistic reports claiming a rout of Vietnamese units from Laos. . . . We run the risk of losing most of our high-level political support for prosecuting Lam Son 719 to a successful conclusion and of undermining widespread confidence in the success of Vietnamization to date."[7]

Back in Laos at Lolo, the 4th Battalion, left in contact when the rest of the regiment moved off the escarpment, found itself fighting a rear-guard action against increasing enemy pressure. What ensued was a desperate battle that raged for two days. Despite repeated calls by the NVA to surrender, the battalion fought its way back toward the bank of the Xe Pon River. However, on 17 March, as the ARVN neared the river, NVA forces were waiting for them there. The bitter battle continued for the rest of the day, with US tac air and gunships providing support to the grossly outnumbered ARVN soldiers, who took cover in a ravine. During the course of the intense fighting, which extended through the night and into the next day, both the battalion commander and his deputy were killed. Three helicopters were shot down, and one fighter-bomber was hit and exploded in midair.[8]

As the fighting continued, Lt. Col. Archie Rider, new commander of 2nd Squadron, 17th Cavalry, and Lieutenant Colonel Kirklighter, commander of 223rd Combat Aviation Battalion, put together a plan to rescue the beleaguered battalion. By the time they arrived on the scene late in the afternoon of 18 March, a group of ARVN survivors led by a sergeant had made it to a clearing where they took refuge in a bomb crater, but several attempts to rescue them were turned away by intense fire.

Capt. Keith A. Brandt, leading an attack helicopter section from

D Company, 101st Aviation Battalion, arrived on the scene. The ARVN sergeant on the ground radioed Brandt, saying, "We're completely surrounded." Brandt assured the sergeant, "We are going to get you out of there." For the rest of the afternoon, Brandt and his copilot, 1st Lt. Alan B. Boffman, stayed over the ARVN, returning to Khe Sanh for refueling and rearming three times. When rescue ships from 173rd Assault Helicopter Company, the "Robin Hoods," arrived on the scene, Brandt volunteered to lead them in to the landing zone, radioing, "This is Music One Six. Follow me Robin Hood 3 [the lead UH-1H], and I'll lead you to the friendlies." As they were making their final approach to pick up the ARVN soldiers, the ground fire intensified, and Brandt's AH-1G Cobra was hit. He radioed, "There it is Robin Hood! Twelve o'clock, 100 meters—I'm going to try to make it to the river." However, shortly thereafter, he radioed, "I've lost my engine and my transmission is breaking up. Good-bye. Send my love to my family. I'm dead."[9] The helicopter crashed, exploding in a ball of flame just before it hit the ground; because of the intense fighting in the area, the bodies of Brandt and Boffman were not recovered at the time.[10] This is just one example of the courage and sacrifice demonstrated time and again by the American helicopter pilots who supported the operation in Laos.

Despite the loss of their comrades, the lift pilots from the 173rd carried on with the mission, landing under intense fire to pick up the survivors of the 4th Battalion, and then flew them to Khe Sanh in the rear. The first UH-1H, grossly overloaded, came out with twenty-two ARVN soldiers on board, some of them clinging to the helicopter skids. When the helicopters landed at Khe Sanh, reporters crowded around the airstrip, photographing the ARVN soldiers hanging from the skids as the Hueys approached. They spoke with the aircrews, who related stories about the panicked soldiers who would do anything to get out of Laos alive. Like the earlier Ranger incident, this contributed to the perception that the ARVN were being run out of Laos, which became the story line that would be transmitted back to the States.

The whole story of this incident and the battalion's performance in the bitter fighting was much more than it seemed; the 4th Battalion, which had been fighting a desperate battle for six weeks, successfully fought a rear-guard action to protect the withdrawal of the regimental headquarters and the rest of the regiment. They were surrounded and out of ammunition when they were extracted. On 19 March, after another small group of survivors was extracted, the 4th Battalion, 1st ARVN Regiment, could muster only eighty-eight survivors of the bitter fighting at the riverbank; all of the officers had been killed, and sixty-one of the survivors were wounded. Nevertheless, the South Vietnamese troop had held their own in the heavy fighting at Lolo and the subsequent withdrawal: the NVA had sustained an estimated eleven hundred to seventeen hundred killed in action, severely damaging the two main force regiments of the 2nd Division.[11]

That is a much different story than the one told by photos of the ARVN soldiers clinging to the helicopter skids. "I don't know what the press was trying to prove," said Lieutenant Colonel Kirklighter. "I didn't see him [the ARVN soldier] hanging from the skids. It does not mean that the unit panicked or acted unmilitarily. It only means that some soldier looked around and, hell, he's the last son of a bitch on the ground, and he's not going to be left behind. I'd jump on the skid, too. And so would you."[12] Nevertheless, the perceptions fostered by the images of panicked ARVN soldiers being driven out of Laos persisted.

By that time, the story of the withdrawal was being covered heavily in the news media back in the United States. Despite the attempts by MACV to put the best face on the situation, most of the reports were very critical of the South Vietnamese troops and questioned the progress of Vietnamization. One of these reports, which is fairly representative, quoted an army pilot who said, "They can talk about helicopter mobility all they want, but from where I'm flying there's only one way to describe it—retreat, and a bad one."[13]

In Washington, the president and Kissinger, alarmed at the negative media coverage, were becoming increasingly dissatisfied with the reports from Abrams that indicated the South Vietnamese were curtailing the operation prematurely and planned to abandon the continued interdiction of Route 914 and the clearing of Base Area 611. They were concerned not only with the fact that a chance would be missed to inflict heavier damage on the North Vietnamese forces, but also that an early withdrawal would only add fuel to the current wave of pessimistic press reports claiming a rout of South Vietnamese forces in Laos. They were also upset with what they saw as late, incomplete, inaccurate information on what was unfolding in Laos. White House statements to the press based on these reports were often contradicted by events, increasing the skepticism in the media.[14] It was almost inevitable that Nixon's and Kissinger's ire would fall on Abrams, who had maintained a steady stream of extremely positive reports. To get a better assessment of the situation in Laos, Kissinger sent Haig on a fact-finding mission to Saigon.

While Haig was en route to the South Vietnamese capital, enemy activity in the Marine sector increased significantly. The 147th Marine Brigade headquarters at FSB Delta sustained four hundred artillery rounds, which killed four Marines. The brigade's 7th Battalion, conducting operations outside the base, also came under indirect fire that effectively pinned down the unit. The South Vietnamese Marines were surrounded by two regiments of the NVA 324th Division, the 1st and 3rd, which had moved into Laos from the A Shau Valley.[15] The NVA positioned antiaircraft guns in the hills around Delta, attempting to close down air access to the base while they continued to pound it with 130-mm artillery.

At FSB Delta 1, 1st Battalion of the 3rd ARVN Regiment remained to secure the base, but the regimental headquarters and 4th Battalion had been picked up and taken to Ham Nghi base at Khe Sanh on 16 March. The 3rd Battalion had been evacuated two days before.

As the battle at Lolo and the subsequent withdrawal by the 1st Regiment developed, elements of the 2nd Regiment, 1st ARVN Division, continued to conduct search operations in the vicinity of FSBs Brown and Sophia East, coming under increasing enemy pressure. On the afternoon and evening of 18 March, three of the regiment's battalions, located on the high ground immediately south of FSB Brown, came under heavy attacks from enemy infantry using flamethrowers. The regiment's 5th Battalion at FSB Delta 1 was also under attack. During these firefights the ARVN fought hard: 2nd Battalion killed 85 enemy soldiers, the 3rd Battalion reported 85 enemy killed, and the 4th Battalion reported killing 195 communist soldiers.[16] During the course of the battle, 2nd Battalion discovered an abandoned NVA encampment where they found over 130 buildings, sheds, and bunkers. The camp had apparently been evacuated because of a nearby Arc Light strike.

As these events unfolded in Laos, the bases in South Vietnam that were supporting the Laos operation repeatedly came under fire. The FSB at Khe Sanh was hit by mortar fire for two days in a row. Four Americans were wounded and two helicopters were damaged. North Vietnamese gunners also shelled FSBs Phu Loc and Lao Bao with 130-mm field guns. There were daily ambushes and mine attacks along Route 9 from Dong Ha to Khe Sanh, while US and ARVN logistical bases came under sapper attacks. At the same time, the North Vietnamese launched a psychological operations campaign touting their victories against ARVN forces in Laos.

Meanwhile, Haig had arrived in Saigon. He traveled to XXIV Corps (Forward) on 18 March, where he told General Sutherland that "Washington would like to see ARVN stay in Laos through April."[17] That may have been Washington's wish, but as far as the South Vietnamese were concerned, that was not going to happen.

On the evening of 18 March, General Lam called for a meeting with his division commanders. He was disturbed by reports of the continuous heavy artillery bombardments and ground attacks supported by tanks; additionally, there were new sightings of more tanks moving in daylight along Routes 92 and 9.[18] The corps commander was particularly upset by the decimation of the 4th Battalion, 1st ARVN Regiment, and the deteriorating situation with the 2nd Regiment at FSBs Brown and Delta 1, both in danger of being surrounded and cut off. It was clear to Lam that the NVA were reinforcing and planned to do everything they could to prevent an orderly ARVN withdrawal. When the general met with his commanders at Ham Nghi, they were in agreement that they should accelerate the withdrawal of their forces.

Unfortunately, the three battalions of the 2nd Regiment were heavily engaged with the NVA and could not break contact. The NVA attempted to surround and destroy the withdrawing South Vietnamese units, and only US tactical air support and attack helicopters prevented a complete disaster. The beleaguered South Vietnamese forces could do nothing but dig in and pray for continued salvation from the air.

By this point in mid-March, the NVA 308th Division (36th, 88th, and 102nd Regiments) was attacking from the north (see Map 7). At the same time, the 64th and 24th Regiments from the 320th and 304th Divisions, respectively, continued to encircle the Ban Dong area. While the NVA 2nd Division was trying to annihilate the remaining forces of the 1st ARVN Division, the NVA 324th Division deployed its 1st and 3rd Regiments to attack the 147th Marine Brigade. At the same time, its 2nd Regiment pinned down the 258th Marine Brigade around Hotel and at Co

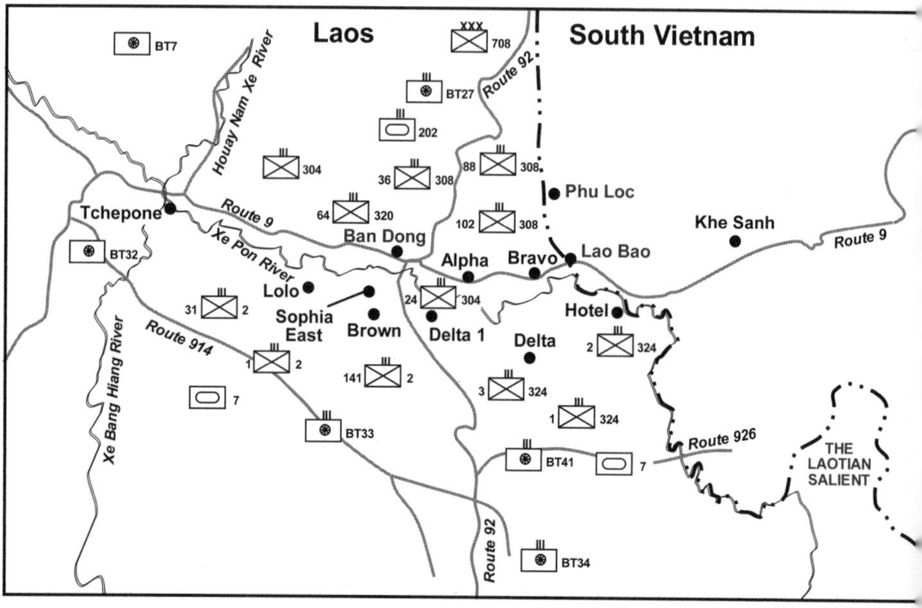

Map 7. Enemy Situation, Mid-March 1971

Roc. The NVA corps commander apparently hoped to catch the entire ARVN force in his trap. As former ARVN general Nguyen Duy Hinh wrote after the war, "In the manner of a hunter, he [the NVA commander] set about to kill his prey by 'Locking its head and gripping its tail.'"[19]

As the action south of the Xe Pon River unfolded, the ARVN forces north of the river were told to hold their positions until the 1st Infantry Division had extracted its forward units from FSBs Sophia and Lolo. However, by 15 March the forces at FSB A Luoi were surrounded and under intense enemy pressure. By 17 March it was apparent that the NVA were preparing to launch a tank-infantry assault similar to the one that had overrun FSB 31; in light of this intelligence, General Lam gave instructions to initiate phase two of the withdrawal. The Airborne Division subsequently directed the armored task force to abandon A Luoi and begin movement to designated positions west of FSB Alpha.

At first light on the morning of 19 March, with almost all of the ARVN battalions in Laos in contact, the armored task force began to withdraw from A Luoi, covered by the 8th and 9th Airborne Battalions operating north of the base. A column of eighteen tanks and armored personnel carriers departed first, towing damaged vehicles and several howitzers. The force had been allocated two US air cavalry troops to cover the move, but General Dong, the Airborne Division commander, diverted them to support other airborne units.

Four kilometers east of Ban Dong, still about halfway to FSB Alpha, the column was ambushed at a stream crossing. North Vietnamese gunners struck the lead vehicles with rocket-propelled grenades, disabling four M41 tanks in the middle of the stream and stranding the vehicles that followed in the ambush zone while at the same time isolating the 11th Armored Cavalry on the west bank of the stream. During the course of the short and violent battle that ensued, about half the ARVN vehicles were damaged or destroyed. The column was immobilized, and the airborne soldiers, refusing to stay with the stranded vehicles, left the cavalry, continuing to march east down Route 9. The cavalry fought on alone, finally getting across the stream after three hours, but lost four tanks and three M113 armored personnel carriers in the process. In addition, they left eighteen disabled vehicles on the west side of the stream. Eventually, tactical air support was called in to destroy the abandoned vehicles to prevent them from falling into enemy hands.

The North Vietnamese did everything possible to prevent the South Vietnamese from escaping, pursuing with tanks and other armored vehicles while continuing to pound them with artillery, rockets, and mortars. Route 9 became a tangle of disabled and destroyed tanks and other vehicles that had run out of gas. The panic that ensued in some South Vietnamese units was reminiscent of that shown earlier by the deserters at Ranger Base North. Lieutenant Colonel Peachey, commander of the 158th Aviation Battalion, described the nature of the South Vietnamese withdrawal: "They [the ARVN troops] would do absolutely anything to get out of Laos. . . . The healthy would run over the dead and wounded. We would hover at six or seven feet, and the crew chief and gunner would lay on their bellies and pull people up. If you got on the ground they would turn the helicopter over. A later tactic was to run and jump on the shoulders of people and grab on to the skids. The helicopters would go up to 3,000 or 4,000 feet, and after five or ten minutes, they'd get tired and turn loose. I can still see the bodies coming through the sky."[20] By nightfall, the battered armored column had finally reached FSB Alpha.

In Washington, Kissinger's frustration with the situation in Laos had reached new heights. On 18 March, Admiral Moorer telephoned with an update from General Abrams, who reported that the withdrawals were "proceeding in an orderly fashion." Kissinger was not buying it; he observed that the ARVN were off Route 914, "strung along like sausage" on Route 9, and did not seem to be headed for Base Area 611. He concluded that it looked like they were "bugging out."[21]

Kissinger's concern only increased when he received a message from Haig in Saigon detailing the deteriorating situation in Laos. Haig reported that "ARVN enthusiasm for continuation of the operation in Laos is completely lacking." Furthermore, he observed, "The extended period of intense combat has convinced the ARVN commanders that the operation should be called off as quickly as possible."[22]

Subsequently, Kissinger sent a message to Ambassador Bunker. He said, "It would be hard to exaggerate the mystification and confusion caused here by ARVN's latest scheme of maneuver which envisages a rapid pull-out from Laos." He concluded: "I hope Thieu understands that the President's confidence is an asset he should not lightly dissipate and that this may be his last crack at massive US support."[23] Kissinger's thinly veiled threat had no effect on Thieu.

Back in Laos, the 147th Marine Brigade at FSB Delta found itself in an increasingly desperate situation. It was effectively surrounded, and ten antiaircraft guns in the hills around the base prevented any aerial resupply. At the same time, NVA gunners pounded the Marine positions with 130-mm artillery shells. The 2nd and 4th Battalions were ordered to move from their positions to relieve the base but were blocked by NVA forces, resulting in a number of sharp firefights. Inside the base, five of ten 105-mm howitzers had been put out of commission, while the number of Marines killed and wounded continued to rise. An NVA defector told the Marine interrogators that the entire 324th Division was committed to the "Route 9 Campaign." He reported that his regiment had been pretty beat up in the fighting, but that his sister regiment was in good shape and engaging the Vietnamese Marines at LZ Hotel.[24]

To the northwest of the Marines, the 1st ARVN Division was hanging in, but the situation was deteriorating rapidly. FSB Delta 1 sustained heavy fire from 122-mm rockets and recoilless rifles, which put four 105-mm howitzers out of action and detonated the 105-mm ammunition supply. The greatly outnumbered 2nd,

3rd, and 4th Battalions from 2nd Regiment west of Sophia East were in contact all day. Late in the afternoon, the NVA mounted determined attacks against all three battalions. During the ensuing battle, which lasted until midnight, the ARVN acquitted themselves well, inflicting heavy casualties on the North Vietnamese. In a number of sustained firefights, the ARVN prevailed, killing 245 NVA soldiers and capturing a large amount of weapons and ammunition while losing only 37 friendly soldiers. The 3rd Battalion reported that they found two company commanders from the NVA 2nd Division among the enemy dead after their battle.

In Saigon on 19 March, Ambassador Bunker and General Abrams met again with President Thieu in Saigon. The South Vietnamese president informed them about the progress of the ongoing withdrawal, saying that it should be completed by 5–8 April. He also said that after the withdrawal was completed, he intended to launch a three-battalion raid in the Muong Nong area, the center of communist Base Area 611, and requested strong US air support for that operation. The US support so far had been substantial. On this day, 686 sorties of helicopter gunships, 246 tac air sorties, and 14 B-52 strikes were flown in support of the ARVN as they continued in their attempts to disengage and withdraw.

Abrams advised Moorer of Thieu's plans, saying, "The support is really lined up and they should be able to pull it off in good shape." The chairman passed the information on, but Kissinger and Nixon were not impressed. According to Moorer, Kissinger, concerned with the flood of negative reports in the media, said, "When they [the ARVN] took Tchepone they should have told us what they wanted to do. Instead they got us babbling about the wrong things and now it looks like a defeat."[25] Continuing, he read a cable that had just come in from Haig in Saigon, stating that "in his [Haig's] judgment, the ARVN have lost their stomach for Laos and the problem isn't to keep them in but rather to influence them to pull out in an orderly fashion."[26] The original plan, which had such promise when it was conceived, had fallen apart.

Meanwhile, in Laos, the NVA were doing their best to prevent the ARVN from escaping; they had decided to do everything they could to cut the ARVN escape routes back toward Vietnam so they could surround and annihilate the South Vietnamese forces.[27] On 20 March, at FSB Brown, just south of Route 9 and southwest of A Luoi, the remnants of four ARVN battalions from the 2nd and 3rd Regiments of the 1st ARVN Division were under heavy enemy attack. Over the course of the previous three days, these troops had battled their way to Brown and had been fighting constantly as the NVA encircled their position. They were low on ammunition and in danger of being overrun. An emergency extraction order was given, and aircraft from the 116th and 174th Assault Helicopter Companies of the 14th Combat Aviation Battalion, supplemented with ten aircraft from 101st Aviation Battalion, responded to the call. As the helicopters approached to pick up the beleaguered South Vietnamese soldiers, the North Vietnamese opened up with everything they had. The situation was total chaos as two ten-ship elements made it into and out of the pickup zone, taking fire the whole time as the terrified ARVN soldiers clamored aboard. Six aircraft in the two lifts were shot down. Other aircraft took so many hits that they had to make forced landings along the flight route back to Khe Sanh.

It was during the attempt to rescue the troops from the 1st ARVN at Brown that Maj. Jack Barker and his crew were lost. Barker, from B company, 101st Aviation Battalion, was leading the third flight of ten helicopters. As they descended toward the pickup zone, Barker's aircraft took automatic weapons fire, forcing him to make a go-around, but this time his aircraft was so badly damaged that he had to return to Khe Sanh. There, he and his copilot, Capt. John Dugan, jumped into a less damaged aircraft and headed back to Brown, with two other aircraft in trail. As Barker and Dugan made their third attempt into the pickup zone, their aircraft was hit by a rocket-propelled grenade, which severed its tail boom; the aircraft exploded in a ball of flame, killing all aboard.[28]

The enemy antiaircraft fire was so heavy that of the forty helicopters involved in the evacuation of the surrounded ARVN soldiers, twenty-eight were hit. By that time visibility throughout the area of operation had been reduced by clouds of dust and smoke, but the pilots did their best to come to the aid of the weary South Vietnamese soldiers. Somehow they managed to extract the 3rd Battalion, but attempts to rescue the remaining ARVN at Brown would continue into the next day. That would be too late for the Black Wolves of the 2nd Battalion, 2nd Regiment. The battalion commander, Lt. Col. Tran Ngoc Hue, an outstanding officer who had been wounded four times and had made a name for himself commanding the Hac Bao "Black Panthers" during the battle for Hue in 1968, was leading his unit in a breakout to find a better landing area for the helicopters when he was seriously wounded by an enemy mortar round, losing parts of four fingers. His men prepared to carry him, but Hue realized that he would only hold his troops back, so he ordered his executive officer to leave him and get his troops to safety. Tearfully, Capt. Nguyen Huu Chuoc complied with the order, leading a small group of sixty survivors in the breakout as the NVA began their final assault. Lieutenant Colonel Hue was captured by the NVA and would endure thirteen years of captivity.[29]

Captain Chuoc and his small group, the last remnants of a once proud battalion, and most of the rest of the 4th Battalion were picked up by helicopter the following day, but the toll on both the pilots and the South Vietnamese soldiers continued to mount. Finally, the 48th Assault Helicopter Company, braving intense antiaircraft fire, was able to rescue the last group of ARVN survivors.

Elsewhere, the ARVN airborne forces on the northern flank were also in heavy contact. On the afternoon of 19 March, an attempt was made to extract the 2nd and 7th Airborne Battalions at FSB Alpha, but they were under intense pressure, and the attempt was canceled after three tries. During the course of this operation, a UH-1H Huey received a direct hit from a mortar round in the pickup zone and went down. Specialist Paul Lagenour, a door gunner, was the only crew member to survive. With shrapnel wounds in his left arm, Lagenour joined four soldiers from the 2nd Airborne Battalion and used their radio to direct air strikes and attack helicopters against the North Vietnamese. Forced to withdraw to the east on foot, Lagenour successfully evaded the enemy for twelve days, dodging enemy patrols and traversing thirty kilometers before he was found by a US armored unit just west of Khe Sanh.[30]

While Lagenour was fleeing for his life, the armored convoy from A Luoi reached FSB Alpha. Lieutenant General Dong ordered the 2nd and 7th Airborne Battalions to maintain blocking positions until the armored brigade, reinforced by the 8th Airborne Battalion, consolidated its position at FSB Alpha. The airborne elements deployed immediately to provide security for Route 9 from Alpha to FSB Bravo. During the night on 19 March, while the armored column was still in transit, the two airborne battalions were attacked by NVA forces, but the paratroopers repulsed the attacks, inflicting heavy casualties on the North Vietnamese. However, by late in the afternoon on the next day, the paratroopers were surrounded and in danger of being overrun. An extraction was attempted, but it ended with the first aircraft being shot down. According to Lieutenant Colonel Rider, commander of the 2nd Squadron, 17th Air Cavalry, "Every time an aircraft would start into the landing zone the mortars would start to rain on the place, and we had the wreckage of a couple of aircraft laying in the landing zone."[31] The fighting continued throughout the day, but when darkness fell the surrounded paratroopers broke out and headed to the south. By nightfall on 20 March the survivors of the 2nd and 7th Airborne Battalions were picked up by helicopter and taken to Khe Sanh.

Meanwhile, the headquarters of the 1st Airborne Brigade, the 5th Battalion, and the remaining artillery elements at FSB Alpha were also safely evacuated on 20 March to Ham Nghi and ultimately to Dong Ha. This meant that by the end of the day, both FSBs Alpha and Delta 1 had been abandoned. ARVN forces along Route 9 had effectively pulled back to FSB Bravo, just five kilometers west of the South Vietnamese border.

South of Route 9, it became increasingly clear that the NVA were determined to annihilate the South Vietnamese Marines at FSB Delta. In fact, unknown to the ARVN commanders at the time, the Central Military Party Committee had sent a message to the NVA units fighting in Laos that said, "It is vital that we win this battle, no matter how many troops and how much equipment and supplies we have to mobilize to do it, and no matter how great are our losses. This is because this is a battle of decisive strategic significance."[32]

Exhorted by this new directive, the 324th Division surrounded FSB Delta with its 1st and 3rd Regiments and at dawn on 21 March opened up on the Marines with an intensive barrage of mortars and direct fire from tanks, which, based on previous patterns, meant they were preparing to launch a major attack on the Marine position. During the course of the day, the NVA launched four combined human wave and tank attacks, but the Marines, with support from 175-mm guns firing from South Vietnam, doggedly held on. Thirteen tactical air support sorties provided additional support, and a B-52 bomber mission was diverted to the area; a prisoner of war later reported that four hundred NVA soldiers from one battalion were killed or wounded in this strike. After the day-long fighting, the Marines had sustained eighty-five killed and were short of ammo and supplies, but they, with the help of several B-52 strikes, had killed more than six hundred enemy soldiers during the heavy fighting.

Also on this day, 21 March, the armored task force continued its movement eastward toward FSB Bravo. At 1100 hours, the column was attacked by a two-battalion NVA force five kilometers west of the border. The 7th and 11th Armored Cavalry Squadrons and the 8th Airborne Battalion found themselves embroiled in heavy combat that lasted for seven hours. The NVA attackers turned the road into "a deadly corridor of death."[33] The ARVN column had to fight its way through ambushes and steady enemy fire, losing many of their vehicles in the process.

During the course of the day, there were 788 gunships sorties, 11 B-52 missions that dropped 921 tons of bombs, and 157 tactical air sorties, which destroyed thirty-seven enemy vehicles and one field gun while damaging eighteen other vehicles. Unfortunately, however, one air strike mistakenly hit the South Vietnamese with napalm, killing twelve soldiers and wounding seventy-five. The NVA broke contact about 1830 hours, but the ARVN sustained over a hundred casualties, including thirty-two more soldiers killed, during the day's heavy fighting. Four M41 tanks and thirteen armored personnel carriers were damaged, leaving Route 9 littered with burnt-out and damaged vehicles that made travel along the road difficult. Marine Lt. Col. Robert Darron, flying over the road as a forward air controller, said, "Route 9 was cluttered full of junk. Tanks and trucks and all kinds of things . . . stretched out about a mile."[34]

Interrogation of a captured NVA soldier revealed that two enemy regiments were waiting in ambush further to the east. As it turned out, the Airborne Division had landed forces by helicopter north of the ambush site and had cleared it of enemy soldiers. Unfortunately, the armored task force commander, Col. Nguyen Trong Luat, was never informed of this fact and, believing that the way ahead on Route 9 was blocked by the enemy, decided to leave the road and look for an alternate route to the border. ARVN Gen. Nguyen Duy Hinh wrote after the war that Luat told him that his unit had taken to the jungle because there was no other alternative; Luat said if they had not done so, he doubted that any of his vehicles would have made it back to Vietnam.[35] Had he been informed that the road had been cleared, he would have been saved two difficult river crossings and a seventeen-kilometer cross-country detour.

During the night, as they prepared for the next day's move, the armored task force and the screening airborne units were harassed by NVA forces, but AC-130 gunships were employed in concert with flare ships to keep the enemy at bay. During the early morning hours of 22 March, the 1st Armored Brigade and the 1st and 8th Airborne Battalions left their positions near FSB Bravo and moved directly east through the jungle in search of a way to cross the Xe Pon River. They were successful in avoiding the NVA until about noon the next day, when the one-hundred-vehicle column reached the banks of the river about one kilometer south of Route 9. The river was relatively shallow during the dry season, but the current was swift and the banks were very steep. The 9th Airborne Battalion had already crossed the river, and they established security on the eastern bank while additional paratroopers fanned out to provide a screen to the north of Route 9. Late in the afternoon, US CH-54 Sky Crane helicopters lifted in two D2 bulldozers and other pieces of equipment that were used to prepare the crossing site.

As the ARVN engineers were working on the site, a forward air controller reported that twenty NVA armored vehicles led by T-54 tanks were headed east along Route 9 about nine kilometers west of the stalled ARVN column. Tac air was called in, and a pair of F-100s responded. One T-54 tank was destroyed, but one F-100 was shot down. A second set of F-100s appeared, and two more enemy tanks were destroyed. Artillery support following the air strikes broke up the enemy attack; the NVA tanks and armored personnel dispersed, pulling into the jungle for cover.

The engineers were not able to prepare the crossing site sufficiently before nightfall, so the column of ARVN vehicles remained on the west bank of the river during the night, which passed without further enemy contact. In the morning hours of 23 March, the engineers completed their work, and the ARVN armored column, along with the accompanying airborne troops, began crossing the river and rolled east to the border. When the crossing began, aerial observers sighted enemy armored vehicles on the Laotian side of the border. US air cavalry elements reported five different sightings of enemy armor near Route 9 and to the south of the road. The US Army helicopters engaged and killed ten tanks.

With the air cavalry screening the crossing, the lead vehicles of the ARVN column crossed the border into South Vietnam, link-ing up with the 1st Battalion, 77th Armor, of the US 1st Brigade, 5th Mechanized Division, at 0915 hours. About noon, the last vehicles of the convoy crossed into South Vietnam. By that time the column numbered only eighty-nine vehicles; more than a hundred vehicles, including more than twenty tanks, fifty armored personnel carriers, and several pieces of heavy engineer equipment, had been left in Laos. Tac air, helicopter gunships, and artillery were used in an attempt to destroy the vehicles to deny them to the NVA.

With the armored task force back in South Vietnam, they joined the 1st ARVN Division and the 1st Ranger Group, leaving only six battalions of South Vietnamese Marines still in Laos to take the brunt of the North Vietnamese counterattack. The 147th Marine Brigade at FSB Delta had weathered an intense attack on 21 March and was still heavily engaged with elements of the 324th Division. However, they were running dangerously low on ammunition and supplies. On 22 March the NVA continued to put pressure on the defenders, but forty tactical air strikes flown in a period of two hours and thirty minutes that morning enabled the Marines to hold their positions. A resupply effort was successful when seven UH-1H helicopters brought in ammunition and took out wounded; however, an eighth helicopter was shot down during the mission. There was another instance of a few panic-stricken South Vietnamese troops clamoring to board the helicopters and escape the battlefield, but most of the Marines stayed with their brothers and fought valiantly.

In the late afternoon, the NVA launched a new attack from their positions inside the Marine perimeter, supported by "a noxious gas" and ten flame-throwing tanks. The Marines destroyed the first two tanks with M72 LAWs (Light Anti-tank Weapons), while another tank hit a mine, and yet another was hit by tac air. Despite these losses, the NVA attackers kept coming, rushing forward over the bodies of their fallen comrades to charge into the base. During a lull in the fighting, the Marines searched several of the enemy bodies, finding on one a piece of paper reading: "We dedicate our lives to the annihilation of the Crazy Buffaloes [what the NVA called the Vietnamese Marines]."[36]

During the battle, the NVA came up on the Marines' radio frequency and called for them to surrender, saying, "You realize too well that we are all around you, and can move in at any time, not because you are bad soldiers, but because you are so few, so lonely, and a little frightened. We are Vietnamese, why do you fight for the American imperialists? You should be fighting for your own country, the Vietnamese people." One South Vietnamese Marine shouted back on the radio, "Sons of bitches, you are working like dogs for the Chinese, for the Russians, you are selling the country to them."[37]

With the Marines refusing to surrender, the fighting continued into the night; at one point, NVA soldiers were firing 75-mm recoilless rifles directly into the Marine command post. Enemy artillery continued to pound the Marines throughout the night and into the early morning hours. After midnight, the 2nd Battalion reported seeing lights presumably from tracked vehicles to the south. With a previously coordinated B-52 strike called in on their own position, the Marines gathered their walking wounded and set out to break through the encircling enemy, leaving behind six artillery pieces that they attempted to disable before departing. They were also forced to leave behind their more seriously wounded comrades. One Marine later recalled, "They lay there crying, knowing the B-52 bombs would fall on them. They asked buddies to shoot them, but none of us could bring himself to do that. So the wounded cried out for grenades. . . . I could not bear it."[38]

The retreating Marines intended to withdraw toward the 258th Brigade at FSB Hotel, but the NVA anticipated this move and ambushed them along the way. A series of bitter battles ensued as the Marines dispersed and fought their way toward Hotel; during the fighting at Delta and the subsequent withdrawal, all three Marine battalion commanders were wounded. Helicopters picked up some of the Marines, and others kept walking toward the border in small groups. One of the Marines who reached FSB Hotel described the night movement: "We moved as ghosts, terrified of being ambushed by the North Vietnamese. We stopped moving many times when there was firing—not daring to breathe. . . . Our group bumped into a North Vietnamese unit, and we ran again like ants."[39]

By the next morning, some of the survivors of the 147th Brigade had pushed through the NVA and linked up with the 258th Brigade at Hotel. It was initially reported that 134 Marines were missing, but several small groups of Marines who had become isolated in the withdrawal straggled in and joined up with their parent units, and in the final count only thirty-seven Marines were unaccounted for. Having crossed the border back into South Vietnam, a young Marine corporal from the 147th Brigade observed, "The papers and the radio kept on saying there was a Laos victory, I have learned now, but what a joke. We ran out like wounded dogs."[40]

The exhausted Marine's comments are understandable, but in the desperate battle at FSB Delta and the fighting withdrawal toward Hotel, the South Vietnamese Marines had turned back four successive tank-supported enemy human wave attacks while killing an estimated two thousand enemy soldiers and seriously damaging the 1st and 3rd Regiments of the NVA 324th Division.[41] Despite the horrific difficulties incurred in breaking out from the encirclement, the Marines at Delta had achieved a remarkable feat, withdrawing in order and bringing out most of their wounded; it was true, the Marines had withdrawn from Laos, but they had made the enemy pay a high price for the real estate they had abandoned. Upon closure of its stragglers, the 147th Brigade, including the 2nd, 4th, and 7th Battalions, was transported by US Army helicopters to an area near Ham Nghi Base.

As the Marines from the 147th Brigade were being extracted, the remaining elements of the 258th Marine Brigade began to experience a series of enemy probes; simultaneously, there were numerous sightings of North Vietnamese tanks. Hoping to avoid a replay of the situation at FSB Delta, the commander of the Marine Division, Lieutenant General Khang, without informing Lieutenant General Lam ordered the 258th to abandon Hotel before the North Vietnamese could encircle and capture it. Late in the afternoon of 24 March, US CH-54 and CH-47 helicopters lifted out all the Marines and six 105-mm and four 155-mm howitzers. When the Marines reached Khe Sanh, the 258th was directed to set up a fire support base at Lang Vei and assume control of the surrounding area of operation.

Lam told Khang to send a battalion to the top of Co Roc Mountain to provide early warning for Khe Sanh as the last of the South Vietnamese forces withdrew from Laos. However, Khang ignored the order, and it was not until the mountain had been pounded by two B-52 strikes that he sent a Marine reconnaissance company to occupy the mountaintop.[42]

While the rest of the Marines were making their way toward Khe Sanh, 1st ARVN Division deployed its 2nd Regiment to provide security for Ham Nghi Base. However, since the 2nd was worn out from its battles in Laos, the 54th Infantry Regiment from Hue was ordered to move to Khe Sanh and relieve the 2nd Regiment. At the same time, 5th Regiment from 2nd ARVN Division was deployed to gradually replace US units west of Quang Tri.

Even as the ARVN and Vietnamese Marines fought their way back to South Vietnam, the communist B5 Front had exerted a concerted effort to disrupt the flow of supplies and support down Route 9 that was sustaining the ARVN effort across the border in Laos. The US truck convoys that plied the road inside South Vietnam were subjected to daily attacks by NVA forces. Additionally, the four combat support bases at Dong Ha, Quang Tri, Khe Sanh, and Da Nang sustained frequent and severe indirect fire attacks from NVA mortars, rockets, and artillery. On 15 March, Da Nang began to take artillery fire, which wounded five South Vietnamese soldiers and three American troops who were providing support for the Laos operation. The base continued to take sporadic but steadily increasing indirect fire for the next week. Elsewhere, on 21 March, NVA sappers penetrated the logistical base at Vandergrift, blowing up forty thousand gallons of aviation fuel and eighty-six hundred rounds of 20-mm ammunition.[43]

On 23 March, Khe Sanh was attacked by forty sappers from the 33rd Sapper Battalion, who penetrated the base, tossing satchel charges into bunkers before heading to the airfield, where they destroyed several aircraft and set two ammunition dumps ablaze. During the course of the attack, the defenders from 2nd Squadron, 17th Cavalry, and 4th Battalion, 77th Field Artillery, engaged the sappers, often in hand-to-hand combat.[44] When the sun came up, fourteen NVA bodies were found inside the wire, many with fatal wounds inflicted by machete. The attack left three Americans dead and fourteen wounded. The attacks on Vandergrift and Khe Sanh notwithstanding, all other enemy attacks were repulsed, and the supplies never stopped flowing.

During this period, combat teams from the US 1st Brigade, 5th Mechanized Division, experienced frequent sharp contacts with enemy forces. At one point there was evidence of a large enemy buildup in the DMZ area, and, subsequently, US forces in the area were augmented with units of the US 23rd Infantry Division and additional aviation assets. Despite the enemy buildup, a major attack from the DMZ never materialized.

By 25 March, forty-five days after they entered Laos, most South Vietnamese troops had withdrawn back to South Vietnam, leaving only two small Marine recon elements, previously mentioned, that had been inserted in the vicinity of Co Roc Mountain to provide early warning for Khe Sanh base. During his briefing on the withdrawal, President Thieu had told General Abrams and Ambassador Bunker that there would be a regiment-sized raid on Base Area 611, south of Route 9. There were a number of reasons for this, not the least of which was that to the media and many other observers, the Lam Son campaign appeared to be incomplete, having been terminated prematurely. The operation had received too much publicity, and to terminate it at this time, well before the lower Laos rainy season, would surely be branded a failure by public opinion.[45]

Accordingly, the South Vietnamese military spokesman reiterated during a press conference that day that the lower Laos operation was not really over and that Republic of Vietnam forces were still attacking communist logistics routes. This was not really true, but the government of Vietnam now had to do something to get itself off the hook. Consequently, the RVNAF began to focus its efforts on the Muong Nong area in the Laotian Salient approximately forty kilometers southeast of Lang Vei. In preparation for further operations, several B-52 strikes were directed into the area. It was with more than a little trepidation that the planners at I Corps Forward contemplated the conduct of a raid against Base Area 611. The enemy had set up an intensive antiaircraft umbrella over the area and was clearly going to defend its positions with everything it had. Reconnaissance aircraft sent in to look at the area in preparation for an insertion of ARVN forces in the area were driven off by heavy antiaircraft fire that would have, in Lieutenant General Sutherland's opinion, inflicted "unacceptable losses in personnel and equipment."[46] Subsequently, the scheduled raid was postponed until 31 March.

Back in Washington, when Admiral Moorer informed Kissinger that the raid had not come off as planned, a frustrated Kissinger replied, "Our tigers can't go through with it." Moorer assured him that the ARVN would try again to complete the mission.[47]

On the morning of 31 March, B-52s and twenty-two tac air sorties were put in to prepare an LZ south of the Laotian Salient, but these strikes failed to sufficiently suppress the enemy antiaircraft guns, so the operation was postponed while additional close air support was called in on the LZ. At 1130, the Hac Bao "Black Panthers," about two hundred men from the 1st ARVN Division's intelligence and reconnaissance company, supported by the 2nd Squadron, 17th Air Cavalry, from the 101st Airborne Division, landed without incident. With a FAC and communications relay aircraft circling overhead, the Black Panthers searched the area. Experiencing only light contact, they found eighty-five NVA dead and a number of destroyed weapons, apparently the victims of the earlier B-52 strike.

That night, the Black Panthers heard enemy vehicles moving around to their south. They called in tac air support, which reported destroying five vehicles.[48] The following morning, the Black Panthers continued their search of the area, finding an enemy fuel dump hit by air strikes and a destroyed tunnel complex housing tracked vehicles. That afternoon, they were picked up by US Army helicopters and transported to Hue.

President Thieu visited the headquarters of I Corps at Dong Ha to speak with troops who had participated in the attack into Laos. During the course of the visit, he expressed his belief that the Laos operation had been the greatest victory of all and announced a new phase of attacks against the Ho Chi Minh Trail.

Despite Thieu's announcement about new attacks against the communist logistics network, the allied support base at Khe Sanh was in the process of being dismantled. On 2 April, 8th Battalion, 4th Field Artillery, the last US heavy artillery battalion supporting the Laotian operation, departed Khe Sanh, heading southeast. On 4 April the entire South Vietnamese Marine Division left the Laotian border area and redeployed to positions near Quang Tri. By this time, Vietnamese and US logistical units at Vandegrift and Khe San had all relocated to the east. On 5 April the ARVN 4th Armored Squadron and the 77th Ranger Battalion were the last South Vietnamese units to leave the border area, bound for Dong Ha.

On 6 April the South Vietnamese forces made one last foray into Laos. At 1000 hours, after tactical air strikes, the reinforced Black Panthers again landed unopposed in the Lao-Viet border salient, just inside Laos, and conducted a search that lasted until late afternoon without making contact with the enemy. At one location they found fifteen enemy bodies and seventeen weapons along with large quantities of food and an intricate network of tunnels, trenches, and huts, all destroyed, apparently by air strikes. Having completed their sweep of the area, the Black Panthers were extracted at 1700 the same day.

A few hours before the Black Panther unit ended its second raid, the last ARVN and US units were on their way out of Khe Sanh. The ARVN 4th Armored Cavalry Squadron and US 1st Battalion, 77th Armor, provided the rear guard as a long convoy of vehicles made its way along Route 9 toward Vandegrift. The US 1st Battalion, 11th Infantry, boarded helicopters and was the last unit to leave Khe Sanh, thereby ending Operation Lam Son 719, forty-five days after the South Vietnamese forces had first entered Laos.

As Lam Son 719 came to an end, so did the ARVN attack into the Chup Plantation area in Cambodia. Operation Toan Thang 1/71 had seen some success under the command of Gen. Do Cao Tri, but after his death in a helicopter crash on 23 February, the attack bogged down. Ultimately, the South Vietnamese forces withdrew from Cambodia in June, but not without a sharp local setback near the Cambodian town of Snuol.[49] In a very real sense, cross-border operations in both Laos and Cambodia during the 1971 dry season ended with inconclusive results.

CHAPTER TEN

Assessing Lam Son 719

By the end of March, the North Vietnamese declared victory in their Route 9–Southern Laos counterattack. They claimed twenty thousand ARVN killed and more than one thousand captured, eliminating three regiments and brigades, thirteen infantry and artillery battalions, and four armored squadrons from the field.[1] Additionally, the North Vietnamese claimed they destroyed 1,100 vehicles, including 528 tanks and APCs, and more than one hundred artillery pieces, in addition to shooting down more than five hundred helicopters.[2] These claims were grossly exaggerated, but, as will be seen, the actual figures were bad enough.

On 31 March 1971 the Politburo sent a congratulatory message to the troops on the Route 9–Southern Laos front, praising them "for fighting well, securing complete victory, and establishing an outstanding combat record."[3] Col. Gen. Nguyen Huu An, commander of the NVA 308th Division during the fighting in Laos, later wrote in his memoir that General Giap had boasted in the Politburo at the time that the North Vietnamese forces had won a great victory "in a ferocious test of strength" with the "puppets' elite forces supported by the Americans." An concluded that the battle in Laos "was a uniquely Vietnamese victory, and marked the independent and creative development of the Vietnamese combat arms."[4]

The South Vietnamese and American leaders would also claim victory. On the day that his forces reached Tchepone, President Thieu proclaimed Lam Son 719 "the biggest victory ever . . . a moral, political, and psychological Dien Bien Phu," claiming that the ARVN had killed thirteen thousand NVA soldiers during the operation. Likewise, the Nixon administration began a campaign to convince the American public that, despite clear evidence to the contrary, the operation had been a great success. This effort had begun early in the operation; President Nixon had reported in February that "the operation has gone according to plan" and that ARVN was "fighting in a superior way."[5]

With the operation winding down, General Abrams and his headquarters continued the positive slant that they had maintained since the beginning. One of his briefers at MACV described how the ARVN "had performed some pretty doggone professional operations in a complex environment of bad weather, bad terrain, and of course the enemy, and had done a fine soldierly job of it."[6]

While speaking to the press in Saigon on 21 March, General Abrams himself echoed the positive assessment of the operation, saying, "Lam Son 719 has been a milestone in the development of the Armed Forces of the Republic of Vietnam. For the first time the South Vietnamese have conducted a multidivision operation against a strong and determined enemy. The ARVN without US advisors, penetrating into an area which had been controlled for years by the enemy, has faced their sternest test to date and acquitted themselves against an aggressive enemy."[7]

On 22 March the president, in a nationally televised interview with Howard K. Smith of the American Broadcasting Company, declared that Lam Son 719 had been an unqualified success. Referring to the TV news reports showing demoralized South Vietnamese troops clinging to the skids of helicopters in a panic to escape Laos, Nixon insisted that these reports showed "only those men in four battalions . . . that were in trouble. They haven't shown people in the other 18 battalions [committed on the ground in Laos]." He further claimed that the operation had reduced by seventy-five percent the volume of traffic along the Ho Chi Minh Trail. In an attempt to link the operation to the continued withdrawal of US troops, he argued that "the thousands of North Vietnamese who were casualties . . . , the hundreds of millions of rounds of ammunition that was destroyed . . . , the time that was bought . . . , all these things" greatly reduced "the risk to American lives" by preventing an offensive as the last American troops prepared to withdraw from South Vietnam. That, he concluded, "is why the operation was worthwhile in my opinion."[8] Even after the war, Nixon continued to maintain that the operation had achieved its objective. He wrote in his memoirs, "The net result [of Lam Son 719] was a military success but a psychological defeat" brought on by negative television coverage of the withdrawal.[9] Such was to be the Nixon administration's line on the operation and its outcome, despite severe private misgivings about the performance of the South Vietnamese forces.

In that vein, General Abrams continued to accentuate the positive aspects of the operation. In a message to Admiral McCain on 22 March, he wrote that the South Vietnamese forces had operated without US advisers, without the "reassuring presence" of adjacent US units that would render assistance if needed, and they did so concurrently with a major operation in Cambodia in addition to continuing operations in their own country. Abrams concluded that in his opinion Lam Son 719 was an "epoch as [far as] the development of the RVNAF is concerned."[10]

In an assessment for Kissinger, Abrams downplayed the many shortcomings demonstrated by the South Vietnamese in Laos. Acknowledging some "disappointments and failures" in both the Cambodian and Laotian operations, he proclaimed that the operations had "gone well militarily" and produced "the maximum practical benefits." Moreover, the ability of the South Vietnamese to conduct simultaneous cross-border operations "speaks to the success of the Vietnamization program."[11]

Melvin Laird, however, had mixed feelings about the outcome of the operation in Laos. He thought that Lam Son 719 would "prove to be a success, after a period of several months," because the enemy "had taken heavy casualties and their logistics flow had been hampered." However, he feared that adverse media coverage of the fighting in Laos would create a "bad image" of the ARVN. Moreover, he saw the abandonment of vehicles and equipment in Laos by the South Vietnamese as a "fiasco."[12]

Henry Kissinger's feelings were decidedly not mixed; there was little doubt in his mind about Lam Son 719 and its outcome. After the war, he described the operation as "conceived in doubt and assailed by skepticism, [that] proceeded in confusion." The chief drawback of the operation, according to Kissinger, "was that it in no way accorded with Vietnamese realities. South Vietnamese divisions had never conducted major offensive operations against a determined enemy outside Vietnam and only rarely inside. . . . The South Vietnamese divisions were simply not yet good enough for such a complex operation as the one in Laos."[13]

Nevertheless, at the time, continuing the Nixon administration line, Kissinger tried to put the best face on the operation publicly. Repeating Nixon's earlier figures, Kissinger asserted, "The ARVN fought extremely well. Eighteen out of twenty-two of the battalions turned in a credible performance. Reports of a rout are largely exaggerated. Even the photographs of ARVN troops clinging to the skids of outbound choppers provide proof of their order and discipline—particularly when one sees that the troops are bringing with them their rifles and other gear, hardly the characteristic of panic-stricken soldiers."[14] Such statements strained the credibility of the administration for all who had actually seen those images; for them a picture was worth a thousand words.

The administration was deeply concerned about the damage done to Vietnamization and would continue to focus on what they characterized as biased reporting. It would prove to be an uphill battle. In a memorandum to Nixon on 22 March, Kissinger wrote, "Here [in the United States], particularly because of the very one-sided press treatment of the operation, the consequences of the operation were probably most adverse. Laos has again brought the war to the front pages, in a way which shows that no early and easy end is in sight. Opponents of Vietnamization will probably be encouraged to push harder for a unilateral US withdrawal."[15]

It is clear that many in the US news media took almost violent exception to administration pronouncements about South Vietnamese performance and the results of the operation. Despite administration efforts to put a positive spin on the story, many in the media agreed with the story in *Life* magazine that declared that "the NVA drove the invading force out of Laos with their tails between their legs."[16]

Similar stories appeared in many newspapers across the country. James McCartney wrote in the *Philadelphia Inquirer*, "The South Vietnamese have invented a new kind of warfare in Laos. They avoid fighting whenever they can, they flee an area when the Communists start showing up on the battlefield, and they consistently claim 'victory' or 'success' when the operation involved is over. . . . Many US military men used to criticize the South Vietnamese for a tendency to 'cut and run' when a battle loomed in Vietnam. Now, when the South Vietnamese flee, Pentagon spokesmen are inclined to praise their 'mobility.'"[17]

The *Cleveland Plain Dealer* also challenged the administration's characterization of the operation, writing, "Rather than the military success President Nixon has acclaimed, it appears the Laos incursion was a defeat that has bolstered Hanoi's confidence." A US soldier put the general perception more succinctly when he said to John Saar of *Life* magazine, "ARVN is making an orderly withdrawal they say. In other words, they got their asses kicked and they are hightailing it back." Even a relatively balanced account of the operation in the *Philadelphia Bulletin* observed, "Without our air cover and without 51 battalions of US troops holding the fort . . . [one] can only guess at how much worse the situation might have been."[18]

The Nixon administration continued its efforts to counter these reports with a steady drumbeat of positive comments about the operation in Laos. A set of White House talking points published in April reported that "the operation . . . achieved its primary objective of carrying the fight to the enemy's sanctuaries and disrupting his principal lines of communications." The paper concluded "that the foundation for Vietnamization in South Vietnam is sound and that the process has been enhanced by the disruptions Lam Son has caused the enemy and by the increased confidence it has given the South Vietnamese in meeting their own defense needs."[19]

Thus, there were two distinctly different story lines about the outcome of the bitter fighting in Laos. An objective assessment of the Laotian campaign reveals that while the operation may not have been the total debacle portrayed in the US media, it had been a costly campaign for the South Vietnamese forces. Saigon reported that the operation had cost 1,160 government troops killed, 4,271 wounded, and 240 missing. Many in the media, including The Associated Press and *Newsweek* magazine, challenged those figures and put the actual casualty count at 3,800 killed, 5,200 wounded, and 775 missing.[20]

According to XXIV Corps official figures, which were close to those reported by the media, Saigon casualties included more than 7,000 killed, wounded, and captured, a casualty rate of nearly 40 percent. US casualties included 253 killed or missing in action and 1,149 wounded. In terms of equipment, the US lost 107 helicopters destroyed and 601 damaged (20 percent of which were so badly damaged that they were expected never to fly again). The US Air Force lost six fighter-bombers and a FAC aircraft, and four pilots were killed in action (or were declared missing). The ARVN lost 211 trucks, eighty-seven combat vehicles, fifty-four tanks, ninety-six artillery pieces, and most of the combat engineer equipment (bulldozers, graders, and the like) that had accompanied the attackers.[21]

On the plus side of the account, the allies claimed over nineteen thousand enemy soldiers killed. Abrams reported that of thirty-three enemy battalions engaged, at least sixteen had been rendered combat ineffective. The allies also reported 1,963 crew-served and 5,170 individual weapons captured; additionally, 106 tanks, thirteen artillery pieces, 2,001 vehicles, 170,346 tons of munitions, ninety thousand gallons of fuel, and 1,250 tons of rice were destroyed.[22] It is important to note that while these results are impressive, most of them occurred in the earlier part of the campaign before the South Vietnamese lost the initiative. Additionally, there is ample evidence that a large number of the casualties and most of the destruction of NVA vehicles and equipment resulted from air strikes.

It is also important to note that despite the destruction of enemy materiel by South Vietnamese forces in Laos, the operation came nowhere near the "75 percent" reduction of traffic along the Ho Chi Minh Trail claimed by President Nixon. There is no doubt that the operation disrupted activities along the trail in February and March 1971, but electronic sensors indicated that traffic throughout southern Laos increased immediately after Lam Son.[23]

Despite the casualties inflicted on the North Vietnamese and the capture or destruction of enemy supplies and equipment, the South Vietnamese combat performance in the heavy fighting in Laos had been, at best, uneven. The truth was that three of the finest South Vietnamese divisions—the 1st Infantry, Airborne, and Marine Divisions—had generally been bested by the North Vietnamese and were heavily battered in the bitter fighting in Laos.

Even before the operation was over, Lieutenant General Sutherland acknowledged that the North Vietnamese had all but wiped out the 1st Armored Brigade, destroying or capturing 60 percent of the unit's tanks and half of its armored personnel carriers, a total of 163 vehicles, rendering the brigade combat ineffective. Additionally, the brigade lost fifty-four 105-mm and twenty-eight 155-mm howitzers.[24]

The problems were not just with the armored force; severe losses were also incurred by a number of other units. One infantry, one airborne, and two ranger battalions were also rendered combat ineffective because they were all but destroyed in the fighting. Additionally, another airborne battalion was considered doubtful because of inept leadership and poor morale.[25]

President Nixon, again trying to put the best face on what he knew had been a near disastrous performance in some units, credited the South Vietnamese with having done a laudable job against the best that the North Vietnamese could throw against them. Citing General Abrams's early claim that eighteen out of twenty-two battalions had fought well in Laos, the president said the ARVN had "conducted themselves with high morale, with great confidence, and they are able to defend themselves man for man against the North Vietnamese."[26] This assessment is highly questionable. Some units, such as those of the 1st ARVN Division, the Rangers, and the South Vietnamese Marines, fought heroically against overwhelming odds in some of the hardest fighting of the war; five of the ARVN Airborne Division's battalion commanders were killed leading their men in the bloody fighting. Some of the units fought well as individual elements but lacked cohesion at the higher echelons of command. This was particularly true of the Airborne and Marine Divisions, who were unaccustomed to fighting in larger formations; the armor units fought well at times but were poorly employed. Some units, even those considered among the best South Vietnamese troops, fell apart under the intense enemy pressure, scrambling in a panic on any helicopter that tried to land. For example, the airborne infantry battalion commander at FSB 30 was one of those who forced himself aboard one of the medevac flights, even though he was not seriously wounded.[27]

There are a number of explanations for the outcome of the operation. Chief among these factors was poor South Vietnamese senior leadership. This started at the top when President Thieu repeatedly interfered in operational matters best left to the senior commander on the ground. He was also less than steadfast in his support of the operation once it was underway. Having given enthusiastic support to the operation in the beginning, he then became too cautious when the battle was joined. As historian George Donelson Moss suggests, "In Thieu's hierarchy of priorities, political self-preservation ranked well ahead" of the long-term success of the attack into Laos.[28] His decision to intervene on 12 February effectively brought the operation to a halt and all but predetermined the outcome when the North Vietnamese rushed reinforcements to the area.

The politicized senior leadership within the chain of command under the president also had a tremendously negative impact on the outcome of the operation. Most of the senior commanders charged with leading the effort in Laos were unable to set aside petty jealousies and desire for personal gain in favor of the greater good for the nation. Although Lieutenant General Lam was the overall ground commander, he was virtually ignored by the commanders of the Airborne and Marine Divisions, both themselves lieutenant generals who were more accustomed, as commanders of national strategic reserve forces, to answering directly to Saigon rather than responding to a corps commander. An assessment conducted after the operation was terminated noted that the Airborne and Marine Division commanders "seemed sure enough of their position in the Vietnamese political/military hierarchy to act quite independently. In consequence, many orders given by the I Corps Commander were ignored or were violated with impunity."[29] The situation for Lam was made even more difficult when General Khang sent a message denying a rumor that the Marine commander was going to take over for Lam. A new US adviser to the I Corps forward command post, Maj. Tom Jaco, later observed that there was "more political intrigue than you can ever imagine."[30]

With his major subordinates contesting his orders at every opportunity, Lam appealed to President Thieu for support, but Thieu refused to reprimand Lam's subordinate commanders, even when their actions bordered on insubordination to Lam during the heat of the battle. Thieu did not wish to offend the two other generals, one of whom commanded his primary anticoup force (the Airborne Division) and the other of whom commanded a large portion of his strategic reserve. Once again, as was the case so often during the course of the war, political considerations proved more important than military necessity. Former ARVN major general Nguyen Duy Hinh summed up the situation when he wrote after the war, "The unsubmissive attitude of the Marine and Airborne Division commanders was actually inexcusable in that they placed themselves above the national interest and let their personal pride interfere with the task of defeating the enemy. . . . At least, the I Corps commander should have been given the authority to require that his orders be strictly carried out."[31] The lack of unity of effort that resulted from this situation played a major role in the outcome of the operation.

Lam, for his part, was certainly not blameless. As General Bruce Palmer wrote after the war, Lam's reputation as a combat commander was only "mediocre," but he "was considered to be a loyal, capable administrator." Prior to Lam Son 719, Lam, who had been in command since 1966, had survived as a corps commander because of his political skills and his support of President Thieu. He had been adequate as a military region commander in low-intensity warfare, but he had very little experience in directing several divisions and supporting arms in conventional operations. He, according to historian Keith William Nolan, was more of an administrator who gave broad directives and left tactical planning to his division and regimental commanders.[32]

The intensity of combat in Laos and the demands of the operation were too much for Lam. Lieutenant Colonel Darron of the US XXIV Corps headquarters later discussed Lam's actions during the operations: "I remember seeing him one morning toward the end of the operation when things were worms in Laos. . . . He was laying back, kind of in a crucified position, leaning back against his bunker . . . looking up at the sky with his eyes closed, and he was obviously under a terrible, terrible strain. Frankly, I think he was just in over his head." Lam's ineptitude was evident throughout the operation; he spent little time in the forward command areas and failed to exert sufficient control on his forces during the operation. Brigadier General Berry, assistant commander of the 101st Airborne Division, reported after the operation that "planning and coordination for Lam Son 719 were, at the Corps Commander's level, of unacceptably low quality."[33]

The South Vietnamese staffs at the upper echelons of command were also ill-prepared for the level of combat that prevailed during the planning and conduct of the operation. Colonel Batreall, senior adviser to the armored brigade who observed the operation from I Corps forward command post at Khe Sanh, concluded that neither the corps headquarters nor subordinate units "truly grasped the responsibilities inherent in attachment, the differences between a zone of action and an axis of advance, or the full meaning of the word 'secure.'" For example, the indecisiveness and overall ineptitude of the forward command element at Khe Sanh played a major role in the fall of FSB 31. On 27 February, as the situation in Laos worsened, Abrams sent a message to General Sutherland, saying, "I am concerned with the adequacy of General Lam's control element at Khe Sanh. It does not appear adequate in staff strength or organization for the task of controlling an operation the size and complexity of Lam Son 719."[34]

While Lam and his staff were found wanting, they were not alone, and, unfortunately for the South Vietnamese, planning and coordination inadequacies were not limited solely to the corps level. ARVN commanders at all echelons displayed serious difficulties in command and control, particularly with regard to coordinating combined arms operations, including the ability to employ infantry, armor, and artillery in concert and the proper use of reserve forces. Former ARVN major general Hinh wrote, "During the operation, there were several instances in which division commanders lost control of their units. Even the I Corps commander sometimes did not know the major events affecting his division."[35] This situation was compounded on several occasions when subordinate commanders, having received no orders from above, failed to seize the initiative. Colonel Battreall later observed, "Initiative by a subordinate, unhappily, never became part of the ARVN character and many, many opportunities were lost."[36] Historian Andrew Wiest, summing up the leadership shortcomings in the South Vietnamese armed forces, observed that "command weaknesses that had once been obscured by the ARVN's normal role as an adjunct to the American war . . . came into stark relief as the ARVN's leadership struggled to come to grips with the big-unit war [in Laos]."[37]

Another important factor that impacted the outcome of the operation was the hurried way in which it was planned. The preparations and planning for the operation were done in a rush; there was no time to explore any potential weaknesses in the plan or to consider alternate courses of action. Additionally, the complexity of the operation and the number of both South Vietnamese and US units involved demanded detailed coordination, but the short planning time did not permit that coordination and the myriad of other tasks necessary to promote mission accomplishment. The planning problem was compounded by the necessity to maintain secrecy for the sake of operational security. These considerations meant that subordinate units had little time to plan and prepare for the complex operation.

In the planning arena, the US planners were not without blame. According to Colonel Battreall, the planners at XXIV Corps, not part of the US adviser structure, did not know their counterparts at I Corps. So they wrote "a perfectly good plan using standard US military terminology, not realizing that the Vietnamese would often nod politely even when they disagreed and that, even when they did agree, they sometimes understood terms differently than the American authors intended." Gen. Phillip Davidson, reflecting the same observations, later concluded that "the Americans embarked on their support mission with inadequate planning, deficient cooperation with ARVN, and major service differences over the concept and execution of the operations."[38]

The resulting combined plan, as characterized by Andrew Wiest, was "fatally predictable." Built on a best-case scenario predicated on a flawed understanding of the enemy and his intentions, it called for attacking a well-defended piece of terrain along a single axis of advance. As General Hinh wrote, "The operational plan for Lam Son 719 was adequate only so long as the operation progressed smoothly and ARVN forces were able to hold the initiative. It should have taken contingencies into full consideration and been able to respond to them with resourcefulness." Such was not the case, and when the attack did not go as planned, the situation deteriorated rapidly.[39]

Once the enemy saw that the South Vietnamese were going to attack along Route 9 toward Tchepone, it was very easy, given the nature of the area of operation, to predict how the plan would unfold and respond accordingly. After the North Vietnamese determined where the main effort was to be, they reacted rapidly, committing more than sixty thousand troops to the battle, ultimately outnumbering the South Vietnamese forces more than three to one.

Under these conditions it was almost inevitable that the plan would fail. When it began to unravel, the shortcomings of the ARVN were magnified. On the ground, the ARVN tactics, developed over nearly a decade of battle against a low-tech threat, proved completely inadequate against an enemy equipped with modern armor, heavy artillery, and sophisticated air defense weapons.

Compounding the problem were the repeated security lapses during the operation. According to the XXIV Corps after action report, communications security "was virtually ignored by the [South] Vietnamese." On 10 March, Lieutenant General Sutherland complained to Abrams, "The enemy has had foreknowledge of every move planned by I Corps in Lam Son 719."[40] This had a disastrous effect at the tactical level, where the NVA were often able to monitor ARVN radio nets and make adjustments on the battlefield to counter ARVN planned moves. In one case the NVA called a false check fire in the middle of a battle with airborne troops on the northern flank, effectively shutting down critical artillery fires when the paratroopers really needed them.[41]

General Vien, former chairman of the RVNAF JGS, described the results of these difficulties after the war: "Deployed in an unfavorable terrain, our 300-vehicle armored force was impotent against enemy tanks and unable to assist the Airborne Division in breaking the enemy encirclement or regaining the initiative. By contrast, the enemy armor had proved aggressive and dangerous; it had taken advantage of a familiar though unfavorable terrain to lay ambushes or close in on our strongpoints and finally combine with infantry to assault and overrun them." Vien is unstinting in his criticism of the South Vietnamese infantry units, which he maintains "shunned maneuvers when engaged and failed to use their organic fire to destroy the enemy, relying entirely on supporting firepower." He concludes, "The I Corps and the division commanders involved all had reserves, but they failed to use them to overcome difficulties and regain the initiative. Even our available firepower was not properly used especially during the first month of the operation because of poor coordination."[42]

In the wake of the termination of Lam Son 719, President Nixon had declared that "the South Vietnamese had demonstrated that without American advisers they could fight effectively against the best troops North Vietnam could put in the field." However, in truth, the South Vietnamese had grown far too dependent on US advisers and American support. Many of the things that the ARVN commanders had routinely relied upon their US advisers to accomplish were not done or were done poorly. Army Chief of Staff William Westmoreland wrote, "Long accustomed to working with American advisers, subordinate ARVN commanders had difficulty without them in arranging fire support and resupply."[43]

Given the complex operational plan, once Lam Son 719 was launched, the South Vietnamese leaders demonstrated an inability to effectively coordinate modern combined arms warfare. A good example of this can be seen in the performance of the airborne commander, who clearly did not know how to employ the armored brigade. As a result, both the armored force and the airborne infantry, employed independently, suffered higher casualties and losses than if they had fought as a combined team. The South Vietnamese also demonstrated an inability to coordinate the fires of their own organic artillery. An official US Marine history, citing a Marine adviser, noted that the South Vietnamese Marines were "loath to bring it [artillery fire] closer than 1000 meters to friendlies."[44] This problem affected the entire force in Laos, not just the Vietnamese Marines.

The South Vietnamese inability to coordinate their own organic fire support led to a subsequent overreliance on external US assets. General Sutherland, in a late March message to General Abrams, asserted that the South Vietnamese casualties might have been reduced by half if US advisers had been present to help direct the large amounts of tactical air, helicopter, B-52, and artillery support available.[45]

Flying against intense antiaircraft artillery and ground fire, US Army and Marine helicopters flew over 160,000 sorties. The helicopter pilots had performed magnificently in an environment that demanded intense commitment and extreme measures. As Andrew Wiest observed, "It was the actions of US helicopter pilots, who braved their own personal hell in a stream of missions into and out of stricken ARVN bases while facing constant enemy fire, that made the ARVN operation and the survival of the ARVN soldiers themselves possible."[46]

Close air support was also critical. During the operation, US Air Force, Navy, and Marine tactical fighter-bombers flew more than nine thousand attack sorties, dropping some twenty thousand tons of bombs and napalm on targets within an area of just 550 square miles. Additionally, B-52s flew more than thirteen hundred sorties, dropping some thirty-two thousand tons of bombs. USAF C-130 aircraft dropped twenty-five fifteen-thousand-pound BLU-82 bombs on proposed LZs, while Air Force gunships and flare ships provided support at night. General Sutherland acknowledged the importance of American air power, pointing out that the South Vietnamese had survived "principally because of TAC [tactical] air [support] and B-52s strikes."[47]

In addition to close air support and B-52s, the Air Force also provided tactical airlift during the deployment, employment, and subsequent resupply phases of the operation. This support was essential to marshaling and supplying the ground combat troops necessary for the operation in Laos.

From the time that the South Vietnamese crossed into Laos on 8 February until the operation ended, Military Airlift Command flew more than 2,000 sorties in support of Lam Son 719, carrying twenty-one thousand tons of cargo and almost fourteen thousand passengers. With the operation over and forces redeploying, Air Force C-130 cargo planes flew 195 sorties into Phu Bai and Quang Tri City to retrieve one thousand tons of cargo and redeploy almost ten thousand troops.[48]

It is clear that the South Vietnamese forces on the ground in Laos, outnumbered and on unfamiliar terrain, would never have survived without air support in all its forms. Many in both MACV and the RVNAF Joint General Staff realized that this support was the only thing that stood between the South Vietnamese forces and a total rout in Laos. This overdependence on US air support was extremely troubling, for these resources would disappear when US troop withdrawals were completed.

Operation Lam Son 719 had a number of lasting impacts, not the least of which was its devastating effect on South Vietnamese morale and esprit. Despite President Thieu's bombastic statements about the success of the operation, the South Vietnamese forces who retreated from Laos believed they had been defeated. Even General Abrams acknowledged that "field reports indicate that morale of certain combat units in the 1st ARVN Division, Marine Division, and the Airborne Division suffered as a result of the Lam Son 719 operation."[49]

Maj. William Dabney, USMC, senior adviser, 3rd Battalion, 258th VNMC Brigade, who flew over Laos as an airborne coordinator, contrasted the Vietnamese Marines before and after the operation, saying, "These were brave men, well led, well supplied, who had a certain elan and a certain confidence in themselves when they went in. When they came out, they'd been whipped. They knew they'd been whipped and they acted like they had been whipped."[50]

The same sentiment was true in the ARVN; they also felt like they had been defeated. Gen. Vu Van Giai of the 1st ARVN Division observed after the operation, "Yes, the morale of 1st Division was damaged after Lam Son 719." Many in the ARVN thought like Lt. Col. Pham Van Dinh of the 54th Regiment, which had remained at Hue during the Laotian operation, who observed that the ultimate outcome in Laos was part of "the sacrifice of a fine army for political purposes and vanity."[51]

New York Times reporter Gloria Emerson, having interviewed a number of the ARVN survivors upon their return to Khe Sanh, concluded that South Vietnamese morale was "shattered," saying, "What has dramatically demoralized many of the South

Vietnamese troops is the large number of their own wounded who were left behind, begging for their friends to shoot them or to leave hand grenades so they could commit suicide before the North Vietnamese or the B-52s killed them." The Laotian operation had been a test, "and now most South Vietnamese forces admit frankly that their forces failed."[52]

In the process of retreating from Laos under heavy pressure, many South Vietnamese dead had been left on the battlefield. Former ARVN major general Nguyen Duy Hinh later described the situation: "This came as a horrendous trauma to those unlucky families who, in their traditional devotion to the cult of the dead and their attachment to the living, were condemned to live in perpetual sorrow and doubt. . . . Vietnamese sentiment would never forget."[53]

While Thieu claimed victory, the soldiers and their families had no illusions about the outcome of the operation, and they were demoralized by what they saw as a clear defeat at the hands of the North Vietnamese. Thieu took steps to lessen the downward spiral of morale. He banned US news magazines *Time* and *Newsweek* and several opposition newspapers whose coverage trumpeted the negative aspects of the operation in Laos. Additionally, he kept the hard-hit Airborne and Marine Divisions in I Corps, rather than return them to their normal bases around Saigon. He did not want those troops telling stories about the near disaster in Laos. Nevertheless, South Vietnamese morale and confidence had been dealt a serious blow.

Despite the negative outcomes of the operation, Lam Son 719 still achieved a modicum of its original objectives. There is ample evidence that the operation at least temporarily disrupted the NVA buildup in Laos, costing the communists dearly in men and equipment that probably would have been used in a major NVA offensive against Military Region I later in 1971. While the South Vietnamese losses had been severe, the North Vietnamese forces suffered as badly, if not worse, losing by some counts up to one-half of the troops committed to the operation.[54]

A XXIV Corps report predicted that "the enemy will not be able to rebuild his logistics system and his tactical units for a major offensive before late September 1971. . . . It may even have forestalled any major offensive until the spring of 1972." Similarly, a CIA report sent to Secretary of Defense Laird by the CIA's Office of Economic Research stated that "large-scale enemy military operations in South Vietnam for the remainder of 1971 were probably impossible and that Hanoi would have to undertake a major resupply campaign before any offensive could be launched in 1972."[55]

Despite the shortcomings demonstrated by the South Vietnamese forces in Laos, Lam Son 719 was an important factor in delaying the next major communist offensive; it would take nearly a year for the North Vietnamese to replace the men and equipment lost in the effort to destroy the South Vietnamese along Route 9. This gave the South Vietnamese a very brief but needed respite from NVA pressure.

However, any assessment of the operation must include a consideration of its impact on the Vietnamization effort. In late March, General Sutherland provided his own evaluation of the operation and South Vietnamese combat performance. Noting some of the ARVN weaknesses demonstrated in Laos, Sutherland was nevertheless very upbeat, reporting "continuing progress towards the goal of Vietnamization." He concluded: "Lam Son 719 has been expensive in terms of US support costs, but its achievement so far indicates that in terms of damage inflicted upon the enemy, disruption of his expected offensive operations, evidence of the effectiveness of the Vietnamization program, and benefits which will accrue in the future [it] has been an unquestionably a highly valuable and productive operation."[56]

In his debriefing report, prepared as his tenure in command of XXIV Corps came to an end, Sutherland again acknowledged some major shortcomings, including "a lack of effective long-range planning by higher staffs, a serious disregard for communications security, a general lack of supply discipline, and a failure to delegate authority to subordinates." Still, he pointed out that the South Vietnamese forces without US advisers had "carried the war into an enemy controlled area, far removed from the familiar confines of their normal areas of operation." He concluded, "The forces that participated in LAMSON 719 proved that the Republic of Vietnam possess[es] a viable military organization that is significantly more capable, cohesive and better led than the military organization that existed during TET 1968, only three years ago." Furthermore, he wrote, "the NVA's losses of personnel and supplies have surely disrupted plans for an early offensive."[57]

Sutherland's assessments may have been overblown, and his comments about the effectiveness of Vietnamization are certainly subject to debate. Nevertheless, this is what the administration wanted to hear; Nixon needed Vietnamization to be a success, or at least appear to be successful, so that he could carry through with his plan to disengage totally from the war.

In that vein, the president prepared his message for the American people. In an address to the nation on 7 April, President Nixon proclaimed, "Tonight I can report that Vietnamization has succeeded." Continuing, he said, "Because of the increased strength of the South Vietnamese . . . and because of the achievements of the South Vietnamese operation in Laos I am announcing an increase in the rate of American withdrawals." He then said that an additional one hundred thousand troops would be brought home by November 1971. He promised that "American involvement in Vietnam is coming to an end" but refused to set a date for total withdrawal, saying that doing so would give away "our principal bargaining counter to win release of the American prisoners of war . . . [and] would remove the enemy's strongest incentive to end the war sooner by negotiation."[58]

The newly announced withdrawals would leave 184,000 American troops remaining in South Vietnam at the end of 1971. In June 1971, Secretary of Defense Laird declared that 90 percent of combat responsibility had been turned over to the ARVN, and two months later he announced that Phase I of Vietnamization had been completed.[59] This meant that from that time on, ground combat responsibility would be entirely assumed by the RVNAF.

Despite administration claims about the success of Lam Son 719 and the state of the South Vietnamese armed forces, the operation raised serious questions about the progress of Vietnamization, and Nixon was privately distressed with how poorly the South Vietnamese had performed. During the next phase of Vietnamization, the South Vietnamese were to develop air and naval support systems and artillery, logistical, and maintenance systems to replace those that since 1965 had been supplied by the United States. How long this would take was unknown, but Lam Son 719 had demonstrated that the RVNAF still had a way to go toward the final objective of self-sustainment on the battlefield. It was acknowledged that while the South Vietnamese worked toward this goal, the United States would need to maintain a level of combat support, particularly air support, which had been so critical in Laos, while it gradually pulled out the remaining American ground forces. General Davidson, former MACV J2, later described the situation in 1971 as follows: "Lam Son 719 demonstrated that, while Vietnamization had made progress, the South Vietnamese government and its armed forces had deep flaws which made final success of the concept years, probably decades, away. Above all, the operation showed ARVN's complete dependence on the United States forces. . . . The operation revealed the inherent flaws of the RVNAF, which doomed any realistic hopes of successful Vietnamization."[60]

Over and above what Lam Son 719 said about the Vietnamization effort, the operation had a significantly negative impact on the relations between the White House and President Thieu. On 26 March, Kissinger cabled Bunker complaining about Thieu's role in the outcome of the operation, saying, "I hope Thieu understands that the president's confidence is an asset he should not lightly dissipate and that this [Lam Son 719] may be his last crack at massive US support."[61]

Lam Son 719 also had a similar impact on the relationship between Nixon and General Abrams, as evidenced by the 23 March conversation between the president and Kissinger. According to Nixon's chief of staff, H. R. Haldeman, who recorded the conversation in his diary, Kissinger and the president talked about how Abrams had not gotten enough "push" into the operation, that he had stayed too long with his initial plan, that American support for the South Vietnamese set them up for failure, that MACV had become too inbred, and that "our people let us down." Moreover, they felt "they were misled by Abrams on the original evaluation of what might be accomplished and that Abrams went ahead with the plan even though it was clear that it wasn't working."[62]

According to Alexander Haig, Nixon was so frustrated with Abrams that he ordered Haig to fly out to Saigon to take command of the US forces there. But the next day, the president had apparently cooled off and changed his mind; Haldeman wrote in his diary, "The P[resident] made the point that this is the end of the military operations anyway so what difference does it make." Historian Lewis Sorley disputes this claim, citing an interview with Henry Kissinger in January 1989 in which Kissinger stated, "There is no truth to the idea that Nixon ever thought of relieving and replacing Abrams, after Lam Son 719 or at any other point, with Haig or anyone else."[63]

Regardless, it is clear that Kissinger and Nixon were frustrated with Abrams, and this frustration continued to grow. During a phone conversation with Nixon on 6 April 1971, Kissinger, echoing their 23 March conversation, declared, "Abrams in this whole operation has been a disaster."[64] Part of the resentment toward Abrams and MACV evolved from what the White House saw as incomplete reporting from MACV during the course of the operation; the White House statements to the press based on these reports were often contradicted by events, increasing skepticism in the media and contributing to the confrontation between the White House and the press.[65]

Haig's reports from Saigon during his March fact-finding trip had contributed to the dissatisfaction with Abrams. He sent a message back to Kissinger saying that "it was clear that the operation was not receiving the kind of leadership and management from the American force structure that it should have."[66]

The situation did not change with the end of the operation. If anything, Kissinger's ire increased. On 10 April, Rear Adm. R. C. Robinson, the JCS chairman's liaison with the National Security Staff, told the chairman that Kissinger was "furious" with Abrams and General Weyand, his deputy, for going on leave at the crucial time of the ARVN withdrawal from Laos. Additionally, he criticized them for not ensuring better support coordination for the ARVN forces.[67] How far the relationship between Abrams and the White House had deteriorated was demonstrated in a 7 June conversation between the president and Kissinger in which the national security adviser said, "I wouldn't believe a word Abrams says anymore."[68]

Admiral Moorer was also upset with General Abrams and his overly optimistic reporting about Laos. He later said he was "appalled" that Abrams and his field commanders, "two full generals [Abrams included] and four [lieutenant generals]," had given him no reason to believe that General Lam and the South Vietnamese forces might not be able to hack it. Furthermore, if Abrams and his generals had believed that Lam and his subordinates were unable to conduct such an ambitious operation, "they never should have let this operation be approved."[69]

As for the American people, their perceptions of the outcome of the operation in Laos were only too clear. Secretary of Defense Melvin Laird was concerned that the adverse coverage of the operation would create a "bad image" of the South Vietnamese army among the American people.[70] His concerns would be borne out. The vivid images of ARVN soldiers clinging to helicopter skids as they fled the combat zone in terror "froze the American public's perception of their South Vietnamese allies."[71] This perception was not a positive one. A May 1971 Harris poll revealed that by a margin of 45 to 24 percent, Americans believed that the South Vietnamese incursion into Laos had been a "failure."[72] Despite Nixon's protestations about the efficacy of Vietnamization, many Americans were now convinced that the South Vietnamese would never be able to stand on their own and that further American sacrifices to bolster their combat capability were just not worth the cost.

For the South Vietnamese themselves, Lam Son 719 raised doubts about the willingness of the United States to accept risks on behalf of their ally. President Thieu had hoped to hold down casualties for political reasons. The worst of the South Vietnamese losses were incurred after Abrams and Sutherland had pressed Thieu to continue the attack from Ban Dong to Tchepone and after the Americans had declined to intervene with US ground troops. Stanley Karnow, a journalist in Saigon, later wrote that during the period following the conclusion of the operation in Laos he could detect a growing distrust of Americans.[73] There was a wave of anti-American demonstrations in Saigon. George Donelson Moss describes a poster that appeared in Saigon in the wake of Lam Son which depicted Nixon standing over a pile of dead South Vietnamese soldiers, with a message that Vietnamization meant that the United States would fight to the last South Vietnamese.[74]

For their part, the North Vietnamese leaders in Hanoi were also left with lasting and important impressions of Lam Son 719 that would have a significant impact on the war in the aftermath of the fighting in Laos. In an official history of the Route 9–Southern Laos campaign, written shortly after it ended, the North Vietnamese ridiculed Lam Son 719 and called it "the heaviest defeat ever" for "Nixon and company. . . . A fine picture of Vietnamization indeed!"[75]

CHAPTER ELEVEN

Aftermath

Despite the internal negative assessments and lingering concerns about Operation Lam Son 719, the Nixon administration continued to attempt to put the best face on it publicly. Even Henry Kissinger joined in the effort. In a report to Carl Albert, speaker of the House, Kissinger said that the North Vietnamese would have fewer options in 1972 because of the impact of the operation. He concluded, "The combination of enemy manpower and logistics setbacks resulting from the Lam Son operation make it unlikely that the enemy will mount major offensive activities in South Vietnam or in Cambodia, despite evidence that the enemy planned to mount such offensives."[1] As it turned out, Kissinger could not have been more wrong. The months after Lam Son 719 proved to be only the calm before the gathering of a new storm.

Immediately following the termination of Lam Son 719, General Abrams instituted new programs in an attempt to overcome the weaknesses and correct the deficiencies of the ARVN that had been so apparent during the operation. In Laos, the North Vietnamese had clearly demonstrated that they had turned away from guerrilla tactics to conventional warfare, which the South Vietnamese forces had great difficulty in trying to counter. The only way to combat this type of warfare was with combined arms operations that focused on the synchronization of infantry, armor, artillery, and air support. Abrams urged General Vien to appoint a committee to develop a combined arms doctrine suitable for RVNAF use; this was done, and the committee produced the *Combined Arms Doctrinal Manual,* which was approved late in 1971.[2]

Additionally, command post exercises for ARVN units were initiated to teach air-ground coordination and combined tank-infantry operations. General Abrams directed his corps senior advisers to put together mobile advisory and support groups to work directly with the South Vietnamese corps commanders to provide "dynamic support to the early introduction of the new mode of [combined arms] tactics" within the RVNAF. He also directed that a joint support group be established in each ARVN corps area command patterned on the one XXIV Corps had established during Lam Son 719. The purpose of these groups was to help improve the coordination of US air and artillery support to South Vietnamese corps and division staffs, particularly with regard to the employment of B-52s, helicopter gunships, and artillery fire. Later, Abrams assigned an additional senior Army officer as "air-mobile adviser" in each corps zone to help coordinate US helicopter support to South Vietnamese field units.[3]

MACV also took steps to improve RVNAF weaponry. The T-54 tanks and heavy artillery that the NVA used in Laos outmatched the ARVN M41 tanks and the lighter South Vietnamese artillery. In an attempt to counter the heavier communist weapons, MACV equipped one South Vietnamese tank battalion in Military Region I with the US M48 main battle tank, which was much more capable than the M41. Additionally, one ARVN artillery battalion received 175-mm self-propelled guns to combat the Soviet 130-mm long-range guns that the NVA possessed. Those new weapons were steps in the right direction, but the amounts provided were in such small numbers as to have little significant impact. As General Davidson, former MACV J2, wrote after the war, these efforts would eventually prove to be part of the continual story of "too little, too late."[4]

Modern equipment for the ARVN was not the most important consideration in improving the fighting ability of the South Vietnamese forces. General Abrams noted in July 1971 that poor leadership remained the most critical South Vietnamese weakness.[5] This had only been too apparent during Lam Son 719. Abrams and his senior generals began a campaign to convince Thieu to replace weaker leaders at the top of the ARVN chain of command. Although the South Vietnamese president made a few changes, the criteria for senior command in the ARVN remained political loyalty rather than proven combat ability. A 1971 assessment of the RVNAF officer corps noted that the army had not been able to divorce itself from politics and that family relationships, personal loyalties, and regional, school, and business ties determined entrée into the upper levels of the officer corps.[6]

Even senior South Vietnamese generals realized that something had to be done. General Vien wrote after the war that "the problem of [ARVN] leadership should have been reviewed especially at corps and division levels. The appointment of general officers to these key command jobs should have been devoid of political considerations and based entirely on military professionalism and competence. . . . Military discipline should have been strictly enforced even with general officers especially when the conduct of a major and decisive operation was at stake."[7] President Thieu was obviously more concerned about his political support and refused to relieve incompetent officers who were loyal to him. This situation, long prevalent in the ARVN, had dire consequences in Laos and left unremedied would also have serious ramifications in battles to come.

Another aspect of the leadership crisis was the need to develop sufficient leaders for the expanding South Vietnamese forces. To combat this problem, Abrams urged more emphasis on the early identification of men with leadership potential, expanding the number and length of leadership training courses, and elevating the standards of the leader-producing schools, to include the Vietnamese Military Academy and the Command and General Staff College.[8] These were steps in the right direction, but only time would tell if they would have a significant impact on the situation.

These concerns notwithstanding, reports on the progress of Vietnamization in the aftermath of the Cambodian and Laotian operations continued to be upbeat. In October 1971, General Abrams sent a message to CINCPAC and the chairman of the JCS asserting that, in his opinion, the JGS and the four ARVN corps commanders were performing very well. Further, he said of the thirteen division commanders (including the commander of the newly formed 3rd Division), Abrams considered only one ineffective and one marginal. He assured CINCPAC and the chairman that senior officer manning in the RVNAF remained one of his personal priorities and that he would continue to do everything he could to convince the JGS to replace those who did not measure up, and that so far the senior South Vietnamese military leadership had been receptive.[9] However, as receptive as they may have been, little was done to remedy the situation.

Despite the difficulties involved in increasing the combat capability of the RVNAF while at the same time continuing to withdraw US troops, General Abrams was relatively pleased with the progress of Vietnamization. In early 1972 he declared that "the state of readiness, the alertness and activity on the part of the armed forces here in this country [South Vietnam] is the highest that I've ever seen it, though some are still asleep at the switch." However, the US troop withdrawals continued, and Abrams and his advisers in the field realized that time was running short to get the South Vietnamese ready to take over when all Americans were gone.[10] Nevertheless, the White House would continue to trumpet the "successes" of Vietnamization as more US troops departed.

However, on the streets of America, Lam Son 719 had, like the Cambodian incursion the year before, brought out antiwar dissidents in force. Although the reaction was not as violent or widespread as in 1970, the numbers of dissidents appeared to grow daily. Media coverage of the South Vietnamese retreat from Laos had a devastating effect on many Americans, most of whom were fed up with the inconclusive nature of a seemingly unending war. Popular support for President Nixon and his policies in South Vietnam fell to an all-time low. A Gallup Poll on 7 March 1971, while the battle continued to rage along Route 9 in Laos, indicated that seven out of ten Americans doubted the president had told them all they needed to know about the events in Laos and South Vietnam. A Harris Poll published the next day revealed that only 39 percent of the population supported Nixon's handling of the war. Forty-one percent were concerned that the fighting in Laos would delay the evacuation of US troops from South Vietnam, and 51 percent indicated they would favor a congressional resolution requiring the withdrawal of all US troops from Southeast Asia by the end of the year.[11]

During April and May there were six weeks of demonstrations against continued US involvement in the war. On 24 April, 150,000 people demonstrated in San Francisco, and on the same day, 200,000 demonstrators, including a large contingent of Vietnam Veterans Against the War, hit the streets in Washington, demanding an immediate withdrawal of all US troops. In the week leading up to May Day 1971, demonstrators threatened to shut down the federal government, so the mayor of the District of Columbia asked for federal help. The National Guard was called out, and 12,000 protesters were arrested, effectively ending the demonstration. Nevertheless, sentiment against the war and the administration's handling of it continued unabated.

Nixon's Democratic opponents in Congress seized the moment. Between 1 March and 1 July 1971, seventeen House or Senate votes sought to restrict Nixon's authority to conduct the war and/or fix a date for unilateral withdrawal. House Democrats approved a resolution in late March 1971 calling for the termination of US involvement in Indochina by 1 January 1973. When Nixon approved more bombing of North Vietnam during Lam Son 719, Senator George McGovern (Democrat, South Dakota) charged that the new bombing was "the most barbaric act committed by any modern state since the death of Adolph Hitler."[12] McGovern subsequently proposed to the Senate Foreign Relations Committee a bill that would force Nixon to have US troops out of Southeast Asia by 31 December 1971. Committee Chairman William Fulbright (D-AR) conducted hearings on the proposal, in which supporters of McGovern's bill called for unilateral US withdrawal regardless of North Vietnamese reciprocity. McGovern's bill eventually appeared in a slightly modified form as an amendment to the military conscription bill; however, on 16 June the Senate defeated the amendment. Nevertheless, this clearly demonstrated the growing confrontation between the White House and the Democrats in Congress.

The anti-Nixon forces did not give up. On 22 June the Senate passed the Mansfield Amendment, which declared that all American troops were to be withdrawn from Vietnam within nine months after the approval of the extension of the draft. The wording was later changed in conference committee from "nine months from passage" to "earliest practicable date."[13] Such legislation increased the pressure on the administration and later would seriously undermine the US bargaining position at the Paris peace negotiations.

To quiet his critics, the president made a series of speeches in April 1971 stressing plans for continued US troop withdrawals. At the same time, the Nixon administration tried throughout 1971 and into the new year to get the North Vietnamese to enter into serious and meaningful negotiations in Paris. Official talks with the North Vietnamese at the Majestic Hotel in Paris had been going on for four years and had settled little except the shape of the negotiating table. Accordingly, Kissinger had begun secret negotiations with the North Vietnamese in a Paris suburb in August 1969. Little more progress than in the official talks occurred during 1970 and well into 1971. Lam Son 719 interrupted the secret sessions, but shortly after the operation was ended, Kissinger, his negotiating position somewhat weakened by the outcome in Laos, requested a resumption of the clandestine talks.

On 31 May 1971, Kissinger met secretly with Xuan Tuy, who was heading the North Vietnamese delegation while his colleague, Le Duc Tho, was temporarily in Hanoi. Kissinger repeated the five-part proposal made by Nixon in October 1970 in which he called for a standstill cease fire and a peace conference to bring a permanent end to the fighting. Kissinger also proposed that all prisoners of war be exchanged immediately and indicated that the United States was prepared to discuss a deadline for complete US withdrawal and a subsequent cease-fire when the final withdrawals began. In turn, he asked that the North Vietnamese agree to no further infiltration of outside forces into South Vietnam, Laos, and Cambodia. The North Vietnamese refused Kissinger's proposal, saying that it did not provide sufficient guarantees that NVA troops could remain in South Vietnam. Additionally, they rejected the timing of Kissinger's offer, because the proposed US withdrawal would come after the cease-fire and the exchange of prisoners, which effectively removed two of their key bargaining chips. Despite Xuan Tuy's rejection of his proposals, Kissinger left the meeting believing that "serious negotiations seemed in the offing for the first time."[14]

On 26 June, at Le Duc Tho's request, Kissinger again met secretly with the North Vietnamese in Paris. The Hanoi regime's diplomats presented nine counterproposals to Kissinger's earlier offer. Kissinger believed that seven of the proposals could be successfully negotiated but had major objections to the last two, in which Hanoi demanded reparations and that the United States "stop supporting Thieu-Ky-Khiem so that a new administration could be set up in Saigon."[15] Nevertheless, Kissinger was encouraged by the ongoing discussions.

On 1 July, as Nixon and Kissinger were considering Hanoi's nine points, Madame Nguyen Thi Binh, the representative of the Provisional Revolutionary Government (PRG) at the official Paris negotiations, publicly issued a seven-point plan of her own, which was similar to but not the same as the one presented by Le Duc Tho during the secret meetings with Kissinger. Binh called for reunification of Vietnam, a guarantee of Vietnamese neutrality, an end to Vietnamization, dismantling of US military bases, inclusion of the PRG in the South's government before any elections, and a release of all political prisoners. Kissinger was stunned and asked Le Duc Tho what constituted the official North Vietnamese position; Le Duc Tho replied that his was the approved position.[16]

Kissinger concluded that this contretemps was a ploy to force the United States to negotiate on Le Duc Tho's terms; the North Vietnamese wanted to negotiate in secret but used Madame Binh's announcement as a way to appeal to the antiwar contingent in the United States. After the war, it was revealed that this may not necessarily have been the case. Truong Nhu Tang, former minister of justice of the PRG, wrote in his book that the conflicting communist peace proposals in Paris were a result of the conflict in Hanoi between the North Vietnamese and the South Vietnamese in the PRG. Regardless of the reason for Madame Binh's announcement, it caused Congress, the news media, and the antiwar dissidents, unaware of Kissinger's secret negotiations with Le Duc Tho in Paris, to condemn Nixon for failing to respond to Binh's overture.[17]

Kissinger, who had just come from a two-day meeting with Zhou Enlai in Beijing to discuss Nixon's visit to China, set for 1972, met again with Tho on 12 July to discuss the discrepancies between the two North Vietnamese proposals. Le Duc Tho reiterated his original nine proposals as the basis for further negotiations. Kissinger said that reparations might be discussed, but that dismantlement of the Thieu government was nonnegotiable. At an impasse, the meeting broke up, but the participants agreed to meet again on 26 July.

At the next session, the discussions went well, again only to hit a wall when the Thieu issue came up. Another meeting was called for 16 August, but no progress was made. This pattern repeated itself at the next session on 13 September.

Kissinger made one more attempt to negotiate with the North Vietnamese in 1971. Trying to reach a compromise over the fate of the Thieu government, Kissinger sent the communist negotiators a letter on 3 October proposing "that a new presidential election be held within six months after the signing of a final agreement. The election would be run by an electoral commission, including communists, under international supervision. One month before the election, Thieu would resign and his function would be assumed by the president of the South Vietnamese Senate." Additionally, the proposal included a new formula for the withdrawal of US troops, saying that most of the troops would be gone within seven months of an agreement, leaving only a small residual force to provide "technical advice, logistics, and observation of the ceasefire."[18] The North Vietnamese agreed to discuss this proposal on 20 November, but on 17 November they canceled the meeting without commenting on Kissinger's letter.

After the war, Truong Nhu Tang wrote that the whole scenario of North Vietnamese negotiations in 1971 was a classic example of "talking while preparing to fight," in which Le Duc Tho "was treating Henry Kissinger to a brilliant display of 'talking and fighting,' using the negotiations to cover as long as possible the next real move in the war, the upcoming dry season campaign in the South."[19] While they talked in Paris, the North Vietnamese used this time well to prepare for their next offensive.

In an attempt to bring the North Vietnamese back to the table, Nixon revealed to the public in a nationwide radio and television broadcast on 25 January 1972 that Kissinger was conducting secret negotiations with the North Vietnamese in Paris. While Nixon's announcement did not quiet all his critics, it nevertheless boosted the president's political fortunes early in the election year. Unfortunately, the speech had no impact on the North Vietnamese. The day after the broadcast, Washington sent Hanoi a private note indicating a willingness to resume the secret talks. The North Vietnamese refused and withdrew all previous peace proposals, saying, "You should realize the difference of the conditions in 1971 and the present conditions in 1972." The major condition that had changed, not yet apparent to Nixon and Kissinger, was that the North Vietnamese were preparing to launch a general offensive in the South.[20]

In South Vietnam the effort continued to bolster the combat capabilities of the RVNAF. In early November 1971, Secretary Laird and Admiral Moorer went to see for themselves how the effort was going. In Saigon they met with General Abrams, who briefed them on the ARVN improvements made in planning ability and air-ground coordination, asserting that "leadership throughout Vietnam was good—the Military Region commanders are outstanding."[21]

In a similar vein, a 1971 year-end report provided the following assessment: "Gradual improvement in the ARVN has occurred partially as a result of the assumption of a greater portion of combat responsibilities as US forces redeploy. The experience gained in the planning and execution of complex, large-scale, cross-border operations, starting with Lam Son 719 early in 1971, has been invaluable. While the ARVN command and control system has a long way to go, it has demonstrated that it can and will function under demanding combat conditions."[22]

Concurrent with the ongoing effort to improve the fighting ability of the ARVN, US troop withdrawals continued unabated. By the end of 1971, only 139,000 Americans remained in South Vietnam, the lowest number since 1965. While Kissinger continued to negotiate with the North Vietnamese in Paris, Nixon, no doubt driven by domestic political concerns, contemplated a new round of US troop withdrawals. On 13 January 1972, the president announced that 70,000 more troops would depart Vietnam by 1 May, reducing MACV strength to 69,000; he also promised an announcement of an additional reduction by the end of April. By this point, between 1 July 1969 and 31 January 1972, MACV had already carried out ten redeployment increments for a total reduction of 410,500 troops, including 102 infantry and other maneuver battalions, sixty-six artillery battalions, and thirty-three attack and fighter squadrons as well as support units of all services.[23]

As the number of US forces in South Vietnam spiraled steadily and rapidly downward, the North Vietnamese leaders in Hanoi were devising new plans. Despite the problems that the South Vietnamese forces had experienced in Laos, the bitter fighting had nevertheless exacted a heavy toll on the North Vietnamese supply network, which resulted in a dampening of the level of military activity during the remainder of 1971. In the immediate aftermath of the operation, the North Vietnamese began again to build up their forces in Laos and Cambodia to replace the men, weapons, and equipment lost in the fighting earlier in the year.

At the same time, the leadership in Hanoi came to the conclusion that the outcome of the campaign in Laos "signaled a new step forward in the development of Vietnam's campaign arts" and meant that the army had "moved into a new era" in which it was now capable of conducting large-scale, conventional, combined arms operations.[24] A North Vietnamese historian later recalled that Lam Son 719 was seen as "proof that we could defeat the best [South Vietnamese] units. We had not been certain we could do this before."[25] The NVA official history declared that the Route 9–Southern Laos victory marked "a new level of maturity for our army and was a concrete demonstration . . . that our army and people were strong enough to militarily defeat the 'Vietnamization' strategy of the American imperialists."[26]

In the eyes of Lao Dong Party First Secretary Le Duan and his supporters among the senior political and military leadership in Hanoi, the performance of the ARVN during Lam Son 719 was proof that the South Vietnamese were incapable of standing up to the NVA, even with US air support. In a very real sense, as historian Dale Andradé writes, "Lam Son 719 became an epiphany for Hanoi, a leap of faith from the doctrine of irregular warfare to the final stage of Mao Zedong's guerrilla strategy—conventional war."[27]

Some in the North Vietnamese leadership differed with Le Duan, recognizing that the operation had not gone flawlessly. A number of weaknesses were acknowledged in the performance of higher headquarters and their staff officers. A postwar report noted that several command posts were deployed late and that some of them were located too far from the fighting to effectively control rapidly unfolding situations. Additionally, the report pointed out that a number of weaknesses had manifested themselves in problems with the support of large-scale operations and that some staff officers were "not fully proficient in their professional skills."[28]

With this in mind, the North Vietnamese set out to redress these shortcomings while continuing to build up their forces in Cambodia and Laos. At the same time, they watched the US withdrawals closely; the steady departure of American troops convinced them that the time was rapidly approaching to put the South Vietnamese forces to the final test. Historian Lien-Hang T. Nguyen further suggests that the North Vietnamese leadership may have incorrectly assumed that they had dealt a decisive blow against Vietnamization, and this perhaps blinded them to the resistance they would encounter in South Vietnam in 1972.[29]

Nevertheless, there were some troubling issues that weighed heavily on their decision making. Le Duan and his supporters were worried about Nixon's overtures to the People's Republic of China and the Soviet Union, watching the evolving diplomacy between Washington and both Moscow and Beijing with more than a little apprehension. They were unsure how these warming relations would affect the continued relationship with their communist benefactors and support for the North Vietnamese war effort.

Thus, the North Vietnamese leaders in Hanoi were faced with a quandary. They had been emboldened by the outcome of the bitter fighting in Laos, but they were concerned about losing support from China and the Soviet Union in the wake of Nixon's diplomatic moves. At the same time, there was growing evidence that the pacification effort in the Vietnamese countryside was beginning to make some headway, and this had to be addressed. With all of these issues on the table, and believing that the United States did not have enough combat power left in South Vietnam to prevent a South Vietnamese defeat, the Politburo in Hanoi ordered a massive invasion of South Vietnam to "win a decisive victory."[30] For all of these reasons, the idea of a general offensive gained support in the Politburo, particularly among those who believed that it was the only way to ensure that Hanoi might force a settlement on its own terms.[31]

This was not a new idea; the Politburo had begun discussing the possibility of a new general offensive in South Vietnam even before South Vietnamese forces crossed the border into Laos. At the 19th Plenary Session of the Lao Dong Party in December 1970 and January 1971, Le Duan strongly advocated an all-out offensive; he believed that the total subjugation of the South was the only ideologically proper path to follow. There was some opposition from a more conservative faction within the Politburo, whose members wanted to concentrate on rebuilding the North while prosecuting a more protracted approach to the war in the South. However, historian Lien-Hang T. Nguyen cites new evidence that suggests that "there was more general consensus regarding the 1972 offensive, and that disagreements were only minor ones over tactics."[32]

In May 1971 the Party Central Committee met in Hanoi to discuss the outcome of the South Vietnamese operation in Laos. Lam Son 719 seemed to reinforce the belief that North Vietnamese forces, with modern weapons and conventional tactics, could defeat South Vietnam's armed forces easily once the rest of US combat troops were withdrawn. The weaknesses demonstrated by the South Vietnamese in Laos, Saigon's lack of substantial strategic reserves, and their inability to shift forces rapidly within South Vietnam were all too apparent; additionally, with the preponderance of US combat forces already departed, South Vietnamese forces were stretched very thin along a six-hundred-mile border.

With regard to the potential for American intervention in any contemplated offensive, the North Vietnamese felt that with continued US troops reductions, eventually there would be a point where the US would not have enough forces left to influence the strategic situation. Furthermore, Le Duan, although wary of how Nixon might react, did not think that the political situation in the United States would permit Nixon to commit any new ground troops or combat support to assist the South Vietnamese once the NVA launched their offensive. Additionally, he believed that Nixon, "preoccupied with his historic visits [to China and the Soviet Union]," would be reluctant to take any extreme measures to blunt an offensive that might upset the strategic arms control talks.[33] In the end, Le Duan would be proven drastically wrong on this point, an error that would have disastrous consequences for the North Vietnamese forces in 1972.

The objectives of the new offensive, which would be called the Nguyen Hue campaign, named for a Vietnamese hero who had defeated the Chinese on the outskirts of Hanoi in 1788, were to defeat the pacification effort, destroy the South Vietnamese army, further discredit Vietnamization, and topple the Saigon government once and for all.[34] At the very least, they hoped to "win a significant victory obliging the US to end the war in a losing position through a political solution that the US must and can accept, but advantageous to us." If the invasion was successful, during a time when there was still a small residual US presence in Vietnam, North Vietnamese forces would humiliate Nixon, destroy his war politics, and perhaps foil his reelection bid. Also, according to former PRG minister of justice Truong Nhu Tang, an additional objective of the offensive was to spur antiwar dissidence in the United States.[35]

In a very real sense, at least in theory, the new offensive would be a win-win situation. If the offensive were successful, the war would be won. If it were less than completely successful, at least it would better position North Vietnam for the ongoing negotiations in Paris. As an article in a 1972 Lao Dong Party journal stated, "It doesn't matter whether the war is promptly ended or prolonged. . . . Both are opportunities to sow the seeds; all we have to do is to wait for the time to harvest the crop."[36]

Once the Politburo decided to launch a general offensive, then the question became one of deciding where and when to attack. North Vietnamese leaders had watched closely the US troop withdrawals and calculated that American troop strength would probably fall below sixty-five thousand in April 1972. This number would not include many combat units but would comprise primarily headquarters and combat support elements. There were those in the Politburo who argued that the best course of action was to wait until 1973, when virtually all US troops would be gone, but Le Duan and his supporters prevailed, arguing that the new offensive had to be launched before the pacification and Vietnamization programs gained more traction. He maintained that if these programs were allowed to develop unimpeded for the rest of 1972, the US would continue to pump weapons and equipment into South Vietnam, and the ARVN would grow stronger, thus making the future military conquest of South Vietnam that much more difficult. In the end, Le Duan convinced his colleagues in the Central Party Military Committee at a meeting in June 1971 that they should not wait. Subsequently, the decision was made to "develop our strategic offensive posture in South Vietnam to defeat the American 'Vietnamization' policy, gain a decisive victory in 1972, and force the US imperialists to negotiate an end to the war from a position of defeat."[37]

The final discussions on the new offensive were conducted during the Twentieth Party Plenum in Hanoi from 27 January to 2 February 1972, during which it was decided to go for a complete military victory. This was followed by subsequent discussions in the Central Military Committee to work out the details for the new offensive.[38]

As always, the monsoon seasons dictated the best times for combat operations in Vietnam. If the North Vietnamese waited until too late in the spring dry season to start their offensive, they risked torrential rains in May that could seriously impede the later phases of the operation. The communist leaders also wanted to initiate the invasion in time to have a maximum impact on the US election in November, and that could only be done by starting the offensive earlier in the year rather than later. For those reasons, the decision was made to launch the offensive in March 1972.

The preparations for the new offensive did not go unnoticed in Saigon or Washington. Intelligence estimates indicated an intensification of enemy activity that pointed toward a new buildup in both Laos and Cambodia and the likelihood of a new enemy general offensive. On 20 January, in a message to Admiral McCain, General Abrams reported that "the enemy is preparing and positioning for a major offensive." Further, he said he foresaw "a hard battle involving sophisticated weaponry and as much ground combat power as the enemy can generate." The question for MACV intelligence officers was not if there was to be a new offensive, but rather where and when the offensive would be launched. By the end of January, General Abrams expected the coming offensive to come in the northern half of South Vietnam and that it would "evolve into the maximum military effort the North is capable of making in the next few months."[39]

In the beginning days of February there were almost daily sightings of enemy forces in western Military Region II near the border with Laos. At the same time, there was an increase in activity in both the Quang Tri Province and the A Shau Valley in Thua Thien Province Military Region I. Earlier, MACV intelligence predicted that the new attack would target the northern regions and begin sometime after the last week in February, following the Tet holidays. When the offensive failed to materialize, there was some confusion in both Saigon and Washington about Hanoi's intentions.[40]

However, those intentions were made only too clear on 30 March 1972, Maundy Thursday, when the North Vietnamese launched what would be referred to in the American media as the Easter Offensive.[41] Although the new offensive was not unexpected, when it came it was stunning in its scope and ferocity.

The full force of the enemy attack began in the north with a devastating artillery barrage against 3rd ARVN Division, located in outposts all along a line just south of the DMZ that separated North and South Vietnam. These artillery fires were followed by the attack of two NVA divisions from the B5 Front south across the DMZ toward Quang Tri, while another NVA division attacked eastward from Laos toward Hue in Thua Thien Province.[42] The unexpected enemy attack across the DMZ by the NVA 304th and 308th Divisions reinforced by three separate infantry regiments, two tank regiments, and at least one sapper battalion caught the 3rd Division repositioning forces and not ready for a fight. The 3rd Division, which had only recently been formed, was not prepared for large-scale conventional tank-infantry attacks supported by massive heavy artillery strikes, and they reeled from the intensity of the NVA onslaught.

The next day, three more North Vietnamese divisions under the command of the B3 Front attacked from the tri-border area into the western Central Highlands toward Pleiku and Kontum, while additional forces targeted Binh Dinh Province along the coast in an attempt to cut South Vietnam in half. On 5 April, after a feint against Tay Ninh Province, three NVA divisions under command of the B2 Front moved from sanctuaries in Cambodia and pushed into Binh Long Province, in Military Region III, northwest of Saigon. Meanwhile, one NVA division attacked into the Mekong Delta to seize food and to pin down South Vietnamese forces in the region.

A total of fourteen NVA infantry divisions and twenty-six separate regiments (more than 130,000 troops and approximately twelve hundred tanks and other armored vehicles) participated in the offensive, which was characterized by large-scale conventional infantry tactics supported by tanks and massive amounts of artillery fire and rockets. Having seen the impact of American air support in Laos, the North Vietnamese attackers were accompanied by surface-to-air missiles and increased numbers of antiaircraft guns. The result of the massive conventional invasion was a scale of warfare that the South Vietnamese had seldom experienced—even more intense than the fighting in Laos the year before.

In the north, General Lam, who had retained command of I Corps after Lam Son 719, was not prepared for a communist attack of such scope. He had expected any attack in his area of responsibility to come from the west out of Laos rather than across the relatively flat and open DMZ, so he was caught completely by surprise when the NVA poured across it in force. The North Vietnamese attackers in Military Region I almost totally overwhelmed the South Vietnamese defenders; by 2 April, six firebases had fallen, and two more fell by the end of the day; the 3rd Division's 57th Regiment broke under the onslaught, and the commander of the 56th Regiment, defending Camp Carroll, surrendered the camp and his fifteen hundred troops to the enemy with hardly a shot.[43] This left only three major bases in the northern part of Quang Tri Province; ultimately, these, too, succumbed as the ARVN and Vietnamese Marines fell back toward Quang Tri City in the face of the NVA juggernaut.

On 2 April, Ambassador Bunker cabled Kissinger and Nixon that "ARVN forces are on the verge of collapse in I Corps."[44] Nixon realized that if the North Vietnamese succeeded in inflicting a major defeat on the South Vietnamese forces, his Vietnamization policy would be exposed as a fraud, and his bid for reelection in November might be imperiled. Further, Nixon was scheduled to meet in Russia with Soviet premier Leonid Brezhnev, and he could not go to Moscow in the wake of a military defeat inflicted largely by Soviet-supplied weapons.[45] Nixon was in a difficult position. If he responded in a strong fashion to the North Vietnamese invasion, it might cause the Soviets to cancel the summit and destroy his hopes for détente. It no doubt would anger the Chinese, who Nixon was also trying to court. Yet if Nixon did not use bombing, virtually the only weapon left to him with most of the US combat troops already having departed South Vietnam, the North Vietnamese would most likely overrun Saigon's troops, inflict a military defeat on ARVN, and compromise the US strategic position throughout the world. At home, it was an election year, and Nixon would be condemned by one segment of American for failing to act to prevent the collapse of South Vietnam and by another if he responded with anything that looked like an escalation of the war. Despite the dangers involved, Nixon had come to the conclusion that "defeat . . . was simply not an option." He and Kissinger agreed that something had to be done quickly to assist the faltering South Vietnamese, and they determined that the best way to do that was to "carry the war to North Vietnam."[46] Given this situation, bombing was the only answer to prevent the fall of South Vietnam.

Accordingly, the president directed a strong response, increasing the amount of airpower in-theater and removing many long-standing restraints. Unleashing the bombers on Hanoi and Haiphong, to include eventually mining the harbor there, Nixon ordered additional aircraft and warships to Vietnam to reinforce the assets already there.[47] However, it would take some time for the reinforcements to have an impact; meanwhile, the North Vietnamese offensive continued unchecked.

As the air campaign focused on Hanoi and Haiphong, further to the south in Binh Long the communist B2 Front began its move against An Loc, which was located only sixty-five miles from Saigon. The battle began with the 5th VC Division, supported by twenty-five T-54 tanks, overrunning the border town of Loc Ninh. The town fell on 6 April, after two days of hard fighting. The NVA then turned their attention on An Loc, the province capital, ten miles to the south along Highway 13, which led directly to Saigon. The main attack on An Loc would be made by the 9th VC Division, while the 7th NVA Division would block the highway to the south of the city to prevent ARVN reinforcements from reaching the town.[48]

Having surrounded the city, which was defended by the 5th ARVN Division, the 9th Division launched its attack on 13 April. The defenders and their American advisers, employing massive amounts of US airpower, turned back the initial attack but sustained heavy casualties in the door-to-door fighting. The NVA lay siege to the city and continued to pound the ARVN defenders with artillery as they prepared for another attack. Meanwhile, President Thieu ordered the 21st ARVN Division to move from its normal area of operation in the Mekong Delta to break the roadblock on Highway 13. Additionally, he ordered the 1st Airborne Brigade to be inserted by helicopter to the east of An Loc to reinforce the defenders.

It was at this point that the relations between President Nixon and General Abrams, which had become frayed over the operation in Laos, once again became strained. The president had ordered an all-out attack on petroleum storage areas, truck parks, and logistical facilities in the Hanoi-Haiphong area. General Abrams, supported by Admiral McCain, requested a postponement of that operation in order to generate enough air support to defend An Loc and support a counterattack in Military Region I. According to Admiral Moorer, the president reacted angrily, replying that he "did not understand why Abrams needs all of the forces in the country regardless of how many forces are sent there. The strike on Haiphong is part of a progressive and heavy escalation being made for political purposes in an effort to negotiate [an end to] the war."[49] Nixon rejected Abrams's request to postpone the air operation in North Vietnam, and it was conducted 15–16 April.

The NVA launched the second major attack on An Loc on 19 April. This time they were successful in seizing the northern half of the town, but the defenders managed to hold out in the south, again supported by the massive application of US airpower. During the first two weeks of the battle for An Loc, despite the conflict over the use of aircraft between the president and Abrams, there was still sufficient airpower to aid the beleaguered defenders during the bitter fighting; over twenty-five hundred air strikes were flown in and around the city in support of the South Vietnamese defenders and their American advisers.[50]

On 11 May, after a seven-thousand-round artillery barrage, the NVA made another big push to take An Loc. The 5th VC Division, reinforced with several other regiments, launched what turned out to be the last major attack on An Loc. The attackers succeeded in forging two salients in the South Vietnamese lines, but ultimately the defenders prevailed, once again relying heavily on US airpower, including thirty B-52 strikes in one twenty-five-hour period. Although there were other smaller attacks during the rest of the month of May, the NVA had peaked, and with reinforcements brought in by helicopter, the ARVN began to push the NVA back from the city. The siege was effectively broken by early June. Although there were sporadic NVA attacks during the rest of the month, the ARVN expanded the perimeter and began to clear the surrounding area.[51] The ARVN had stopped the NVA just sixty-five miles away from Saigon.

As the battle in Binh Long Province unfolded, the fighting had continued to rage in the Central Highlands, where elements of the 2nd and 320th NVA Divisions launched an attack toward Kontum. By 15 April the ARVN bases at Dak To and Tan Canh had been overwhelmed in four days of heavy fighting, resulting in the destruction of both the 42nd and 47th Regiments of the 22nd ARVN Division. During the battle, the division commander, Col. Le Duc Dat, broke under pressure. Col. Phillip Kaplan, senior adviser to the division, later recalled that Dat said, "We're going to lose, we're going to be overrun, we will all be killed or captured."[52]

The II Corps commander, Lt. Gen. Ngo Dzu, was totally ineffective during the battles for Dak To and Tan Canh.[53] When the NVA next turned their attention directly on Kontum, President Thieu relieved him and replaced him with Maj. Gen. Nguyen Van Toan, the former deputy for operations in Military Region I, who set about to organize Kontum's defenses for the coming battle. The NVA launched their main attack on Kontum on 14 May, but Toan's forces, directed by Col. Ly Tong Ba, the new commander of the 23rd Division, and their American advisers, assisted by the massive application of US airpower, successfully defended the city in bitter fighting that lasted for two weeks.

Unfortunately, far to the north, the story was very much different. There, the situation had rapidly deteriorated as the NVA tightened its grip on Quang Tri. On 23 April, reinforced by another division, the forces surrounding the city had launched a new attack. As the battle in Quang Tri developed, General Abrams remained cautiously optimistic. In a message to Washington on

24 April, the general said of the unfolding situation, "On the whole the effective far outweighs the ineffective." He described the leadership in Military Region I under General Lam as "outstanding: aggressive and confident."[54] Such statements, given the way the situation turned out in I Corps, further strained the general's credibility with the White House.

At the time, however, Nixon, no doubt convinced that things were not as bad as they seemed by Abrams's continual upbeat assessments from Saigon, announced on 26 April that twenty thousand more US troops would be withdrawn in the next two months. He asserted that "if we continue to provide air and sea support, the enemy will fail."[55]

Such was not going to be the case, at least at Quang Tri. On 27 April the North Vietnamese forces mounted another effort to take the city. As the NVA tried to outflank and envelop the city, the South Vietnamese defenses began to crumble. On 1 May, after a sustained artillery attack, panic set in, the defenders broke, and the city was abandoned to the NVA. Abrams, sobered by the fall of Quang Tri City, cabled Washington: "I must report that as the pressure has mounted and the battle has become brutal, the [South Vietnamese] senior military leadership has begun to bend and in some cases to break. In adversity it is losing its will and cannot be depended on to take the necessary measures to stand and fight." He closed by saying that he saw "no basis for confidence" that either Hue or Kontum could be held.[56]

With the South Vietnamese forces falling back in disarray, the North Vietnamese continued to push south along Route 1. At that point President Thieu relieved Lieutenant General Lam, who had demonstrated the same kind of performance during the fight for Quang Tri that had marked his command during the earlier operation in Laos. Faced with a situation in which he risked losing the northern third of the country to Lam's ineptitude, Thieu replaced him with Lt. Gen. Ngo Quang Truong, arguably the best general in the South Vietnamese military. Truong arrived on 2 May and immediately took charge, organizing the defenses of Hue and stabilizing the situation. He gave the Vietnamese Marines responsibility for defending the city in the north and northwest and charged the 1st ARVN Division with manning the defenses to the west of the city. On 13 May, having halted the NVA advance, Truong's forces, reinforced with an airborne brigade, launched a counterattack to retake Quang Tri Province. Supported by massive amounts of US firepower, including B-52s and naval gunfire from US warships standing off the coast, Truong's forces advanced deliberately against the opposing North Vietnamese forces, now numbering six divisions, recapturing many of the firebases that had been lost earlier. On 16 September, Truong's troops retook Quang Tri City, turning back the NVA attack in the north.

The South Vietnamese, bolstered by their American advisers and supported by massive amounts of US air support, halted the NVA offensive, holding in Kontum and An Loc and successfully counterattacking to retake Quang Tri and regain lost ground in Military Region I. The North Vietnamese sustained more than one hundred thousand casualties and lost more than 50 percent of their tanks and artillery. The South Vietnamese had prevailed, but they, too, had paid a heavy price, suffering over twelve thousand soldiers killed, thirty-four thousand wounded, and fifteen thousand missing.[57]

Despite the high number of casualties, the South Vietnamese had held against everything the NVA could throw at them, emerging victorious after months of bitter fighting at a sustained level never before seen during the earlier years of the war. As Douglas Pike observed, "ARVN troops and even local forces stood and fought as never before."[58] The victory seemed a turning point for South Vietnam.

The South Vietnamese had been victorious, but it had been a very near thing. They continued to demonstrate a heavy dependence on US advisers and even more so on US airpower. As Dale Andradé, observed, "Despite Vietnamization, the South Vietnamese army exhibited many of the same problems in 1972 as it had ten years earlier, a fact made painfully clear during the Easter Offensive."[59] The problems that were prevalent during Operation Lam Son 719 in Laos in 1971 were still there in 1972. As it had been in Laos, leadership, particularly at the senior levels, was, according to General Abrams, the single most critical failing in the RVNAF.[60] General Lam, who had proven so inept in Laos in 1971, was so ineffective in 1972 that Thieu had no choice but to replace him with General Truong. Lam's counterparts in II and III Corps also proved not up to the demands of high-intensity warfare.[61] The same was true of several division commanders. The leadership problem went further down the chain of command. After the battle, one US general said that the regimental commanders at An Loc, with a few exceptions, were no better than mediocre, stating that "there was no control. There was no supervision; there was no command emphasis to get out in the crew positions."[62] Despite these lapses in leadership, many South Vietnamese soldiers fought valiantly, as many did in Laos in 1971. When ably led, the South Vietnamese soldiers fought hard and in many instances heroically.

Nevertheless, what enabled the defenders to survive against the North Vietnamese onslaught was, more often than not, the support provided by US airpower, on which the South Vietnamese depended heavily in 1972, just as they had a year earlier in Laos. The type of large-scale conventional operations that characterized the NVA offensive in 1972 was exactly the type of confrontation that the US had been seeking since the arrival of American ground troops in 1965. These operations exposed the North Vietnamese forces to devastating US firepower from the air, and they paid dearly. General Abrams, who departed Saigon in June 1972 to become US Army chief of staff, earlier observed that American airpower, and not South Vietnamese arms, had caused the enemy's losses. Gen. Fred C. Weyand, who assumed command of MACV upon Abrams's departure, summed up the collective role of airpower in all its forms when he said that it was "unlikely that the South Vietnamese forces could have stopped the invasion without the tremendous effectiveness of airpower."[63]

One of the key differences between the South Vietnamese performance in Laos and turning back the NVA Easter Offensive in 1972 was the presence of US advisers. In Laos, the advisers were precluded from crossing the border by congressional legislation. In 1972, the advisers, in most cases, fought right alongside their South Vietnamese counterparts. In doing so, the advisers played several important roles. Maybe most important, the advisors, who usually stayed with their counterparts throughout the battle and shared their fate on a daily basis, provided a tangible demonstration of American resolve, which encouraged their counterparts, raising their spirits during the darkest hours of the deadly fighting. The advisers also provided the critical link that was missing in Laos between the ARVN and the tactical aircraft and helicopters that supported them. In times of extreme duress, the advisers provided stability and expertise in coordinating combined arms, making up for the inabilities of the South Vietnamese commanders to command and control conventional battles against massed tank and infantry attacks. In many cases, one senior US officer observed, the advisers "were the glue that kept them [ARVN] together."[64]

It is true that the South Vietnamese had held when they had to do so, but Nixon administration spokesmen downplayed the role of US airpower and American advisers while praising the steadfastness of the South Vietnamese. On 26 April, even as the fighting raged on three fronts, Nixon had gone on national television, reporting, "The South Vietnamese will have demonstrated their ability to defend themselves on the ground against future enemy attacks. . . . I have decided that Vietnamization has proved itself sufficiently that we can continue our program of withdrawing American forces without detriment to our overall goal of insuring South Vietnam's survival as an independent country."[65]

This became the story line trumpeted by the Nixon administration in the wake of the Easter Offensive. Citing the "fierce determination of . . . [the] Vietnamese defenders," the administration proclaimed the victories at An Loc and Kontum as clear proof that the policy of turning the war over to the South Vietnamese was working.[66] This was in one sense true, but it was also true that the ARVN had prevailed with a tremendous amount of US support in the form of advisers and airpower.

On 29 August, President Nixon announced another redeployment of twelve thousand troops, to be completed by 30 November. This would bring MACV's strength down to twenty-seven thousand. Meanwhile, the negotiations between Kissinger and Le Duc Tho continued in Paris. In September, with the NVA offensive having failed, the North Vietnamese negotiators became more willing to make concessions, and the discussions began to achieve some momentum. However, President Thieu, who was concerned that the Americans, in a rush to disengage, would sign an agreement that would disadvantage South Vietnam, began to drag his feet. In October the North Vietnamese announced that they would accept a cease-fire in place. President Thieu rejected the proposal, but Nixon announced a halt to all bombing north of the twentieth parallel in North Vietnam.

By mid-October, Kissinger and the North Vietnamese negotiators worked out a tentative peace agreement; on 26 October, Kissinger proclaimed, "peace is at hand." This proved to be premature when President Thieu denounced the draft proposal as, effectively, a surrender to the communists. In November, Kissinger and the White House attempted to convince Thieu to accept the proposed agreement, but he submitted sixty-nine amendments, which incensed the North Vietnamese negotiators. The talks bogged down, and when the North Vietnamese negotiators departed the negotiations to return to Hanoi for consultation, Nixon launched Operation Linebacker II, the bombing of Hanoi and Haiphong, on 15 December. On 26 December the North Vietnamese agreed to return to the negotiations. After a flurry of new talks, the Paris Peace Accords were signed on 27 January 1973. Thieu acceded to Nixon's wishes and agreed to the accords only after Nixon threatened to sign them without South Vietnam's concurrence.[67]

As for the battlefield, according to the official history of MACV, a "rough equilibrium had been established."[68] In accordance with the Peace Accords, all US military personnel, less a small contingent that remained behind as part of the Defense Attaché Office in Saigon, departed Vietnam on 29 March after the dissolution of Military Assistance Command, Vietnam.

In conclusion, just as the outcome in 1972 was not the total victory that the Nixon administration touted, the South Vietnamese performance in Laos was not the total debacle that it was portrayed in the American media. The story in each case was much more complex.

As for Operation Lam Son 719, perhaps Henry Kissinger said it best when he wrote in his memoir, "We allowed ourselves to be carried away by the daring conception, by the unanimity of the responsible planners in both Saigon and Washington, by the memory of the success in Cambodia, and by the prospect of a decisive turn."[69]

As the last major military event before the preponderance of US forces were withdrawn from Vietnam, Lam Son 719 represented the first real test of Nixon's Vietnamization policy. In the end, although the operation resulted in heavy NVA casualties, it nevertheless demonstrated the long-standing weaknesses and vulnerabilities of the South Vietnamese armed forces and caused many to question the efficacy of Nixon's exit strategy, which focused on turning over the war as US troops were withdrawn. It is noted that South Vietnamese performance on the battlefield improved between 1971 and 1972, but the shortcomings that had bedeviled the RVNAF from the earliest days of existence and were so clearly revealed in Laos in 1971 had not been sufficiently addressed. Nixon and his advisers trumpeted the idea that the South Vietnamese victory demonstrated that Vietnamization had been a success. Jeffrey Kimball writes that Nixon "needed Vietnamization to succeed, and because he did, he wanted to believe it could."[70] Thus, for better or worse, Vietnamization was officially validated, and the South Vietnamese victory became one of the underlying rationales for complete US withdrawal and Nixon's "peace with honor."

However, as the official Marine Corps history points out, "Vietnamization, whatever progress could be reported, remained an unequal contest between the slow pace of RVNAF improvement and the inexorably quickening pace of American withdrawal."[71] The success of Vietnamization rested on the ability of the South Vietnamese to carry the war on their own. Progress was made in preparing the South Vietnamese to stand on their own between 1971 and 1972, and the South Vietnamese performance during the Easter Offensive is testament to that. However, in the final test the South Vietnamese would continue to suffer from the same shortcomings that they had demonstrated so clearly along Route 9 in Laos in 1971.

Epilogue: Endgame

The war was over for the United States, but, as it turned out, decidedly not so for the Vietnamese. Unfortunately for the South Vietnamese, the Paris Peace Accords did not address over one hundred thousand North Vietnamese troops inside the borders of South Vietnam. The cease-fire was short-lived, and the fighting resumed as both sides tried to grab as much territory as possible. For the rest of 1973 and most of 1974, the North and South Vietnamese fought each other throughout South Vietnam.

Nixon had coerced Thieu into acquiescing to the Paris Accords, promising that the United States would come to the aid of the South Vietnamese if North Vietnam tried another major offensive. With this in mind, and using weapons and equipment stockpiled during 1972, the South Vietnamese initially held their own against the North Vietnamese. However, as these stocks began to wane, Thieu had no one to turn to for support. Nixon, reeling from the impact of the Watergate investigation, was fighting for his political life and was unable to generate any interest in the plight of the South Vietnamese. On 9 August 1974, Nixon resigned from the presidency. Thieu and his countrymen had always relied on Nixon's promises to intervene if the North Vietnamese violated the cease-fire. Now Nixon was gone. Nixon's successor, Gerald Ford, promised that "the existing commitments this nation has made in the past are still valid and will be fully honored in my administration."[1]

This was a commitment that Ford could not keep, given the prevailing sentiment in Congress. With Nixon gone, the North Vietnamese decided to test the South Vietnamese with a corps-level attack against Phuoc Long Province. This was effectively to be a test case to see how the South Vietnamese would handle a multidivision attack, but, more important, to see how the United States would react if the South Vietnamese got into trouble on the battlefield. The battle was launched in mid-December. The outnumbered ARVN fought poorly, and the North Vietnamese routed the defenders, killing or capturing three thousand soldiers, taking control of vast quantities of war materiel, and "liberating" the entire province. The United States did nothing.

Both Saigon and Hanoi were shocked. Thieu finally realized that his forces had been relegated to fighting a "poor man's war," while the North Vietnamese, still being resupplied by China and the Soviet Union, got stronger every day. The North Vietnamese decided that the time was ripe for a knockout blow. Believing the United States would not or could not intervene, they planned a two-year strategy that called for large-scale offensives in 1975 to create conditions for a "general offensive, general uprising" in 1976.[2]

The North Vietnamese launched what they called Campaign 275 on 10 March 1975 with an attack on Ban Me Thuot in the Central Highlands. They overran the city in two days and then turned their attention on Pleiku and Kontum. The South Vietnamese, realizing they were on their own without any hope of US support, fell back in panic. When Thieu decided to shorten his lines by withdrawing his forces out of the Highlands, supposedly to concentrate his forces for a major effort to retake Ban Me Thuot, the retreat rapidly turned into a rout. While the communist forces in the highlands attacked toward the sea, additional communist troops in the northern provinces drove southward from Quang Tri down Highway 1. One by one, the cities and bases fell as the communists drove rapidly down the coast. On 30 April 1975, it all came to an abrupt end when North Vietnamese tanks crashed through the gates of the Presidential Palace in Saigon, and the war was over.[3] The war was over; the South Vietnamese forces, beset by their long-standing shortcomings and demoralized by America's failure to honor the promises that had been made by Presidents Nixon and Ford, had collapsed in less than fifty-five days. In the end, the RVNAF failed in its ultimate test, and so, too, did Nixon's Vietnamization program.

Appendixes

Task Organization, ARVN and US

- I Corps (ARVN)*
    - Hq, I Corps
    - I Corps Arty
        - 64th FA Bn
    - 1st ALC I Corps
        - 71st Med Gp
        - I Corps Sig Bn
        - 1st MP Bn
        - 111th Trans Co
        - 116th Trans Co
        - 118th Trans Co
    - 1st Armored Bde
        - 7th Ar Cav Sqdn
        - 11th Ar Cav Sqdn
        - 17th Ar Cav Sqdn
        - 4th Ar Cav Sqdn (Prov) (OPCON) (D+40)
        - 1st/3rd Ar Cav
        - 1st/8th Ar Cav
    - 1st Ranger Gp (+)
        - 21st Rgr Bn
        - 37th Rgr Bn
        - 39th Rgr Bn
        - 77th Rgr Border Defense Bn
            - 3rd Co/79th Rgr Border Defense Bn
    - 10th Engr Gp
        - 101st Engr Bn (OPCON to Abn Div)
        - 102nd Engr Bn
        - 118th Engr LC Co
    - 1st Inf Div
        - 1st Inf Regt
            - 1st Bn/1st Inf
            - 2nd Bn/1st Inf
            - 3rd Bn/1st Inf
            - 4th Bn/1st Inf

*Maj. Gen. Nguyen Duy Hinh, *Lam Son 719*, Indochina Monographs, 172–74; Headquarters, XXIV Corps, After Action Report: LAM SON 719, 30 Jan.–6 Apr. 1971, 14 May 1971, A-2-5.

- 2nd Inf Regt
  - 1st Bn/2nd Inf (OPCON 54 Regt D+53 to D+68)
  - 2nd Bn/2nd Inf
  - 3rd Bn/2nd Inf
  - 4th Bn/2nd Inf
  - 5th Bn/2nd Inf
- 3rd Inf Regt
  - 1st Bn/3rd Inf
  - 2nd Bn/3rd Inf
  - 3rd Bn/3rd Inf
  - 4th Bn/3rd Inf
- 54th Inf Regt
  - 1st Bn/54th Inf
  - 2nd Bn/54th Inf
  - 4th Bn/54th Inf
- 1st Inf Div Arty
  - 48th FA Bn (–)
  - 14th FA Bn (–)
  - 62nd FA Bn
  - 11th FA Bn (–)
- 1st Engr Bn
- 1st Med Bn
- 1st Sig Bn
- 1st Log Bn

Abn Div (+) (OPCON)

- 1st Abn Bde
  - 1st Abn Bn
  - 8th Abn Bn
  - 9th Abn Bn
  - 1st FA Bn
- 2nd Abn Bde
  - 5th Abn Bn
  - 7th Abn Bn
  - 11th Abn Bn
  - 2nd FA Bn
- 3rd Abn Bde
  - 2nd Abn Bn
  - 3rd Abn Bn
  - 6th Abn Bn
  - 3rd FA Bn
- Abn Div Arty (–)
  - 44th FA Bn (155)
- 1st Abn Med Bn
- 1st Abn Service Bn
- 1st Abn Signal Bn

Marine Div (OPCON)

- Hq Bn
- 147th Bde (D+1)
  - 2nd Inf Bn
  - 4th Inf Bn

- 7th Inf Bn
- 2nd FA Bn
- C/20th FA Bn (155)

258th Bde
- 1st Inf Bn
- 3rd Inf Bn
- 8th Inf Bn
- 3rd FA Bn
- D/48th FA Bn (–) (155)

369th Bde (D+32)
- 5th Inf Bn
- 6th Inf Bn
- 9th Inf Bn
- 1st FA Bn

A Btry/48th FA Bn (–) (155)
Service Bn
Medical Bn

5th Inf Regt/2nd Inf Div
- 1st Bn/5th Inf
- 2nd Bn/5th Inf

XXIV Corps (US)†
- Hq, XXIV Corps
- 108th Arty Gp
  - 8th Bn, 4th FA
  - 2nd Bn, 94th FA
  - 1st Bn, 39th FA (–) (D+30)
  - 1st Bn, 44th FA AWSP (–)
- 45th Engr Gp (OPCON D–13 to D+23)
  - 14th Engr Bn (CBT)
    - 630th Engr Co (LE)
    - 511th Engr Co (PB)
    - 59th Engr Co (–) (LC)
  - 27th Eng Bn (CBT) (–)
    - 59lst Engr Co (LE)
- 504th MP Bn (–)
  - 300th MP Co (OPCON)
- 212th CAB
  - 131st Surv Aerial Co
  - 220th Recon Airplane Co
- 101st Abn Div (Ambl) (–)
  - 101st Abn Div Arty (–)
    - 2nd Bn (Ambl), 11th Arty
    - 2nd Bn (Ambl), 319th Arty
    - 4th Bn, 77th ARA (Ambl)
      - B/2nd Bn, 20th ARA (OPCON)
      - B/326th Engr Bn (Ambl)
  - 1st Bde, 101st Abn Div (Ambl) (Res)

†Headquarters, XXIV Corps, After Action Report: LAM SON 719, 30 Jan.–6 Apr. 1971, 14 May 1971, A-1–3.

3rd Bde, 101st Abn Div (Ambl) (D+30 to D+67)
- 1st Bn, 501st Abn Inf (D+25 to D+67)
- 2nd Bn, 502nd Abn Inf (OPCON 3d Bde, 101st Abn Div) (D+26 to D+67)
- 1st Bn, 506th Abn Inf (D+47 to D+67)
- 2nd Bn, 327th Abn Inf (D+29 to D+48)

TF 326th (–) (OPCON) (D–1 to D+67)
- A/326th Engr Bn (Ambl) (+)
- 59th EOD Det (–)

101st Combat Aviation Group‡
- 101st Avn Bn (AH) (Ambl)(D–1 to D+67)
- 158th Avn Bn (AH) (Ambl)(D–1 to D+67)
- 159th Avn Bn (ASH) (Ambl)(D–1 to D+67)
  - 132nd ASHC (OPCON)
  - 176th AHC (OPCON)
  - 179th AHC (OPCON)
  - 478th HHC (OPCON)
- 5th Trans Bn (D–l to D+67)
- 14th Avn Bn (OPCON) (D+2 to D+63)
  - 71st AHC (D+25 to D+59)
  - 116th AHC (D+34 to D+36 & D+50 to D+53)
  - 174th AHC (D+25 to D+67)
  - 176th AHC (OPCON)
- 223rd Avn Bn HHC (OPCON) (D+2 to D+67)
  - 48th AHC (D+2 to D+67)
  - 173rd AHC (D+2 to D+67)
  - 282rd AHC (D+34 to D+36 & D+50 to D+51)
  - 235th AWC (D+38 to D+56)
  - 238th AWC (D+2 to D+56)
  - D/227th AWC (D+28 to D+66)
  - 179th ASHC (D+23 to D+66)
  - 756th Med
- 2nd Sqdn (Ambl), 17th Air Cav
  - C/7/17 Cav Sqdn (OPCON)
  - B/7/1 Cav Sqdn (OPCON)
- 67th Med Gp
  - 326th Med Bn
  - 498th Med Co
  - 237th Med Det
  - 571st Med Det
- 34th Gen Spt Gp (–)
  - 34th Avn Det (DS)
  - 34th Co Spt Gp (AM&S)
- 58th Trans Bn
  - 610th SG Trans Co
  - 142nd DS Trans Co
  - 263rd GS Avel Co

‡Vietnam Helicopter Pilots Association, *1994 Membership Directory,* Section IX—History of Lam Son 719, 288. This listing of aviation units and command relationships differs slightly from the one in the XXIV Corps After Action Report.

HMH-463, 1st MAW (OPCON D+1)[§]
163rd Avn Co (GS)
1st Bde, 5th Inf Div (Mech) (+) (OPCON 101st Abn Div (Ambl) D+32 to D+67)
1st Bn, 11th Inf (Mech)
3rd Bn, 187th Abn Inf, 101st Abn Div (OPCON D–1 to D+67)
1st Bn, 61st Inf (Mech) (OPCON 101st Abn Div (Ambl) D+26 to D+31 and D+57 to D+67) (11th Bde, 23rd Div D+32 to D+56)
3rd Sqdn, 5th Cav
1st Bn, 77th Armor
5th Bn, 4th FA (DS)
1st Bn, 82nd FA (–) 23rd Div (Atch) (DS) (D–1)
A/4th Bn, 12th Armor
A/7th Engr
P/75th Ranger
298th Sig Co
Co B, 23rd Med Bn, 23rd Div (OPCON D+31 to D+48)
75th Support Bn
F/8th Cav (OPCON D+2 to D+67)
11th Bde, 23rd Inf Div (OPCON 101st Abn Div (Ambl) D+32 to D+66)
1st Sqdn, 1st Cav (OPCON 1st Bde, 5th Inf Div (Mech) D–1 to D+56) (OPCON 101st Abn Div (Ambl D+67)
2nd Bn, 1st Inf (D+21)
4th Bn, 3rd Inf, 23rd Inf Div (OPCON 1st Bde, 5th Inf Div (Mech) D–1 to D+56)
H/17th Cav
C/26th Engr Bn
6th Bn, 11th FA (–)
C/1st Bn, 82nd FA
C/6th Bn, 11th FA
A/3rd Bn, 82nd FA
11th Spt En (Prov)
Hq, USASUPCOM–Da Nang
26th GSG
8th Trans Gp
39th Trans Bn
57th Trans Bn
C/11th Motor Trans Bn (+)
2nd Maint Bn
63rd Maint Bn
FSA Maint Bn
FSA 26-1
FSA 26-2

[§]The Marine CH-53D Sea Stallions were usually escorted in the missions into Laos by AH-1G Cobras from HML-367.

APPENDIX 2

Order of Battle, People's Army of Vietnam

Northern Military Regions and Laos, 1971

Overall Command: Headquarters 702 (Gen. Le Trong Tan, commander)
- B70 Corps (or corps-sized group): (Gen. Cao Van Khanh, commander)
  - 308th Division (Col. Nguyen Huu An, commander)
    - 36th Infantry Regiment (in reserve)
    - 88th Infantry Regiment
    - 102nd Infantry Regiment
  - 304th Division (minus 9th Regiment) (Col. Hoang An, commander)
    - 24th Infantry Regiment
    - 66th Infantry Regiment
  - 320th Division (minus 52nd Regiment) (Col. Nguyen Cong Tien, alias Kim Tuan, commander)
    - 48th Infantry Regiment
    - 64th Infantry Regiment
- B5 Front (Col. Nguyen Anh De, commander)
    - 27th Infantry Regiment
    - 270th Infantry Regiment
- Tri-Thien Military Region (B4 Front)
  - 324th Division (Col. Chu Phuong Doi, commander)*
    - 1st Infantry Regiment
    - 2nd Infantry Regiment
    - 3rd Infantry Regiment
- Military Region 5
  - 2nd Division (minus 31st Regiment) (Col. Nguyen Chon, commander)
    - 1st "Ba Gia" Regiment
    - 141st Regiment

Source: Military History Institute of Vietnam, *Chiến dịch phản công Đường 9–Nam Lào, Nam 1971* [The Route 9–Southern Laos counteroffensive campaign, 1971].

*Many references list the subordinate regiments of the 324th Division as the 803rd, 812th, and 29th Regiments. However, according to the division history, *Lịch sử sư đoàn bộ binh 324, 1955–2005* [History of the 324th Infantry Division, 1955–2005], accessed 19 Oct. 2009 at http://www.quansuvn.net/index.php?topic=103.0 and translated by Merle Pribbenow, these were the old designations of the regiments during the time of the 324A Division, which was disbanded in 1966. After the division was reformed in 1969, the regiments were renumbered as the 1st, 2nd, and 3rd Regiments.

Group 559 (the Ho Chi Minh Trail command) (Gen. Dong Si Nguyen, commander)
- Area Headquarters 470 (division-sized transportation and combat support unit)
  - Binh Tram 9 (Way Station 9)†
  - Binh Tram 27
  - Binh Tram 31
  - Binh Tram 32
  - Binh Tram 33
  - Binh Tram 41

Combat Support:
- Artillery
  - 38th Field Artillery Regiment
  - 45th Field Artillery Regiment
  - 368th Field Artillery Regiment
  - 84th Artillery Regiment (heavy mortars and rockets)
- Armor
  - 198th Battalion/202nd Tank Regiment
  - 397th Battalion/202nd Tank Regiment
- Anti-Aircraft Artillery
  - 230th AAA Regiment
  - 241st AAA Regiment
  - 591st AAA Regiment
- Surface-to-Air Missiles (SA-2)
  - 237th Missile Regiment
- Engineer
  - 7th Engineer Regiment
  - 83rd Engineer Regiment
  - 219th Engineer Regiment
- Sappers (not including divisional sapper battalions)
  - 126th Water Sapper Group (operating along the Dong Ha River)
  - 33rd Sapper Battalion
  - 35th Sapper Battalion
- Reconnaissance
  - 74th Reconnaissance Battalion (directly subordinate to the General Staff)

†A *binh tram* was a regimental-sized combat support unit with its own organic battalion-sized infantry, engineer, antiaircraft, transportation, and supply/administrative elements.

APPENDIX 3

Casualties, Operation Lam Son 719

8 February–24 March 1971

US Armed Forces*

Unit	Killed in Action	Wounded in Action	Missing in Action
101st Airborne Div	68	26	17
1st Bde, 5th Infantry Div	55	431	3
11th Bde, 23rd Infantry Div	47	256	7
223rd Combat Aviation Bn	19	59	11
XXIV Corps Artillery	9	76	0
US Army Support Cmd	8	40	0
45th Engineer Gp	6	11	0
504th MP Bn	3	15	0
7th US Air Force	3	0	0
Totals	**219**	**919**	**38**

South Vietnamese Armed Forces†

Unit	Killed in Action	Wounded in Action	Missing in Action
1st Infantry Div	537	1,607	537
1st Airborne Div	455	1,993	0‡
VNMC Div	355	770	63
1st Ranger Gp	93	435	27
1st Armored Bde	54	364	0
I Corps units	55	314	24
Totals	**1,549**	**5,483**	**651**

North Vietnamese Army

	Killed in Action	Wounded in Action	Missing in Action
	19,360	Unknown	Unknown§

*Headquarters, XXIV Corps, After Action Report: LAM SON 719, 30 Jan.–6 Apr. 1971, 14 May 1971; Headquarters, XXIV Corps, An Assessment of the Performance of South Vietnamese Forces during Operation LAM SON 719 (30 January–6 April 1971), 3 May 1971.

†Maj. Gen. Nguyen Duy Hinh, *Vietnamization and the Cease-Fire*, Indochina Monographs, 129.

‡This number is obviously in error, since Colonel Tho, 3rd Airborne Brigade commander, and several of his troops were captured during the battle for LZ 31.

§Maj. Gen. Nguyen Duy Hinh, *Lam Son 719*, Indochina Monographs, 131. Additionally, fifty-seven NVA soldiers were captured. The number of reported casualties on both sides was a contentious issue after the operation was completed.

APPENDIX 4

US Army Aviation Summary, Operation Lam Son 719

30 January–7 April 1971

Rotary-wing Aircraft Assets Available to Support Operation

OH-6A (Cayuse)	5
OH-58 (Kiowa)	59
UH-1C (Huey gunship)	60
UH-1H (Huey)	312
AH-1G (Cobra)	117
CH-47 (Chinook)	80
CH-53 (Sea Stallion)	16
CH-54 (Skycrane)	10
Total	**659**

Sorties

Type Sortie	In RVN	In Laos
Gunship	17,159	17, 014
Troop Lift	37,681	13,098
Medevac	1,829	909
Air Cavalry	10,603	7,284
Logistic Support	51,342	7,523
Total	**118,614**	**45,828**

Losses

Type Aircraft	Nonhostile		Hostile	
	Damaged	Lost	Damaged	Lost
OH-6A (Cayuse)	—	1	25	9
OH-58 (Kiowa)		—	15	6
UH-1C (Huey gunship)	1	—	62	8
UH-1H (Huey)	2	1	314	52
AH-1G (Cobra)	1	2	157	24
CH-47 (Chinook)	—	—	26	3
Total	4	4	601	102*

Sources: Headquarters, US Military Assistance Command, Vietnam, Command History, 1971, 2: E-38–39; Headquarters, 101st Airborne Division (Airmobile), Final Report: 101st Airborne Division Airmobile Operations in Support of Operation Lam Son 719, 8 February–6 April 1971, 2 vols., Camp Eagle, RVN, 1 May 1971.

Note: One USMC CH-53D Sea Stallion from HMH-463 was lost to ground fire on 23 February while attempting to lift a howitzer from FSB Hotel II. Another CH-53D exploded in midair and crashed northeast of Marble Mountain after returning from a support mission in Laos (Graham A. Cosmas and Lt. Col. Terrence P. Murray, *US Marines in Vietnam: Vietnamization and Redeployment, 1970–1971*, 204). The South Vietnamese Air Force lost seven helicopters during the operation.

*Maj. Gen. Nguyen Duy Hinh, *Lam Son 719*, Indochina Monographs, 135. Hinh reports 108 helicopters destroyed and 618 damaged; several 101st Airborne Division documents reflect 107 helicopters destroyed.

APPENDIX 5

US Air Force Summary, Operation Lam Son 719

30 January–7 April 1971

Tactical Air Support Summary

	In Laos	In South Vietnam	Total
Total Sorties Flown	7,104	2,010	9,114
Average Sorties/Day	103	29	132
Highest Number of Sorties on Any One Day (8 March 1971)			277
Total Tons of Ordnance Delivered	10,931	3,100	14,031
Aircraft Lost			7

B-52 "Arc Light" Summary

Strikes	Phase I (8 Feb–5 Mar)	Phase II (6 Mar–15 Mar)	Phase III (16 Mar–7 Apr)	Phase IV	Total
I Corps US	0	189	97	135	421
	7	37	20	137	201
Total	7	226	117	272	622
Tonnage	456.75	14,435.50	9,261.75	22,705.25	46,859.25

Gunship Summary (AC-119/AC-130 sorties)

3–9 Feb.	9
10–16 Feb.	26
17–23 Feb.	34
24 Feb.–2 Mar.	38
3–9 Mar.	40
10–16 Mar.	34
17–23 Mar.	58

Tactical Airlift Support Summary

Date	Mission	Sorties	Passengers	Cargo (Short Tons)
26 Jan.–6 Feb.	Deploy US Support Forces	338	2,045	2,633.8
30 Jan.–6 Feb.	Deploy Contingency Forces	247	9,254	1,711.5
5 Feb.–3 Apr.	Resupply and Reinforcement	2,083	15,545	20,513.7
28 Mar.–6 Apr.	Redeployment	141	4,638	1,261.7
	Total	**2,809**	**31,482**	**26,120.7**

Source: Maj. Gen. Nguyen Duy Hinh, *Lam Son 719*, Indochina Monographs, 135, 137; US Air Force, Headquarters, Pacific Air Forces, Directorate of Operations Analysis, *Contemporary Historical Examination of Current Operations (CHECO) Report: LAM SON 719, 30 January–24 March 71, The South Vietnamese Incursion into Laos*, 123, 134, 137–38.

APPENDIX 6

US/ARVN Artillery Summary, Operation Lam Son 719

30 January–7 April 1971

Caliber	Number of Tubes	Missions in South	Rounds	Number of Tubes Lost in Combat
US				
105-mm	6	111	3,197	0
155-mm	28	5,738	132,278	0
175-mm	20	6,946	36,695	4
8-inch	8	2,373	16,392	0
Total	**62**	**15,168**	**208,962**	**4**
ARVN				
105-mm	152	Unknown	240,709	70
155-mm	48	Unknown	79,228	26
Total	**200**	**Unknown**	**310,937**	**96**
Grand Total	**262**	**15,168 (US only)**	**519,899**	**100**

Source: Maj. Gen. Nguyen Duy Hinh, *Lam Son 719*, Indochina Monographs, 139.

Notes

Introduction

1. Distinguished Service Cross citation, Maj. Jack Lamar Barker, accessed 7 May 2012 at http://www.arlingtoncemetery.net/jlbarker.htm.
2. Earl Swift, *Where They Lay: Searching for America's Lost Soldiers*. The author discusses the unsuccessful 2001 mission by members of Joint Task Force–Full Accounting, to recover the remains of Major Barker and his crew; JTF-FA was a Department of Defense agency created in 1992 to resolve the cases of Americans still unaccounted for as a result of the Vietnam War. In his book, Swift addresses not only the search for the crew, but also their family backgrounds and the circumstances of their loss. The remains of Barker and his crew were finally recovered during a mission mounted in 2005 by the Joint POW/MIA Accounting Command, successor to JTF-FA. Barker, Dugan, Dillender, and Chubb were buried in Arlington National Cemetery with full military honors on 12 April 2006; twenty-three former "Kingsmen" from B Company, 101st Aviation Battalion attended the services.
3. Capt. James E. Fulbrook, "Part II: The Battle," *US Army Aviation Digest*, July 1986, 40. The North Vietnamese Army (NVA) was more accurately the People's Army of Vietnam (PAVN), but for the purposes of this narrative they will be referred to as NVA, as that was the more commonly used name for the PAVN during the war.
4. Andrew Wiest, *Vietnam's Forgotten Army, Heroism and Betrayal in the ARVN*, 207.
5. Bernard C. Nalty, *Air War over South Vietnam, 1968–1975*, 247.
6. Phillip B. Davidson, *Vietnam at War: The History, 1946–1975*, 617.

Chapter 1

1. Robert B. Semple, "Nixon Vows to End War with a 'New Leadership,'" *New York Times*, 6 Mar. 1968; Robert B. Semple, "Nixon Withholds His Peace Ideas," ibid., 11 Mar. 1968.
2. Larry Berman, *No Peace, No Honor: Nixon, Kissinger, and Betrayal*, 45–46.
3. Quote in Roger Morris, *Uncertain Greatness: Henry Kissinger and American Foreign Policy*, 156.
4. Henry A. Kissinger, Special Assistant for National Security, National Security Study Memorandum (NSSM) 1, for the Secretaries of State and Defense and the Director of Central Intelligence, 21 Jan. 1969, DepCORDS Papers, US Army Center of Military History, Washington, DC (hereafter referred to as CMH); Henry Kissinger, *White House Years*, 238.
5. In December, Nixon had seen an intelligence assessment made by the CIA that was very critical of the Thieu government and the capabilities of the RVNAF. This assessment is contained in Wheeler to Abrams, message, 120217Z Dec. 1968, subj.: RVNAF Capabilities, Abrams Papers, CMH.

6. Henry A. Kissinger, memorandum for Members of the National Security Council Review Group, 14 Mar. 1969, subj.: Summary of Responses to NSSM 1 Vietnam Questions, DepCORDS Papers, CMH. Actual agency responses are found in the Thomas C. Thayer Papers, Folders 13, 20, 134, and 136, CMH.
7. Ibid.
8. Kissinger, *White House Years,* 239.
9. Ibid., 227–28.
10. Gen. Andrew J. Goodpaster, interview by Col. William D. Johnson and Lt. Col. James C. Ferguson, 1976, Andrew J. Goodpaster Papers, US Army Military History Institute, Carlisle Barracks, Pennsylvania (hereafter referred to as MHI); Willard J. Webb, *The Joint Chiefs of Staff and the War in Vietnam, 1969–1970,* 64.
11. Lewis Sorley, *Thunderbolt, from the Battle of the Bulge to Vietnam and Beyond: Creighton Abrams and the Army of His Times,* 254–56. The original impetus to improve the RVNAF and turn over the war effort lay with former secretary of defense Clark Clifford, who directed the Joint Chiefs of Staff to draw up plans to make the South Vietnamese forces more self-sufficient, saying, "We have embarked on a course of gradually shifting the burden of the war to GVN force." Headquarters, US Military Assistance Command, Vietnam (MACV), Command History, 1968, Military History Branch, Saigon, 1969, 1:152–253 (hereafter MACV histories are cited as MACV Command History and year).
12. Jerry Friedheim, Deputy Assistant Secretary of Defense, 1969–73, interview by William M. Hammond, 3 Oct. 1986, CMH.
13. Laird to the President, memorandum, 13 Mar. 1969, subj.: Trip to Vietnam and CINCPAC, March 5–12, 1969, White House Special Files (WHSF), Richard Nixon Presidential Library and Museum, National Archives and Records Administration, Yorba Linda, California (hereafter referred to as Nixon Library).
14. Minutes of National Security Council Meeting, March 28, 1969, Document 49 in US Department of State, *Foreign Relations of the United States, 1969–1976,* 6:164–76 (hereafter cited as *FRUS, 1969–1976,* with appropriate volume and page numbers); Kissinger, *White House Years,* 272; Webb, *Joint Chiefs of Staff, 1969–1970,* 13. By all accounts, *Vietnamization* became the accepted term for Nixon's new policy at this meeting. However, Abrams biographer Lewis Sorley, in *Thunderbolt,* 254–56, maintains that Abrams started the process of helping the South Vietnamese armed forces become more capable when he assumed command from General Westmoreland in 1968 and that Nixon and Laird merely adopted the *Vietnamization* label and formalized it as administration policy (accompanied by US troop withdrawals). Nixon said virtually the same thing earlier in *No More Vietnams,* 105.
15. US Congress, House of Representatives, Committee on Armed Services, *Hearings on Military Posture,* Part I, 91st Cong., 2nd sess., 1970, 7023–24.
16. Alexander M. Haig Jr., *Inner Circles: How America Changed the World—A Memoir,* 226; Kissinger, *White House Years,* 262.
17. Richard M. Nixon, *RN: The Memoirs of Richard Nixon,* 392; Haig, *Inner Circles,* 225–29; National Security Decision Memorandum 9, to Vice President, Secretary of State, Secretary of Defense, Director of Central Intelligence, Director, Office of Emergency Preparedness, Washington, April 1, 1969, subj.: Vietnam, Document 51 in *FRUS, 1969–1976,* 6:179–80.
18. Henry Kissinger to Secretary of State, Secretary of Defense, and Director of Central Intelligence, National Security Study Memorandum (NSSM) 36, 10 Apr. 1969, subj.: Vietnamizing the War, NSC Files, Nixon Library; Nixon, *RN,* 392; Kissinger, *White House Years,* 272.

19. Webb, *Joint Chiefs of Staff, 1969–1970,* 77.
20. Kissinger, memorandum for the President, 9 May 1969, subj.: Talking Points for Use in Private Discussion with Gen. Abrams, NSC Files, Nixon Library.
21. Richard M. Nixon, *Public Papers of the Presidents of the United States: Richard M. Nixon, 1969,* 443.
22. Nixon, *RN,* 392; Nguyen Duy Hinh, *Vietnamization and the Cease-Fire,* Indochina Monographs, 18. The Indochina Monographs are a series of studies written by former South Vietnamese generals and published by the US Army Center of Military History, Fort McNair, DC.
23. Kissinger, *White House Years,* 274.
24. Office of the Assistant Secretary of Defense, talking paper, 3 Oct. 1969, subj.: US Objectives in Southeast Asia, Thomas C. Thayer Papers, CMH.
25. Wheeler to McCain and Abrams, message, 6 Aug. 1969, Abrams Papers, CMH; Laird, memorandum for the President, 7 Aug. 1969, subj.: Statement of Mission of US Forces in Southeast Asia, NSC Files, Nixon Library.
26. US Congress, House of Representatives, Committee on Appropriations, Subcommittee on Department of Defense, *Hearings on Department of Defense Appropriations for 1971,* Part I, 91st Cong., 2nd sess., 1970, 311.
27. Even before Nixon assumed office, plans had been developed to increase the size of the RVNAF. Under what became known as the May-68 Plan, MACV had instituted a program to increase and modernize the South Vietnamese armed forces. This program focused on developing the RVNAF into a balanced force with command, administration, and self-support capabilities to continue the fighting successfully after the withdrawal of US and NVA troops. However, it is important to note that at no time during the discussion and implementation of the May-68 Plan did anyone, including MACV, ever consider the "prospect of a unilateral American withdrawal that would leave South Vietnam facing a combined Viet Cong and North Vietnamese threat." This was to change under Nixon and Laird.
28. Jeffrey C. Clarke, *Advice and Support: The Final Years, 1965–1973,* The US Army in Vietnam, 353–54. Strangely, General Abrams did not mention obvious corruption in the RVNAF senior ranks, but he was, nevertheless, joined in this overall assessment by Adm. John S. McCain Jr., Commander, US Pacific Command.
29. Chairman of the Joint Chiefs of Staff (Wheeler) to Secretary of Defense Laird, memorandum, 21 July 1969, Document 100 in *FRUS, 1969–1976,* 6:307–15.
30. Laird to Moorer, memorandum, 10 Nov. 1969, subj.: Vietnamization—RVNAF Improvement and Modernization Aspects and Related US Planning, Abrams Papers, CMH.
31. Clarke, *Advice and Support,* 356; MACV Command History, 1970, 2: VII-4–16.
32. Nguyen Duy Hinh, *Vietnamization and the Cease-Fire,* 39.
33. Ibid., 42.
34. Clark Clifford, "A Viet Nam Reappraisal," *Foreign Affairs* 47, no. 4 (July 1969): 610.
35. Kissinger, *White House Years,* 275.
36. Military History Institute of Vietnam, *Report to General Vo Nguyen Giap: A Consolidated Report on the Fight against the United States for the Salvation of Vietnam by Our People,* 26. The North Vietnamese found that they could not sustain the August attacks because they had not fully recovered from the losses incurred during the 1968 Tet Offensive.

37. Kissinger, *White House Years*, 283; Kissinger to Nixon, memorandum, 10 Sept. 1969, subj.: Our Course in Vietnam, Document 117 in *FRUS, 1969–1976*, 6:370–84.

38. The war was decidedly not over. One of the battles of the war occurred in May 1969. The bitter ten-day battle for Dong Ap Bia, which became known as Hamburger Hill, resulted in the death of fifty-six American soldiers from the 101st Airborne (Airmobile) Division and an estimated 650 NVA killed during the intense fighting.

39. Nixon, *Public Papers: Richard M. Nixon, 1969*, 901–9.

40. Charles DeBenedetti, *An American Ordeal: The Antiwar Movement of the Vietnam Era*, 259.

41. Samuel Lipsman and Edward Doyle, *Fighting for Time*, The Vietnam Experience, 70.

42. Wheeler to Abrams, message, 4 July 1969, subj.: Publicizing ARVN Performance; Abrams to Wheeler, message, 8 Aug. 1969, subj.: Publicizing ARVN Achievements, both in Abrams Papers, CMH.

43. Bunker to the President, message, 27 Apr. 1970, NSC Files, Nixon Library.

44. For the most comprehensive accounts of the campaign in Cambodia, see John M. Shaw, *The Cambodian Incursion: The 1970 Offensive and America's War*, and Tran Dinh Tho, *The Cambodian Incursion*, Indochina Monographs.

45. William M. Hammond, *Public Affairs: The Military and the Media, 1968–1973*, 401–92.

46. MACV Command History, 1970, 3: Annex A; Maj. Gen. Nguyen Duy Hinh, *Lam Son 719*, Indochina Monographs, 7; Tran Dinh Tho, *Cambodian Incursion*, 193–94; Shaw, *Cambodian Incursion*, 161.

47. Abrams quote in Document 313, *FRUS, 1969–1976*, 6:1016–28; Nixon quote in *Public Papers, 1970*, 536. In a memorandum from Nixon to Haldeman on 11 May 1970, the president said that he wanted Haldeman to devise "a positive, coordinated administration program for getting across the fact that this mission has been enormously successful." This would prove difficult, because the announcement of the move into Cambodia resulted in a firestorm of antiwar demonstrations, one of which resulted in the shooting of four students by the National Guard at Kent State.

48. II Field Forces Vietnam (IIFFV), Operational Report–Lessons Learned (OR-LL) for period ending 31 July 1970, dated 14 Aug. 1970, 108, Histories Division, CMH.

Chapter 2

1. Robert Dallek, *Nixon and Kissinger: Partners in Power*, 255.

2. Lien-Hang T. Nguyen, *Hanoi's War: An International History of the War for Peace in Vietnam*, 201.

3. David Fulghum and Terrence Maitland, *South Vietnam on Trial, Mid-1970 to 1972*, The Vietnam Experience, 65.

4. National Security Council, memorandum, 16 Mar. 1971, LAM SON 719—The South Vietnamese Operation in Laos, NSC files, Nixon Library.

5. MACV Command History, 1971, 2: E-15, E-17. What were previously known as Corps Tactical Zones were renamed Military Regions in 1970. Military Region I, previously known as I Corps Tactical Zone, included the five northernmost provinces of South Vietnam.

6. Alexander M. Haig Jr., *Inner Circles: How America Changed the World—A Memoir*, 273.

7. Memorandum, 19 Jan. 1971, subj.: Meeting between the President, Secretary Rogers, Secretary Laird, the Chairman of the Joint Chiefs of Staff,

Henry Kissinger, Richard Helms, Vietnam Subject Files, Nixon Library; Dallek, *Nixon and Kissinger*, 257; MACV Command History, 1971, 2: E-15; Henry Kissinger, *White House Years*, 986–89.

8. Memorandum of conversation, 19 Oct. 1970, Washington, DC, Document 55 in *FRUS, 1969–1976*, 7:137–38.
9. Willard J. Webb and Walter S. Poole, *The Joint Chiefs of Staff and the War in Vietnam, 1971–1973*, 3–5; Robert Mann, *A Grand Delusion: America's Descent Into Vietnam*, 659–66.
10. Kissinger, *White House Years*, 990.
11. Ibid., 990–91.
12. McCain to Moorer, message, 230420Z Aug. 1970, Abrams Papers, CMH.
13. Lewis Sorley, *A Better War: The Unexamined Victories and Final Tragedy of America's Last Years in Vietnam*, 231–32.
14. McCain to Abrams, message, 110253Z Oct. 1970, Abrams Papers, CMH.
15. McCain to Moorer, message, 100556Z Nov. 1970, Abrams Papers, CMH.
16. Webb and Poole, *Joint Chiefs of Staff, 1971–1973*, 2.
17. William C. Westmoreland, *A Soldier Reports*, 272; Bruce Palmer Jr., *The 25-Year War*, 105–6; John M. Collins, *Military Geography for Professionals and the Public*, 367–84; John M. Collins, "Going to Tchepone: OPLAN El Paso," *Joint Force Quarterly*, Autumn/Winter 1997–98, 118–29. The mission of the proposed operation was to seize and hold as long as possible key choke points astride the Ho Chi Minh Trail in Laos to block infiltration of North Vietnamese troops, supplies, and equipment through the Laotian panhandle to South Vietnam and communist sanctuaries inside Cambodia.
18. Nguyen Duy Hinh, *Lam Son 719*, Indochina Monographs, 8.
19. Kissinger, *White House Years*, 992–94.
20. Col. Hoang Ngoc Lung, *Strategy and Tactics*, Indochina Monographs, 73.
21. Nguyen Duy Hinh, *Lam Son 719*, 10–11, 16, 32; Graham A. Cosmas, *MACV: The Joint Command in the Years of Withdrawal, 1968–1973*, 324.
22. Nguyen Duy Hinh, *Lam Son 719*, 53–54.
23. Bui Diem (with David Chanoff), *In the Jaws of History*, 284–85.
24. Sorley, *A Better War*, 230–36; Haig, *Inner Circles*, 273; Palmer, *The 25-Year War*, 106.
25. McCain to Abrams, message, 062132Z Dec. 1970, Abrams Papers, CMH.
26. McCain to Abrams, message, 080435Z Dec. 1970, Abrams Papers, CMH; Kissinger to Bunker, message, 10 Dec. 70, Box 1011, NSC files, Nixon Library.
27. Cosmas, *MACV, 1968–1973*, 322; Kissinger, *White House Years*, 990.
28. Keith William Nolan, *Into Laos: The Story of Dewey Canyon II/Lam Son 719, Vietnam 1971*, 14–15.
29. Nguyen Duy Hinh, in *Lam Son 719*, 33–35, maintains that this meeting took place in early January, but all US accounts agree that it occurred in early December.
30. Moorer to Abrams, message, 100051Z Dec. 1970, Abrams Papers, CMH.
31. Abrams to McCain, message, 120925Z Dec. 1970, Abrams Papers, CMH; McCain to Moorer, message, 150236Z Dec. 1970, Abrams Papers, CMH; Moorer quote in Webb and Poole, *Joint Chiefs of Staff, 1971–1973*, 3.
32. Memorandum of conversation, subj.: Meeting between President Thieu, Ambassador Bunker and General Haig, Saigon, December 17, 1970, Document 91 in *FRUS, 1969–1976*, 7:223–30.

33. MACV Command History, 1971, 2: E-17; Webb and Poole, *Joint Chiefs of Staff, 1971–1973*, 3.
34. President's Deputy Assistant for National Security Affairs (Haig) to the President's Assistant for National Security Affairs (Kissinger), backchannel message, Saigon, 15 Dec. 1970, Document 89 in *FRUS, 1969–1976*, 7:219–21.
35. Abrams to McCain, message, 120925Z Dec. 1970, Abrams Papers, CMH.
36. Memorandum of conversation, subj.: Meeting between President Thieu, Ambassador Bunker and General Haig, Saigon, December 17, 1970, Document 91 in *FRUS, 1969–1976*, 7:223–33.
37. Kissinger, *White House Years*, 994.
38. Memorandum for the record, Washington, December 23, 1970, Document 96 in *FRUS, 1969–1976*, 7:240–44; Kissinger, memorandum for the President, subj.: Meeting with Secretary of Defense Laird, Chairman of the Joint Chiefs of Staff Moorer and Henry A. Kissinger, 23 Dec. 1970, NSC Files/Alexander M. Haig Chronological Files, Nixon Library; Webb and Poole, *Joint Chiefs of Staff, 1971–1973*, 4. Dale Van Atta, *With Honor: Melvin Laird in War, Peace, and Politics*, 346, says that Laird directed the planning for the cross-border operation into Laos, but documentary evidence suggests otherwise.
39. Kissinger, *White House Years*, 994–95
40. Ibid., 999.

Chapter 3

1. Lt. Gen. James W. Sutherland, US Army Senior Officer Debriefing, 31 August 1971, Senior Officer Debriefing Reports, MHI, 25.
2. Quote in Keith William Nolan, *Into Laos: The Story of Dewey Canyon II/Lam Son 719, Vietnam 1971*, 31; Headquarters, XXIV Corps, After Action Report, LAM SON 719, 30 Jan.–6 Apr. 1971, 14 May 1971, Records Group (RG) 472, National Archives, College Park, MD (hereafter referred to as XXIV Corps, AAR, LAM SON 719). Most Army and Marine Corps records for this study were drawn from RG 472; hereafter, unless otherwise noted, these records will cite RG 472, NARA as source.
3. The numerical designation for Operation Lam Son 719 came from combing the year, '71, and the main highway used, Route 9.
4. Headquarters, 101st Airborne Division (Airmobile), memorandum for the record, subj.: Airmobile Operations in Support of Operation LAMSON 719, Camp Eagle, RVN, 20 Mar. 1971, RG 472, NARA.
5. MACV Command History, 1971, 2: E-19.
6. Headquarters, 101st Airborne Division (Airmobile), Final Report: Airmobile Operations in Support of Operation LAMSON 719, 8 Feb. 1971–6 Apr. 1971, Camp Eagle, RVN, 1 May 1971, I-4, RG 472, NARA; MACV Command History, 1971, 2: E-17.
7. MACV Command History, 1971, 2: E-19.
8. The original Dewey Canyon had been a 1969 Marine operation directed in the area south of Khe Sanh in the Da Krong Valley, and it was hoped that designating Phase I of Lam Son 719 as Dewey Canyon II would have some deception value by diverting enemy attention in that direction rather than toward Laos.
9. XXIV Corps, AAR, LAM SON 719, 2.
10. Directorate of Operations Analysis, Headquarters Pacific Air Forces, *Contemporary Historical Examination of Current Operations (CHECO) Report—LAM SON 719, 30 January–24 March 71: The South Vietnamese Incursion Into Laos,*

Honolulu, 24 Mar. 1971, 24 (hereafter referred to as *CHECO Report—LAM SON 719*).

11. Donn A. Starry, *Armored Combat in Vietnam*, 190–91.
12. XXIV Corps, AAR, LAM SON 719, 2–3.
13. Headquarters, 101st Airborne Division (Airmobile), memorandum for the record, subj.: Airmobile Operations in Support of Operation LAMSON 719, Camp Eagle, RVN, 20 Mar. 1971, 4, RG 472, NARA.
14. MACV Command History, 1971, 2: E-20; XXIV Corps, AAR, LAM SON 719, A-1–A-2.
15. Quote in Nolan, *Into Laos*, 109.
16. The Marine CH-53Ds were normally escorted on the missions into Laos by Marine AH-1Gs or AH-1Js from Marine Light Helicopter Squadron 367 (HML-367).
17. Michael Sloniker, "History of Dewey Canyon II/Lam Son 719," manuscript, Vietnam Helicopter Pilots Association (VHPA) Collection: Lam Son 719, Vietnam Center and Virtual Archive, Texas Tech University, Lubbock (hereafter referred to as Sloniker, "History of Dewey Canyon II/Lam Son 719").
18. Headquarters, 101st Airborne Division (Airmobile), Final Report: Airmobile Operations in Support of Operation LAMSON 719, 24 Apr. 1971, I-44, RG 472, NARA.
19. MACV Command History, 1971, 2: E-20.
20. Bernard C. Nalty, *Air War over South Vietnam, 1968–1975*, 253.
21. Graham A. Cosmas and Lt. Col. Terrence P. Murray, *US Marines in Vietnam: Vietnamization and Redeployment, 1970–1971*, 207–9. Admiral McCain had proposed a much larger diversion, but General Abrams declared that he could not spare the US or South Vietnamese forces to carry out the plan. McCain then assigned the mission to the Seventh Fleet, and Amphibious Ready Group (ARG) Alpha, with the 31st Marine Amphibious Unit (MAU) embarked, was tasked to conduct the feint during the period 5 February–7 March.
22. Pham Van Chung, Tran Ve, To Van Cap, Nguyen Kim Tien, Kieu Cong Cu, *Hai Mười Một Năm Chiến Trận của Binh Chủng Thủy Quân Lục Chiến Việt Nam (1954–1975)* [The Vietnamese Marine Corps' Twenty-One Years of Warfare (1954–1975)], 231.
23. Secretary of Defense Melvin Laird, memorandum for the President, 16 Jan. 1971, subj.: Trip to Paris, Bangkok, South Vietnam, and CINCPAC January 5–15, 1971, NSC Files/Vietnam Subject Files, Operations in Laos and Cambodia, Nixon Library.
24. Abrams to Sutherland, message, 12 Jan. 1971, Sutherland Papers, MHI.
25. H. R. Haldeman, *The Haldeman Diaries: Inside the Nixon White House*, 239.
26. Willard J. Webb and Walter S. Poole, *The Joint Chiefs of Staff and the War in Vietnam, 1971–1973*, 4.
27. President's Deputy Assistant for National Security Affairs (Haig), memorandum for the President's file, subj.: Meeting between The President, Secretary Rogers, Secretary Laird, Admiral Moorer, Director Helms, and Dr. Kissinger, Washington, January 18, 1971, Document 104 in *FRUS, 1969–1976*, 7:275–86.

Chapter 4

1. Donn A. Starry, *Mounted Combat in Vietnam*, Vietnam Studies, 190–91.
2. Nguyen Duy Hinh, *Lam Son 719*, Indochina Monographs, 34.

3. XXIV Corps, AAR, LAM SON 719, 100.
4. Col. Arthur S. Pence, interview by 1st Lt. Thomas Turlenko, 6 May 1971, Vietnam Series, CMH; Keith William Nolan, *Into Laos: The Story of Dewey Canyon II/Lam Son 719, Vietnam 1971,* 109. Pence would later be relieved by Sutherland in a dispute over air support for the ARVN forces in Laos.
5. Lewis Sorley, *A Better War: The Unexamined Victories and Final Tragedy of America's Last Years in Vietnam,* 235.
6. Weekly Intelligence Estimate Update (WIEU), 30 Jan. 1971, in Lewis Sorley, ed., *Vietnam Chronicles: The Abrams Tapes 1968–1972,* 525.
7. Final Report: 101st Airborne Division Airmobile Operations in Support of Operation LAM SON 719, 8 Feb.–6 Apr. 1971, 2 vols., Camp Eagle, RVN, 1 May 1971, 1:7–8, RG 472, NARA.
8. Quote in Nolan, *Into Laos,* 104.
9. According to Nolan, *Into Laos,* 105, Khang, perhaps miffed that he was not placed in command of the operation, remained in Saigon and visited the Quang Tri headquarters only intermittently, leaving command of the Vietnamese Marines to his deputy commander, Col. Bui Thi Lan.
10. Bruce Palmer Jr., *The 25-Year War,* 110. Palmer served as vice chief of staff of the army from 1968 to 1973.
11. Central Intelligence Agency report, Analysis of Probable Reactions of Various Concerned Parties to a Possible Allied Action in South Laos, 21 Jan. 1971, NSC Files/Vietnam Subject Files, Nixon Library.
12. Henry Kissinger, *White House Years,* 998–99; Willard J. Webb and Walter S. Poole, *The Joint Chiefs of Staff and the War in Vietnam, 1971–1973,* 4.
13. Moorer to McCain and Abrams, message, 262124Z Jan. 1971, Abrams Papers, CMH; Webb and Poole, *Joint Chiefs of Staff, 1971–1973,* 5; Abrams to McCain, message, 27 Jan. 1971, subj.: Planning for Laos, Abrams Papers, CMH.
14. Webb and Poole, *Joint Chiefs of Staff, 1971–1973,* 447n11.
15. President's Deputy Assistant for National Security Affairs (Haig), memorandum for the President's file, subj.: Meeting of the President, Secretary of State Rogers, Secretary of Defense Laird, Director of CIA Helms, Chairman of JCS Moorer, Henry A. Kissinger, and Alexander M. Haig, Washington, January 27, 1971, Document 112 in *FRUS, 1969–1976,* 7:319–32.
16. McCain to Moorer, message, 192121Z Jan. 1971; Moorer to McCain, message, 262240Z Jan. 1971; Moorer to McCain and Abrams, message, 280125Z Jan. 1971, all in Abrams Papers, CMH.
17. President's Deputy Assistant for National Security Affairs (Haig), memorandum for the President's file, Subject: Meeting of the President, Secretary of State Rogers, Secretary of Defense Laird, Director of CIA Helms, Chairman of JCS Moorer, Henry A. Kissinger, and Alexander M. Haig, Washington, January 27, 1971, Document 112 in *FRUS, 1969–1976,* 7:319–32.
18. Ibid.; Henry Kissinger, *Ending the Vietnam War,* 196; Robert Dallek, *Nixon and Kissinger: Partners in Power,* 259.
19. Haig, memorandum for Kissinger, 1 Feb. 1971, subj.: Meeting with the Vice President, et al., 29 Jan. 1971, White House Central Files, Nixon Library; Kissinger, *White House Years,* 999–1000.
20. Kissinger, *White House Years,* 999–1000.
21. Memorandum for the record, subj.: Minutes of the WSAG Meeting, Washington, January 19, 1971, Document 105 in *FRUS, 1969–1976,* 7: 286–92.
22. President's Deputy Assistant for National Security Affairs (Haig), memorandum for the President's file, subj.: Meeting of the President, Secretary of State Rogers, Secretary of Defense Laird, Director of CIA Helms, Chair-

man of JCS Moorer, Henry A. Kissinger, and Alexander M. Haig, Washington, January 27, 1971, Document 112 in *FRUS, 1969–1976*, 7:319–32; Webb and Poole, *Joint Chiefs of Staff, 1971–1973*, 5; Kissinger, *White House Years*, 997–1000.

23. Alexander M. Haig Jr., *Inner Circles: How America Changed the World—A Memoir*, 273.

Chapter 5

1. Larry Berman, *Perfect Spy: The Incredible Double Life of Pham Xuan An, Time Magazine Reporter and Vietnamese Communist Agent*, 286; Thomas A. Bass, *The Spy Who Loved Us: The Vietnam War and Pham Xuan An's Dangerous Game*, 278.
2. Richard Pyle and Horst Faas, *Lost over Laos: A True Story of Tragedy, Mystery, and Friendship*, 99; Gen. Cao Van Vien and Lt. Gen. Dong Van Khuyen, *Reflections on the Vietnam War*, Indochina Monographs, 100–101; Headquarters, XXIV Corps, Senior Officer Debriefing Report: Lieutenant General James W. Sutherland, Jr., Commanding General, XXIV Corps (18 June 1970–9 June 1971), undated; H. R. Haldeman, *The Haldeman Diaries: Inside the Nixon White House*, 239.
3. "Tin sớm về cuộc "hành quân xa'" [Advance information about a 'distant operation'"], *Quan Doi Nhan Dan* [People's Army newspaper], 14 Mar. 2011, accessed 14 March 2011 at http://www.qdnd.vn/QDNDSite/vi-VN/89/70/79/79/79/141555/Default.aspx.
4. Col. Gen. Dong Si Nguyen with Duy Tuong and Ky Van, *Duong Xuyen Truong Son: Hoi Ky* [The road through the Annamite Mountains: A memoir], 181–83.
5. Col. Gen. Nguyen Huu An and Nguyen Tu Duong, *Chien Truong Moi: Hoi Uc* [New battlefield: A memoir], 107. Col. Gen. Nguyen Huu An was the commander of 308th Division before and during the fighting in Laos.
6. Military History Institute of Vietnam, *Victory in Vietnam: The Official History of the People's Army of Vietnam, 1954–1975*, trans. Merle L. Pribbenow, 272.
7. Nguyen Huu An and Nguyen Tu Duong, *Chien Truong Moi* [New battlefield], 104.
8. Pham Huy Thuong, Dang Ngoc Tinh, Le Moc, and Nguyen Van Dieu, *Su Doan Dong Bang (Binh Doan Tay Nguyen), Tap Ba* [The Lowlands Division (Central Highlands Corps), vol. 3], 100.
9. Each *binh tram* was a regimental-sized combat support unit with its own organic battalion-sized infantry, engineer, antiaircraft, transportation, and supply/administrative elements.
10. Military History Institute of Vietnam, *Victory in Vietnam*, 273.
11. WIEU, 6 Feb. 1971, in Lewis Sorley, ed., *Vietnam Chronicles: The Abrams Tapes, 1968–1972*, 529–30, states: "Our analysis indicated that the enemy is improving his defensive positions and is currently increasing his alert status in preparation for anticipated allied operations into his LOC [line of communication]. However, the widespread area of his preparations and the general nature of his communications indicate that he is still uncertain as to the time and location of friendly operations."
12. Nguyen Huu An and Nguyen Tu Dong, *Chien Truong Moi* [New battlefield], 106.
13. Vo Nguyen Giap, *Tổng Tập Luận Văn, Đại tướng Võ Nguyên Giáp* [Collected essays of Gen. Vo Nguyen Giap], 1143–77.
14. Pham Huy Thuong, Dang Ngoc Tinh, Le Moc, and Nguyen Van Dieu, *Su Doan Dong Bang* [The Lowlands Division], 111; *Su Doan 304, Tap II* [304th Division, vol. II], 160; *Su Doan 308 Quan Tien Phong* [308th 'Vanguard' Division], 222.

15. Lt. Gen. Nguyen Huy Chuong, Chỉ Một Con Đường [Only one road to take], Vietnamese Military History website, accessed 15 Mar. 2011 at http://www.quansuvn.net/index.php/topic,19999.0.html.

16. Military Region 4 Headquarters and the Current Affairs Committee of the MR-4 Party Committee (with the personal assistance of Maj. Gen. Tran Van An), *Quan Khu 4: Lich Su Khang Chien Chong My Cuu Nuoc, 1954–1975* [Military Region 4: History of the resistance against the Americans to save the nation, 1954–1975], 308.

17. *Su Doan 308 Quan Tien Phong* [The 308th 'Vanguard' Division], 223; Nguyen and Nguyen, *Chien Truong Moi: Hoi Uc* [New battlefield], 104 Once the campaign in Laos began, part of the 64th Regiment was attached to the 2nd Division.

18. Military Science Council, Armor Branch, *Lich Su Binh Chung Thiet Giap, Quan Doi Nhan Dan Viet Nam 1959–1975* [History of the Armor Branch, People's Army of Vietnam 1959–1975], 85.

19. Col. Gen. Dong Si Nguyen with Duy Tuong and Ky Van, *Duong Xuyen Truong Son* [The road through the Annamite Mountains], 181.

20. Lt. Gen. Hoang Nghia Khanh, *Đường Lên Cơ Quan Tổng Hành Dinh* [The road to the General Headquarters Staff], 140–42, 215; "Chiến dịch phản công Đường 9—Nam Lào (Kỳ 1)" [The Route 9–Southern Laos Counter-offensive (installment 1)], *Quan Doi Nhan Dan* [People's Army newspaper], Friday, 11 Feb. 2011, accessed 15 Feb. 2011 at http://www.qdnd.vn/QDNDSite/vi-VN/61/43/56/57/57/138304/Default.aspx. Pinpointing the actual date of the formation of the new headquarters is problematic. Various other Vietnamese accounts give different dates, ranging from 4 to 8 February 1971.

21. Merle Pribbenow, e-mail to the author, 5 Jan. 2012.

22. "Chiến dịch phản công Đường 9—Nam Lào (Kỳ 1)."

23. Ibid.; Military History Institute of Vietnam, *Chiến dịch phản công Đường 9—Nam Lào, 1971* [The Route 9–Southern Laos counteroffensive campaign, 1971], 21.

24. "Chiến dịch phản công Đường 9—Nam Lào (Kỳ 1)."

25. Military History Institute of Vietnam, *Victory in Vietnam*, 273; *Van Kien Dang, Toan Tap 31, 1970* [Collected party documents, vol. 31, 1970], 330; *Su Doan 304, Tap II* [304th Division, vol. II], 160; *Su Doan 308 Quan Tien Phong* [The 308th 'Vanguard' Division], 222; Pham, Dang, Le, and Nguyen, *Su Doan Dong Bang (Binh Doan Tay Nguyen), Tap Ba* [The Lowlands Division (Central Highlands Corps), vol. 3], 100; Vo Nguyen Giap, *Tổng Tập Luận Văn, Đại tướng Võ Nguyên Giáp* [Collected essays of Gen. Vo Nguyen Giap], 1172–73. There are several other sources that indicate that Hanoi was very concerned about a South Vietnamese attack into Military Region 4.

26. "Chiến dịch phản công Đường 9—Nam Lào (Kỳ 1)."

27. Military History Institute of Vietnam, *Victory in Vietnam*, 272–75; Ho Chi Minh National Political Studies Institute, Party History Institute, *Lịch Sử Biên Niên Xứ Ủy Nam Bộ và Trung Ương Cục Miền Nam, 1954–1975* [Historical chronicle of the Cochin China Party Committee and the Central Office for South Vietnam, 1954–1975], 833.

28. Military History Institute of Vietnam, *Chiến dịch phản công Đường 9–Nam Lào, Nam 1971* [The Route 9–Southern Laos Counteroffensive Campaign, 1971], 28, 30–31.

29. Nguyen Duy Hinh, *Lam Son 719*, Indochina Monographs, 164; Military History Institute of Vietnam, *Victory in Vietnam*, 274; Webb and Poole, *Joint Chiefs of Staff, 1971–1973*, 6.

30. Phillip B. Davidson, *Vietnam at War: The History, 1946–1975*, 579.

Chapter 6

1. Westmoreland to McCain, message, 29 Jan. 1971, Abrams Papers, CMH.
2. "News Blackout Continues in Indochina," *Washington Post*, 1 Feb. 1971; Terence Smith, "US B-52's Strike Foe's Laos Bases around the Clock," *New York Times*, 1 Feb. 1971; Terence Smith, "US Officials Say Allied Drive Is On in Area near Laos," *New York Times*, 2 Feb. 1971; Chalmers Roberts, "Laos Border Activities Still a Secret," *Washington Post*, 2 Feb. 1971; "Blindfolding the Public," *Chicago Daily News*, 3 Feb. 1971; "Some Daylight on the Blackout," *Washington Daily News*, 4 Feb. 1971; Ralph Blumenthal, "US News Blackout in Saigon Tried to Keep Even Its Existence Secret," *New York Times*, 5 Feb. 1971; Henry Kissinger, *White House Years*, 1000.
3. Sloniker, "History of Dewey Canyon II/Lam Son 719."
4. *CHECO Report—LAM SON 719*, 36; Bernard C. Nalty, *Air War over South Vietnam*, 253.
5. XXIV Corps, AAR, LAM SON 719, 6.
6. Willard J. Webb and Walter S. Poole, *The Joint Chiefs of Staff and the War in Vietnam, 1971–1973*, 5; Moorer to McCain, message 041600Z Feb. 1971, NSC Files/Vietnam Subject Files, Nixon Library; President's Assistant for National Security Affairs (Kissinger) to President Nixon, memorandum, subj.: Meeting between the President, Secretary Rogers, Secretary Laird, Director of CIA Helms, Chairman of the Joint Chiefs of Staff Moorer, Washington, February 2, 1971, Document 116 in *FRUS, 1969–1976*, 7:339–46.
7. Quote in Webb and Poole, *Joint Chiefs of Staff, 1971–1973*, 5; William M. Hammond, *Public Affairs: The Military and the Media, 1968–1973*, 423.
8. Dick Smyser, memorandum for Henry A. Kissinger, subj.: The Significance of the Special Operation, Feb. 6, 1971, NSC Files/Vietnam Subject Files, Nixon Library. Smyser was not the only dissenter. Undersecretary of State U. Alexis Johnson quietly surfaced objections during the discussions leading up to the president's decision, but to no avail. He later recalled, "The action was ill-conceived from the start. It required an unproven group of soldiers to strike at an objective that the enemy could defend stoutly in any region where it had superior logistics. I argued against the operation . . . but Nixon and Thieu ordered it." Ulysses Alexis Johnson and Jef Olivarius McAlister, *The Right Hand of Power*, 533.
9. Moorer to McCain and Abrams, message, 4 Feb. 1971, subj.: Press Guidance, Abrams Papers, CMH.
10. William M. Hammond, *Reporting Vietnam: Media and Military at War*, 237–38; Hammond, *Public Affairs*, chaps. 17–19.
11. Nguyen Duy Hinh, *Lam Son 719*, Indochina Monographs, 61–63; XXIV Corps, AAR, LAM SON 719, 8.
12. Keith William Nolan, *Into Laos: The Story of Dewey Canyon II/Lam Son 719, Vietnam 1971*, 89–90. The Americans were upset with ARVN convoy discipline and their "more casual outlook in war."
13. Nguyen Duy Hinh, *Lam Son 719*, 64. In *Spymaster: My Life in the CIA*, 244, former CIA station chief Ted Shackley claims that Thieu set the date for Lam Son 719 with his astrologer, but George J. Veith, *Black Sunday: The Fall of South Vietnam 1973–75*, 502*n*12, writes that Hoang Duc Nha, Thieu's cousin and close adviser, denied this when Veith interviewed him.
14. Pham Van Chung, Tran Ve, To Van Cap, Nguyen Kim Tien, Kieu Cong Cu, *Hai Mười Một Năm Chiến Trận của Binh Chủng Thủy Quân Lục Chiến Việt Nam (1954–1975)* [The Vietnamese Marine Corps' twenty-one years of warfare (1954–1975)], 232; "President Thieu's Message on Vietnamese Operations in Laos, February 8, 1971," *Vietnam Bulletin* 5, no. 7 (15 Feb. 1971), 2, 3.
15. Nolan, *Into Laos*, 112.

16. During the course of the operation, US Army aviators performed magnificently in a high-threat environment. For a more detailed account of their courage and valor, see Nolan, *Into Laos.*
17. Sloniker, "History of Dewey Canyon II/Lam Son 719."
18. Akihiko Okamura, "Crossroads at Tchepone," *Life*, 26 Mar. 1971.
19. Military History Institute of Vietnam, *Chiến dịch phản công Đường 9–Nam Lào, Nam 1971* [The Route 9–Southern Laos Counteroffensive Campaign, 1971], 70.
20. Military History Institute of Vietnam, *Victory in Vietnam: The Official History of the People's Army of Vietnam, 1954–1975*, 273.
21. *Su Doan 308 Quan Tien Phong* [The 308th 'Vanguard' Division], 224; Col. Gen. Nguyen Huu An and Nguyen Tu Duong, *Chien Truong Moi: Hoi Uc* [New battlefield: A memoir], 106; 2nd Division Party Committee and Division Headquarters, *Su Doan 2, Tap 1* [2nd Division, vol. 1], 153–54, 157; Lt. Gen. Nguyen Huy Chuong, Chỉ Một Con Đường [Only one road to take], Vietnamese Military History website, accessed 15 Mar. 2011 at http://www.quansuvn.net/index.php/topic,19999.0.html.
22. 2nd Division Party Committee and Division Headquarters, *Su Doan 2, Tap 1* [2nd Division, vol. 1], 156.
23. Military History Institute of Vietnam, *Chiến dịch phản công Đường 9–Nam Lào, Nam 1971* [The Route 9–Southern Laos Counteroffensive Campaign, 1971], 28; Col. Gen. Dong Si Nguyen with Duy Tuong and Ky Van, *Duong Xuyen Truong Son* [The road through the Annamite Mountains], 188.
24. Nguyen Duy Hinh, *Lam Son 719*, 69; Secretary of Defense to Dr. Kissinger, memorandum, subj.: Status Report on Operations in Laos and Cambodia, 10 Feb. 1971, NSC Files/Vietnam Subject Files, Nixon Library.
25. Graham A. Cosmas and Terrence P. Murray, *US Marines in Vietnam: Vietnamization and Redeployment, 1970–1971*, 207–9.

Chapter 7

1. Lewis Sorley, *A Better War: The Unexamined Victories and Final Tragedy of America's Last Years in Vietnam*, 247.
2. Bob Houdek to Henry A. Kissinger, memorandum, subj.: Latest Figures on Enemy Strength in Laos, 10 Feb. 1971, NSC Files/Vietnam Subject Files, Nixon Library; CIA, Directorate of Intelligence, 3 Mar. 1971, Intelligence Memorandum: Major Deployments of Communist Combat Units in South Laos, Southern North Vietnam and South Vietnam's Military Region since 1 February 1971, NSC Files/Vietnam Subject Files, Nixon Library.
3. Military History Institute of Vietnam, *Victory in Vietnam: The Official History of the People's Army of Vietnam, 1954–1975*, 274–75; *CHECO Report—LAM SON 719*, 48–50.
4. Abrams to Sutherland, message 131017Z Feb. 1971, Abrams Papers, CMH; Nguyen Duy Hinh, *Lam Son 719*, Indochina Monographs, 73; Phillip B. Davidson, *Vietnam at War: The History, 1946–1975*, 646; Sorley, *A Better War*, 247.
5. Henry Kissinger, *White House Years*, 1004; Nguyen Duy Hinh, *Lam Son 719*, 79. Nguyen Tien Hung and Jerold L. Schecter, *The Palace File*, 44, wrote, "Thieu insists he never gave such an order." However, the evidence suggests otherwise.
6. Sutherland to Abrams, message, 14 Feb. 1971, Abrams Papers, CMH.
7. Headquarters, XXIV Corps, After Action Report, LAM SON 719, C-12.
8. Abrams to Moorer, message, 141435Z Feb. 1971, Abrams Papers, CMH; Kissinger to the President, memorandum, 14 Feb. 1971, subj.: General

Abrams Report on Laos Operation, NSC Files/Vietnam Subject Files, Nixon Library.

9. Sloniker, "History of Dewey Canyon II/Lam Son 719."

10. Quote in George Weiss, "CO 2/17 AirCav: 'Gunships Took Tanks, Survived Flak' in Laos," *Armed Forces Journal*, 19 Apr. 1971, 22.

11. Roy R. Stephenson, "Road to Downfall: Lam Son 71/9 and US Airmobility Doctrine," PhD diss., University of Kansas, 1991, 156–57.

12. Sorley, *A Better War*, 250–53; Keith William Nolan, *Into Laos: The Story of Dewey Canyon II/Lam Son 719, Vietnam 1971*, 122–25

13. Headquarters, XXIV Corps, After Action Report, LAM SON 719, C-12.

14. Ho Chi Minh National Political Studies Institute, Party History Institute, *Lịch Sử Biên Niên Xứ Ủy Nam Bộ và Trung Ương Cục Miền Nam, 1954–1975* [Historical chronicle of the Cochin China party committee and the Central Office for South Vietnam, 1954–1975], 833.

15. Dave Richard Palmer, *Summons of the Trumpet*, 306.

16. "The World: Indochina: Tough Days on the Trail," *Time*, 8 Mar. 1971.

17. The pipeline was later determined to run from Vinh in North Vietnam through the Mu Gia Pass into southern Laos. The pipeline would play a significant role in further stretching the Nixon administration's credibility. At a 24 February press conference in the Pentagon, Secretary of Defense Laird and Gen. John W. Vogt of the Air Force displayed a three-foot section of the Russian-made pipe from Laos. However, it was leaked in the press that the pipe had not been taken by the ARVN during the attack into Laos, but rather had been seized earlier by special forces during clandestine cross-border operations, which had been long denied by the White House.

18. MACV Command History, 1971, 2: E-27.

19. Col. Gen. Nguyen Huu An and Nguyen Tu Duong, *Chien Truong Moi* [New battlefield], 114–20.

20. Nguyen Duy Hinh, *Lam Son 719*, 79; Abrams to Moorer and McCain, message, 221355Z Feb. 1971, NSC Files/Vietnam Subject Files, Nixon Library.

21. *Su Doan 308 Quan Tien Phong* [The 308th 'Vanguard' Division], 226.

22. Headquarters, 101st Airborne Division (Airmobile), memorandum for the record, subj.: Airmobile Operations in Support of Operation LAM SON 719, 20 Mar. 1971, RG 472, NARA II; David Fulghum and Terrence Maitland, *South Vietnam on Trial, Mid-1970 to 1972*, The Vietnam Experience, 76; 2nd Division Party Committee and Division Headquarters, *Su Doan 2, Tap 1* [2nd Division, vol. 1], 168.

23. Graham A. Cosmas and Terrence P. Murray, *US Marines in Vietnam: Vietnamization and Redeployment, 1970–1971*, 203.

24. Abrams to McCain, message, 201215Z Feb. 1971, Abrams Papers, CMH.

25. Bernard C. Nalty, *Air War over South Vietnam, 1968–1975*, 261.

26. Nolan, *Into Laos*, 134.

27. Ibid., 128–29, 134–37. After the action, Fujii was awarded the Distinguished Service Cross for his courage under fire.

28. Fulghum and Maitland, *South Vietnam on Trial*, 78.

29. MACV Command History, 1971, 2: E-27; Fulghum and Maitland, *South Vietnam on Trial*, 78–79.

30. Craig Whitney, "Saigon's Rangers Driven from an Outpost in Laos," *New York Times*, 22 Feb. 1971; "Hanoi Troops Attack," *Washington Post*, 21 Feb. 1971.

31. Quoted in Fulghum and Maitland, *South Vietnam on Trial*, 79–80.

32. *CHECO Report—LAM SON 719*, 52.
33. Abrams to Moorer and McCain, message, 21 Feb. 1971, Abrams Papers, CMH; McCain to Abrams, message, 23 Feb. 1971, subj.: LAM SON 719, Abrams Papers, CMH.
34. Transcript of a telephone conversation between President Nixon and the Chairman of the Joint Chiefs of Staff (Moorer), Washington, February 22, 1971, Document 134 in *FRUS, 1969–1976*, 7:411–15.
35. Quote in William M. Hammond, *Public Affairs: The Military and the Media, 1968–1973*, 451–52; Willard J. Webb and Walter S. Poole, *The Joint Chiefs of Staff and the War in Vietnam, 1971–1973*, 8.
36. Kissinger, *White House Years*, 1004.
37. Alexander M. Haig to the President, memorandum, subj.: The President's Meeting with Admiral Moorer and Henry A. Kissinger, Feb. 25, 1971, NSC Files/Alexander M. Haig Chronological Files, Nixon Library.
38. Abrams to Moorer and McCain, message, 221355Z Feb. 1971, Abrams Papers, CMH; Quote in Webb and Poole, *Joint Chiefs of Staff, 1971-1973*, 8.
39. Webb and Poole, *Joint Chiefs of Staff, 1971–1973*, 8–9.
40. Headquarters, US Army Advisory Group, 1st Infantry Division (ARVN), Combat Operation After Action Feeder Report, Lam Son 719, 13 Mar. 1971, RG 472, NARA II.
41. Sloniker, "History of Dewey Canyon II/Lam Son 719." The gun platoon, known as the Jokers, lost four pilots MIA, two pilots KIA, and one door gunner KIA and three more MIA during the operation in Laos.
42. Sutherland to McCaffey, message, 231600Z Feb. 1971, Abrams Papers, CMH.
43. Sorley, *A Better War*, 251–53; WIEU, 24 Feb. 1971, in Lewis Sorley, ed., *Vietnam Chronicles: The Abrams Tapes, 1968–1972*, 544–46.
44. Nguyen Duy Hinh, *Lam Son 719*, 81.
45. WIEU, 24 Feb. 1971, in Sorley, *Vietnam Chronicles*, 544; "The Death of a Fighting General," *Time*, 8 Mar. 1971, 21.
46. Nolan, *Into Laos*, 139.
47. Nguyen Duy Hinh, *Lam Son 719*, 80.
48. Ibid., 82. This supports the earlier discussion that the North Vietnamese high command were concerned about a South Vietnamese move into Laos along Route 9 but did not know the exact timing of any planned ARVN operation.
49. Fulghum and Maitland, *South Vietnam on Trial*, 82.
50. Ibid., 82–83.
51. Ibid. Donn A. Starry, *Mounted Combat in Vietnam*, Vietnam Studies, 192; Headquarters, USARV, 17th MHD, interview with Col. James B. Vaught, Senior Advisor, ARVN Airborne Division, 20 May 1971, RG 472, NARA. Battreall was officially the senior advisor, RVNAF Armor Command in Saigon. Vaught, who took over as senior advisor on 2 March, later credited a lot of the confusion to the fact that the airborne and armor forces had never before worked together, and "the result was that of poor coordination."
52. Military Science Council, Armor Branch, *Lich Su Binh Chung Thiet Giap, Quan Doi Nhan Dan Viet Nam, 1959–1975* [History of the Armor Branch, People's Army of Vietnam, 1959–1975], 88; Col. Gen. Nguyen Huu An and Nguyen Tu Duong, *Chien Truong Moi* [New battlefield], 126.
53. *CHECO Report—LAM SON 719*, 57–69; Nalty, *Air War over South Vietnam*, 262–63.

54. Nguyen Cong Luan, *Nationalist in the Viet Nam War: Memoirs of a Victim Turned Soldier*, 387.
55. Quote in Fulghum and Maitland, *South Vietnam on Trial*, 83.
56. "Trận đánh trên đồi Không Tên" [The Battle of No Name Hill"], *Quan Doi Nhan Dan* [People's Army Newspaper], 18 Mar. 2011, accessed 19 Mar. 2011 at http://www.qdnd.vn/QDNDSite/vi-VN/89/70/78/78/78/142038/Default.aspx; "Trung Tướng Nguyễn Ân và ký ức về trận đánh 40 năm trước" [Lieutenant General Nguyen An and his memories of a battle fought 40 years ago], *Quan Doi Nhan Dan* [People's Army Newspaper], 20 Mar. 2011, accessed 21 Mar. 2011 at http://www.qdnd.vn/QDNDSite/vi-VN/61/43/296/296/296/142282/Default.aspx; Nguyen Duy Hinh, *Lam Son 719*, 85n6.
57. Col. Gen. Nguyen Huu An and Nguyen Tu Duong, *Chien Truong Moi* [New battlefield], 126.
58. Cosmas and Murray, *Marines in Vietnam, 1970–1971*, 200.
59. Quote in William M. Hammond, *Reporting Vietnam: Media and Military at War*, 248.
60. William P. Head, *Shadow and Stinger: Developing the AC-119G/K Gunships in the Vietnam War*, 232. During the fighting in Laos, AC-119 gunships reported twenty-four enemy tanks destroyed during the course of thirty-nine missions.
61. Sutherland to Abrams, message, 021420Z Mar. 1971, Abrams Papers, CMH. By that time Sutherland had also lost confidence in Dong's senior advisor, Colonel Pence, who had lodged a complaint about the handling of tactical air support during the fall of FSB 31. He was relieved as adviser to the ARVN airborne and replaced by Col. Benjamin Harrison, who also served as senior adviser to the 1st ARVN Division.
62. XXIV Corps, AAR, LAM SON 719, 31.
63. Ibid., 42.
64. Sutherland to Abrams, message, 040740Z Mar. 1971, Abrams Papers, CMH.
65. Cosmas and Murray, *Marines in Vietnam, 1970–1971*, 204.
66. Sutherland to Abrams, message, 040952Z Mar. 1971, Abrams Papers, CMH; Headquarters, US Army Combat Assistance Team, First Division (ARVN), Advisory Team 3, Combat Operations After Action Report—LAM SON 719, 13–14, RG 472, NARA.
67. Jonathan Bernstein, *US Army AH-1 Cobra Units in Vietnam*, 73.
68. "LAM SON 719," http://www.militaryimages.net/forums/sowthread.php?t=9746, accessed 29 October 2010.
69. US Marine Corps Historical Center, *Vietnam Revisited: Conversation with William Broyles, Jr.*, 27.
70. "'Laos Drive on Schedule,' Laird Says," *Washington Post*, 9 Mar. 1971.
71. Quote in Dale Van Atta, *With Honor: Melvin Laird in War, Peace, and Politics*, 349.
72. Hammond, *Reporting Vietnam*, 249.
73. WIEU, 24 Feb. 1971, in Sorley, *Vietnam Chronicles*, 543.
74. Lieutenant General Knowles, memorandum for the record, JCS Meeting, 1430, Wednesday, 24 Feb. 1971, Abrams Papers, CMH.
75. Kissinger, *White House Years*, 1005; Webb and Poole, *Joint Chiefs of Staff, 1971–1973*, 9.
76. Kissinger, memorandum for the President, subj.: Southeast Asia Operational Status, 26 Feb. 1971, NSC Files/Vietnam Subject Files, Nixon Library.

Chapter 8

1. Quote in Lewis Sorley, *A Better War: The Unexamined Victories and Final Tragedy of America's Last Years in Vietnam*, 250.
2. In fact, North Vietnamese radio had boasted that the battle for Tchepone would be the second Dien Bien Phu.
3. Nguyen Duy Hinh, *Lam Son 719*, Indochina Monographs, 89.
4. Kissinger to Bunker, message, 1 Mar. 1971, NSC Files/Vietnam Subject Files, Nixon Library; Willard J. Webb and Walter S. Poole, *The Joint Chiefs of Staff and the War in Vietnam, 1971–1973*, 11; Henry Kissinger, *White House Years*, 1006–7.
5. *CHECO Report—LAM SON 719*, 28; Nguyen Duy Hinh, *Lam Son 719*, 91.
6. Graham A. Cosmas and Terrence P. Murray, *US Marines in Vietnam: Vietnamization and Redeployment, 1970–1971*, 204.
7. Bruce Palmer Jr., *The 25-Year War*, 112.
8. Nguyen Duy Hinh, *Lam Son 719*, 95.
9. Capt. James E. Fulbrook, "Part I: Prelude to Air Assault," *US Army Aviation Digest*, June 1986, 3; quote in Keith William Nolan, *Into Laos: The Story of Dewey Canyon II/Lam Son 719, Vietnam 1971*, 260; Brig. Gen. Sidney Berry, "LAM SON 719—The Assault into Laos 8 February–6 April 1971," undated, Abrams Papers, CMH.
10. Sloniker, "History of Dewey Canyon II/Lam Son 719";
11. Quote in David Fulghum and Terrence Maitland, *South Vietnam on Trial, Mid-1970 to 1972*, The Vietnam Experience, 85.
12. *CHECO Report—LAM SON 719*, 62.
13. Capt. James E. Fulbrook, "Part II: The Battle," *US Army Aviation Digest*, July 1978, 41.
14. Kissinger, memorandum for the President, 4 Mar. 1971, subj.: Situation Report from General Abrams, NSC Files/Vietnam Subject Files, Nixon Library; Webb and Poole, *Joint Chiefs of Staff, 1971–1973*, 11; Richard M. Nixon, *Public Papers of the Presidents: Richard M. Nixon, 1971*, 387.
15. Sloniker, "History of Dewey Canyon II/Lam Son 719."
16. Secretary of Defense, memorandum for Dr. Kissinger, subj.: Status Report on Operations in Laos and Cambodia, 5 Mar. 1971, NSC Files/Vietnam Subject Files, Nixon Library; XXIV Corps, AAR, LAM SON 719, 47; *CHECO Report—LAM SON 719*, 64.
17. Military History Institute of Vietnam, *Chiến dịch phản công Đường 9–Nam Lào, Nam 1971* [The Route 9–Southern Laos counteroffensive campaign, 1971], 57. The official history admits "that we [the NVA] did not detect and move quickly enough to attack and destroy the enemy troops who landed at Tchepone."
18. Fulbrook, "Part II: The Battle," 42.
19. *CHECO Report—LAM SON 719*, 7, 13, 92–93. The BLU-82 was nicknamed the daisy cutter and was usually used to clear an area for a landing zone.
20. Ibid., 65–66.
21. Alvin Shuster, "Laos Battle in Crucial Phase with Outcome Uncertain," *New York Times*, 7 Mar. 1971; Michael Parks, "It's Up To Saigon's Army (with a Little Help from US)," *Baltimore Sun*, 7 Mar. 1971.
22. Tom Marshall, *The Price of Exit*, 227–28.
23. Military History Institute of Vietnam, *Chiến dịch phản công Đường 9–Nam Lào, Nam 1971* [The Route 9–Southern Laos Counteroffensive Campaign, 1971], 71; quote in *Su Doan 304, Tap II* [304th Division, vol. II], 163.
24. Donn A. Starry, *Mounted Combat in Vietnam*, Vietnam Studies, 195.

25. Abrams to McCain and Moorer, message, 8 Mar. 1971, Abrams Papers, CMH; Webb and Poole, *Joint Chiefs of Staff, 1971–1973*, 11.
26. Kissinger to Bunker, message, 9 Mar. 1971, NSC Files, Nixon Library.
27. Sutherland to Abrams, message, 100850Z Mar. 1971; Abrams to McCain, message, 091232Z Mar. 1971, Abrams Papers, CMH.
28. Abrams to Moorer, message, 140425Z Mar. 1971, Abrams Papers, CMH.
29. Palmer, *The 25-Year War*, 112.
30. President's Assistant for National Security Affairs (Kissinger) to the Ambassador to Vietnam (Bunker), backchannel message, Washington, DC, March 9, 1971, Document 147 in *FRUS, 1969–1976*, 7:450.
31. William M. Hammond, *Public Affairs: The Military and the Media, 1968–1973*, 466–67; quote in Nguyen Duy Hinh, *Lam Son 719*, 103.

Chapter 9

1. Headquarters, 101st Airborne Division (Airmobile), Final Report: Airmobile Operations in Support of Operation LAMSON 719, 24 April 1971, 1: I-12, RG 472, NARA II; Military History Institute of Vietnam, *Victory in Vietnam: The Official History of the People's Army of Vietnam, 1954–1975*, 272–75.
2. Memorandum of briefing, Participants: Henry A. Kissinger, General Haig, and Colonel Martin (briefer), subj.: Laos/Cambodia Briefing, 11 Mar. 1971, Alexander M. Haig Chronological Files, Nixon Library.
3. Willard J. Webb and Walter S. Poole, *The Joint Chiefs of Staff and the War in Vietnam, 1971–1973*, 13.
4. Ambassador to Vietnam (Bunker) to the President's Assistant for National Security Affairs (Kissinger), backchannel message, Saigon, March 12, 1971, Document 149 in *FRUS, 1969–1976*, 7:452–53.
5. Keith William Nolan, *Into Laos: The Story of Dewey Canyon II/Lam Son 719, Vietnam 1971*, 273–74.
6. Quotes in Webb and Poole, *Joint Chiefs of Staff, 1971–1973*, 12.
7. Abrams to McCain, message, 171045Z Mar. 1971, Abrams Papers, CMH; Moorer to McCain and Abrams, message, 172317Z Mar. 1971, Abrams Papers, CMH.
8. *CHECO Report—LAM SON 719*, 70.
9. Sloniker, "History of Dewey Canyon II/Lam Son 719."
10. "Keith A. Brandt, Captain, United States Army," Arlington National Cemetery Website, http://www.arlingtoncemetery.net/kabrandt.htm. In January 1990 the crash site was excavated by a joint US/Lao team from Joint Task Force Full Accounting; the remains of both Brandt and Boffman were recovered and buried in Arlington Cemetery.
11. Nguyen Duy Hinh, *Lam Son 719*, Indochina Monographs, 108; *CHECO Report—LAM SON 719*, 119.
12. Quote in Nolan, *Into Laos*, 281.
13. "Viet Forces in Laos Said to Retreat," *Washington Post*, 18 Mar. 1971.
14. Howe, memorandum for Kissinger, 24 Mar. 1971, subj.: White House View of Laotian Planning (February 8–March 20), NSC Files, Nixon Library.
15. *Lịch sử sư đoàn bộ binh 324, 1955–2005* [History of the 324th Infantry Division, 1955–2005], 33, 35–36, accessed 19 October 2009 at http://www.quansuvn.net/index.php?topic=103.0; Nguyen Duy Hinh, *Lam Son 719*, 109, references the 803rd , 812th, and 29th Regiments of the 324B Division. These were the old designations of the regiments during the time of the 324A Division, which was disbanded in 1966. After the division was reformed in 1969, the regiments were renumbered as the 1st, 2nd, and

3rd. In spite of the official redesignation, soldiers of the division often used the old designations for the regiments rather than the new ones, which created a lot of confusion and led to the use of the earlier designations in reports, etc.

16. *CHECO Report—LAM SON 719*, 71.
17. Sutherland to Abrams, message, 181425Z Mar. 1971, Abrams Papers, CMH.
18. *CHECO Report—LAM SON 719*, 8.
19. Nguyen Duy Hinh, *Lam Son 719*, 113.
20. Quote in David Fulghum and Terrence Maitland, *South Vietnam on Trial, Mid-1970 to 1972*, The Vietnam Experience, 90.
21. Quote in Webb and Poole, *Joint Chiefs of Staff, 1971–1973*, 13.
22. Henry Kissinger, memorandum for the President, subj.: Situation in Laos, March 19, 1971, NSC Files/Vietnam Subject Files, Nixon Library; General Haig to Henry A. Kissinger, memorandum, 19 Mar. 1971, NSC Files/Alexander M. Haig Chronological Files, Nixon Library.
23. Kissinger to Bunker, message, 18 Mar. 1971, NSC Files/Vietnam Subject Files, Nixon Library; President's Assistant for National Security Affairs (Kissinger) to the Ambassador to Vietnam (Bunker), backchannel message, Washington, DC, March 18, 1971, Document 156 in *FRUS, 1969–1976*, 7:467.
24. Nguyen Duy Hinh, *Lam Son 719*, 109.
25. Abrams to Moorer and McCain, message, 191325Z Mar. 1971, Abrams Papers, CMH; quote in Webb and Poole, *Joint Chiefs of Staff, 1971–1973*, 13.
26. President's Deputy Assistant for National Security Affairs (Haig) to the President's Assistant for National Security Affairs (Kissinger), backchannel message, Saigon, March 19, 1971, Document 158 in *FRUS, 1969–1976*, 7:475–77; Webb and Poole, *Joint Chiefs of Staff, 1971–1973*, 13.
27. Military History Institute of Vietnam, *Chiến dịch phản công Đường 9–Nam Lào, Nam 1971* [The Route 9–Southern Laos counteroffensive campaign, 1971], 57.
28. As previously stated, the remains of Barker and his crew were recovered in 2005 and returned to the United States for burial.
29. *CHECO Report—LAM SON 719*, 71. Tran Ngoc Hue's story is told in detail in Andrew Wiest, *Vietnam's Forgotten Army: Heroism and Betrayal in the ARVN*; the NVA version of the capture is found in 2nd Division Party Committee and Division Headquarters, *Su Doan 2, Tap 1* [2nd Division, vol. 1], 172. Lieutenant Colonel Hue was promoted on the spot for his role in occupying Tchepone.
30. "Wounded GI Tells of 13-Day Ordeal," *Pacific Stars & Stripes*, 4 Apr. 1971.
31. Quote in Roy R. Stephenson, "Road to Downfall: LAM SON 71/9 and US Airmobility Doctrine." PhD diss., University of Kansas, 1991, 228.
32. Col. Gen. Nguyen Huu An and Nguyen Tu Duong, *Chien Truong Moi: Hoi Uc* [New battlefield: A memoir], 138.
33. Fulghum and Maitland, *South Vietnam on Trial*, 93.
34. Ibid., 90.
35. Nguyen Duy Hinh, *Lam Son 719*, 118.
36. Col. Hoang Tich Thong, "LAM SON 719 Operation," http://www.vnafmamn.com/lamson_719.html, accessed 29 Oct. 2010.
37. Quotes in Nolan, *Into Laos*, 345.
38. Quote in Fulghum and Maitland, *South Vietnam on Trial*, 87.
39. Ibid.
40. Quote in Nolan, *Into Laos*, 347–48.

41. Col. Hoang Tich Thong, "LAM SON 719 Operation," http://www.vnafmamn.com/lamson_719.html, accessed 29 Oct. 2010; Graham A. Cosmas and Terrence P. Murray, *US Marines in Vietnam: Vietnamization and Redeployment, 1970–1971*, 378.
42. Sutherland to Abrams, message, 250430Z Feb. 1971, Abrams Papers, CMH; Nguyen Duy Hinh, *Lam Son 719*, 151.
43. MACV Command History, 1971, 2: E-33.
44. Sp4 Michael J. Fitzmaurice, Troop D, 2nd Squadron, 17th Cavalry, later rreceived the Medal of Honor for his actions during the sapper attack at Khe Sanh.
45. Nguyen Duy Hinh, *Lam Son 719*, 122.
46. Sutherland to Abrams, message, 290600Z Mar. 1971, Abrams Papers, CMH; Nguyen Duy Hinh, *Lam Son 719*, 122.
47. Quote in Webb and Poole, *Joint Chiefs of Staff, 1971–1973*, 14.
48. Sutherland to Abrams, message, 311418Z Feb. 1971, Abrams Papers, CMH.
49. MACV Command History, 1971, 2: E-5–E-13; Ha Mai Viet, *Steel and Blood: South Vietnamese Armor and the War for Southeast Asia*, 56–67.

Chapter 10

1. Military History Institute of Vietnam, *Victory in Vietnam: The Official History of the People's Army of Vietnam, 1954–1975*, 277.
2. "Chiến dịch phản công Đường 9–Nam Lào (Kỳ 3)" [The Route 9–Southern Laos Counteroffensive (Final Installment)], *Quan Doi Nhan Dan* [People's Army newspaper], 11 Feb. 2011, accessed 15 Feb. 2011 at http://www.qdnd.vn/QDNDSite/vi-VN/61/43/56/57/57/138304/Default.aspx. These figures are obviously a gross exaggeration.
3. Military History Institute of Vietnam, *Victory in Vietnam*, 277–78.
4. Col. Gen. Nguyen Huu An and Nguyen Tu Duong, *Chien Truong Moi: Hoi Uc* [New battlefield: A memoir], 138–39.
5. Thieu quote in David Fulghum and Terrence Maitland, *South Vietnam on Trial: Mid-1970 to 1972*, The Vietnam Experience, 90; Richard M. Nixon, *Public Papers of the Presidents of the United States: Richard M. Nixon, 1971*, 160.
6. WIEU, 18 Mar. 1971, in Sorley, ed., *Vietnam Chronicles: The Abrams Tapes, 1968–1972*, 563–64.
7. Kissinger, memorandum for the President, 21 Mar. 1971, subj.: General Abrams Remarks to the Press on LAM SON 719, NSC/Vietnam Subject Files, Nixon Library.
8. Nixon, *Public Papers, 1971*, 450–52.
9. Richard M. Nixon, *RN: The Memoirs of Richard Nixon*, 499.
10. Abrams to McCain, message, subj.: Assessment of the Effects of Operation LAM SON 719 and TOAN THANG 01-71, 22 Mar. 1971, NSC/Vietnam Subject Files, Nixon Library.
11. Kissinger, memorandum for the President, 22 Mar. 1971, subj.: Assessment by General Abrams, NSC Files, Nixon Library.
12. Phil Odeen, memorandum for the record, 25 Mar. 1971, Vietnamization Meeting with Secretary Laird, Thomas Thayer Papers, CMH.
13. Henry Kissinger, *White House Years*, 992, 1002.
14. Quote in Willard J. Webb and Walter S. Poole, *The Joint Chiefs of Staff and the War in Vietnam, 1971–1973*, 15.
15. Kissinger to Nixon, memorandum, 22 Mar. 1971, NSC/Country Files, Nixon Library.

16. "Retreat from Laos," *Life*, 2 Apr. 1971, 24. The most comprehensive study of the Nixon administration's confrontation with the US news media over the conduct and meaning of Lam Son 719 can be found in William M. Hammond, *Public Affairs: The Military and the Media, 1968–1973*, 401–92.
17. James McCartney, "S. Vietnamese 'Succeed' by Backing Away," *Philadelphia Enquirer*, 18 Mar. 1971.
18. "Hanoi Supplies Still Moving," *Cleveland Plain Dealer*, 12 Apr. 1971; John Saar, "An Ignominious and Disorderly Retreat," *Life*, 2 Apr. 1971, 28; "'Hacking' It in Laos," *Philadelphia Bulletin*, 23 Mar. 1971.
19. LAM SON 719 Talking Points, 19 Apr. 1971, NSC Files/Vietnam Subject Files, Nixon Library.
20. "Assessing the Laos Invasion," *Newsweek*, 5 Apr. 1971, 25–26. The NVA claimed 16,400 allies killed, including 200 Americans.
21. XXIV Corps, AAR, LAM SON 719, 90; *CHECO Report—LAM SON 719*, 123; Graham A. Cosmas, *MACV: The Joint Command in the Years of Withdrawal, 1968–1973*, 335; Phillip B. Davidson, *Vietnam at War: The History, 1946–1975*, 585. MACV Command History, 1971, 2: E-39, indicates 102 US helicopters lost during Lam Son 719, but several 101st Airborne Division (Airmobile) documents reflect 107 helicopters were lost to hostile fire during the operation. Lt. Gen. (ret.) Sidney Berry, assistant division commander of the 101st, who was the aviation support coordinator for the entire operation in 1971, confirmed this number in a letter to the editor of the *Washington Post*, 18 May 1995.
22. Kissinger, memorandum for the President, 22 Mar. 1971, subj.: Assessment by General Abrams, NSC Files, Nixon Library; XXIV Corps, AAR, LAM SON 719, 91; Nguyen Duy Hinh, Lam Son 719, Indochina Monographs, 128, 131–32. XXIV Corps AAR acknowledges that there was some difference in numbers between the US reports and those by the ARVN.
23. MACV Command History, 1971, 2: E-33–35.
24. Sutherland to Abrams, message, 251155Z Mar. 1971, subj.: Periodic Appraisal of the Progress of LAM SON 719 for the Period 180000H Feb 71 to 242400H Mar 71, Abrams Papers, CMH; XXIV Corps, AAR, LAM SON 719, 69.
25. Sutherland to Abrams, message, 040740Z Mar. 1971, subj.: Periodic Appraisal of the Progress of LAM SON 719 for the Period 250000H Feb 71 to 032400H Mar 71, Abrams Papers, CMH.
26. Nixon quote in Fulghum and Maitland, *South Vietnam on Trial*, 91.
27. Michael Martin, *Angels in Red Hats: Paratroopers of the Second Indochina War*, 19; Sutherland to Abrams, message, 021420Z Mar. 1971, Abrams Papers, CMH.
28. George Donelson Moss, *Vietnam: An American Ordeal*, 304.
29. XXIV Corps, "An Assessment of the Performance of South Vietnamese Forces during Operation LAM SON 719 (30 January–6 April 1971)," undated staff study, 1971, 13, RG 472, NARA; Headquarters, Naval Advisory Group, Office of the Senior Marine Advisor, subj.: Combat Operations After Action Report LAM SON 719, 21 March 1971, 6, RG 472, NARA.
30. Memorandum for the record, Briefing of 22 Mar. 1971 (Kissinger, Zais, Haig, Lieutenant Colonel Martin, David R. Young), NSC Files/Vietnam Subject Files, Nixon Library; Jaco quote in Andrew Wiest, *Vietnam's Forgotten Army: Heroism and Betrayal in the ARVN*, 210.
31. Nguyen Duy Hinh, *Lam Son 719*, 158.
32. Bruce Palmer Jr., *The 25-Year War*, 109; Keith William Nolan, *Into Laos: The Story of Dewey Canyon II/Lam Son 719, Vietnam 1971*, 104.
33. Quotes in Fulghum and Maitland, *South Vietnam on Trial*, 72, 91.

34. Battreall quote in Lewis Sorley, *A Better War: The Unexamined Victories and Final Tragedy of America's Last Years in Vietnam*, 257; Abrams to Sutherland, message (MAC 02079), 27 Feb. 1971, Sutherland Papers, MHI.
35. Nguyen Duy Hinh, *Lam Son 719*, 159.
36. Battreall quote in Nolan, *Into Laos*, 119.
37. Wiest, *Vietnam's Forgotten Army*, 209.
38. Battreall quote in Nolan, *Into Laos*, 119; Davidson, *Vietnam at War*, 655.
39. Wiest, *Vietnam's Forgotten Army*, 201; Nguyen Duy Hinh, *Lam Son 719*, 157.
40. XXIV Corps, AAR, LAM SON 719, 100; Sutherland to Abrams, message, 100715Z Mar. 1971, Abrams Papers, CMH.
41. Maj. Kenneth C. Fogelquist, G3 Advisor, ARVN Airborne Division, transcript of interview, 19 May 1971, RG 472, NARA.
42. Gen. Cao Van Vien and Lt. Gen. Dong Van Khuyen, *Reflections on the Vietnam War*, Indochina Monographs, 102.
43. Nixon, *Public Papers, 1971*, 523; Westmoreland quote in Nolan, *Into Laos*, 360.
44. Graham A. Cosmas and Terrence P. Murray, *US Marines in Vietnam: Vietnamization and Redeployment, 1970–1971*, 199.
45. Sutherland to Abrams, message, 281110Z Mar. 1971, Abrams Papers, CMH.
46. John J. Tolson, *Vietnam Studies: Air Mobility, 1961–1971*, 251–52; Wiest, *Vietnam's Forgotten Army*, 211.
47. *CHECO Report—LAM SON 719*, 13–14; Headquarters, USMACV, Command History, 1971, 2: E-37; Sutherland to Abrams, message, 251155Z Mar. 1971, subj.: Periodic Appraisal of the Progress of LAM SON 719 for the Period 180000H Mar 71 to 242400H Mar 71, Abrams Papers, CMH.
48. Ronald D. Merrell, *Tactical Airlift in SEA*, 52–53, 61.
49. Abrams to McCain, message, 230100Z Mar. 1971, Abrams Papers, CMH.
50. Quote in Fulghum and Maitland, *South Vietnam on Trial*, 90.
51. Both quotes in Wiest, *Vietnam's Forgotten Army*, 226.
52. Gloria Emerson, "Spirit of Saigon's Army Shaken in Laos," *New York Times*, 28 Mar. 1971, 1, 4.
53. Nguyen Duy Hinh, *Lam Son 719*, 140.
54. Nolan, *Into Laos*, 360.
55. Headquarters, XXIV Corps, An Assessment of the Performance of South Vietnamese Forces during Operation LAM SON 719 (30 January–6 April 1971), Undated, 2–7, RG 472, NARA; CIA report quoted in Gen. Bruce Palmer Jr., "US Intelligence and Vietnam," *Studies in Intelligence* 28, special edition (1984): 90.
56. Sutherland to Abrams, message, 211040Z Mar. 1971, Abrams Papers, CMH.
57. Headquarters, XXIV Corps, Debriefing Report: Lieutenant General James W. Sutherland, Jr., Commanding General, XXIV Corps (18 June 1970–9 June 1971), RG 472, NARA II.
58. Nixon, *Public Papers, 1971*, 523–26.
59. Nguyen Duy Hinh, *Vietnamization and the Cease-Fire*, Indochina Monographs, 68.
60. Davidson, *Vietnam at War*, 588, 651–52.
61. Kissinger to Bunker, message, 18 Mar. 1971, NSC Files/Haig Special Files, Nixon Library.
62. Oval Office Conversation 472–13, Nixon, Kissinger, Haldeman, 12:16–1:07 P.M., 23 Mar. 1971, White House Tapes, Nixon Library; H. R. Haldeman, *The Haldeman Diaries: Inside the White House*, 313.

63. Alexander M. Haig Jr., *Inner Circles: How America Changed the World—A Memoir*, 273–78; Haldeman, *Haldeman Diaries*, 313; Sorley, *A Better War*, 442n11. In *Ending the Vietnam War*, 199, Kissinger writes "General Abrams was one of the ablest soldiers, greatest patriots, and finest human beings it has been my privilege to meet." In fact, he dedicated *Ending the Vietnam War* to Abrams and Bunker. Nevertheless, the evidence is clear that he and the president were very unhappy with Abrams in 1971 because of the outcome of the Laotian operation.
64. Transcript, Presidential Recordings Program, Conversation between Richard Nixon and Henry Kissinger, 6 Apr. 1971, accessed 15 Jan. 2012 at http://whitehousetapes.net/transcript/nixon/001–004; White House views on MACV shortcomings in Kissinger, *Ending the Vietnam War*, 199, and Hammond, *Public Affairs*, 489.
65. Howe, memorandum for Kissinger, 24 Mar. 1971, subj.: White House View of Laotian Planning (February 8–March 20), NSC Files, Nixon Library.
66. Quote in Dale Andradé, *America's Last Vietnam Battle: Halting Hanoi's 1972 Easter Offensive*, 3.
67. Webb and Poole, *Joint Chiefs of Staff, 1971–1973*, 16.
68. Conversation between President Nixon and His Assistant for National Security Affairs (Kissinger), Washington, June 7, 1971, Document 211 in *FRUS, 1969–1976*, 7:674.
69. Quote in Graham A. Cosmas, *MACV: The Joint Command in the Years of Withdrawal, 1968–1973*, 338.
70. Phillip A. Odeen, memorandum, 25 Mar. 1971, subj.: Vietnamization Meeting with Secretary Laird, Thayer Papers, CMH.
71. Stephen Randolph, *Powerful and Brutal Weapons: Nixon, Kissinger, and the Easter Offensive*, 15.
72. Louis Harris poll, 3 May 1971, White House Subject Files/Haldeman Files, Nixon Library.
73. Stanley Karnow, *Vietnam—A History*, 3rd ed., 646.
74. Moss, *Vietnam: American Ordeal*, 305.
75. Quote in Fulghum and Maitland, *South Vietnam on Trial*, 90.

Chapter 11

1. Henry Kissinger to the Honorable Carl Albert, memorandum, 29 Mar. 1971, NSC Files/Vietnam Subject Files, Nixon Library.
2. MACV Command History, 1971, 1: VIII-42–43.
3. Abrams to Major Subordinates, message, 18 Apr. 1971, Abrams Papers, CMH; Abrams to Major Subordinates, message, 300448Z Nov. 1971, subj.: VNAF/RVNAF Helicopter Operations, Abrams Papers, CMH.
4. Phillip B. Davidson, *Vietnam at War: The History, 1946–1975*, 594.
5. Abrams to Major Subordinates, message, 050611Z July 1971, Abrams Papers, CMH. For additional observations with regard to South Vietnamese leadership during Lam Son 719, see Lewis Sorley, *A Better War: The Unexamined Victories and Final Tragedy of America's Last Years in Vietnam*, 257–59.
6. Department of Defense (Vietnam Task Force), report, 27 Aug. 1971, subj.: Daily Highlights of Vietnamization and Pacification: An Assessment of the RVNAF Officer Corps, Abrams Papers, CMH.
7. Cao Van Vien and Dong Van Khuyen, *Reflections on the Vietnam War*, Indochina Monographs, 103.
8. MACV Command History, 1971, 1: VIII-45.
9. Abrams to McCain and Moorer, message, 090944Z Oct. 1971, Abrams Papers, CMH. A 1971 US Joint Chiefs of Staff assessment of RVNAF leader-

ship found the South Vietnamese improving, but still marginal in most aspects.

10. Sorley, *A Better War*, 223–24, quote at 309.
11. George Gallup, "The Gallup Poll," *Washington Post*, 7 Mar. 1971; Louis Harris, "The Harris Survey," *Washington Post*, 8 Mar. 1971.
12. Terrence Smith, "Fulbright Hopes to Force Nixon's Advisers to Testify," *New York Times*, 1 Mar. 1971.
13. Louis A Fanning, *Betrayal in Vietnam*, 85–86.
14. Memorandum of Conversation, Paris, May 31, 1971, Document 207 in *FRUS, 1969–1976*, 7:651–67; Henry Kissinger, *White House Years*, 1020.
15. Kissinger, *White House Years*, 1023; Memorandum of Conversation, Paris, June 26, 1971, Document 223 in *FRUS, 1969–1976*, 7:746–70.
16. *Van Kien Dang, Toan Tap 32, 1971* [Collected party documents, vol. 32, 1971], 409; Kissinger, *White House Years*, 1024; Qiang Zhai, *China and the Vietnam Wars, 1950–1975*, 197.
17. Kissinger, *White House Years*, 1025.; Truong Nhu Tang, *Vietcong Memoir*, 186–200.
18. Kissinger, *White House Years*, 1039.
19. Truong Nhu Tang, *Vietcong Memoir*, 194.
20. "The Same Old Shell Game," *Washington Post*, 27 Jan. 1972; *New York Times*, 26 Jan. 1972; North Vietnamese quote in David Fulghum and Terrence Maitland, *South Vietnam on Trial, Mid-1970 to 1972*, The Vietnam Experience, 111.
21. Quote in Willard J. Webb and Walter S. Poole, *The Joint Chiefs of Staff and the War in Vietnam, 1971–1973*, 102.
22. MACV Command History, 1971, 1:I-2.
23. Kissinger, *White House Years*, 1101; MACV History, 1972–73, 2: F-56; Graham A. Cosmas, *MACV: The Joint Command in the Years of Withdrawal, 1968–1973*, 175.
24. Military History Institute of Vietnam, *Chiến dịch phản công Đường 9–Nam Lào, Nam 1971* [The Route 9–Southern Laos counteroffensive campaign, 1971], 63.
25. Quote in William S. Turley, *The Second Indochina War*, 138.
26. Military History Institute of Vietnam, *Victory in Vietnam: The Official History of the People's Army of Vietnam, 1954–1975*, 278.
27. Dale Andradé, *America's Last Vietnam Battle: Halting Hanoi's 1972 Easter Offensive*, 3.
28. *Van Kien Dang, Toan Tap 32, 1971* [Collected party documents, vol. 32, 1971], 339; Military History Institute of Vietnam, *Chiến dịch phản công Đường 9–Nam Lào, Nam 1971* [The Route 9–Southern Laos counteroffensive campaign, 1971], 105.
29. Nguyen, *Hanoi's War*, 228.
30. War Experiences Recapitulation Committee of the High-Level Military Institute, Vietnam, *The Anti-US Resistance War for National Salvation, 1954–1975: Military Events*, 138.
31. William J. Duiker, *Sacred War: Nationalism and Revolution in a Divided Vietnam*, 234–35; Qiang Zhai, *China and the Vietnam Wars, 1950–1975*, 202.
32. Kimball, *Nixon's Vietnam War*, 284; Randolph, *Powerful and Brutal Weapons*, 4–5, 22–31; Nguyen, *Hanoi's War*, 234.
33. Nguyen, *Hanoi's War*, 242.

34. Military History Institute of Vietnam, *Victory in Vietnam,* 289. The offensive was also known as Chien dic Xuan he 1972 [1972 Spring-Summer Offensive].
35. Luu Van Loi and Nguyen Anh Vu, *Le Duc Tho–Kissinger Negotiations in Paris,* 218–19; Central Office of South Vietnam (COSVN), Directive 42, Dec. 1971, Douglas Pike Indochina Collection, Texas Tech University Vietnam Archive; Institute of Military History of Vietnam, *Report to General Vo Nguyen Giap: A Consolidated Report on the Fight against the United States for the Salvation of Vietnam by Our People,* 30; Troung Nhu Tang, *Vietcong Memoir,* 204, 210.
36. Quote in Fulghum and Maitland, *South Vietnam on Trial,* 122.
37. Military History Institute, *Victory in Vietnam,* 283. Historian Lien-Hang T. Nguyen, in *Hanoi's War,* 232, notes that the key decisions for launching the new offensive were made between May and October 1971.
38. Nguyen, *Hanoi's War,* 239.
39. MACV Command History, 1972–1973, 1:9, 11; Commander, Military Assistance Command, Vietnam (Abrams), to the Commander in Chief, Pacific (McCain), message, Saigon, January 20, 1972, Document 1 in *FRUS, 1969–1976,* 8:1–7; Laird, memorandum for the Assistant to the President for National Security Affairs, 26 Jan. 1972, subj.: The Current Situation in SVN, NSC Files, Nixon Library.
40. Abrams to McCain (info Moorer), message, 11 Jan. 1972, Abrams Papers, CMH; John D. Negroponte of the National Security Council Staff to the President's Assistant for National Security Affairs (Kissinger), memorandum, subj.: The Enemy's Dry Season Campaign, Washington, February 29, 1972, Document 30 in *FRUS, 1969–1976,* 8:111–12.
41. For the most comprehensive treatment of the 1972 Easter Offensive, see Andradé, *America's Last Vietnam Battle,* and Lt. Gen. Ngo Quang Truong, *The Easter Offensive of 1972.*
42. For a complete discussion of the 1972 NVA Easter Offensive in Military Region I, see Gerald R. Turley, *Easter Offensive: The Last American Advisors, Vietnam, 1972,* reprint ed.
43. Andrew Wiest, *Vietnam's Forgotten Army: Heroism and Betrayal in the ARVN,* 235–62.
44. Bunker quote in James S. Olson and Randy Roberts, *Where the Last Domino Fell: America and Vietnam, 1945 to 1990,* 247.
45. Kissinger, *White House Years,* 1098–99.
46. Richard M. Nixon, *RN: The Memoirs of Richard Nixon,* 588; Kissinger, *White House Years,* 1113.
47. The most comprehensive account of Nixon's response to the 1972 NVA offensive is in Stephen P. Randolph, *Powerful and Brutal Weapons: Nixon, Kissinger, and the Easter Offensive.*
48. Although the 5th and 9th Divisions carried VC designations, by this time in the war they were North Vietnamese Army formations—manned, trained, and equipped just like the other NVA divisions. For a complete discussion of the 1972 NVA Easter Offensive in Military Region III, see Lam Quang Thi, *Hell in An Loc: The 1972 Easter Invasion and the Battle That Saved Saigon*; Mike McDermott, *True Faith and Allegiance: An American Paratrooper and the 1972 Battle for An Loc*; Tran Van Nhut, *An Loc: The Unfinished War*; James H. Willbanks, *The Battle of An Loc.* The author served as an adviser with the South Vietnamese forces in An Loc during the siege.
49. Quote in Webb and Poole, *Joint Chiefs of Staff, 1971–1973,* 158.
50. A. J. C. Lavalle, *Airpower and the 1972 Spring Invasion,* 85.

51. The artillery and local attacks continued into the summer months. On 9 July, Brig. Gen. John Tallman, deputy senior adviser to III Corps, and four others were killed during an artillery attack shortly after arriving in An Loc by helicopter. The author was also wounded in this incident.

52. Kaplan quote of Dat in Fulghum and Maitland, *South Vietnam on Trial,* 154. For a complete discussion of the 1972 NVA Easter Offensive in Military Region II, see Thomas P. McKenna, *Kontum: The Battle to Save South Vietnam.*

53. Andradé, *America's Last Vietnam Battle,* 276–77.

54. Abrams to SECDEF, message, 241111Z Apr. 1972, Abrams Papers, CMH.

55. Richard M. Nixon, *Public Papers of the Presidents of the United States: Richard M. Nixon, 1972,* 550–54.

56. Abrams to SECDEF, message, 011601Z May 1972, Abrams Papers, CMH.

57. Davidson, *Vietnam at War,* 634; US Information Agency, Office of Policy and Plans, "Talking Paper: Facts on the Current North Vietnamese Invasion," 20 July 1972, Douglas Pike Indochina Collection, Texas Tech University Vietnam Archive, Lubbock; Craig A. Whitney, "US Aides Believe Saigon Can Withstand Foe's Drive," *New York Times,* 29 June 1972.

58. Douglas Pike, *PAVN: People's Army of Vietnam,* 224–25.

59. Andradé, *America's Last Vietnam Battle,* 487–88.

60. Abrams to SECDEF, message, 020443Z May 1972, Abrams Papers, CMH. Some South Vietnamese generals agreed; see Gen. Cao Van Vien and Lt. Gen. Dong Van Khuyen, *Reflections on the Vietnam War,* Indochina Monographs, 105.

61. Andradé, *America's Last Vietnam Battle,* 141–45; Jeffrey C. Clarke, *Advice and Support: The Final Years, 1965–1973,* The US Army in Vietnam, 483–86.

62. Brig. Gen. John R. McGiffert, interview by Walter S. Dillard, 10 Oct. 1972, MACV, SJS-History, Abrams Papers, CMH, 23.

63. Abrams to SECDEF, message, 011601Z May 1972, subj.: Personal Assessment of the Situation in RVN as of 1 May 1972, Abrams Papers, CMH; Weyand quote in Edgar Ulsamer, "Airpower Halts an Invasion," *Air Force Magazine,* Sep. 1972, 61.

64. McGiffert interview, 27.

65. Nixon, *Public Papers, 1972,* 551–52.

66. "A Record of Sheer Endurance," *Time,* 26 June 1972, 26.

67. Kissinger, *White House Years,* 1399, 1469–70.

68. Graham A. Cosmas, *MACV: The Joint Command in the Years of Withdrawal, 1968–1973,* 379.

69. Kissinger, *White House Years,* 994.

70. Kimball, *Nixon's Vietnam War,* 182.

71. Graham A. Cosmas and Terrence P. Murray, *US Marines in Vietnam: Vietnamization and Redeployment, 1970–1971,* 210.

Epilogue

1. Ford to Thieu, 10 Aug. 1974, White House Central Files, Gerald R. Ford Library, Ann Arbor, Michigan.

2. Van Tien Dung, *Our Great Spring Victory: An Account of the Liberation of South Vietnam,* 19–20.

3. The most complete accounting of the fall of South Vietnam can be found in George J. Veith, *Black Sunday: The Fall of South Vietnam 1973–75.*

Glossary

AAA	antiaircraft artillery
Abn	airborne
ABCCC	airborne command and control center
AFA	aerial field artillery
AFCCC	Air Force command and control center
AHB	assault helicopter battalion
AHC	assault helicopter company
ALC	area logistics command
Ambl	airmobile
AMC	air mission commander
AM&S	aircraft maintenance and support
AO	area of operation
APC	armored personnel carrier
Ar	armor
ARA	aerial rocket artillery
ARG	amphibious ready group
ARVN	Army of the Republic of Vietnam
ASHB	assault support helicopter battalion
ASRT	air support radar team
Arty	artillery
Atch	attached
Avn	aviation
AWC	aerial weapons company
AWSP	automatic weapon, self-propelled
BDA	bomb damage assessment
Bde	brigade
Bn	battalion
BSA	base support area
Btry	battery
CAB	combat aviation battalion
CAS	close air support
Cav	cavalry
CBU	cluster bomb unit
Cbt	combat
C&C	command and control (helicopter)
CG	commanding general
CIA	Central Intelligence Agency
CIDG	Civilian Irregular Defense Group
CINCPAC	commander in chief, Pacific
CJCS	chairman of the Joint Chiefs of Staff
Cmd	command
CO	commanding officer
Co	company
COMSEC	communications security
COMUSMACV	commander, US Military Assistance Command, Vietnam
CORDS	Civil Operations and Rural Development Support
COSVN	Central Office for South Vietnam
CP	command post
CRIMP	Consolidated RVNAF Improvement and Mobilization Plan
DASC	direct air support center
DCAT	division combat assistance team
Det	detachment

DISCOM	division support command
Div	division
DMZ	Demilitarized Zone
DRV	Democratic Republic of Vietnam (North Vietnam)
DS	direct support
Engr	engineer
EOD	explosive ordnance disposal
FA	field artillery
FAC	forward air controller
FARP	forward arming and refueling point
FDC	fire direction center
FSA	forward support area
FSB	fire support base
FSCC	fire support coordination center
Gp	group
GS	general support
GSG	general support group
GVN	government of South Vietnam
HE	high explosive
HEAT	high-explosive antitank
HHC	heavy helicopter company
HHC	headquarters and headquarters company
HMH	Marine heavy helicopter squadron
HML	Marine light helicopter squadron
IFFV	I Field Force Vietnam
IIFFV	II Field Force Vietnam
Inf	infantry
JGS	Joint General Staff (RVNAF)
JCS	Joint Chiefs of Staff (US)
JTF-FA	Joint Task Force–Full Accounting
JPAC	Joint POW/MIA Accounting Command
KIA	killed in action
LAW	light antitank weapon (M72)
LC	land clearing
LE	light equipment
LOC	line of communication
Log	logistics
LOH	light Observation Helicopter (also known as "Loach")
LZ	landing zone
MACV	Military Assistance Command, Vietnam
MAU	Marine Amphibious Unit
MAW	Marine Air Wing
Med	medical
Medevac	medical evacuation (helicopter)
MIA	missing in action
MP	military police
NLF	National Liberation Front
NVA	North Vietnamese Army (PAVN)
OB	order of battle
OPCON	operational control
OPLAN	operations plan
PAVN	People's Army of Vietnam (NVA)
PB	panel bridge
POL	petroleum, oil, and lubricants
POW	prisoner of war
Prov	provisional
PRG	Provisional Revolutionary Government
PSP	pierced steel plating
PZ	pickup zone
Recon	reconnaissance
Regt	regiment
Res	reserve
Rgr	Ranger
RPG	rocket-propelled grenade
RVN	Republic of (South) Vietnam
RVNAF	Republic of (South) Vietnam Armed Forces
SAR	search and rescue
SAC	Strategic Air Command
SECDEF	secretary of defense
SECSTATE	secretary of state

Sig	signal
SP	self-propelled
Spt	support
SUPCOM	support command
Surv	surveillance
Tac air	tactical air (support)
TACP	tactical air control party
TASS	tactical air support squadron
TOC	tactical operations center
Trans	transportation
UH	utility helicopter
USAF	US Air Force
USARV	US Army, Vietnam
USN	US Navy
USMC	US Marine Corps
VC	Viet Cong
VNAF	[South] Vietnamese Air Force
VNMC	[South] Vietnamese Marine Corps
WIA	wounded in action
WP	white phosphorus
WSAG	Washington Special Actions Group

Archives

Combined Arms Research Library (CARL), US Army Command and General Staff College, Fort Leavenworth, Kansas

Gerald R. Ford Presidential Library, Ann Arbor, Michigan

National Archives and Records Administration (NARA), College Park, Maryland

Richard M. Nixon Presidential Library, Yorba Linda, California

US Army Center of Military History (CMH), Fort McNair, Washington, DC

US Army Military History Institute (MHI), Carlisle Barracks, Pennsylvania

Vietnam Center and Virtual Archive, Texas Tech University, Lubbock

US Government Publications

Berger, C., J. S. Ballard, and R. L. Bowers. *The United States Air Force in Southeast Asia: 1961–1973*. Washington, DC: Office of Air Force History, 1977.

Cao Van Vien, Gen. *Leadership*. Indochina Monographs. Washington, DC: US Army Center of Military History, 1977.

Cao Van Vien, Gen., and Lt. Gen. Dong Van Khuyen *Reflections on the Vietnam War*. Indochina Monographs. Washington, DC: US Army Center of Military History, 1980.

Cao Van Vien, Gen.; Lt. Gen. Ngo Quang Truong; Lt. Gen. Dong Van Khuyen; Maj. Gen. Nguyen Duy Hinh; Brig. Gen. Tran Dinh Tho; Col. Hoang Ngoc Lung; and Lt. Col. Chu Xuan Vien. *The US Adviser*. Indochina Monographs. Washington, DC: US Army Center of Military History, 1980.Clarke, Jeffrey C. *Advice and Support: The Final Years, 1965–1973*. The US Army in Vietnam. Washington, DC: US Army Center of Military History, 1987.

Collins, James Lawton, Jr. *The Development and Training of the South Vietnamese Army, 1950–1972*. Washington, DC: US Government Printing Office, 1975.

Cosmas, Graham A. *MACV: The Joint Command in the Years of Escalation, 1962–1967*. Washington, DC: US Army Center of Military History, 2006.

———. *MACV: The Joint Command in the Years of Withdrawal, 1968–1973*. Washington, DC: US Army Center of Military History, 2007.

———, and Lt. Col. Terrence P. Murray. *US Marines in Vietnam: Vietnamization and Redeployment, 1970–1971*. Washington, DC: Headquarters, US Marine Corps, History and Museums Division, 1986.

Dillard, Walter S. *Sixty Days to Peace: Implementing the Paris Peace Accords, Vietnam, 1973*. Washington, DC: National Defense University, 1982.

Goodman, Allan E. "The Dual-Track Strategy of Vietnamization and Negotiation." In *The Second Indochina War: Proceedings of a Symposium Held at Airlie, Virginia, 7–9 November 1984*. Ed. by John Schlight, pp. 143–52. Washington, DC: US Army Center of Military History, 1986.

Hammond, William M. *Public Affairs: The Military and the Media, 1968–1973*. Washington, DC: US Army Center of Military History, 1996.

Hoang Ngoc Lung, Col. *Strategy and Tactics*. Indochina Monographs. Washington, DC: US Army Center of Military History, 1980.

Johnson, Lt. Col. Richard M. *LAM SON 719: Perils of Strategy*. Carlisle, PA: US Army War College, 1996.

Lavalle, A. J. C., ed. *Airpower and the 1972 Spring Invasion*. USAF Southeast Asia Monograph Series, vol. 2, no. 3. Maxwell Air Force Base, AL: Air Command and Staff College, 1976.

Le Gro, William E. *Vietnam from Cease-Fire to Capitulation*. Washington, DC: US Army Center of Military History, 1981.

Melson, Charles D., and Curtis G. Arnold, *US Marines in Vietnam: The War That Would Not End, 1971–1973*. Washington, DC: US Government Printing Office, 1991.

Merrell, Ronald D. *Tactical Airlift in SEA*. Honolulu: Directorate of Operations Analysis, Headquarters Pacific Air Forces, February 15, 1972.

Momyer, William W. *The Vietnamese Air Force, 1951—1975: An Analysis of Its Role in Combat*. USAF Southeast Asia Monograph Series, vol. 3. Washington, DC: US Government Printing Office, 1975.

———. *Airpower in Three Wars (WWII, Korea, Vietnam)*. Washington, DC: US Government Printing Office, 1978.

Nalty, Bernard C. *Air War over South Vietnam, 1968–1975*. Washington, DC: Air Force History and Museums Program, 2000.

Ngo Quang Truong, Lt. Gen. *The Easter Offensive of 1972*. Indochina Monographs. Washington, DC: US Army Center of Military History, 1980.

———. *RVNAF and US Operational Cooperation and Coordination*. Indochina Monographs. Washington, DC: US Army Center of Military History, 1980.

Nixon, Richard M. *Public Papers of the President of the United States: Richard M. Nixon*. 6 vols. Washington, DC: US Government Printing Office, 1971–75.

Ott, David Ewing. *Vietnam Studies: Field Artillery, 1954–1973*. Washington, DC: Department of the Army, 1975.

Starry, Gen. Donn A. *Mounted Combat in Vietnam*. Vietnam Studies. Washington, DC: Department of the Army, 1989.

Tolson, John J. *Air Mobility, 1961–1971*. Vietnam Studies. Washington, DC: US Department of the Army, 1973.

Tran Dinh Tho, Brig. Gen. *The Cambodian Incursion*. Indochina Monographs. Washington, DC: US Army Center of Military History, 1979.

———. *Pacification*. Indochina Monographs. Washington, DC: US Army Center of Military History, 1980.

Trask, Roger R. *The Secretaries of Defense: A Brief History, 1947–1985*. Washington, DC: Historical Office, Office of the Secretary of Defense, 1985.

US Air Force, Headquarters Pacific Air Forces, Directorate of Operations Analysis. *Contemporary Historical Examination of Current Operations*

(CHECO) Report: LAM SON 719, 30 January–24 March '71, The South Vietnamese Incursion into Laos. Honolulu: Headquarters Pacific Air Forces, 24 March 1971.

US Department of State, Office of the Historian. *Foreign Relations of the United States, 1969–1976*, Vol. 6, *Vietnam, January 1969–July 1970*. Washington, DC: US Government Printing Office, 2006.

———. *Foreign Relations of the United States, 1969–1976*, Vol. 7, *Vietnam, July 1970–January 1972*. Washington, DC: US Government Printing Office, 2010.

———. *Foreign Relations of the United States, 1969–1976*, Vol. 8, *Vietnam, January–October 1972*. Washington, DC: US Government Printing Office, 2010.

———. *Foreign Relations of the United States, 1969–1976*, Vol. 9, *Vietnam, October 1972–January 1973*. Washington, DC: US Government Printing Office, 2010.

———. *Foreign Relations of the United States, 1969–1976*, Vol. 10, *Vietnam, January 1973–July 1975*. Washington, DC: US Government Printing Office, 2010.

US Marine Corps Historical Center. *Vietnam Revisited: Conversation with William Broyles, Jr.* Washington, DC: Histories and Museums Division, Headquarters, US Marine Corps, 1984.

Webb, Willard J. *The Joint Chiefs of Staff and the War in Vietnam, 1969–1970*. The History of the Joint Chiefs of Staff. Washington, DC: Office of Joint History, Office of the Joint Chiefs of Staff, 2002.

———, and Walter S. Poole, *The Joint Chiefs of Staff and the War in Vietnam, 1971–1973*. The History of the Joint Chiefs of Staff. Washington, DC: Office of Joint History, Office of the Joint Chiefs of Staff, 2007.

Communist Vietnamese Sources (Trans. by Merle Pribbenow unless otherwise noted)

Armor Branch, Military Science Council. *Lich Su Binh Chung Thiet Giap, Quan Doi Nhan Dan Viet Nam 1959–1975* [History of the Armor Branch, People's Army of Vietnam, 1959–1975]. Hanoi: People's Army Publishing House, 1982.

Armored Command. *Một Số Trận Đánh của Bộ Đội Tăng-Thiết Giáp Việt Nam trong Kháng Chiến chống Mỹ và chiến tranh bảo vệ tổ quốc, Tập 1* [A number of battles fought by Vietnamese armor troops during the War against the United States and the War to Defend the Fatherland, vol. 1]. Hanoi: People's Army Publishing House, 1995.

Artillery Command and Artillery Party Current Affairs Committee. *Phao Binh Nhan Dan Viet Nam: Nhung Chang Duong Chien Dau, Tap II* [People's artillery of Vietnam: Combat history, vol. 2]. Hanoi: The Artillery Command, 1986.

Bui Tin. *Following Ho Chi Minh: The Memoirs of a North Vietnamese Colonel*. Honolulu: University of Hawaii Press, 1995.

———. *From Enemy to Friend*. Annapolis, MD: Naval Institute Press, 2002.

"Chiến dịch phản công Đường 9–Nam Lào (Kỳ 1)" [The Route 9–southern Laos Counteroffensive (Installment 1)]. *Quan Doi Nhan Dan* [People's Army newspaper], Friday, 11 February 2011. Accessed 15 February 2011 at http://www.qdnd.vn/QDNDSite/vi-VN/61/43/56/57/57/138304/Default.aspx.

"Chiến dịch phản công Đường 9–Nam Lào (Kỳ 3)" [The Route 9–southern Laos Counteroffensive (Final Installment)]. *Quan Doi Nhan Dan* [People's Army newspaper], Friday, 11 February 2011. Accessed 15 February 2011 at http://www.qdnd.vn/QDNDSite/vi-VN/61/43/56/57/57/138304/Default.aspx.

Cong An Nhan Dan [People's Public Security newspaper].

Cong Tac Chien Dich Duong 9 Nam Lao 9 (Tu 28/2 Den 23/3/1971) [Route 9–southern Laos Campaign rear services operations (28 February–23 March 1971]Hanoi: General Rear Services Department, 1987.

Dong Si Nguyen, Col. Gen., with Duy Tuong and Ky Van. *Duong Xuyen Truong Son: Hoi Ky* [The road through the Annamite Mountains: A memoir]. Hanoi: People's Army Publishing House, 2001 (second printing, with corrections and additions).

Hoang Nghia Khanh, Lt. Gen. *Đường Lên Cơ Quan Tổng Hành Dinh* [The road to the General Headquarters Staff]. Hanoi: People's Army Publishing House, 2008.

Hoang Van Thai, Gen. *History of the People's Army*, Vol. II. Hanoi: People's Army Publishing House, 1994.

———. *The Decisive Years: Memoirs of Vietnamese Senior General Hoang Van Thai*. Joint Publications Research Service Report JSPS-SEA-87-084. Springfield, VA: Foreign Broadcast Information Service, 1987.

———. *How South Vietnam Was Liberated*. Hanoi: The Gioi Publishers, 1992.

Ho Chi Minh National Political Studies Institute, Party History Institute. *Lịch Sử Biên Niên Xứ Ủy Nam Bộ và Trung Ương Cục Miền Nam, 1954–1975* [Historical chronicle of the Cochin China party committee and the central office for South Vietnam, 1954–1975]. Hanoi: National Political Publishing House, 2002.

Ho Si Huu, Sr. Col.; Sr. Col. Chu Thai; Col. The Ky; and Lt. Le Duan. *Letters to the South*. Hanoi: Su That Publishing House, 1985.

Lịch sử sư đoàn bộ binh 324, 1955–2005 [History of the 324th Infantry Division, 1955–2005]. Hanoi: People's Army Publishing House, 2005. Accessed 19 October 2009 at http://www.quansuvn.net/index.php?topic=103.0.

Lich Su Quan Chung Phong Khong, Tap II [History of the Air Defense Service, vol. 2]. Hanoi: People's Army Publishing House, 1993.

Luu Van Loi and Nguyen Ahn Vu. *Le Duc Tho–Kissinger Negotiations in Paris*. Hanoi: The Gioi, 1996.

Military History Institute of Vietnam. *Chiến dịch phản công Đường 9–Nam Lào, Nam 1971* [The Route 9–Southern Laos Counteroffensive Campaign, 1971]. Hanoi: Ministry of Defense, 1987.

———. *History of the People's Army of Vietnam*, vol. 2. Hanoi: People's Army Publishing House, 1994.

———. *Report to General Vo Nguyen Giap: A Consolidated Report on the Fight against the United States for the Salvation of Vietnam by Our People*. Trans. by Duong Bui, Defense Language Institute Foreign Language Center, Presidio of Monterey, California. Hanoi: Military History Institute of Vietnam, 1987.

———. *Victory in Vietnam: The Official History of the People's Army of Vietnam, 1954–1975*. Trans. by Merle L. Pribbenow. Lawrence: University Press of Kansas, 2002.

Military Region 4 Headquarters and the Current Affairs Committee of the MR-4 Party Committee, with the personal assistance of Maj. Gen. Tran Van An. *Quan Khu 4: Lich Su Khang Chien Chong My Cuu Nuoc, 1954–1975* [Military Region 4: History of the resistance against the Americans to save the nation, 1954–1975]. Hanoi: People's Army Publishing House, 1994.

Mot So Tran Danh Cua Bo Doi Thiet Gap, Tap IV [A number of battles fought by our armor troops, vol. IV]. Hanoi: Armor Command, General Staff Printing Plant, 1983.

Nguyen Dinh Uoc, ed. *Lich Su Mat Tran Duong 9-Bac Quang Tri, 1966–1973* [History of the Route 9–northern Quang Tri front, 1966–1973]. Hanoi: People's Army Publishing House, date unknown.

Nguyen Huu An, Col. Gen., and Nguyen Tu Duong. *Chien Truong Moi: Hoi Uc* [New battlefield: A memoir]. Hanoi: People's Army Publishing House, 2002.

Nguyen Huy Chuong, Lt. Gen. *Chỉ Một Con Đường* [Only one road to take]. Danang: Danang Publishing House, 2001. Vietnamese military history website, accessed 15 March 2011 at http://www.quansuvn.net/index.php/topic,19999.0.html.

Pham Huy Thuong, Dang Ngoc Tinh, Le Moc, and Nguyen Van Dieu. *Su Doan Dong Bang (Binh Doan Tay Nguyen), Tap Ba* [The Lowlands Division (Central Highlands Corps), vol. 3]. Hanoi: People's Army Publishing House, 1984.

Phan Huu Dai. *Trường Sơn Ngày Ấy* [The Annamite Mountains back then]. Hanoi: People's Army Publishing House, 1995.

Rear Services Department Headquarters and Party Current Affairs Committee. *Lich Su Bo Doi Truong Son Duong Ho Chi Minh* [History of the Annamite Mountain troops on the Ho Chi Minh Trail]. Hanoi: People's Army Publishing House, 1994.

2nd Division Party Committee and Division Headquarters. *Su Doan 2, Tap 1* [2nd Division, vol. 1], Danang: Danang Publishing House, 1989.

Su Doan 9 [9th Division]. Trans. by Foreign Broadcast Information Service, October 1995. Hanoi: People's Army Publishing House, 1990.

Su Doan 304, Tap II [304th Division, vol. 2]. Hanoi: People's Army Publishing House, 1990.

Su Doan 308 Quan Tien Phong [The 308th Vanguard Division]. Hanoi: People's Army Publishing House, 1999.

324th Infantry Division Headquarters and Division Party Committee. *Lịch sử sư đoàn bộ binh 324 1955–2005* [History of the 324th Infantry Division, 1955–2005]. Hanoi: People's Army Publishing House, 2005. http://www.quansuvn.net/index.php?topic=103.0, accessed 19 October 2009.

"Tin sớm về cuộc "hành quân xa" [Advance information about a "distant operation"]. *Quan Doi Nhan Dan* [People's Army newspaper], 18 November 2010. Accessed 6 December 2010 at http://www.qdnd.vn/QDNDSite/vi-VN/89/70/79/79/79/130010/Default.aspx.

"Trận đánh trên đồi Không Tên" [The Battle of No Name Hill]. *Quan Doi Nhan Dan* [People's Army Newspaper], 18 March 2011. Accessed 19 March 2011 at http://www.qdnd.vn/QDNDSite/vi-VN/89/70/78/78/78/142038/Default.aspx.

Tran Van Don. *Our Endless War*. San Rafael, CA: Presidio Press, 1978.

Tran Van Tra. *Vietnam: History of the Bulwark B2 Theater*, Vol. 5, *Concluding the 30-Year War*. Southeast Asia Report, No. 1247. Ho Chi Minh City: Van Nghe Publishing, 1982.

"Trung Tướng Nguyễn Ân và ký ức về trận đánh 40 năm trước" [Lt. Gen. Nguyen An and his memories of a battle fought 40 years ago]. *Quan Doi Nhan Dan* [People's Army Newspaper], 20 March 2011. Accessed 21 March 2011 at http://www.qdnd.vn/QDNDSite/vi-VN/61/43/296/296/296/142282/Default.aspx.

Truong Nhu Tang. *A Vietcong Memoir: An Insider Account of the Vietnam War and Its Aftermath*. New York: Harcourt Brace Jovanovich, 1985.

Van Kien Dang, Toan Tap 31, 1970 [Collected party documents, vol. 31, 1970]. Hanoi: Nha Xuat Ban Chinh Tri Quoc Gia [National Political Publishing House], 2004.

Van Kien Dang, Toan Tap 32, 1971 [Collected party documents, vol. 32, 1971]. Hanoi: Nha Xuat Ban Chinh Tri Quoc Gia [National Political Publishing House], 2004.

Vo Nguyen Giap. *Tổng Tập Luận Văn, Đại tướng Võ Nguyên Giáp* [Collected essays of Gen. Vo Nguyen Giap]. Hanoi: People's Army Publishing House, 2006.

———. *How We Won the War*. Philadelphia: Recon Press, 1976.

———. *People's War, People's Army*. New York: Praeger, 1968.

War Experiences Recapitulation Committee of the High-Level Military Institute, Vietnam. *The Anti-US Resistance War for National Salvation, 1954–1975: Military Events*. Trans. by Joint Publications Research Service. Hanoi: People's Army Publishing House, 1980.

Published Works

Ambrose, Stephen E. *Nixon*, Vol. 2, *The Triumph of a Politician, 1962–1972*. New York: Simon and Schuster, 1989.

———. *Nixon*, Vol. 3, *Ruin and Recovery, 1973–1990*. New York: Simon and Schuster, 1991.

Anderson, David L., ed. *Shadow on the White House: Presidents and the Vietnam War, 1945–1975*. Lawrence: University Press of Kansas, 1993.

Andradé, Dale. *America's Last Vietnam Battle: Halting Hanoi's 1972 Easter Offensive*. Lawrence: University Press of Kansas, 2001.

Bass, Thomas A. *The Spy Who Loved Us: The Vietnam War and Pham Xuan An's Dangerous Game*. New York: Public Affairs, 2009.

Bendix Aerospace Systems Division, Department of Applied Science and Technology. *Analysis of Vietnamization: Summary and Evaluation*. Ann Arbor, MI: Bendix Aerospace Systems Division, 1973.

Berman, Larry. *No Peace, No Honor: Nixon, Kissinger, and Betrayal*. New York: Free Press, 2001.

———. *Perfect Spy: The Incredible Double Life of Pham Xuan An,* Time *Magazine Reporter and Vietnamese Communist Agent*. Washington, DC: Smithsonian, 2007.

Bernstein, Jonathan. *US Army AH-1 Cobra Units in Vietnam*. Oxford, UK: Osprey, 2003.

Bui Diem (with David Chanoff). *In the Jaws of History*. Boston: Houghton Mifflin Company, 1977.

Bundy, William. *A Tangled Web: The Making of Foreign Policy in the Nixon Presidency*. New York: Hill and Wang, 1998.

Chanoff, David, and Doan Van Toai. *Portrait of the Enemy*. New York: Random House, 1986.

———. *Vietnam: A Portrait of Its People at War*. London: I. B. Tauriis Publishers, 1996.

Colby, William. *Lost Victory*. Chicago: Contemporary Books, 1989.

Coleman, J. D. *Incursion*. New York: St. Martin's Press, 1991.

Collins, John M. *Military Geography for Professionals and the Public*. Washington, DC: Brassey's, 1998.

Cook, John L. *Rescue Under Fire: The Story of DUST OFF in Vietnam*. New York: Schiffer, 1998.

Currey, Cecil B. *Victory at Any Cost: The Genius of Viet Nam's General Vo Nguyen Giap*. Washington: Brassey's, Inc., 1997.

Daddis, Gregory A. *No Sure Victory: Measuring US Army Effectiveness and Progress in the Vietnam War*. New York: Oxford University Press, 2011.

Dallek, Robert. *Nixon and Kissinger: Partners in Power*. New York: HarperCollins Publishers, 2007.

Davidson, Phillip B. *Secrets of the Vietnam War*. Novato, CA: Presidio Press, 1990.

———. *Vietnam at War: The History, 1946–1975*. Novato, CA: Presidio Press, 1988.

Dawson, Joseph G., ed. *Commanders in Chief: Presidential Leadership in Modern Wars*. Lawrence: University Press of Kansas, 1993.

DeBenedetti, Charles. *An American Ordeal: The Antiwar Movement of the Vietnam Era*. Syracuse, NY: Syracuse University Press, 1990.

Doleman, Edgar C. *The Vietnam Experience: Tools of War*. Boston: Boston Publishing Company, 1984.

Dong Van Khuyen, Lt. Gen. *The RVNAF*. Indochina Monographs. Washington, DC: US Army Center of Military History, 1979.

Dougan, Clark, and David Fulghum. *The Vietnam Experience: The Fall of the South*. Boston: Boston Publishing Company, 1985.

Duiker, William J. *Sacred War: Nationalism and Revolution in a Divided Vietnam*. New York: McGraw-Hill, 1995.

Dunstan, Simon. *Armor of the Vietnam Wars*. London: Osprey Press, 1985.

———. *Vietnam Tracks: Armor in Battle, 1945–75*. Novato, CA: Presidio Press, 1982.

Ehrlichman, John. *Witness to Power: The Nixon Years*. New York: Simon & Schuster, 1982.

Errington, Elizabeth Jane, and B. J. C. McKercher, eds. *The Vietnam War As History*. New York: Praeger, 1990.

Esper, George. *The Eyewitness History of the Vietnam War, 1961–1975*. New York: Ballantine Books, 1983.

Fanning, Louis A. *Betrayal in Vietnam*. New Rochelle, NY: Arlington House Publishers, 1976.

Fulghum, David, and Terrence Maitland. *South Vietnam on Trial, Mid-1970 to 1972*. The Vietnam Experience. Boston: Boston Publishing Company, 1984.

Gaiduk, I. V. *The Soviet Union and the Vietnam War*. New York: Ivan R. Dee, 1996.

Gettleman, Marvin E.; Jane Franklin; Marilyn B. Young; and H. Bruce Franklin, eds. *Vietnam and America*. New York: Grove Press, 1995.

Goodman, Allan E. *An Institutional Profile of the South Vietnamese Officer Corps*. Santa Monica, CA: Rand Corporation, 1970.

Gross, Chuck. *Rattler One-Seven*. Denton: University of North Texas Press, 2004.

Haig, Alexander M., Jr., with Charles McCarry, *Inner Circles: How America Changed the World—A Memoir*. New York: Warner Books, 1992.

Haldeman, H. R. *The Haldeman Diaries: Inside the Nixon White House*. New York: Berkley, 1995.

———, with Joseph DiMona. *The Ends of Power*. New York: Times Books, 1978.

Ha Mai Viet. *Steel and Blood: South Vietnamese Armor and the War for Southeast Asia*. Annapolis, MD: Naval Institute Press, 2008.

Hammond, William M. *Reporting Vietnam: Media and Military at War*. Lawrence, KS: University Press of America, 1998.

Harris, Louis. *The Anguish of Change*. New York: W. W. Norton, 1973.

Head, William P. *Shadow and Stinger: Developing the AC-119G/K Gunships in the Vietnam War*. College Station: Texas A&M University Press, 2007.

Head, William, and Lawrence E. Grinter, eds. *Looking Back on the Vietnam War*. Westport, CT: Praeger, 1993.

Hersh, Seymour. *The Price of Power: Kissinger in the Nixon White House*. New York: Summit Books, 1983.

Hess, Gary R. *Vietnam and the United States: Origins and Legacy of the War*. Boston: Twayne Publishers, 1990.

Hoff, Joan. *Nixon Reconsidered*. New York: Harper Collins, 1994.

Isaacson, Walter. *Kissinger: A Biography*. New York: Simon & Schuster, 1992.

Joes, Anthony James. *The War for South Viet Nam, 1954–1975*. New York: Praeger, 1989.

Johns, Andrew L. *Vietnam's Second Front: Domestic Politics, the Republican Party, and the War*. Lexington: University Press of Kentucky, 2012.

Johnson, Ulysses Alexis, with Jef Olivarius McAlister. *The Right Hand of Power*. Englewood Cliffs, NJ: Prentice-Hall, 1984.

Karnow, Stanley. *Vietnam—A History*. 3rd ed. New York: Penguin, 1997.

Katsiaficas, George, ed. *Vietnam Documents: American and Vietnamese Views of the War*. New York: M. E. Sharpe, 1992.

Keough, James. *President Nixon and the Press*. New York: Funk & Wagnalls, 1972.

Kimble, Jeffrey. *Nixon's Vietnam War*. Lawrence: University Press of Kansas, 1998.

———. *The Vietnam War Files: Uncovering the Secret History of Nixon-Era Strategy*. Lawrence: University Press of Kansas, 2004.

Kissinger, Henry. *Ending the Vietnam War*. New York: Simon & Schuster, 2003.

———. *White House Years*. Boston: Little, Brown and Company, 1979.

———. *Years of Renewal*. New York: Simon & Schuster, 1999.

———. *Years of Upheaval*. Boston: Little, Brown, 1989.

Kutler, Stanley I., ed. *Abuse of Power: The New Nixon Tapes*. New York: The Free Press, 1997.

Laird, Melvin R. *Town Hall Meeting: The Nixon Doctrine*. Washington, DC: American Enterprise Institute for Public Policy Research, 1972.

Lam Quang Thi. *Hell in An Loc: The 1972 Easter Invasion and the Battle That Saved Saigon*. Denton: University of North Texas Press, 2011.

———. *The Twenty-Five Year Century*. Denton: University of North Texas Press, 2001.

Lanning, Michael Lee, and Dan Cragg. *Inside the VC and the NVA: The Real Story of North Vietnam's Armed Forces*. New York: Fawcett Columbine, 1992.

Lewy, Guenther. *America in Vietnam*. New York: Oxford University Press, 1978.

Lien-Hang T. Nguyen. *Hanoi's War: An International History of the War for Peace in Vietnam*. Chapel Hill: University of North Carolina Press, 2012.

Lind, Michael. *Vietnam: The Necessary War*. New York: The Free Press, 1999.

Lipsman, Samuel, and Edward Doyle. *Fighting for Time*. The Vietnam Experience. Boston: Boston Publishing Company, 1983.

MacDonald, Peter. *Giap: The Victor in Vietnam*. New York: W. W. Norton & Company, 1993.

Marshall, Tom. *The Price of Exit*. New York: Ballentine Books, 1998.

Martin, Michael. *Angels in Red Hats: Paratroopers of the Second Indochina War*. Louisville, KY: Harmony House, 1995.

Matthews, Lloyd J., and Dale E. Brown, eds. *Assessing the Vietnam War*. Washington, DC: Pergamon-Brassey's, 1987.

Maurer, Henry. *Strange Ground: Americans in Vietnam, 1945–1975*. New York: Henry Holt, 1989.

McDermott, Mike. *True Faith and Allegiance: An American Paratrooper and the 1972 Battle for An Loc*. Tuscaloosa: The University of Alabama Press, 2012.

McGarvey, Patrick J., ed. *Visions of Victory: Selected Vietnamese Communist Military Writings, 1964–1968*. Stanford, CA: Hoover Institution of War, Revolution and Peace, Stanford University, 1969.

McKenna, Thomas P. *Kontum: The Battle to Save South Vietnam*. Lexington: The University Press of Kentucky, 2011.

Morris, Roger. *Uncertain Greatness: Henry Kissinger and American Foreign Policy*. New York: Harper & Row, 1977.

Morrocco, John. *The Vietnam Experience: Rain of Fire, Air War, 1969–1973*. Boston: Boston Publishing Company, 1985.

Moss, George Donelson. *Vietnam: An American Ordeal*. 6th ed. Upper Saddle River, NJ: Prentice Hall, 2010.

Natkiel, Richard. *Atlas of Battles: Strategy and Tactics, Civil War to Present*. New York: The Military Press, 1984.

Nguyen Cong Luan. *Nationalist in the Vietnam Wars: Memoirs of a Victim Turned Soldier*. Bloomington: Indiana University Press, 2012.

Nguyen Duy Hinh, Maj. Gen. *Lam Son 719*. Indochina Monographs. Washington, DC: US Army Center of Military History, 1979.

———. *Vietnamization and the Cease-Fire*. Indochina Monographs. Washington, DC: US Army Center of Military History, 1980.

Nguyen Tien Hung and Jerold L. Schester. *The Palace File*. New York: Harper Collins, 1989.

Niksch, Larry A. *Vietnamization: The Program and Its Problems*. Washington, DC: Congressional Research Service, January 5, 1972.

Nixon, Richard M. *In The Arena: A Memoir of Victory, Defeat and Renewal.* New York: Simon and Schuster, 1990.

———. *No More Vietnams*. New York: Touchstone, 1990.

———. *RN: The Memoirs of Richard Nixon*. New York: Warner Books, 1978.

———. *Setting the Course: Major Policy Statements by President Richard Nixon.* New York: Funk & Wagnalls, 1970.

———. *The Real War*. New York: Warner Books, 1980.

Nolan, Keith William. *Into Laos: The Story of Dewey Canyon II/Lam Son 719, Vietnam 1971*. Novato, CA: Presidio, 1986.

Olson, James S., and Randy Roberts. *Where the Last Domino Fell: America and Vietnam, 1945 to 1990*. New York: St. Martin's Press, 1991.

Palmer, Bruce, Jr. *The 25-Year War*. Lexington: University Press of Kentucky, 1984.

Palmer, Dave Richard. *Summons of the Trumpet*. San Rafael, CA: Presidio Press, 1978.

Pauker, G. J. *An Essay on Vietnamization*. Santa Monica, CA: Rand Corporation, March 1971.

Pham Van Chung, Tran Ve, To Van Cap, Nguyen Kim Tien, and Kieu Cong Cu. *Hai Mươi Một Năm Chiến Trận của Binh Chủng Thủy Quân Lục Chiến Việt Nam (1954–1975)* [The Vietnamese Marine Corps' Twenty-One Years of Warfare (1954–1975)] . 2 vols. Santa Ana, CA: Vietnamese Marine Association in the United States (Tong Hoi TQLC/VN tai Hoa Ky), 2005.

Phillips, Rufus. *Why Vietnam Matters: An Eyewitness Account of Lessons Not Learned*. Annapolis, MD: Naval Institute Press, 2008.

Pike, Douglas. *PAVN: People's Army of Vietnam*. Novato, CA: Presidio Press, 1986.

Pike, Douglas, ed. *The Bunker Papers: Reports to the President from Vietnam, 1967–1973*, Vols. 1–3. Berkeley: Institute of East Asian Studies, University of California, 1990.

Pimlott, John, ed. *Vietnam: The History and the Tactics*. New York, Crescent Books, 1982.

Pratt, John Clark, ed. *Vietnam Voices: Perspectives on the War Years, 1941–1982*. New York: Viking, 1984.

Prados, John. *Vietnam: The History of an Unwinnable War, 1945–1975*. Lawrence: University Press of Kansas, 2009.

———. *The Blood Road: The Ho Chi Minh Trail and the Vietnam War*. New York: John Wiley and Son, 1999.

Pyle, Richard, and Horst Faas. *Lost over Laos: A True Story of Tragedy, Mystery, and Friendship*. Cambridge, MA: Da Capo Press, 2003.

Randolph, Stephen P. *Powerful and Brutal Weapons: Nixon, Kissinger, and the Easter Offensive*. Cambridge, MA: Harvard University Press, 2007.

Rockett, Frederick C., and A. A. Berle. *RVNAF Effectiveness Evaluation*. Washington, DC: Simulmatics Corporation, 1967.

Rosenburgh, Bob. *Snake Driver: Cobras in Vietnam*. New York: Ivy Books, 1993.

Schulzinger, Robert D. *A Time for War: The United States and Vietnam, 1941–1975*. New York: Oxford University Press, 1997.

———. *Henry Kissinger: Doctor of Diplomacy*. New York: Columbia University Press, 1989.

Schurmann, Franz. *The Foreign Policy of Nixon: The Grand Design*. Berkeley, CA: Institute of International Studies, 1987.

Shackley, Ted. *Spymaster: My Life in the CIA*. Dulles, VA: Potomac Books, 2005.

Shaplen, Robert. *Bitter Victory*. New York: Harper & Row, 1986.

Shaw, John M. *The Cambodian Campaign: The 1970 Offensive and America's Vietnam War*. Lawrence: University Press of Kansas, 2005.

Sorley, Lewis. *A Better War: The Unexamined Victories and Final Tragedy of America's Last Years in Vietnam*. New York: Harcourt Brace, 1999.

———. *The Vietnam War: An Assessment by South Vietnam's Generals*. Lubbock: Texas Tech University Press, 2010.

———. *Thunderbolt, from the Battle of the Bulge to Vietnam and Beyond: Creighton Abrams and the Army of His Times*. New York: Simon & Schuster, 1992.

———, ed. *Vietnam Chronicles: The Abrams Tapes, 1968–1972*. Lubbock: Texas Tech University Press, 2004.

Spector, Ronald H. *After Tet: The Bloodiest Year in Vietnam*. New York: The Free Press, 1993.

Stanton, Shelby L. *Vietnam Order of Battle*. New York: Galahad Books, 1986.

Starry, Gen. Donn A. *Armored Combat in Vietnam*. New York: The Bobbs-Merrill Company, 1980.

Steinberg, Blema. *Shame and Humiliation: Presidential Decision Making on Vietnam*. Pittsburgh: University of Pittsburgh Press, 1996.

Stephenson, Roy R. "Road to Downfall: LAM SON 71/9 and US Airmobility Doctrine." PhD diss., University of Kansas, 1991.

Stevens, Richard L. *The Trail: A History of the Ho Chi Minh Trail and the Role of Nature in the Vietnam War*. New York: Garland Publishing, 1993.

Summers, Harry C., Jr. *Historical Atlas of the Vietnam War*. New York: Houghton Mifflin Company, 1995.

Swift, Earl. *Where They Lay: Searching for America's Lost Soldiers*. New York: Houghton Mifflin, 2003.

Tilford, Earl H., Jr. *Crosswinds: The Air Force's Setup in Vietnam*. College Station: Texas A&M University Press, 1993.

Tin Nguyen. *Major General Nguyen Van Hieu, ARVN*. San Jose, CA: Writers Club Press, 2000.

Tran Van Nhut. *An Loc: The Unfinished War*. Lubbock: Texas Tech University Press, 2009.

Tucker, Spencer C. *Vietnam*. Lexington: University Press of Kentucky, 1999.

Turley, Gerald R. *Easter Offensive: The Last American Advisors, Vietnam, 1972*. Reprint ed. Annapolis, MD: Naval Institute Press, 2010.

Turley, William S. *The Second Indochina War*. Boulder: Westview Press, 1986.

Van Atta, Dale. *With Honor: Melvin Laird in War, Peace, and Politics*. Madison, WI: University of Wisconsin Press, 2008.

Van Dyke, Jon M. *North Vietnam's Strategy for Survival*. Palo Alto, CA: Pacific Books, 1972.

Veith, George J. *Black Sunday: The Fall of South Vietnam 1973–75*. New York: Encounter Books, 2012.

Walton, C. Dale. *The Myth of Inevitable US Defeat in Vietnam*. London: Frank Cass, 2002.

Warner, Denis A. *Certain Victory: How Hanoi Won the War*. Kansas City: Sneed, Andrews and McKeel, 1978.

Warner, Roger. *Shooting at the Moon: The Story of America's Clandestine War in Laos*. South Royalton, VT: Steerforth Press, 1996.

Werner, Jayne S., and David Hunt, eds. *The American War in Vietnam*. Ithaca, NY: Southeast Asia Program, Cornell University, 1993.

Werner, Jayne S., and Luu Doan Huynh. *The Vietnam War: Vietnamese and American Perspectives*. New York: M. E. Sharpe, 1994.

Westmoreland, William C. *A Soldier Reports*. New York: Doubleday and Co., 1976.

Wiest, Andrew. *Vietnam's Forgotten Army: Heroism and Betrayal in the ARVN*. New York: New York University Press, 2008.

Willbanks, James H. *Abandoning Vietnam: How America Left and South Vietnam Lost Its War*. Lawrence: University Press of Kansas, 2008.

———. *The Battle of An Loc*. Bloomington: Indiana University Press, 2005.

Willenson, Kim. *The Bad War: An Oral History of the Vietnam War*. New York: New American Library, 1987.

Woodruff, Mark W. *Unheralded Victory: The Defeat of the Viet Cong and the North Vietnamese Army, 1961–1973*. Arlington, VA: Vandemere Press, 1999.

Zhai, Qiang. *China and the Vietnam Wars, 1950–1975*. Chapel Hill: University of North Carolina Press, 2000.

Newspapers and Periodicals:

Air Force Magazine
Armed Forces Journal
Armor
Army
Baltimore Sun
Christian Science Monitor
Cleveland Plain Dealer
Foreign Affairs
Joint Forces Quarterly
Life
Los Angeles Times
Newsweek
New York Times
Pacific Stars and Stripes
Philadelphia Bulletin
Philadelphia Enquirer
Studies in Intelligence
Time
US Army Aviation Digest
Vietnam Bulletin
Wall Street Journal
Washington Daily News
Washington Post
Washington Star

Index

Abrams, Gen. Creighton W.: assessment of ARVN performance in Cambodia, 21; assessment of Lt. Gen. Lam, 124; assessment of upcoming operation, 53–54, 55–56; concerned about lack of ARVN progress in Laos, 89; confers with Vien, 90; consults with Nixon on Vietnamization, 11–12; directs Sutherland to prepare detailed plan, 36; foresees new enemy offensive in 1972, 190–91; given new mission, 11–12, 13; imposes press embargo, 71–72,74–75, institutes new programs in wake of Lam Son 719, 178–79; maintains positive slant on Lam Son 719, 159, 160, 180–81; on Cambodian incursion, 21; on South Vietnamese leadership, 185; on Vietnamization, 180–81, 185–86; plan for Lam Son 719, 33–34; provides 1971 year-end report, 185–86; relations with Nixon and Kissinger, 175–76, 194, 240*n*63; responds to Kissinger's concerns, 56–57; responds to mission change in Laos, 118–19; responds to new mission from president, 14, 15, 19; response to NSSM 1, 6–7; role in Lam Son 719 planning, 28, 32, 33; meets with HAIG, 33; meets with Thieu, 32, 101, 134; in Easter Offensive, 190–91, 194, 195–96, 197; urges South Vietnamese to continue the attack, 90–91; worried about premature withdrawal from Laos, 129–30; urges Thieu to commit additional forces, 129;

Agreement on Ending the War and Restoring the Peace in Vietnam. *See* Paris Peace Accords

advisers, American: Abrams' post-Laos directions to, 178–79; accompany ARVN into Cambodia, 21; assessment by, of ARVN performance in Laos, 113, 114, 170, 171; forbidden from crossing Laotian border, 35, 37, 51, 54, 58; not available to coordinate fire support in Laos, 48, 56, 75, 103, 169; opinions about RVNAF combat capability, 20; role during 1972 NVA offensive, 194, 195, 197,198–99

Albert, Carl, 178

Andersen Air Base, Guam, 97

An Loc, battle of, 193–95, 197, 243*n*51

An, Gen. Nguyen Huu. *See* Nguyen Huu An, Gen.

An, Pham Xuan. *See* Pham Xuan An

antiwar movement, 19, 181, 222*n*47

Arc Light, See B-52 bombers

Army of the Republic of Vietnam (ARVN)

ARVN Corps:

- I Corps, 3, 32, 37, 39, 72, 73, 74, 207–209
- II Corps, 195, 197
- III corps, 31, 33, 102, 197

ARVN Divisions:

- Airborne Division, 43, 44, 45, 53, 61, 75, 76, 90, 105, 107, 109, 118, 120, 129, 130, 142, 165
- 1st Division, 36, 41, 42, 44, 86, 90, 91, 118, 121, 124, 132, 133, 171, 196

ARVN Divisions (*continued*)
- 2nd Division, 129, 154
- 3rd Division, 16, 180, 191, 192
- 5th Division, 194
- 21st Division, 194
- 22nd Division, 20, 195
- 23rd Division, 195

ARVN Brigades/Regiments/Groups:
- 1st Airborne Brigade, 52, 75, 148, 194
- 1st Armored Brigade, 42, 43, 44, 52, 75, 77, 82, 107, 132, 150
- 1st Ranger Group, 43, 45, 73
- 2nd Airborne Brigade, 43, 53
- 3rd Airborne Brigade, 52, 79, 105
- 54th Infantry Regiment, 154, 171
- 56th Infantry Regiment, 192
- 57th Infantry Regiment, 192
- 1st Airborne Battalion, 52
- 2nd Airborne Battalion, 52, 109, 111, 147
- 3rd Airborne Battalion, 52, 85, 105
- 4th Armored Cavalry Squadron (Composite), 134, 156, 157
- 5th Airborne Battalion, 53, 148
- 6th Airborne Battalion, 52
- 7th Airborne Battalion, 53, 147
- 8th Airborne Battalion, 52, 82, 93, 109, 142, 147
- 9th Airborne Battalion, 52, 84, 142, 150
- 11th Airborne Battalion, 53
- 11th Armored Cavalry Squadron, 52, 77, 143
- 17th Armored Cavalry Squadron, 52, 77, 85, 93, 106, 109, 111, *gallery*
- 21st Ranger Battalion, 41, 73, 79, 82, 85, 98, 104, 111
- 37th Ranger Battalion, 41, 73
- 39th Ranger Battalion, 41, 73, 85, 92, 94, 98, 104
- 44th Artillery Battalion, 52
- 51st Infantry Battalion, 20
- 77th Ranger Battalion, 156
- 101st Engineer Battalion, 52, 77, 81

ARVN 1st Logistics Command, 48
A Shau Valley, 26, 41, 71, 132, 191

Ba, Col. Le Tong. *See* Ly Tong Ba, Col.
Ban Dong, 43, 78, 83
Ban Karai Pass, 24, 26
Ban Me Thuot, battle of, 203
Ban Raving Pass, 24
Barker, Maj. Jack, 1, 146, 219*n*1, 219*n*2, 236*n*28
Base Areas, 604, 24, 26, 38; 611, 25, 26, 34, 38, 45, 90, 101, 129, 132, 134, 145; 612, 25
Base Support Area (BSA), 48
Battreal, Col, Raymond, 107, 166, 167, 232*n*51
Berry, Brig. Gen. Sidney B., Jr., 45, 78, 122, 166, 238*n*21
B-52 bombers, 20, 40, 42, 47, 56, 77, 81, 85, 94, 96–97, 102, 110, 112, 121, 122, 126, 128, 133, 136, 145, 148, 152, 155, 170
binh tram, 24, 63, 96, 132
Boffman, 1st Lt. Alan B., 138, 235*n*10
bombing of North Vietnam, 193
Brandt, Capt. Keith A., 137–38, 235*n*10
Brezhnev, Leonid, 193
Bui Diem, 30
Bui Thi Lan, Col., 226*n*9
Bunker, Ambassador Ellsworth: conveys Nixon's assurance of support to Thieu, 12; corresponds with Kissinger, 119, 129, 144, 175; favors plan, 34; meets with Haig, 33; meets with Thieu, 134, 145, 155; returns to Washington for consultation, 27

Ca Lu, 40, 70, 75
Cambodian incursion, 21–23, 24, 27, 28, 30, 54–55, 62, 74, 181, 222*n*47
Campaign 275, 203
Camp Carroll, 70, 192
Cam Ranh Bay, 18
Cao Khee Nhat, Col., 52
Cao Van Khanh, Sr. Col., 63, 66

Cao Van Vien, Gen., 30, 33, 60, 90, 169, 179–80
casualties, 158, 162, 163, 214
Cathey, Capt. William, 98
Central Intelligence Agency, 7, 50
China, People's Republic of, 184, 187, 188, 189
Chuoc, Capt. Nguyen Huu. *See* Nguyen Huu Chuoc, Capt.
Chubb, Pfc. John, 1, 219n2
Chup Rubber Plantation, 31, 32, 33, 59, 157
Clay, Gen. Lucius D., Jr., 37
Cleveland Plain Dealer, 161
Clewell, Maj. Bob, 123
Clifford, Clark, 17, 220*n*11
close air support, 42, 81, 105, 170, 171, 216
Cockerham, Col. Sam, 102
Combined Arms Doctrinal Manual, 178
Commando Vault, BLU-82, 126, 170, 234*n*19
Congress, US *See* U. S. Congress
Consolidated RVNAF Improvement & Modernization Program (CRIMP), 16
Cooper-Church Amendment, 27, 35, 58, 129
Co Roc, 38, 39, 80, 142, 153, 155
Cowles, Maj. Gen. Donald, 31

Dabney, Maj. William, 171
Darron, Lt. Col. Robert, 149, 166
Dat, Col. Le Duc. *See* Le Duc Dat, Col.
Davidson, Lt. Gen. Phillip B., 2, 69, 168, 174–75, 179
Davison, Gen. Michael S., 31, 32
De, Dinh Ve. *See* Dinh Van De
Defense Attache Office (DAO), 200
Demilitarized Zone (DMZ), 33, 70, 86, 154, 191
Dewey Canyon II. *See* Operation Dewey Canyon II
Diem, Bui. *See* Bui Diem
Dillender, Sgt. William, 1, 219n2
Dinh, Col. Pham Van. *See* Pham Van Dinh, Col.
Dinh Van De, 61
Direct Air Support Center (DASC), 42
Do Cao Tri, Lt. Gen., 21, 104
Dong, Lt. Gen. Du Quoc. *See* Du Quoc Dong, Lt. Gen.
Dong Si Nguyen, Gen., 61, 66
Doody, Warrant Officer Thomas, 79
Duong, Capt. Nguyen Van. *See* Nguyen Van Duong, Capt.
Dugan, Capt. John, 1, 146, 219*n*2
Dung, Gen. Van Tien. *See* Van Tien Dung, Gen.
Du Quoc Dong, Lt. Gen., 52, 105, 107, 108, 110, 143, 147
Dzu, Lt. Gen.Ngo. *See* Ngo Dzu, Lt. Gen.

Easter Offensive, 1972, 185, 186, 187–98
El Paso, Operations Plan, 29, 116, 223*n*17

Faas, Horst, 60
Farrar, Lt. Col. Raymond E., 71
Fire Support Bases:
- Alpha, 134, 142, 143, 147, 148
- A Luoi, 84, 87, 132, 136, 142
- Bastogne, 71
- Blue, 80
- Bravo, 93, 148, 149, 150
- Brick, 132
- Brown, 1, 86, 125, 132, 133, 141, 145
- Delta, 80, 83, 85, 120, 122, 128, 140, 144, 148, 151, 152, 153
- Delta 1, 80, 86, 125, 132, 140, 141, 144, 144
- Don, 80, 85, 86, 112
- Flexible, 72
- Hope, 121, 125
- Hotel, 80, 63, 86, 120, 152
- Hotel II, 112, 113
- Kilo, 37
- Liz, 121, 124, 125, 130, 133, 134
- Lolo, 121, 122, 123–124, 125, 126, 128, 130, 132, 134, 135, 136, 137, 139
- Moon, 134
- Phu Loc, 127, 141
- Ranger North, 85, 92, 94, 98
- Ranger South, 79, 82, 84, 97, 98, 99, 100, 104

Fire Support Bases (*continued*)
 Sophia, 121, 124, 125,128, 130, 131, 133, 135
 Sophie East, 134, 145
 30, 79, 94, 104, 109
 31, 79, 85, 104, 109
 Vandegrift, 40, 41, 70, 71, 72, 75, 156, 157, *gallery*
 Veghel, 71
 Yellow, 80, 84
 Zon, 71
Fishhook, 21
Fitzmaurice, SP4 Michael J., 237*n*44
Ford, Gerald R., 202
Foreign Affairs, 17
Forward Air Controller (FAC), 42, 85, 105, 107, 162
Forward Support Area 26–1, 48, 75
Forward Support Area 26–2, 49, 75
fratricide, 75, 104
Friedheim, Jerry, 8–9
Fujii, SP5 Dennis, 95, 97, 99, 231*n*27
Fulbright, William, 182

Gallup Poll, 181
Geneva Accords, 1962, 29
Gentry, Warrant Officer Robert B., 80
Giai, Brig. Gen. Vu Van. *See* Vu Van Giai, Brig. Gen.
Giap, Gen. Vo Nguyen. *See* Vo Nguyen Giap
Goodpaster, Gen. Andrew, 9

Hac Bao Company, 47, 78, 146, 155–56
Haig, Brig. Gen. Alexander M.: assessment of ARVN performance in Laos, 145; briefs Abrams' plan to president, 34–35; dispatched to Saigon, 32, 33, 140; meets with Nixon, 57; Nixon considers sending to Saigon to replace Abrams, 175; on Laird's Vietnamization plan, 10; optimistic about the plan, 59; pushes plan, 30; trip to Saigon postponed, 100
Haldeman, H. R., 60, 175, 222*n*47
Hamburger Hill, 222*n*38
Ham Nghi, 42, 70, 119, 140, 144, 153
Harris Poll, 177, 181
Harrison, Col. Ben, 36, 233*n*61
Helicopters: AH-1G Cobra, 47, 75, 83, 91, 94, 104, 113, 114, 123, 124, 215, 135, 137–38, 225*n*16, *gallery;* AH-1J Sea Cobra, 120, 225*n*16; CH-47 Chinook, 113, 153; CH-53 Sea Stallion, 112, 120, *gallery;* CH-54A Sky Crane, 150, 153; OH-6, 83, 114; OH-58, 114; UH-1C, 124; UH-1H Huey, 1, 78, 80, 91, 95, 113, 114, 123, 124, 125, 138, 147, 151, 215, *gallery*
Helms, Richard, 50, 51, 57
Hemingway, Brig. Gen. Jack, 119–120
Hill, Brig. Gen. John J., 40
Hoang Phuong, Sr. Col., 63
Hoang Xuan Lam, Lt. Gen.: aware of impending operation, 36; approves Airborne Division plan, 53; assessment of leadership of, 55, 165–66; background of, 55; briefs plan to Thieu, 37, 52; complains about US support, 90; confers with Thieu, 89–90, 95, 118–19; difficulties with subordinate commanders, 55, 165; establishes headquarters at Khe Sanh, 48; named overall commander for operation in Laos, 37; relieved in 1972, 196, 197; reluctance to postpone operation, 76; responds to mission change in Laos, 118–19; unprepared for 1972 Easter offensive, 192; , 52, 55, 84, 165–66, 192, 196, 197, *gallery*
Ho Chi Minh Trail, 24–25, 26, 32, 33, 54, 55, 57, 62, 61
Hue, Maj. Tran Ngoc. *See* Tran Ngoc Hue, Maj.
Humphrey, Hubert, 4

Jaco, Maj. Tom, 165
Johnson, Lyndon B., 4, 13, 29
Johnson, U. Alexis, 229*n*8
Joint Chiefs of Staff, 8, 15, 16,55
Joint General Staff, 16, 30, 31, 52
Joint POW/MIA Accounting Command, 219*n*2
Joint Task Force—Full Accounting, 1, 219*n*2, 235*n*10

Kaplan, Col. Phillip, 195
Khang, Lt. Gen. Le Nguyen. *See* Le Nguyen Khang, Lt. Gen.
Khanh, Sr. Col. Can Van. *See* Cao Van Khanh, Sr. Col.
Khe Sanh, 1, 24, 33, 37, 40, 41, 42, 43, 44, 47, 48, 49, 65, 67, 70, 71–72, 73, 75, 76, 88, 89, 95, 96, 110, 113, 118, 119, 121–22, 126, 138, 140, 141, 146, 153, 154, 155, 157, *gallery*
Kirklighter, Lt. Col. Gerald W., 80, 123, 137, 139
Kissinger, Henry: against going into Laos, 28, 30; assesses Lam Son 719, 160–161, 178, 200; critical of South Vietnamese performance, 144; meets with Westmoreland, 115–16; misgivings before operation commenced, 56–57; on ending the war, 5; on genesis of Lam Son 719, 30; on media coverage of the operation, 72, 139–40, 145; purpose of NSSM 1, 5–6; on reports from MACV, 109, 145; peace talks, 10–11, 182–85, 199–200; proclaims Peace is at hand," 199; provides assessment to president, 116; relations with General Abrams, 99–100, 119, 140, 175–76, 240*n*63; on troop withdrawals, 18; sends warning to Thieu, 130–131
Klose, Maj. John A. G., 46, 136
Kontum, battle of, 195, 197

Lagenour, Spec. Paul, 147
Laird, Melvin R.: assessment of Vietnamization after Lam Son, 174; concerned about press coverage, 176–77; driving force behind Vietnamization effort, 13–14, 15–16; meets with Nixon, 13, 34–35. 57; mixed feelings about outcome in Laos, 160; names Vietnamization, 9; plans for US withdrawal from Vietnam, 7–8; pushes US troop withdrawals, 17–18; press conference of, 115, 231*n*17; travels to Vietnam, 49–50;
Lam, Lt. General Hoang Xuan. *See* Hoang Xuan Lam, Lt. Gen.
Lam Son 719: ARVN halts along Route 9, 87; assault on Tchepone, 120–128; casualties in, 158, 162, 163; comparison with Cambodian incursion, 53–54; concept for, 33–34, 38; decision to launch operation, 76; difficult terrain and weather in, 38–39, 54–55; diversion in support of, 86; flaws in plan, 167–68; impact on Vietnamization, 173; named, 37; advance halted, 87; plan for, 37–49; North Vietnamese advance notice of, 60–64; North Vietnamese assessment of, 177, 186–87; North Vietnamese reaction to outcome, 158, 186; operations security in, 168–69; performance of South Vietnamese forces in, 163–64, 165–66, 169–70; Phase II commences, 77; positive outcomes of, 172–73; secrecy in planning of, 52; South Vietnamese morale after, 171–72; staff work in, 166–67; Thieu changes mission in Laos, 117.
Lang Vei, 72, 78, 80, 86, 94, 153, 155, *gallery*
Lao Bao, 86, 141
Lao Dong (Workers') Party, 187, 188
Laotian Salient, 45, 88, 132, 155
leadership, South Vietnamese, 164–65, 166–67, 169–70, 178–80, 196, 197–98
Le Duan, 187, 190
Le Duc Tho, 183, 185, 199
Le Loi, 37
Le Nguyen Khang, Lt. Gen., 55, 153, 165, 226*n*9
Le Trong Tran, Maj. Gen., 66
Life, 161, 162
Lloyd, Maj. Jim, 97
logistics, 48–49, 75–76, 92, 94, 102
Lon Nol, 20, 24, 28, 31
Luat, Col. Nguyen Trong. *See* Nguyen Trong Luat, Col.
Lung, Col. Hoang Ngoc. *See* Hoang Ngoc Lung, Col.

Ly Tong Ba, Col., 195
LZ. *See* Fire Support Bases

Mansfield Amendment, 182
Mao Zedong, 187
May-68 Plan, 221*n*27
McCaffrey, Lt. Gen. William, 102
McCain, Adm. John S., Jr., 6, 28–29, 30, 32–33, 56, 58, 221*n*28
McGovern, George, 182
media coverage, 71–72, 74–75; 139, 159–60, 161–62, 176–77
Meyer, Lt. Col. Richard, 70
Midway Conference, 12
Military Region I, 26, 32, 34, 37, 71, 172, 191, 192, 194, 195, 222*n*5
Military Region III, 32, 34, 192
Molinellli, Lt. Col. Robert, 78, 91–92, 98–99
Moorer, Adm. Thomas H.: advises against termination date; 74; asks for McCain's plan, 28; concurs with plan for Lam Son 719, 33; authorizes Abrams to finalize planning, 36; directs Abrams to prepare contingency plan, 31; favors attack into Cambodia, 28; forwards Kissinger's concerns before operation, 56–57; meets with president, 50–51; reassures president about South Vietnamese progress in Laos, 137; role in planning Lam Son 719, 28, 32, 33, 34–35, 36; visits Saigon with Laird, 49–50
morale, South Vietnamese, 171–72
Moratorium Day, 19
Mu Gia Pass, 24, 231*n*17

National Security Council (NSC), 18
National Security Decision Memorandum (NSDM) 9, 10
National Security Study Memorandum (NSSM) 1, 5–7
National Security Study Memorandum (NSSM) 36, 11
Newton, Lt. Col. George, 110
news embargo, 71–72, 74–75
Newsweek, 162, 172
New York Times, 171
Ngo Dzu, Lt. Gen., 195
Ngo Quang Truong, Lt. Gen., 196, 197
Ngo Tavak, 45
Nguyen, Dong Si, Gen. *See* Dong Si Nguyen, Gen.
Nguyen Hue campaign. See *Easter* Offensive
Nguyen Huu An, Col. Gen., 61, 64, 158
Nguyen Huu Chuoc, Capt., 147
Nguyen Thi Binh, 181
Nguyen Trong Luat, Col., 77, 106, 107, 149
Nguyen Van Duong, Capt., 108
Nguyen Van Thieu: actions after operation, 172; agrees with Lam Son 719 plan, 33, 34, 50; at Midway Conference, 12; changes mission in Laos, 117–18; confers with Lam, 89, 95, 118–19; fighting "poor man's war;" 203; interference in operation, 164; meets with Abrams, 101, 129, 134; meets with Haig, 33; proclaims victory, 158; reaction to announcement of Vietnamization, 12–13; relationship with commanders, 55, 89–90, 165; relieves Lt. Gen. Lam, 196; relieves Maj. Gen. Toan, 195; role in halting the attack, 89–90
Nguyen Van Tho, Col., 105, 108
Nguyen Van Toan, Maj. Gen., 195
Nhat, Col. Cao Khee. *See* Cao Khee Nhat, Col.
Nixon, Richard M.: alarmed at build-up in Laos, 27; announcement of Vietnamization, 12; assessment of Cambodian incursion, 24; approves Phase I of the operation, 59; approves plan for Lam Son 719, 34, 35; assessment of Lam Son 719, 159, 161, 162, 164, 169, 174; assessment of Vietnamization, 169, 199; campaigns for presidency, 1968, 4; concerns about Vietnam, 6; concerns about operation in Laos, 58; concerns about withdrawal from Laos, 134; decides on preemptive strike, 27;

declares Vietnamization a success after Cambodian incursion, 21; declares Vietnamization a success after Easter Offensive, 199, 201; declares Vietnamization a success after Lam Son 719, 174, 199; dilemma upon taking office, 17; discusses mission change for MACV, 13; dissatisfied with media reports, 139, 159–60, 161; gives order to launch Phase II, 74; interview with Howard K. Smith, 159; issues NSDM 9, 10; issues NSSM 1, 5–7; issues NSSM 36, 11; meets with advisors before Lam Son 179, 34–35, 50–51, 57; meets with Thieu at Midway conference, 12; on ending the war, 5; on purpose of Vietnamization, 10, 13; orders Cambodian incursion, 21; promotes success of Cambodian incursion, 222*n*47; relations with General Abrams, 175–76; relations with Thieu, 12, 175, 200, 202; reports progress in Laotian operation, 158–59; resigns from office, 202; response to 1972 North Vietnamese invasion, 193; role in genesis of Lam Son 719, 30–31; "Secret plan" for ending the war, 4; silent majority speech of 3 Nov 1969, 19; troop withdrawals, 17–19, 174, 186, 196, 199; wins 1968 election, 4

Nol, Lon. *See* Lon Nol

Norodom Sihanouk, 20, 24

North Vietnam Army (NVA)

- 2nd Division, 67, 82, 88, 95, 135, 141, 195
- 7th Division, 193–94
- 304th Division, 65, 67, 88, 96, 105, 115, 141, 191
- 308th Division, 61, 64, 67, 82, 88, 92, 94, 107, 109, 115, 141, 158, 191
- 312th Division, 66
- 320th Division, 64, 65, 67, 88, 90, 115, 141, 195
- 324th Division, 64, 67, 88, 140, 141, 144, 148, 151, 235*n*15

NVA Regiments:

- Ba Gia Regiment, 83
- 1st Infantry Regiment, 67, 135
- 9th Infantry Regiment, 67, 88
- 24B Regiment, 88
- 24th Infantry Regiment, 65, 67, 96, 105, 109, 141
- 27th Infantry Regiment, 67, 88
- 31st Infantry Regiment, 88
- 36th Infantry Regiment, 109, 141
- 38th Artillery Regiment, 67, 88
- 52nd Infantry Regiment, 65
- 64th Infantry Regiment, 88, 108, 141
- 66th Infantry Regiment, 67, 88, 107
- 84th Artillery Regiment, 67
- 88th Infantry Regiment, 141
- 102nd Infantry Regiment, 94, 98, 141
- 141st Infantry Regiment, 67, 135
- 202nd Tank Regiment, 65, 109
- 203rd Tank Regiment, 65
- 270th Infantry Regiment, 67
- 675th Artillery Regiment, 96

NVA Senior Commands:

- B2 Front, 192
- B3 Front, 191, 191
- B4 Front, 67
- B5 Front, 66, 67, 154, 191
- B70 Corps, 63, 66, 67, 82, 87, 112, 115, 133, 212–213
- General Rear Services Department, 63, 66, 67
- Group 559, 63, 66, 67
- Headquarters 702, 65, 66, 67, 68
- Military Region 4, 62, 64, 65, 66, 68
- Military Region 5, 67
- Military Region Tri Thien, 65, 66, 67
- Route 9-Northern Quang Tri Front, 66

NVA Transportation Group 559, 25

North Vietnam, Politburo, 62–63, 158, 188, 190

North Vietnam, Central Military Committee, 66, 68, 83, 148, 190

North Vietnam, Party Central Committee, 61, 64, 69, 83

Objectives: A Luoi, 43, 45, 79; A-Ro, 102; Bravo, 120; 30, 30; 31, 90
Okamura, Akihiko, 81, 93
Operation Dewey Canyon, 224*n*8
Operation Dewey Canyon II, 40, 70, 224*n*8
Operation Linebacker II, 200
Operation Market-Time, 24
Operation Menu, 20
Operation Toan Thang 1–71, 59, 157
operations security, 168–9

Palmer, Gen. Bruce, 30, 55, 165, 226*n*10
Paris Peace Accords, 200, 202
Parrot's Beak, 21
Pathet Lao, 26, 66
peace negotiations, 10–11, 182–85, 199–200
Peachey, Lt. Col. William N., 106, 108, 110, 143
Pence, Col. Arthur W., 53, 105–106, 226*n*4, 233*n*61
People's Army of Vietnam (PAVN). *See* North Vietnam. Army
People's Republic of China. *See* China, People's Republic of
Pham Van Dinh, Col., 171
Pham Van Phu, Brig. Gen., 36, 43, 112
Pham Xuan An, 60
Philadelphia Inquirer, 161
Phnom Penh, 31
Phouc Long, battle of, 202–203
Phu Loc, 73, 141
Phuong, Sr. Col. Hoang. *See* Hoang Phuong, Sr. Col.
Phu, Pham Van. *See* Pham Van Phu, Brig. Gen.
Popular Forces (PF), 16, 17
Potts, Brig. Gen. William C., 31, 50
Provisional Revolutionary Government (PRG), 183, 184
Pyle, Richard, 60

Quang, Tran Van. *See* Tran Van Quang
Quang Tri, battle of, 192, 195–97

Red Devil Road, 71
Regional Forces (RF), 16, 17
Republic of Vietnam Armed Forces (RVNAF), 1, 29
Rider, Lt. Col. Archie A., 137, 148
Robinson, R. Adm. R. C., 176
Rockpile, 70
Rogers, William P., 50, 57–58
Route 9—Southern Laos Counteroffensive Campaign, 68, 144

Saigon, fall of, 203
Sihanouk, Norodom. *See* Norodom Sihanouk
Sihanoukville, 24
Smith, Howard K., 159
Smyser, Dick, 74, 229*n*8
South Vietnamese Air Force. *See* Vietnamese Air Force (VNAF)
South Vietnamese Army. *See* Army of the Republic of Vietnam (ARVN)
Souvanna Phouma, 29, 58
Soviet Union, 187, 188, 189, 203
Spring Offensive. *See* Easter Offensive
Stewart, Warrant Officer Paul, 79
Sutherland, Lt. Gen. James W.: assesses operation, 170, 173; assessment of Lam before operation, 55; briefs plan to Abrams, 37, 52; concerned about discipline in Airborne Division, 110–111; concerned about helicopter losses, 102; confers with Lam, 91; directed to develop plan, 31 36; meets with Abrams, 37; on casualties, 112, 163, 170; on enemy's prior knowledge of plan, 60; on enemy situation, 117; on impact of operation on Vietnamization, 173; on initial planning, 36–37

tactical airlift, 73, 170–71, 216
Tallman, Brig. Gen. John, 243*n*51
Tan, Le Trong, Maj. Gen. *See* Le Trong Tran, Maj. Gen.
Tarpley, Maj. Gen. Thomas M., 41
Tet Offensive, 1968, 4, 7, 40, 47, 73, 115

Thieu, Nguyen Van Thieu. *See* Nguyen Van Thieu
Tho, Le Duc. *See* Le Duc Tho
Tho, Nguyen Van. *See* Nguyen Van Tho, Col.
Time, 172
Toan, Maj. Gen. Nguyen Van. *See* Nguyen Van Toan, Maj. Gen.
Tong, Brig. Gen. Le Van. *See* Le Van Tong, Brig. Gen.
Tran Ngoc Hue, Maj., 125, 146–7, 236*n*29
Tran Van Quang, 66
troop withdrawals, US, 10, 11, 12, 17–19, 174, 186, 196, 189
Truong, Lt. Gen. Ngo Quang. *See* Ngo Quang Truong, Lt. Gen.
Truong Nhu Tang, 184, 185
"twenty-nine questions," 5–6

US Air Force: Seventh Air Force, 42, 47; 23rd Tactical Air Support Squadron (TASS), 42; 40th Tactical Fighter Squadron, ; 834th Air Division, 49
US Army Corps, XXIV Corps, 32, 36, 53, 70, 167–68, 209–211
US Army Divisions:
- 1st Cavalry Division, 21
- 1st Infantry Division, 23
- 4th Infantry Division, 23
- 9th Infantry Division, 17
- 23rd Infantry Division, 120, 154
- 25th Infantry Division, 21, 23
- 82nd Airborne Division, 21
- 101st Airborne Division, 41, 44, 45, 71, 78, 120, 129, 238*n*21

US Army Brigades/Regiments/Groups:
- 1st Aviation Brigade, 102
- 1st Brigade, 5th Infantry Division (Mechanized), 40, 41, 42, 44, 47, 70, 72, 129, 151, 154
- 3rd Brigade, 82nd Airborne Division, 23
- 11th Armored Cavalry Regiment, 21
- 11th Brigade, 23rd Infantry Division, 120
- 26th General Support Group, 48
- 45th Engineer Group, 41, 71
- 101st Airborne Division Support Command, 38, 80, 94
- 101st Aviation Group, 45–46
- 108th Artillery Group, 47, 72, 77

US Army Battalions/Squadrons:
- 1st Battalion, 11th Infantry, 71, 157
- 1st Battalion, 61st Infantry, 70
- 1st Battalion, 77th Armor, 70, 151, 157
- 1st Squadron, 1st Cavalry, 72
- 2nd Squadron, 17th Cavalry (Air), 44, 46, 72, 73, 77, 78, 91–92, 137, 148, 154, 237n44, 156
- 1st Battalion, 396th Artillery, 47
- 2nd Battalion, 94th Artillery, 47, 72
- 3rd Battalion, 187th Infantry, 71
- 3rd Squadron, 5th Cavalry, 70–71, 75
- 4th Battalion, 3rd Infantry, 71
- 4th Battalion, 77th Artillery (Aerial Rocket Artillery), 47, 135, 154, *gallery*
- 5th Battalion, 4th Artillery, 47, 72
- 7th Engineer Battalion, 71
- 7th Squadron, 1st Cavalry, 78
- 8th Battalion, 4th Artillery, 47, 72, 156
- 14th Combat Aviation Battalion, 46, 122, 146
- 14th Engineer Battalion, 71
- 61st Medical Battalion, 95
- 101st Aviation Battalion, 1, 123, 124, 138, 146, *gallery*
- 158th Assault Helicopter Battalion, 46, 78, 79, 97, 106, 122, 124, 143
- 159th Assault Support Helicopter Battalion, 46, 91, 113
- 212th Combat Aviation Battalion
- 223rd Assault Helicopter Battalion, 46, 78, 80, 112, 121, 122, 123, 125, 136, 137

US Army Companies/Troops:
- B Troop, 2nd Squadron, 1st Cavalry, 94
- B Troop, 7th Squadron, 1st Cavalry, 47, 78
- 48th Assault Helicopter Company, 80, 101–102, 112, 147
- 116th Assault Helicopter Company, 146
- 173rd Assault Helicopter Company, 138
- 174th Assault Helicopter Company, 80, 146, *gallery*

US Support Command, Da Nang, 48
US Congress, 5, 82, 181–82
US Department of Defense, 7, 8, 74
US Department of State, 7
US House of Representatives, 182
US Marine Corps: 1st Marine Air Wing, 42, 46, 109; 3rd Battalion, 9th Marines, 86; 3rd Marine Division, 23; 31st Marine Amphibious Unit (MAU), 225*n*21; Heavy Helicopter Squadron 463 (HMH-463), 46, 112, 120; Light Helicopter Squadron-367 (HML-367), 120, 225*n*16
US Navy: diversion by, 86; Seventh Fleet, 225*n*21; USS *Hancock*, 4; USS *Kitty Hawk*, 42; USS *Ranger*, 42, 75, 104
US Senate, 182
U-Tapao Air Base, Thailand, 97

Van Di, 127
Van Tien Dung, Gen., 68
Vien, Gen. Cao Van. *See* Cao Van Vien, Gen.
Viet Cong: 5th Division, 194–95, 242*n*48; 9th Division, 193, 194, 242*n*48
Vietnamese Air Force (VNAF), 42, 74
Vietnamese Marine Division, 43, 49, 61, 118, 119, 156, 165
Vietnamese Marine Brigades: 147th Marine Brigade, 44, 45, 49, 120, 132, 140, 141, 144, 151, 152, 153; 258th Marine Brigade, 44, 45, 75, 120, 132, 141, 152, 171; 369th Marine Brigade, 119
Vietnamization: and 1972 North Vietnamese offensive, 197–99; assessment by Nixon, 21, 199, 200–201; assessment by North Vietnamese, 177, 186; Davidson's assessment of, 174–75; early progress of, 20–21; genesis of, 4–23; Haig's assessment of, 59; Lam Son 719 as a test of, 51; objectives of, 9–10; phases of, 13–14; risk of Lam Son 719 to, 56; Sutherland's assessment of, 173
Vogt, Gen. John W., 231*n*17
Vo Nguyen Giap, 64, 82, 158
Vuong Thua Vu, 66
Vu Van Giai, Brig. Gen., 121, 171
Vu, Vuong Thua. *See* Vuong Thua Vu

Wasko, Maj. Michael J., 112
Westmoreland, Gen. William C., 29, 58, 115, 136, 169
Weyand, Gen. Fred, 31, 176, 198
Wheeler, Gen. Earle G., 8, 15, 28
Whiting, Cliff, 101–102

Xuan Thuy, 183

Zhou Enlai, 184